AMERICAN VISTAS

1877 to the Present

American Vistas

1877 to the Present

Fourth Edition

Edited by
LEONARD DINNERSTEIN
UNIVERSITY OF ARIZONA

and

KENNETH T. JACKSON
COLUMBIA UNIVERSITY

New York Oxford
OXFORD UNIVERSITY PRESS
1983

Copyright © 1971, 1975, 1979, 1983 by Oxford University Press, Inc.

LIBRARY OF CONGRESS CATALOGING IN PUBLICATION DATA

Main entry under title:
American vistas.

 Contents: [1] 1607-1877—[2] 1877 to the
present.
 1. United States—History—Addresses, essays,
lectures. I. Dinnerstein, Leonard. II. Jackson,
Kenneth T.
E178.6.A426 1979   973   82-2160
ISBN 0-19-503164-4 (pbk. v. 1.)   AACR2
ISBN 0-19-503166-0 (pbk. v. 2.)

Printing (last digit): 9 8 7 6 5 4 3 2 1

Printed in the United States of America

For
Andrew Dinnerstein and Julie Dinnerstein
and
Kenneth Gordon Jackson and Kevan Parish Jackson

PREFACE TO THE FOURTH EDITION

It is now more than a decade since we first embarked upon our project of bringing together a series of historical essays that combined interest with readability and which could be used in conjunction with a survey text or a wide variety of other books. We have been gratified by the initial reader response as well as the enthusiasm with which our subsequent editions were received. The testaments that we have read indicate that there are a large number of instructors who find the combination of traditional and offbeat essays on the American past suitable to their own teaching styles. We are particularly pleased that *American Vistas* has been used by a wide diversity of people in every region of the country as well as in Canada and overseas. It reaffirms our belief that the American past can be both enlightening and instructive to all people who are fascinated by the development of societies.

For this revision we have retained a larger number of articles from the previous edition than has been our wont in the past. Letters from users and comments from other colleagues and scholars clearly indicated which pieces were most suitable for college classes. We have tried to follow this collective advice whenever possible. Almost all of the respondents believed that historiographical essays were out of place in *American Vistas*. We agreed. Many other selections were so highly praised that we felt it would be an injustice to students and teachers alike if we eliminated them. On the other hand, more recent scholarship and the changing emphasis of societal and classroom interests have resulted in the addition to this volume of selections on Henry George and the single tax, new interpretations on the coming of World Wars I and II, Al Capone, the image of women in film, the TV quiz show scandals of the 1950s, the bus boycotts and civil rights, the Vietnam War, and the issue of illegal Mexican immigration to the United States.

For this fourth edition we would like to thank the following people who provided us with candid analyses of previous selections and/or suggested possibilities for our consideration: Karen Anderson, Kent Anderson, Gottlieb J. Baer, Paul A. Carter, Juan Ramon Garcia, Sidney H. Kessler, Oliver Krug, Constance M. Jones, James M. Morris, Glenn Miller, James Richardson, and Robert E. Smith. Phyllis Deutsch was also particularly helpful in evaluating the book.

We would also like to thank the office staff at the University of Arizona History Department who facilitated the preparation of the manuscript: Dawn Polter, Marilyn Bradian, Dorothy Donnelly, Nikki Matz, Maudie Mazza, and student assistant David Romero.

As in the past, both of us would be grateful for individual comments and suggestions from readers. We also hope that articles included in this edition are as useful for classes as those that were chosen for our earlier volumes.

L.D.
K.T.J.

November 1981

CONTENTS

I INDUSTRIAL DEMOCRACY, 1877–1920

I

Schooling the Hopi: Federal Indian Policy Writ Small, 1887–1917

DAVID WALLACE ADAMS

• *Evidence of Indian existence in what is now North America dates back more than 25,000 years. When Christopher Columbus first sailed to the New World in 1492, there were perhaps two million people already resident on the continent. Europeans called them Indians because of the belief that the Americas were the outer reaches of the East Indies.*

Over the course of the next five centuries, the original Americans were pushed slowly westward, where many died in battle or from strange diseases introduced by the new settlers. Ultimately, the white man decided to confine the Indians to reservations, where they could be kept out of the way until they were properly Americanized. Education was of course a favorite method of changing Indian behavioral patterns and of teaching the superiority of Western ways and European culture.

The Hopi were a particularly sedentary farming people who had special skills in pottery, basketry, and textiles. Concentrated in what is now Arizona, they lived peacefully in mesa villages even after Coronado's men visited the area in 1540. After 1820, their primary enemies were the more numerous Navaho, who in 1843 were even given control of most of the Hopi reservation. The following essay by David Wallace Adams focuses on a less violent but equally serious threat— the educational policies adopted by federal officials whose assumptions about "progress" and "savagery" placed little value on tribal traditions.

© 1979 by the Pacific Coast Branch, American Historical Association. Reprinted from PACIFIC HISTORICAL REVIEW, vol. 48, no. 3, August 1979, 335–356, by permission of the Branch.

Although historians have acknowledged the important role of education in late nineteenth-century federal Indian policy, they have failed
to examine this subject in much depth. To date, a study of the federal Indian boarding school system does not exist. Yet for many years
the "friends of the Indian" looked to the boarding school as an essential ingredient of the government's plan to civilize the "savage." This
void in the literature is striking since the boarding school—its organization, formal instruction, and day to day routine—was a major setting for the clash of Native American and white cultures. A deeper
understanding of this phase of Indian policy can be gained by ex-
amining its application to a single Indian tribe—the Hopi. Several
scholars have highlighted various aspects of Hopi-white relations, but
none has discussed in great depth the critical role of education in
this interaction. This study examines that subject, and in doing so, it
integrates tribal and institutional history within the larger context of
Indian-white relations.

Late nineteenth-century federal Indian policy was essentially philanthropic in its approach to the Indian question. It was rooted in a
series of premises and propositions about what the Indian was and
what he ought to become. The pivotal notion was that all cultures
could be classified on a scale according to their degree of civilization
or savagism. Philanthropists believed that throughout history, which
was viewed as a progressive and evolutionary process, only a few societies in the world had reached the upper levels of this scale; the
greater proportion of the world's population remained steeped in savagism. American civilization, of course, exemplified the former and
Indian culture illustrated the latter.

Those responsible for the formulation of Indian policy were sure of
one thing: the Indian could not continue to exist as an Indian. As
the Commissioner of Indian Affairs William A. Jones stated in 1903:
"As a separate entity he cannot exist encysted, as it were, in the body
politic of this great nation." The Indian had to choose, then, between civilization or extinction. Philanthropists were genuinely sin-
cere when they expressed hope that the Indian would choose to learn
the ways of the white man rather than become a victim of American
progress. By the 1880's the Indian Office had settled upon the means
of achieving absorption into white society. The Indian's willingness
to accept the gift of the common school was presumed to be his only

chance for survival. As Commissioner Jones remarked in 1903: "To educate the Indian in the ways of civilized life . . . is to preserve him from extinction, not as an Indian, but as a human being." Education, then, was the means of moving the Indian along the scale of civilization and ultimately into the mainstream of American culture. Moreover, education was seen as the only way of saving the Indian from extinction, but at a considerable price—by eliminating his Indianness.

In the late 1870's, the Indian Office had found cause for renewed hope in the assimilationist potential of education. The source of this hope lay in the apparent success of Captain Richard Henry Pratt in educating Indians at Carlisle Indian Boarding School. Pratt opened Carlisle in 1879 with the philosophy: "Kill the Indian and save the man." Shortly thereafter, all who visited the institution came away with two key impressions: first, that Indians could be civilized, and second, that education was the way to accomplish it. On the surface, at least, it appeared that, if a young Indian was removed from the savage influence of the reservation and kept for several years in the civilized environment of the boarding school, he might be successfully transformed into a copper-colored white man. Following the Carlisle experiment an elaborate three-tiered system of education was developed in the far West; it was composed of the reservation day school, the reservation boarding school, and, finally the Carlisle-type non-reservation boarding school. In the 1880's the Indian Office began to turn its attention to a remote tribe living on three mesas high above the Arizona desert—the Hopi.

In 1882, Indian agent J. H. Fleming decided to visit the Hopi. With a wagon and mules he followed a very "difficult and circuitous" route and finally reached Oraibi, the largest village of the Hopi. Fleming later recorded that "such an event I am told, had never been known in the history of the town; a span of mules and wagon on the streets of Oribi [*sic*] was indeed a novelty!" Fleming was now part of a continuous stream of Indian agents in the last quarter of the century who formed impressions of this remote people. Those agents who could move beyond their own ethnocentricity—and they were few— noted that the Hopi did not seem to fit the traditional model of savagism. They were not nomadic hunters. The Hopi had achieved instead a high level of agriculture in the almost barren desert. Nor did they live in temporary shelters made of animal skins or brush, but dwelled in well-constructed, stone and plaster houses. Furthermore, they were not warriors, but as the word Hopi implied, a people of peace. Indian agent John H. Sullivan observed in 1881:

> They are a peculiar people, and to me a very interesting branch of the human family, presenting some of the best characteristics known to civilized man, occasionally giving strong proof of the fact of their fathers having once enjoyed the advantages of a high degree of intelligence, the vestiges of which have come to them through a long line of succession from son to son. Their faults as seen by us from our standpoint are the results of their system of education, which being so different from our own, we find cause to complain, and doubtless criticize with unjustifiable severity.

Most agents were not so sensitive to the richness and uniqueness of Hopi culture. In 1890, for instance, agent C. E. Vandever, while admitting that the Hopi had an "unexpected capacity for intelligent reflection," still noted that upon reaching maturity, Hopi children "invariably sink into a state of mental apathy." Leo Crane, one of the most hated of the agents and superintendents during this period, declared in his annual report for 1912 that "the average Hopi has no morals in the white man's sense of morality. They begin as children to live on a moral plane little above their livestock." Crane, who was fond of including snapshots with his reports to Washington to demonstrate "the never-improving moral problem of these people," pointed out on one occasion: "Hopi children of both sexes often go nude in the summer, and in some of the villages boys and girls of twelve and over may be discovered practically nude."

But if nudity bothered Crane's Victorian sensibilities, the cultural characteristic that most offended him was Hopi ceremonialism. "The greatest obstacle to Hopi advancement is the dance," he stated. Crane held a special distaste for one of the most traditional and sacred of Hopi ceremonies, the famous Snake Dance. He noted in 1915 that it showed no signs of "deterioration as a barbaric Indian specticle" [sic]. All agents to the Hopi agreed that while this unique people possessed some enobling characteristics, their religious practices alone condemned them to a lower rung on the ladder of civilization. As one agent noted thirty years prior to Crane's arrival: "The dark superstitions and unhallowed rites of a heathenism still infects them with its insidious poison, which, unless replaced by Christian civilization, must sap their very life blood." In a letter to the Secretary of Interior in 1890, the Commissioner of Indian Affairs Thomas J. Morgan concluded that the solution lay in education: "If their children can be kept in school . . . , they will make very satisfactory progress in the ways of civilization."

The opening of Keams Canyon Boarding School in 1887 signaled the beginning of an uninterrupted effort to educate Hopi youth in the ways of civilization. Initially government officials had every reason for optimism about Hopi responsiveness to education. A boarding school established for the Hopi in 1875 had met with some success before closing a year later. Furthermore, the Hopi agent had written to the Commissioner in 1884 that the Hopi manifested "an earnest desire" for a white education, and he claimed to have received assurances from village leaders that out of a total Hopi population of about two thousand, the government might expect 250 students. It was no surprise, then, that after the Keams Canyon School got under way, Agent James Gallaher reported the venture "a complete success."

Within two years, however, the school was experiencing major difficulties in maintaining enrollments. As a reservation boarding school, students were permitted to return to their village for extended vacation periods. The problem was that many never came back. The Hopi were having second thoughts about turning their children over to the government for education. Thus, just two years after the opening of Keams Canyon, the Commissioner of Indian Affairs received word from agency headquarters that there existed a "disinclination of parents to send children."

At this point five Hopi headmen were invited to Washington for a conference with the Commissioner of Indian Affairs. The government sought to emphasize to the Hopi its determination to enforce school attendance. The trip was also designed to impress this remote people with the wealth and power of white civilization. The journey seems to have had the desired effect. When Chief Lololomai from Oraibi spoke with Commissioner Morgan on June 27, 1890, he began:

> My people are blind. Their ears are closed. I am the only one. I am alone. They don't want to go in the white man's ways, although I am chief . . . I am thankful to see you and I want

your advice as to what to do with my people who are hard
headed.

Rather than reply directly to Lololomai's question, Morgan chose to
discuss the power of white civilization and the importance of education:

> As you see the white people are very much greater in numbers
> than you are. They are increasing very fast, and are very pros-
> perous. They live in good houses and have good clothes and
> plenty to eat. Two things make them prosperous, one is that
> they educate all their children and keep them in school year
> after year, and they learn about books and how to do all kinds
> of things. The white people educate the women too, as you see
> here, and then when they are educated they all work. These are
> the two things, we educate all our children and we all work.

After a visit to Carlisle, Pennsylvania, where the chiefs witnessed the
civilizing power of education in its most developed form, they returned home to proclaim the necessity of cooperating with Washington.
   Their appeal went unheeded. Most Hopi remained adamant in
their refusal to send their children to the Keams Canyon school.
"While the headmen were willing for the children to come," reported the agent, "they had few children of their own, and referred
me to the parents, while the fathers said the mothers controlled the
children, and the mothers said the children would cry, and hence
they would not send them." Finally, at wits end, the Office of Indian
Affairs resorted to force. In December 1890 and again in July 1891
federal troops were sent to the village of Oraibi. After this show of
force, the Hopi peaceably handed over their children. By the end of
1891, the agent was able to boast of a respectable enrollment of a
hundred pupils at Keams Canyon.
   Hopi resistance to education did not end, however. In fact, by the
turn of the century the Hopi had divided into two factions, the
"friendlies" and the "hostiles." As the names imply, the former were
more willing than the latter to cooperate with the government's civilization policy. In the main village of Oraibi relations between the
two groups degenerated. The village split in 1906, and the hostiles
were forced to leave the village. The center of Hopi opposition to
government policy thereafter centered in the new hostile village of
Hotevilla. Its determined leader was Yukeoma, a traditional Hopi who

held an ardent dislike for white ways in general and schools in particular. The persistent refusals of the Hotevilla residents to send their children to school finally brought action in 1911. A troop of cavalry was sent out with orders to force the villagers to give up their children for a white education.

Despite the continued opposition of many Hopi to the government's education policy, a steady stream of Hopi children left the mesas to learn the white man's ways after 1890. While some were eased into the white world by attendance first at one of the village day schools established in the 1890s, many directly entered the reservation boarding school at Keams Canyon. After the turn of the century an increasing number of Hopi attended the nonreservation schools at Phoenix, Arizona, and the Sherman Institute at Riverside, California. It was in the boarding school environment, both reservation and nonreservation, that Hopi pupils received their heaviest dose of civilization.

The Hopi child who came to the boarding school directly from the village received a most abrupt introduction to white society. In the first few days, they were subjected to a process, which for lack of a better term, must be called de-Indianization. The belief was that before Indians could begin to acquire the knowledge, skills, and attitudes of the white world, they must be stripped of all outward signs of their savage heritage. This process involved a threefold attack on their personal appearance and tribal identity. They were forced to abandon traditional dress for a school uniform. For some students, of course, this was a welcome exchange, especially if the Indian clothing was inferior to school apparel in its capacity to keep them warm in winter months. Others objected strongly to the change in dress. Emory Sekaquaptewa, for instance, arrived at Keams Canyon wrapped in a fine new blanket woven for him by his grandfather. At school it was exchanged for the standard issue of blue shirt, mustard-colored pants, and heavy shoes. As for the blanket, he recalled, "I saw it later, in the possession of the wife of the superintendent." After a change of dress, the new recruit was subjected to a haircut. This process, too, many Hopi regarded as an unwelcome assault on their person. Finally, there was the need to change an Indian's name. Where possible the Indian Service preferred that an Indian name be only slightly altered or merely translated into English. Often, however, pupils received a new one altogether; some even acquired names of historical distinction. At Keams Canyon in 1889, for instance, a Ki-Ki-tu was recorded as Albert Gallatin and a Ma-ku-si as Michael Angelo.

De-Indianization was only the beginning stage of an institutional process devoted to totally transforming the subjects. The Hopi received the rudiments of an education; its goal was to teach them to speak and write the English language, provide some knowledge of United States history and constitutional government, and convey an elementary understanding of basic subjects such as science, mathematics, and geography. But if instruction in academic subjects was an important aspect of the Indian's education, it was clearly secondary to instruction in manual and vocational trades. Most male graduates of the boarding school, it was assumed, would return to their western homes and support themselves as farmers or tradesmen. Thus, the average Indian's academic education emphasized reading the local newspaper, writing a short letter, and handling numbers sufficiently well to discover whether the reservation trader was cheating.

The preference for the practical over the theoretical was also rooted in the notion that the Indian's success at agricultural pursuits was the principle measuring rod for indicating his progress toward civilization. This belief found expression in the Phoenix Indian School's weekly newspaper, the *Native American*, which had etched over its masthead the declared purpose of the school: to transform "the man with a gun" into a "man with a hoe." This slogan missed the mark in the case of the Hopi, who were well known for their peaceful nature as well as their capacity to make the desert bloom, but it did serve to emphasize the practical orientation of a boarding school education. Consequently Indian boys at Keams Canyon, Sherman, and Phoenix spent half of their academic day on the school farm or in the shop learning basic carpentry skills. Hopi girls spent an equivalent period learning the skills thought appropriate for their sex in a Victorian age—ironing, sewing, and arranging a table setting consistent with the standards of civilized dining.

The emphasis placed on manual and vocational training had a much deeper purpose than merely teaching skills. It was also a means of instilling in the Indian values and attitudes thought essential to being an "American." Specifically, the Indian had to learn the virtue of work, the principle of private property, and the spirit of acquisitiveness even to the point of selfishness. According to United States Senator Henry L. Dawes, the best solution to the general problem was to take the Indian "by the hand and set him upon his feet, and teach him to stand alone first, then to walk, then to dig, then to plant, then to hoe, then to gather, and then to *keep*." Merrill E. Gates, president of the Lake Mohonk Conference, spoke in similar terms when he told fellow philanthropists that the primary challenge before Indian educators was to awaken "wants" in the Indian child. Only then could the Indian be gotten out "of the blanket and into trousers,—and trousers with a *pocket that aches to be filled with dollars!*" This was to remain an enduring objective of Indian education for years to come, and therefore, it is not surprising that in 1907 Commissioner Francis E. Leupp stressed the same point when speaking to a group of Indian educators in Los Angeles. After noting that a group of Hopi boys from Oraibi had just arrived at Sherman Institute, he pointed to the Sherman flag monogrammed with the letters S.I. and commented that the design came "pretty near being a dollar mark." And then he added: "Sordid as it may sound, it is the dollar that makes the world go around, and we have to teach the Indians at the outset of their careers what a dollar means." This concept was for Leupp "the most important part of their education."

Leupp and other philanthropists were convinced that the Indian's survival hinged on the acceptance of this economic principle. After the Indian had been taught the ways of civilization, including the "value of things," Leupp explained, he must be left alone to "dig out his own future." He admitted that "a considerable number will go to the wall," but "those who survive will be well worth saving." It followed that the message of materialism and rugged individualism must be learned well; so well in fact that it could not be entrusted to any single area of the academic program. It must pervade all aspects of the Indian's education. The *Native American* gave poetic expression to the American ideal of success in a piece entitled "The Man Who Wins."

> The man who wins is the man who works—
> The man who toils while the next man shirks. . . .
> And the man who wins is the man who hears

The curse of the envious in his ears
But who goes his way with head held high
And passes the wrecks of the failures by—
For he is the man who wins.

Another area of Indian education that preoccupied boarding school officials was the student's religious conversion. Because philanthropists had historically perceived an essential relationship between Christianization and civilization, missionaries had always been allowed to assume a prominent role in Indian education. By the turn of the century, Catholic, Mennonite, and other missionaries had had opportunities to convert the Hopi, but with limited success. Undaunted by these failures, the Commissioner of Indian Affairs urged the various religious denominations to exert themselves to the utmost so as not to leave "an inch of pagan territory uncovered." Boarding schools were part of this "pagan territory" in that they housed young Indians, many of whom had never come in contact with Christianity. At Keams Canyon the American Baptist Home Missionary Society was invited to offer Sunday morning services as well as two hours of religious instruction during the week. At the larger nonreservation boarding schools, such as those in Phoenix and Sherman, more than one denomination was permitted to compete for the student's loyalty.

As a result, the Indian student was subjected to religious pressures that struck at the very heart of his tribal heritage. To give in to these pressures was to deny the ways of his ancestors; to reject them was to be condemned to savagery and, if the missionaries were right, to everlasting fire and brimstone. Under these pressures many Hopi, for a time at least, professed conversion to Christianity, if only to please the superintendent. Don Talayesva, a Hopi from Oraibi, rejected the Christian message during his stay at Keams Canyon, but once at Sherman he was moved publicly at one point to declare his intention to return eventually to his village and preach the Scriptures "to my people in darkness." When reflecting on this experience at Sherman, Talayesva later recalled: "At that time I was half-Christian and half-heathen and often wished that there were some magic that could change my skin into that of a white man."

Since the Indian Bureau sought a total transformation of the Indian, every aspect of school life was devoted to this end. The structure and organization of the school environment took on special significance. A careful look at the operation of these schools reveals that they were militaristic in both atmosphere and organization. Literally every aspect of the student's life was regimented and routinized, with each day beginning and closing with the sound of a bugle. Every daily activity—learning, working, sleeping, eating, and playing—was scheduled with the neat precision of a military encampment. The boarding school was not just a place where the Hopi learned the white man's religion, language, and skills; it was also a place where he virtually marched and drilled his way toward civilization. One Hopi who attended Sherman in 1914 later recalled: "When I entered school it was just like entering the school for Army or soldiering. Every morning we were rolled out of bed and the biggest part of the time we would have to line up and put guns in our hands. . . . When a man gave a command we had to stand at attention, another command grab our guns, and then march off at another command."

As this recollection suggests, the emphasis on regimentation was not mandated by the organizational difficulties involved in feeding, housing, and educating several hundred young Indians. The reasons went far deeper and had to do with what anthropologist Bernard L. Fontana has recently called the Indian's sense of "natural time" compared to the European-American's concept of "clock time." Because the notion of clock time was closely associated with such positive virtues as work, money, and progress, school officials assumed that the Indian was hopelessly bound to savagery until he internalized the mechanical and disciplined movements of clockwork and gained an appreciation for the belief that "time" was a valuable resource to be spent on civilized pursuits rather than on savage idleness. The *Sherman Bulletin* reminded its pupils that it was not enough "to do the right thing and in the right way, but it must be done at the right time as well if we would reap the rewards of our labor." Lest students miss the relationship between time and money, they were informed that "many of our most successful businessmen date their success from the time they commenced to practice the virtue of being on time." Indeed, the habit of punctuality was not an end in itself, but rather a habit that, if carried into life, became "one of the main instruments in making real success."

Still another reason for the militaristic organization of the schools was the Indian Office's conviction that the student must be taught the value of obedience. In addition to having close links with punctuality, the emphasis on obedience seems to have been rooted in the philanthropic belief that civilization—especially as it was emerging in the modern context—required the acceptance of rules, regulations, and restraints. Since most believed that the young Indian was the product of a way of life that operated on the principle of wild impulse, the lesson of obedience was seen as an essential element in his elevation. The *Sherman Bulletin*, for example, informed students that the first law of life was the word "obey."

> Obedience is the great foundation law of all life. It is the common fundamental law of all organization, in nature, in military, naval, commercial, political, and domestic circles. Obedience is the great essential to securing the purpose of life. Disobedience means disaster. The first disastrous act of disobedience brought ruin to humanity and that ruin is still going on. "The first duty of a soldier is obedience" is a truth forced upon all soldiers the moment they enter upon the military life. The same applies to school life. The moment a student is instructed to do a certain thing, no matter how small or how great, immediate action on his part is a duty and should be a pleasure. . . . What your teachers tell you to do you should do without question. Obedience means marching right on whether you feel like it or not.

The emphasis on order and regimentation also had a political motivation. A major purpose of the boarding school was to sever forever the ties that bound the Indian to his tribal government and to transfer his loyalty to the nation state. Classroom instruction in American history and government could not be counted upon alone to accomplish this objective. Given the tragic history of Indian-white relations, there were special problems connected with winning the young Indian's allegiance to the federal government. Only by actual participation in patriotic and military rituals, officials thought, could Indians be expected to internalize and then identify with national symbols, institutions, and leaders. The world of flags, uniforms, and parades was devoted to this end. The use of military spectacle, especially when combined with a holiday celebration or the visit of a public figure, was seen as a particularly effective method of forging new political loyalties. One Hopi, for instance, remembered that on Decoration Day at the Keams Canyon school the students were handed small flags and bunches of flowers and then "marched out to the graves of two sol-

diers who had come out here to fight the Hopi and had died." When
President William McKinley visited Phoenix Indian School in May
1901, he watched the entire school population march in rank and assemble before him in perfect military fashion. According to the *Native American* account, "The movement was executed like clockwork,
unmarred by a single mistake or bungle. There they stood for an instant, 700 pairs of eyes gazing sharply and intently at the 'great-
father.'" And then upon the command of a bugle call, the Indians
shouted in unison: "I give my head and my heart to my country; one
country, one language, and one flag."

This was what education for civilization was all about: one country,
one language, and one flag. This goal combined with de-Indianization,
Christianization, and finally, setting the Indian on his feet so that he
might "dig out his own future" outfitted in trousers with a "pocket
that aches to be filled with dollars" together constituted the multiple
purposes of Indian education. These objectives were formulated and
universally agreed upon by philanthropic groups and governmental
agencies devoted to the noble goal of preserving the red man from
extinction in the face of white civilization. The price that the Indian
had to pay for his continued existence is revealed in the remarks
made by Indian Commissioner Morgan at another boarding school
ten years before McKinley visited Phoenix. After listening to some religious songs sung by an Indian choir, Morgan remarked to the students: "As I sat here and listened with closed eyes to your singing,
you were not Indians to me. You sing our songs, you speak our language. In the days that are coming there will be nothing save his
color to distinguish the Indian from the white man."

To the disappointment of the Indian Office, many students, after
returning to their villages, rejected much of their boarding school education and returned to the old Hopi ways. Don Talayesva is a case in
point. Talayesva first attended the day school at Oraibi and then
spent several years at Keams Canyon. A bright student, he recalled
that after one year in boarding school he had learned many English
words, could recite part of the Ten Commandments, knew how to
pray to Jesus, and could eat with a knife and fork. He also learned
that the earth was round, that it was improper to go naked in the
presence of girls, and perhaps most important of all "that a person
thinks with his head instead of his heart." Talayesva then moved on

to Sherman Institute. When he left Sherman in 1909, he considered himself a prosperous young man, possessing among other things a five-dollar watch and a respectable looking suitcase. After a ride on the Santa Fe Railroad and another by horsedrawn wagon, he was back in Hopi country again. Like every other returned student, he tried to fit together the pieces of his life. The first night home he lay on the roof of a Hopi pueblo, and while gazing at the clear Arizona sky, he considered the meaning of his education:

> As I lay on my blanket I thought about my school days and all that I had learned. I could talk like a gentleman, read, write, and cipher. I could name all the states in the Union with their capitals, repeat the names of all the books in the Bible, quote a hundred verses of Scripture, sing more than two dozen Christian hymns and patriotic songs, debate, shout football yells, swing my partners in square dances, bake bread, sew well enough to make a pair of trousers, and tell "dirty" Dutchman stories by the hour.

With the exception of the dirty Dutchman stories, the Indian Office would have been pleased with Talayesva's remembrance. About this returned student's future intentions, however, philanthropic enthusiasm would have been substantially dampened. For after recounting all that he had learned of the white man's world, Talayesva now "wanted to become a real Hopi again, to sing the good old Katcina songs, and to feel free to make love without fear of sin or rawhide."

Don Talayesva became part of what the Indian Office commonly referred to as the "problem of the returned student." The original faith placed in the boarding school was based on the assumption that the returned student would not only withstand the pressures to "backslide" into savagery, but that he would serve as a progressive example to those Indians amenable to advancement up the scale of civilization. This was the theory. In fact, however, the nonreservation boarding school system had scarcely been created when it came under heavy criticism for failing to live up to its promise. The problem was not the inability of the boarding school to bring about a dramatic transformation in the Indian child. Indeed, while under the watchful eye of school officials and within the regimented atmosphere of institutional routine, the young Indian appeared to adopt the ways of civilization rather quickly. The change occurred after the student's return to the reservation. Agents frequently noted the problem of the "retrograde" student or the "return to the blanket."

In a long letter to the Indian Office in 1917, Superintendent Leo Crane described how the process of relapse affected the Hopi. From the time of birth to the age of seven the Hopi child, Crane reminded officials, "learns Indian legends, attends Indian dances and ceremonies much more colorful and appealing than any later white man's entertainment." At the age of seven he attended a day school located near his village and for the next six years continued his education in the shadow of the pueblo. "Everything learned during the day has been ironed out of him by night, through ridicule and adverse criticism of that fool white teacher, who is obeyed only because behind him is a greater and stronger fool, the Agent." During this period the child was subjected to the competing world views of the white man and the Hopi. One day he "hears of Jesus," and on the next he "attends a dance to propitiate the snake gods." After several years the child was understandably "a little confused."

Later he was sent to the reservation boarding school at Keams Canyon. At this point in his education, the Hopi child was only partly won over to the cause of civilization. While he now understood "that white people have a kindly sympathy for him," and while he genuinely appreciated the clean clothes, regular food, and clean bed that came with boarding school life, once beyond the eyes of the teacher he "still plays Indian games" and "will unconsciously sing Indian chants." He was, in effect, "AN INDIAN under instruction." At the end of his term at Keams Canyon, he might even become an "INDIAN CITIZEN," a phrase Crane never defined, but in the context of his remarks seems to imply a half-civilized status; the student essentially retained his Indian identity and manner of life, while simultaneously he felt a strong sense of political loyalty to the national government and possessed a general understanding of white ways. In any event, this outcome was the best that could be hoped for. After the reservation boarding school, Crane thought the Hopi's education should end.

Crane believed the root of the returned student problem was found in the notion that the student should continue his education at the nonreservation boarding school. Crane felt the nonreservation school was an ill-conceived "white washing process," a doomed endeavor to turn the Indian into an "imitation white man." The education the

Hopi received away from the reservation was tragically irrelevant to the conditions under which the returned student lived after graduation. Indeed, surrounded by the modern conveniences at Phoenix or Sherman, the Hopi student might reflect on the contrast with his life at home. "He remembers the thirteenth century mesa, insufficient food at home, shortage of fuel in winter, struggle for crops in summer, lack of water, hard work for everything. Perhaps he thinks he is wasting his time, knowing to what he will return." Perhaps, too, he had learned a trade he would probably never be able to practice. Had anyone ever considered, Crane mused, that he would have to apply his modern skills in a thirteenth-century pueblo "located in the heart of the desert one hundred miles from a town or a railroad?" And finally, the student was sent home with a "little pin-money and WITHOUT TOOLS."

Then came the shock of adjustment. "The hand that has been firmly thrusting between his shoulder blades for fifteen years, has suddenly been removed." At first he traveled to the agency seeking employment and an opportunity to apply his newly acquired skills, but in all likelihood this was an impossibility. He was in the ludicrous position of being a blacksmith where there were no forges, a carpenter where lumber was scarce, a tailor where flour-sacks were used for clothes, a shoemaker where moccasins were worn, and a painter where there was nothing to paint. The inevitable process of relapse soon began: "First, the money goes; then the good clothes and the 'Regal' shoes wear out; third, nature is busy on his hair. He binds up his hair with a gaudy handkerchief, as do the others; he begins to make a pair of moccasins." In the meantime, tribal elders, "in strict patriarchal fashion," remind him of the small corn field, a few horses, and some sheep that they have set aside for him. "Gradually he accepts that which he has. He ceases his visits to the Agency asking for a job. The old life is before him. He has, apparently, become an Indian of the Indians."

Despite this depressing scenario, Crane was unwilling to state that the returned student had gone back to the blanket. The educated Hopi was in fact decidedly different from those Hopi who had never been schooled in the white man's ways. While the returned student might soon appear at the agency a trifle unkempt, "he does speak English when not fearful that some stranger will laugh at his grammar, and he has not come as a beggar." Moreover, if he was shown the advantage of a modern convenience or utility, he was more likely to desire it than the Hopi who had never been to school. And perhaps most importantly: "It will be easier to obtain his children for their education, and the hold of the medicine man has been somewhat loosened." Crane felt these were not unimportant consequences of the Hopi's education. He believed the returned student was a failure only to the extent that he was *"not what the tax-payer expected him to be."* Again, Crane remained critical of the nonreservation school. If the Hopi was destined to live a simple life in the vast Arizona desert, then he asked: "Why insert this artificial period in his education?"

Criticism of the nonreservation school caused school officials to search for ways to prepare their graduating students for reservation life. A psychological tactic often used by schools was the "returned student conference." Such conferences not only enabled recent graduates to renew their institutional association with the source of their cultural elevation and to hear again the inspiring message of civilization, it also offered an opportunity to impress upon graduating students just how immense the pressures for conformity were back on the reservation. In 1910, for instance, one school official at Phoenix told members of a conference:

> I most sincerely trust that you who are leaving the school for your homes this year do not underestimate the influence your homes will have to draw you away from what you have learned at this school. . . . I know you feel so well grounded . . . in your hope of doing good . . . on your reservations that you do not realize what you will have to overcome. Remember you are but one against many and among that many . . . are relatives and friends even dearer than any friendships formed in this school. Remember too, they believe themselves just as much in the right in their beliefs as you do in yours. . . . Your lessons of industry, civilization and Christianity have been taught to you but very few years compared with the many years during which customs have been growing in your people.

There was a fatal flaw in how school officials attacked the problem of relapse, and it goes to the very heart of this chapter in Indian-white relations. They assumed that the difficulty was due to the conservative nature of tribal elders and a certain character flaw of the re-

turning students, their inability to withstand ridicule and hardship
for the sake of civilized principles. They ignored altogether the charge
of superintendent Crane that the nonreservation boarding school was
itself to blame because it prepared the Indian student for a life that
did not exist on the reservation. They ignored too the possibility that
many returning students readopted the old culture out of conscious
preference for the Hopi way. Neither the Indian office in Washington
nor school officials in the field ever considered the possibility that
the real source of the returned student problem lay in the questionable premises that had historically shaped the nation's Indian policy—
premises relating to such ethnocentric conceptions as "savagism," "civilization," and "progress." It is not surprising that this last explanation
was never considered. To have done so would have required a painful
reexamination of the entire rationale by which white Americans had
justified the dispossession of the Indian's land and culture. Given all
that was at stake, it was simply too much to ask.

2

The "Black Codes"

JERRELL H. SHOFNER

• The surrender terms offered by General Ulysses S. Grant to Robert E. Lee's proud but dwindling Army of Northern Virginia were among the most generous in history, especially in view of the suffering, anguish, and emotion which accompanied the Civil War. At Appomattox Court House, the commander of the Union Army was both magnanimous and sensitive. All that was required was that Confederate soldiers put down their arms and go home in peace.

But the battlefield result did not immediately make clear what the political future would be for those Southern whites who had led their states out of the Union. According to tradition, and to a considerable segment of Northern sentiment, such men were traitors to the United States. Southern voters understandably took a different view and promptly returned many leaders of the secessionist movement to Washington as members of Congress. Simultaneously, other firebrands of the old Confederacy gained dominance over the various state legislatures and promptly began to limit the social, political, and economic rights of the former slaves.

The result was a series of racist and repressive laws known to history as the "black codes." They were intended both to guarantee the subservience of the entire black population and to assure the continued division of Southern society along strict racial lines. Although they varied from state to state in severity, the black codes generally prevented Negroes from bearing arms or from working at occupations other than farming and domestic service.

As Jerrell H. Shofner makes clear in the following article, these initial inhibitions proved to be only the first set of a long series of measures designed to preserve the "Southern way of life." The black codes were followed by the "Jim

Crow" laws between 1890 and 1910. These new restrictions, which legalized segregation in public facilities and which introduced such concepts as the literacy test, the "grandfather clause," the white primary, and the poll tax, made it almost impossible for blacks to rise above the lowest rung of the economic ladder, or indeed even to protest effectively. Thus a rigidly enforced segregation system came to dominate all aspects of Southern life. Even after two decades of militant civil rights activity, this legacy has just begun to be erased.

In October 1956, Dr. Deborah Coggins, health officer for Madison, Jefferson, and Taylor counties, sat down to lunch in Madison, Florida, with a public health nurse to discuss a matter of mutual official concern. Because of their busy schedules the lunch hour was the only mutually available time for the meeting. But since the doctor was white and the nurse black, the business luncheon led to the dismissal of the doctor by indignant commissioners of the three counties. Her "breach of social tradition" had been so serious, according to the commissioners, that it rendered her unfit to continue in the office to which she had been appointed about six months earlier. While Governor LeRoy Collins disagreed, and incensed citizens of South Florida condemned the commissioners, most white North Floridians nodded approval. As they saw it, Dr. Coggins had violated one of the strictest taboos of her community when "she ate with the darkies." As a native of Tampa married to a descendant of an old Madison County family, she should have known better.

Social intercourse between whites and blacks was forbidden by both law and custom in Florida in the 1950s. And it had been that way as long as most people then living could remember. The one brief period following the Civil War when things had been different had merely proved that segregation was the best way for all concerned. This belief was reinforced by all the myths and folk tales, social institutions, and statute laws with which Floridians of the 1950s were acquainted.

Those few years following the Civil War had been crucial ones for white Floridians, most of whom had sympathized with and supported the Confederate war effort. Defeated, disorganized, and bankrupt in

1865, they had taken heart when President Andrew Johnson announced his plans for reconstructing the nation. Guaranteeing former Confederates retention of all their property except slaves, he appointed William Marvin as provisional governor to oversee the formation of a new government. To gain readmission to the Union, Florida had only to repudiate slavery, secession, and debts incurred in support of the Confederacy, and recognize all laws enacted by Congress while the state was out of the Union. Marvin repeatedly told white audiences that if they would change the laws to provide civil rights to the newly freed blacks that he believed they would not be required to implement Negro suffrage. Retrospectively this implied promise seems to have been an unfortunate one. Radical congressmen had been contending with Abraham Lincoln and later Andrew Johnson for control of Reconstruction policy. What white Floridians regarded as major concessions to former slaves was far less than Radical congressmen believed necessary. The latter watched with growing concern as the southern state governments created by President Johnson enacted their "black codes" which distinguished between black and white citizens. And the final decision on Johnson's Reconstruction program rested with Congress.

The delegates to the 1865 constitutional convention and the members of the 1865–1866 legislature who enacted the Florida black code had spent their lives as members of the dominant white class in a society whose labor system was based on racial chattel slavery. They brought to their law-making sessions all their past experiences gained from a lifetime acquaintance with a comprehensive ideological and legal framework for racial slavery. They believed that blacks were so mentally inferior and incompetent to order their own affairs that subjection to the superior white race was their natural condition. Whites benefited from the labor of blacks, and they were in turn obligated to provide guidance and welfare for their workers. Now that slavery was abolished these men met to comply with Andrew Johnson's requirements, while, at the same time, trying to salvage as much as possible of that system under which whites with their paternalistic responsibilities to blacks, and Negroes with their natural limitations, had lived peacefully.

Florida had a comprehensive slave code regulating almost every activity touching the lives of blacks. Because "free Negroes" had constituted an anomaly in a society where racial slavery was so central, there was also an extensive set of laws regulating their affairs. It was understandable that the lawmakers of 1865–1866 should draw on their past experiences and on the codes regulating slaves and free blacks. But in doing so they invited criticism from suspicious Radicals in Congress who believed that the president had erred in his lenient requirements.

A three-member committee was named by the constitutional convention of 1865 to recommend to the first legislature, scheduled to meet the following year, changes in the old laws necessary to make them conform to the postwar situation. The committee's report did nothing to assuage congressional suspicions. It urged the legislature to preserve, insofar as possible, the beneficial features of that "benign, but much abused and greatly misunderstood institution of slavery." It strenuously asserted the legislature's power to discriminate. Such power had always been executed by all the states of the Union, including those of New England. Slavery had been abolished, but nothing had been done to the status of the "free negro." Certainly, therefore, "Freedmen" could not possibly occupy a higher position in the scale of rights than had the "free negro" before the war.

Provisional Governor William Marvin, who had been appointed by President Johnson in 1865, warned that Congress was likely to intervene unless the state legislature accepted the concept of Negro freedom and extended to freedmen equal protection of the law. Despite this warning, the legislature followed the committee's recommendations. It enacted laws dealing with crime and punishment, vagrancy, apprenticeship, marriages, taxation, labor contracts, and the judicial system which were collectively referred to as the black code. The code clearly established a separate class of citizenship for blacks, making them inferior to whites.

A long list of crimes was enumerated and penalties assigned. The death penalty was imposed for inciting insurrection, raping a white female, or administering poison. Burglary was punishable by death, a fine not exceeding $1,000, or a public whipping and the pillory. Malicious trespass, buying or selling cotton without evidence of ownership, defacement of public or private property, and other crimes of similar nature were punishable by fines, imprisonment, or whipping and the pillory. Whipping or the pillory was also the prescribed punishment for injuring someone else's livestock, hunting with a gun on another's property, or unauthorized use of a horse whether in the employ of the owner or not. According to an antebellum statute continued in force by the 1865–1866 legislature, Negroes were specifically denied the right to carry firearms, bowie knives, dirks, or swords without a license from the probate judge. The punishment was forfeiture of the weapon and a whipping, the pillory, or both. This provision reflected some concern among white Floridians at the time about a rumored Negro insurrection, which had no substantive basis.

"An act to punish Vagrants and Vagabonds" made all persons subject to arrest who could not demonstrate that they were gainfully employed. Aimed at preventing congregation of freedmen in the towns, this law was especially alarming to Radical congressmen. A convicted vagrant could post bond as a guarantee of good behavior for the following year, but if no bond was posted, he could be punished by the pillory, whipping, prison, or by being sold for his labor up to one year to pay his fine and costs. "An act in relation to Apprentices" allowed the courts to apprentice the children of vagrants or paupers to persons who could supervise their activities, provide for them, and teach them a trade. It applied to both races, but in the aftermath of emancipation most of the children affected were black. This was only a slight extension of an antebellum law requiring that all free blacks over twelve years of age have a duly registered white guardian.

For the first time, a statute defined a Negro as any person with one-eighth Negro blood. Although that standard still left much to interpretation, some such ruling was necessary to the enforcement of several acts intended to separate the races. Both blacks and whites were enjoined from attending the meetings of the other race. They were also required to ride only in railroad cars designated for their respective races. Marriages between Negro men and white women were prohibited. White violators of the enactment could be fined $1,000, jailed for three months, or both. In addition to the fine, Negroes could be made to stand in the pillory for one hour, receive thirty-nine lashes, or both.

One of the most controversial enactments was "An act to establish and enforce the Marriage Relation between Persons of Color." Negro couples were given nine months to decide whether they wished to continue living together. After that time they had either to separate or be legally married. This method of correcting a problem arising from slavery and its abolition caused so much criticism in the northern press that the legislature in November 1866 simply passed a law declaring all freedmen living as man and wife to be legally married.

Even the revenue laws seemed discriminatory. There was a provision for a five-mill property tax on real property and a capitation tax of three dollars on every male between twenty-one and fifty-five. The Negroes often did not learn of the tax in time or did not have the money to pay it. If they were delinquent they could be arrested and sold for their labor for a period long enough to liquidate the obligations incurred. Several cases of tax-delinquent blacks being sold for a year's labor soon caught the attention of the northern press. Such an exorbitant punishment for failure to pay a three-dollar tax seemed to some congressmen to be a substitute for the bonded servitude which had just been abolished.

Although the legislators followed closely a system already established by the military commanders, their "ACT in relation to Contracts of Persons of Color" also distinguished between the races. Contracts were to be in writing and witnessed by two white persons. If Negroes broke their agreements, they could be punished as common vagrants by being whipped, put in the pillory, imprisoned, or sold for up to one year's labor. They could also be found in violation of their contract for "willful disobedience," "wanton impudence," "disrespect" to the employer, failure to perform assigned work, or "abandonment of the premises." If the employer broke the contract, the laborer could seek redress in the courts. Although the state attorney general ruled the law unconstitutional, the next legislature rewrote it so as to apply to both races in occupations limited almost entirely to Negroes.

An early crop lien law was intended to keep tenants on the land. A landlord was empowered to seek a writ placing a lien against growing crops on rented land if the rent was not paid within ten days of the due date. If a tenant did not pay out at the end of the year, the lien could be extended to the next year and he could be legally held on the land. Attracting little attention as part of the black code at the time, this statute, with subsequent additions, contributed largely to an agricultural system which kept many tenants in economic bondage for years after the Civil War.

Central features of the black codes were "AN ACT to extend to all the inhabitants of the State the benefits of the Courts of Justice and the processes thereof" and another "prescribing additional penalties for the commission of offenses against the State, and for other purposes." The convention-appointed committee in its recommendations to the legislature had bemoaned the loss of that highly efficient institution which had existed on the plantations for punishing those "minor offenses to which Negroes are addicted." Since those offenses were now under the jurisdiction of the judiciary, the committee declared that circuit courts would be unable to handle the increased volume of litigation. It accordingly proposed that criminal courts be established in each county and the legislative assembly complied. These courts were soon handling cases, but the heritage of slavery days was too much for them. The legislators had permitted Negroes the right to testify only in cases involving blacks, and juries were made up of white men only. These whites had lived in a society where Negro slaves had had no standing in the courts, and they were now unwilling to accept the word of blacks. The courts were abject failures as legal remedies for freedmen accused of crimes or seeking redress of wrongs committed by whites.

The law "prescribing additional penalties" was a response to the special committee's recommendation that "whenever a crime be punishable by fine and imprisonment we add an alternative of the pillory for an hour or whipping up to thirty-nine lashes or both at the discretion of the jury." This discrimination was "founded upon the soundest principles of State policy, growing out of the difference that exists in social and political status of the two races. To degrade a white man by physical punishment is to make a bad member of society and a dangerous political agent. To fine and imprison a colored man . . . is to punish the State instead of the individual."

The Floridians who enacted the "black code" were surprised and angered by the national reaction they caused. Thomas W. Osborn, assistant commissioner of the Freedmen's Bureau in Florida, intervened to prevent the administration of corporal punishment. Radicals in Congress pointed to the discriminatory legislation to show that Negroes could not expect equal treatment as long as the antebellum Florida leaders remained in power. With similar legislation in other former Confederate states, the Florida black code helped the Radicals convince their moderate colleagues that President Johnson's Reconstruction plan had failed to furnish necessary protection to newly-freed persons. In a mammoth executive-legislative struggle which lasted through most of 1866, Congress overturned the Johnson governments in the South and implemented Congressional Reconstruction in 1867–1868.

Based on Negro suffrage—which Provisional Governor Marvin had said would not happen—and military supervision, the congressional plan seemed to Floridians to be a broken bargain. In late 1866 Governor Walker complained that the state had complied with President Johnson's Reconstruction requirements, but that Floridians were still being denied their rights. The subsequent implementation of Negro suffrage, enactment of the 1868 constitution, and the election victory of the newly-founded Florida Republican party were considered by local whites as unwelcome and unwise invasions of the rights of the state.

These developments also embittered them toward their former slaves. When Negro suffrage was first announced, the planters assumed that they could control the freedman's vote. At assemblages throughout the black belt counties former owners competed with "carpetbaggers" for the allegiance of the new voters. When the blacks quite understandably ignored their former masters in favor of the new Republican leaders, the native whites lost most of their paternalistic sentiment toward the freedmen. They determined to resist Negro suffrage and Republican hegemony by every means they could muster.

Landowners and storekeepers applied economic pressures on black voters. Politicians resorted to ingenious political tactics. Conservatives in the legislature blocked action whenever possible by dilatory parliamentary maneuvers. But by far the most visible, and in the long run the costliest, method was violence. With black legislators sitting in the Capitol, black marshals advertising their tax-delinquent property for sale in the county seats, and white Republicans wielding power dependent on black voting majorities, white Floridians believed that destruction of Republican power was a goal which justified any successful means. According to one sympathetic historian who lived in post-Reconstruction Pensacola, "in this contest for a very necessary supremacy many a foul crime was committed by white against black." According to their reasoning, Republican politicians in Washington had overpowered reasonable, well-meaning President Johnson and had implemented, over his vigorous vetoes and in violation of agreements already made with southern leaders, and contrary to sound constitutional theory, a policy of Negro suffrage. Although it was not the fault of the blacks, this policy had subjected an educated, property-owning class to the mismanagement and corruption of ignorant Negroes and their carpetbagger leaders. This wrong had to be corrected regardless of the methods necessary. But in permitting the use of violence for this purpose, the white leaders unleashed a force which was almost impossible to stop.

As soon as the military commander turned over control of the state to Republican Governor Harrison Reed in July 1868 and withdrew his troops to garrison duty, violence began increasing. At first night-riding bands of hooded horsemen attempted to frighten rural Negroes into submission. But partially because many blacks showed more courage than expected and partially because it was easy to commit excesses against helpless people while shrouded in the anonymity of darkness and disguise, the scare tactics soon degenerated into merciless beatings and murder. Threats were delivered and when they went unheeded, recipients were ambushed. Dozens of white Republicans and Negroes were assassinated throughout the Florida black belt from Jackson County on the Apalachicola River to Columbia County on the Suwannee and southward to Gainesville. In Jackson County alone between 1868 and 1871, more than 150 persons were killed.

Congress responded with corrective legislation. A national elections law empowered the United States government to place supervisors at every polling place in Florida and the other southern states. Military guards were also to be deployed during elections to potentially dangerous locations. Two enforcement acts authorized President Grant to declare martial law and employ soldiers where disorder was beyond the ability of state governments to control. Before the 1872 election the worst of the violence had subsided in Florida, as much from the belief among native whites that it had achieved its purpose as from the presence of United States military forces. This episode nurtured the growth of two important aspects of the evolving myth of the Lost Cause: the idea that helpless white Southerners were being mercilessly suppressed by the military power of a hostile central government, and that they were driven to the use of violence to correct an even greater wrong—dominance of the state by an ignorant Negro electorate.

After years of delay due to opposition from Conservative-Democrats and some of the white Republicans, the legislature of 1873 enacted a civil rights law calling for equal accommodations in public places, although it *permitted*, without requiring, integrated schools. Within months of its enactment it was essentially nullified by a Leon County jurist. When several Negroes complained that they had been denied access to a skating rink in Tallahassee, the judge ruled that private owners or commercial establishments had the right to refuse service to anyone they chose. Although it remained on the books for a time, the 1873 civil rights law was a dead letter. Because its principles were opposed by a majority of white Floridians, it did nothing to change social conduct.

During the four years following President Grant's reelection in 1872 the Reconstruction process continued with diminishing velocity. Most southern states were recaptured by native white Conservative-Democratic parties despite the efforts of the Grant administration. A national depression, repeated scandals in the administration, and other matters caused northern interest in the South to wane. As the 1876 presidential election approached, many Northerners were anxious for a settlement of "the southern question." The stage was set for the final episode in the growth of the myth of the Lost Cause. When the campaign of Samuel J. Tilden and Rutherford B. Hayes for president ended in an uncertain election, the nation was subjected to nearly four months of anxiety. Hayes was ultimately inaugurated after tacitly agreeing to withdraw United States soldiers from the South. This resolution of the disputed election became known as the "compromise of 1877." When he withdrew the troops, all remaining Republican administrations in the South collapsed, and Conservative-Democratic regimes took over in their places. The men who headed those new governments came to be called "Redeemers" who had ousted the carpetbaggers and restored "home rule" in the southern states.

Left to their own devices, white and black Republicans were unable to maintain themselves. During the next few years the southern Republican parties became permanent minorities and eventually almost disappeared. The United States Supreme Court's 1883 decision in the *Civil Rights Cases* was regarded as national acceptance of the failure of Reconstruction and restoration of white supremacy in the South. In that decision the court limited the civil rights guarantees of the fourteenth amendment so that they applied only against official discrimination. Thus, while it was unconstitutional for a state to pass a law discriminating on grounds of race, it was legal for private owners of hotels, restaurants, and theaters to refuse service to blacks.

Cautiously at first, but with increasing confidence, white Floridians began rewriting their laws with a view to establishing a society similar to that envisioned in the black codes of 1865–1866. The 1868 constitution was regarded as a carpetbagger document, imposed on the state by outsiders supported by a black electorate and military force. The demand for its replacement swelled in the early 1880s. Attended by a minority of Republicans, only seven of whom were Negroes, an 1885 convention wrote a constitution which prepared the way for disfranchisement of blacks and dissolution of the Republican Party. It authorized a poll tax as a condition for voting and required that all officeholders post bonds before assuming office. The latter was intended to make it difficult for blacks to qualify for office if they were able to win in the northern counties where there were overwhelming majorities of blacks. But the poll tax provision was most important. The 1889 poll tax law required that potential voters pay their tax for two years immediately prior to elections. If the county records did not show the tax paid, then the would-be voter was required to produce receipts to prove that he was eligible to vote. An accompanying statute required separate ballot boxes for each office. These made it necessary that the voter be able to read the names on the boxes in order to place his ballots in the correct places and have them counted. The result was dramatic. Statewide Republican candidates received more than 26,000 votes in 1888; in 1892 they received fewer than 5,000.

The legal changes were accompanied by incessant racist rhetoric from public officials and the state press. School histories taught young children that the "Redeemers" had saved the state from the excesses of "Radical Reconstruction." When white Floridians divided on policy matters, Conservative-Democratic politicians reminded the voters that whites must stand together or risk a return to "Negro rule."

This tactic prevented the sundering of the paramount white man's party, but it also increased the gap between the races. Violence had declined after 1872, but it had never ceased. As the possibility of federal intervention diminished in the 1880s and the doctrine of white supremacy became more firmly entrenched, violence as a means of repressing blacks increased. The brutal Savage-James lynching at Madison in 1882 went without serious investigation. Another in Jefferson

County in 1888 resulted in the arrest of five white men, but all of
them were acquitted by all-white juries. Two especially repugnant
lynchings in the mid-1890s led Governor William D. Bloxham to deplore the practice in his 1897 inaugural address, but he offered no
remedy. The praise of white supremacy and persistent reminders of its
alternatives from prominent men perpetuated a climate of tolerance for
violence by whites against blacks.

Floridians were reinforced in their views by similar developments in
other southern states. Worse yet, racial developments in the South
coincided with a growing racial theory throughout the United States.
Relying on Joseph Gobineau and other European racist writers, social
theorists in the United States were preaching the idea of Anglo-Saxon
superiority and the corresponding inferiority of blacks to a receptive
audience. At the same time the United States acquired the Philippine
Islands, and a little later Theodore Roosevelt added his "corollary" to
the Monroe Doctrine. Our decision to uplift our "little brown brothers" in the Philippines and "protect" our Latin American neighbors
from European interference by intervening in their internal affairs
added powerful impetus to the growing racial theories in our country.

By the turn of the century the Lost Cause myth was virtually beyond question in the South and was gaining adherents elsewhere. It
placed little emphasis on the demise of slavery and the failure of secession. Rather it focused on the unsuccessful efforts at postwar Reconstruction. President Johnson had been willing to permit Southerners
to reform their society along lines that allowed for the innate inferiority of blacks. But a misguided Radical-controlled Congress had taken
direction of Reconstruction away from him. These crusading Northerners had attempted to change natural conditions by legislative fiat,
causing immense difficulties for all involved in an experiment which
was doomed by nature to failure. Finally seeing the errors of their ways,
they had withdrawn from the struggle, leaving Southerners to solve
their own racial problems. This was a powerful and satisfying rationale
for a caste system which ultimately degraded Negroes to the point
where they had absolutely no defense against the worst excesses of the
most lawless elements of white society.

Beginning in 1889 a series of Jim Crow laws were passed which gave
legal sanction to the segregation which already existed by custom.
These laws went far beyond the earlier black codes in separating the

races, but they did little more than legalize existing conditions. Racial segregation in Florida was more extensive in 1900 than it had been in 1865.

An 1895 statute prohibited anyone from conducting a school in which whites and Negroes attended either the same classes, separate classes in the same building, or classes taught by the same teachers. Fines and jail sentences were provided for violators. Others soon followed. In 1903 intermarriage was forbidden between white persons and Negroes, including anyone with at least one-eighth Negro blood. Either or both parties to such a marriage could be punished by up to ten years imprisonment or $1,000 fine. A 1905 enactment required separation of the races on street cars and required companies operating them to provide separate facilities. Failure of the company to do so was punishable by a $50 fine with each day constituting a separate offense. Passengers violating the statute were subject to fines of $25 or up to thirty days in jail. Negro nurses travelling with white children or sick persons were exempt. Since slavery days there had been almost unlimited contact between the races where the blacks were in a servant capacity, and this continued. Segregation was a class rather than a physical matter.

In 1905 constables, sheriffs, and others handling prisoners were forbidden to fasten white male or female prisoners to colored prisoners, subject to fines up to $100 or sentences up to six months. The same legislature required terminal and railroad companies to provide separate waiting rooms and ticket windows for whites and Negroes. The penalty for failure was a fine up to $5,000. A 1909 statute required "equal" and "separate" railroad cars or divisions of cars.

These legal reinforcements of existing practices had great significance. Law and custom had been in harmony during antebellum slavery days. The 1865–1866 black code reflected the social experiences of those who enacted them. Then it was overturned by national legislation which ran counter to the beliefs of the dominant groups of Florida society. Because they disagreed with the Reconstruction legislation and the circumstances of its enactment, native white Floridians not only overturned the laws but also developed a rationale—the Lost Cause myth and its corollary of the necessity for white supremacy—which justified and reinforced their actions following the celebrated 1876 election dispute. The Jim Crow laws were the final necessary step. By the early twentieth century white Floridians were living in a society whose customs, ideology, and law code were once more in harmony.

The first third of the twentieth century was the nadir of race relations in Florida and the nation. Although segregation seemed to be permanently entrenched, whites did not let the matter rest. Politicians always referred to it in their campaigns. Newspapers carried editorials dealing with racism and news stories casting obloquy and odium on Negroes. Creative writers dealt with the subject in the same way. There was a widespread movement to solve the race problem by sending the blacks to Africa. A strong advocate of the idea was Frank Clark, an influential Florida congressman who once declared that "Mr. Lincoln said that this nation could not exist 'half slave and half free.' I think it is equally true that this nation can not exist *half white* and *half black.*" Likewise, progressive Florida Governor Napoleon B. Broward went so far as to propose mass removal of Negroes from the United States in his 1907 message to the legislature.

Without political rights, economic strength, or legal status, blacks had no defense. Their best hope was to keep away from whites unless they were fortunate enough to identify with someone who would assist them in legal and economic matters. Usually tied to the land by perpetual indebtedness and dependent on the good will of a white man for whatever security they had, blacks in the early twentieth century occupied a social position not significantly different from that of the antebellum "free Negro" who had been obliged by law to have a white guardian. But this unofficial paternalism was not available to all, and it was inadequate to prevent physical abuse on those occasions when blacks came into contact with unruly whites. Insults and petty violence could sometimes be borne in silence. But at other times it was impossible to avoid trouble. With no legal or social restraints, white ruffians and sometimes ordinary citizens angered by some incident assaulted blacks without fear of reprisal.

In 1911 Mark Norris and Jerry Guster of Wadesboro, Leon County, were arrested on a charge of stealing and resisting arrest. B. B. Smith, a sawmill owner who had been deputized especially to arrest them, had struck Norris with a pistol while doing so. In the justice of the peace court in Miccosukee, the two Negroes were acquitted. When they went to Smith's home to talk about the matter, a gun fight ensued, and Smith was killed. A group of blacks gathered to defend the two men against an anticipated mob, but they quietly surrendered when two deputies arrived to arrest them. Ultimately, ten Negroes were arrested, six of whom were charged with murder. A crowd gathered in Tallahassee, and talk of lynching increased. Six of the men were smuggled out of Tallahassee and taken to Lake City for safekeeping. A few evenings later several men drove to Lake City and got the blacks out of jail on a forged release order, took them to the edge of town, and riddled all six with bullets for more than a half hour. No one in Lake City went to investigate the shooting until the assassins were driving away; thus there were no witnesses to the crime. Governor Albert Gilchrist offered a $250 reward for information about the lynching, but a cursory investigation was shortly abandoned without success.

There was almost no provocation for an incident at Monticello in 1913. Sheriff's deputies went into Log Town, a black section, at about eleven o'clock one Saturday evening just "scouting around." Seeing a group of blacks walking down the road, the deputies called on them to stop to be searched. The Negroes ran. The deputies fired and three blacks were wounded; one of them permanently paralyzed by a shot in the back. No weapons were found on any of them. Walking down the road on a Saturday night seemed to be sufficient cause for a presumption of guilt only in the case of blacks.

When J. A. McClellan shot and killed Charlie Perry, a black, in 1918, the coroner's jury found the shooting to have been in self-defense. It was true that an argument between them had been started by Perry. But the reason for the altercation was that McClellan and others had broken into Perry's house and had searched it without either a warrant or the owner's permission. During the 1920 general election, July Perry of Ocoee, Orange County, caused a disturbance when he tried to vote without having paid his poll tax. He even threatened election officials, but it is inconceivable that the aftermath would have been the same had he been white. Whites followed Perry home and ordered him out of his house. He fired on them. When the altercation was over three days later, the entire Negro section of Ocoee had been burned and four innocent people consumed in the fire. The grisly episode ended only after a mutilated July Perry was finally put to death by the mob which had tired of torturing him. Three years later at Rosewood, near Cedar Key, a white mob charged into the black community searching for an alleged rapist, burned six houses and a church, and killed five blacks. This time the blacks fought back and two whites also died.

The lynching of Claude Neal in Jackson County in 1934 was so shocking that it stimulated a renewed effort in Congress to enact anti-lynching legislation. Neal was accused of murdering a white girl with whom it was charged he had had an illicit relationship. Transferred from jail to jail in West Florida and in southern Alabama he was finally overtaken by a mob in the latter state and brought back to Marianna. He was tortured and mutilated, dragged behind a car, and finally displayed on the streets before crowds, including school children, who attacked the then lifeless body. The corpse was hanged on the courthouse square. On the following day mobs threatened blacks on the streets of Marianna, and order was not restored until the militia was called in. The NAACP published a report of the incident which aroused considerable ire across the nation, but nothing was done. The attorney general ruled that the recently enacted federal law against kidnapping across state lines did not apply because a monetary ransom had not been the purpose of the mob. And as always there was no remedy under state law.

Violence was only the extreme and most visible surface of a racially segregated society. Many whites who deplored violence still obeyed the infinite daily reinforcements of their segregated system: separate dining facilities, theaters, restrooms, waiting rooms, railroad cars, and drinking fountains, as well as the customary racial divisions of labor. While blacks and whites often worked at comparable jobs at the lower end of the economic spectrum, nearly all the professional and white collar jobs were limited to whites and the most menial tasks were overwhelmingly filled by blacks. Even where employment of blacks and whites was comparable, compensation was disproportionate. For example, black school teachers in the 1930s in one north Florida county earned from $37.50 to $40 per month, slightly less than half the salaries of their white counterparts. At that time Confederate veterans were drawing pensions of $37.50 per month. Even the New Deal programs of the national government, designed to relieve the poverty of the 1930s, were affected by racism. Relief administration in Jacksonville established a formula which gave forty-five percent of the available funds to Negroes and fifty-five percent to whites, while black relief families outnumbered white by three to one. Florida Negroes were often denied access to the work-relief programs of the Civilian Conservation Corps and the National Youth Administration on the grounds that they were unqualified to meet admission standards.

By the time Claude Neal was lynched in 1934 forces outside the state were already undercutting the racial status quo. Negro migration into northern cities had created potential black political power. Breaking traditional ties with the Republican party, large numbers of urban blacks voted for Franklin D. Roosevelt in 1936, beginning an alliance with the national Democratic party which still exists. The NAACP had gained considerable attention by its publicity of lynching statistics and its lobbying for an antilynch law. It won its first school desegregation case at the graduate level in 1937. In World War II blacks made significant gains in the armed services and in defense jobs at home. Further migrations out of the South occurred. The Truman administration called for fair employment practices and the 1948 Democratic platform endorsed the idea. The military services were integrated in 1949.

Despite all these changes, the 1954 United States Supreme Court decision in *Brown* v. *Board of Education of Topeka* and its 1955 directive to integrate the public schools with "all deliberate speed" fell like a bombshell on Florida and the other southern states. The Florida attorney general sent to the court the results of a study by social scientists showing that attempts to integrate the state's schools would cause violence. On the basis of the report he asked for a stay of execution of the decision. Some public officials said the court decision was too soon; others said it was an invasion of state rights and a usurpation of legislative power by the courts. State Senator John Rawls of Marianna introduced a resolution in the legislature which emphasized that the constitution of Florida added "legal force to the time honored custom and native inclination of the people of Florida, both negro and white, to maintain . . . a segregated public school system . . . integration . . . in the public schools . . . would tend to encourage the . . . unnatural, . . . abhorrent, execrable, and revolting practice of miscegenation."

White Floridians girded themselves to resist. With a full range of laws requiring segregation and the widespread belief in state rights, theirs was a formidable defensive arsenal. Because the segregation laws conformed so closely to the social values of white Floridians, they emphasized the primacy of state legislation and branded the United States Supreme Court an usurper. Opponents of integration eventually destroyed much of the creditability of the national court system by emphasizing the clash of state law with the court. It was at this point that the Jim Crow laws were crucial. Instead of having to face the basic question of how a state could distinguish between its citizens by law, segregationists were able to attack the integrity of the agency which raised the question. It was much more satisfying to defend the right of the state against invasions of the national court than to defend the Jim Crow system on its dubious merits.

Governor LeRoy Collins's unwillingness to defy the court was a setback, but he promised to use all lawful efforts to maintain segregation while at the same time calling on Floridians to obey the law of the land. The legislature went beyond the governor's position, passed a resolution calling on him to interpose the authority of the state to protect Florida citizens from any effort of the national government to enforce the Brown decision, and enacted legislation providing for the closing of the schools if the national government used force to integrate them. Representative Mallory Horne of Leon County led an effort to restrict the authority of the court, and many Floridians prepared to *defend the law by resisting* the Brown decision.

The moderation of Governor Collins made an immense difference in Florida. Despite the attorney general's warnings of incipient violence, and amidst reports of disruptions in other states, Florida passed through this "Second Reconstruction" with markedly little actual violence. Although there was almost no progress toward school integration for years after the Brown decision, the civil rights movement broadened to other areas and accelerated. White Floridians retreated slowly, resisting each attack on their social system by referring to the state laws. Gradually the national court system negated those laws. With constant pressure from the courts, and belatedly from Congress and the president, the legal framework of segregation crumbled.

But the initiative came almost entirely from outside the state. Some Floridians, exasperated at the national government's interference, argued that they had been gradually working out solutions for the racial problem before the Brown decision. Some social scientists argue that as a rural, agricultural society becomes urban and industrialized, racial segregation breaks down because it cannot function in such a society. However that may be, there was little change in the racial caste system in Florida until the nation once more became interested in it. The hideous lynchings of the early twentieth century ceased when Congress started seriously considering antilynching legislation. Education funds went to Negro schools in larger quantity as the NAACP began winning its desegregation cases. New congressional legislation on civil rights, public accommodations, and voting spearheaded changes in these areas.

With assistance from the national courts and marshals, blacks moved from the back of the buses, sat down at public lunch counters, came down out of the theater balconies, attended previously all-white schools at least in small numbers, and moved into the mainstream of Florida society in countless ways which had been denied them by both law and custom in the past. It was still a piecemeal movement, and social approval of segregation was still strong among whites, but the Jim Crow legal system had been nullified by the late 1960s.

Florida society still retains some of its traditional segregation. Negroes still live mostly in the less desirable sections of towns. Many white families have taken their children from the public schools and sent them to "Christian" schools which cropped up rapidly after 1968. But there is a significant difference. Supported by custom *and the law* only a few years ago, segregation and its correlative of white supremacy and black inferiority were taken for granted by most political and other opinion leaders. Some applauded it as beneficial and even necessary for the South. Gubernatorial candidate Bill Hendricks campaigned throughout Florida in the 1950s as the Ku Klux Klan candidate. White supremacists rested confidently and comfortably with their views, knowing that they were supported by the laws of the state.

That has changed. Few Floridians now speak publicly against basic civil rights for blacks. Racial jokes have moved from most drawing rooms into the restrooms. Denial of the legal sanction for segregation has reversed the burden of public approval. It is no longer popular to advocate segregation, at least directly. Those who believe in it are on the defensive. In the 1974 election, Jeff Latham, a candidate for state-wide office, ruined his creditability and his chances for election when he admitted appealing for support from a racist organization.

It is difficult to change the values of society by law—or in the jargon of the capitol hallways "You can't legislate morality"—but it is possible to take away the legal basis for repugnant practices. Jim Crow legislation had provided an immense reinforcement of a segregated society and the rationale for it. Its repeal was difficult because it complemented the values of the most powerful groups of Florida society. But once that legislation was nullified, segregationists found themselves on the opposite side of the law. Interposition was a last-ditch effort to justify the system in terms of state sovereignty along lines enunciated by John C. Calhoun more than a century earlier and negated by the Civil War. The state rights defense was gradually discredited in the 1960s by repeated revelations of southern law enforcement officials using the color of law to commit criminal acts in defense of segregation.

Finally forced to the basic question of how to justify segregation on its merits in terms of mid-twentieth century America and without the support of Jim Crow laws—much as their ancestors had had to deal with the problem of converting slaves to freedmen in 1865–1866— white Floridians have exerted remarkable effort to overcome their segregationist views. They have come far from the time when violence was justified on the ground of the necessity for white supremacy. Many people who still prefer a segregated society restrain themselves from open advocacy of it. And most important of all, most Floridians are willing to accept recent changes, albeit sometimes reluctantly, because they are reinforced by the law.

Racial divisions of American society persist and have become a national problem, but they are no longer being dealt with at the level to which they had descended in the early twentieth century. Americans have probably gone as far toward an integrated society as legal changes will take them. Difficulties encountered with the Supreme Court's "busing" decisions reveal the limits on law as a positive force. Legal provisions cannot diverge too far from custom and belief without disruption. But the disparity is not as great in 1977 as in 1867–1868 when the black code was replaced by laws calling for equality. With time— history—and tolerance, custom and the law will once more coincide as they did for white Floridians before 1860.

3

The East European Jewish Migration

LEONARD DINNERSTEIN

• Jews have been in the United States since 1654. By 1790
they numbered perhaps 1,200 and sixty years later about
15,000. Spread thinly throughout the land they had little
difficulty finding a place for themselves in the greater society
and were accepted as individuals or in small groups. During
the middle of the nineteenth century Jews from the German
states of Europe entered the United States along with Protestant and Catholic Germans and they, too, were absorbed
easily. By the 1880s, however, East European Jews started
coming in the hundreds of thousands. A changing industrial
society, Pan-Slavism, and continual pogroms proved too difficult a combination to combat, especially while opportunities
existed in the United States.

The colonial Jews—mostly Sephardim from the Iberian
Peninsula and Brazil—settled mainly in the port cities of
Newport, New York, Philadelphia, Charleston, and Savannah
and engaged in shopkeeping and mercantile activities. Many
chose to assimilate into the dominant community, married
gentiles, and raised their children as Christians. The Jews
who were a part of the mid-nineteenth-century influx also
gravitated toward cities but they did not remain exclusively
in the East. Many a Jew put a pack on his back, traveled in
different sections of the country, and finally settled down in
places as different as Greenville, Mississippi; Boise, Idaho;
Columbus, New Mexico; Cleveland; Atlanta; Dallas; and Los
Angeles. Other Jews, however, went directly to New York,
Cincinnati, Chicago, Philadelphia, and Detroit, and immediately set down roots. As a result, the families of the mid-
nineteenth-century Jewish migration were spread throughout

From *Uncertain Americans: Readings in Ethnic History* by Leonard Dinnerstein and Frederic Cople Jaher. Copyright © 1977 by Oxford University Press,
Inc. Reprinted by permission.

the United States. They, too, engaged in the traditional commercial activities usually associated with Jews, but they also had children who were trained for the professions. The German Jews achieved a level of prosperity well above those of other ethnic groups. In 1890, when the majority of American Jews were still of Sephardic or German extraction, the Hebrew community was considerably more prosperous than the national average. Two thirds of all Jewish families in the United States had at least one servant, while over ninety percent of the American population failed to earn enough money to maintain a family in moderate circumstances. But the massive influx of Eastern European Jews, most of them poor, was already operating to lower the aggregate wealth of American Jewry to the point where this ethnic minority became collectively an underprivileged group.

The new migrants differed in several ways from their predecessors. They came in the hundreds of thousands and could not disappear into the American population with relatively little notice. They were also more Orthodox in religion, bizarre in dress, and determined to settle in Jewish enclaves and perpetuate Orthodox customs. They also tended to concentrate in a few localities. More than seventy percent remained in New York City and the surrounding area. They threatened the security of the Americanized Jews who had already moved into the middle class and who feared, correctly, that the newcomers might stimulate waves of overt anti-Semitism in the United States which would victimize all of the Jews.

Most knew how to read and write Hebrew or Yiddish, and the men had some urban and vocational skills. But the opportunities originally available to them were as unskilled or semiskilled laborers, and for years they were plagued with poverty and occupied cheap tenements on New York's Lower East Side.

The story of their experiences, and ultimate accomplishments, is discussed in the following selection.

INTRODUCTION

Jewish migration to the United States in the nineteenth and twentieth centuries may be divided into three groups: the German, the East European, and the Central European. During the first period of heavy Jewish immigration to the United States, mainly during the pre-Civil War years but roughly from the 1840s through the 1870s, about 50,000 Jews arrived from the German states. They engaged almost exclusively in trade and commerce, many starting off as peddlers and some moving up quickly into banking and department stores. The second and most important wave, from the 1870s through 1924, came primarily from Eastern Europe. Responding to the economic uprooting of society and the frequent pogroms of the late nineteenth and early twentieth centuries, more than 2,000,000 Jews left Russia, Galicia, Rumania, and Hungary for the great trek to the United States. These people included artisans, skilled workers, small merchants, and shopkeepers. They and their descendants have made the greatest impact of all the Jews in the United States and are the subject of this essay. The third group, from Central Europe, numbering about 365,000, came to America between 1925 and 1953, with approximately 132,000 in the years between 1948 and 1953. Some of these people emigrated for economic reasons, but the overwhelming majority were victims of Hitler's rise to power in Germany. In the 1930s Nazi persecutions and brutalities forced many German Jews to leave the country, and after the Second World War some concentration camp victims and the displaced refugees were granted opportunities to resettle in the United States. This third group quickly moved into the Jewish mainstream in the United States. They made major impacts in the American scientific and intellectual communities.

Before the Second World War these Jewish groups were quite different and easily identifiable: by income, education, jobs, residence, and organized associations. In the past twenty-five years, however, the differences have diminished considerably because of a vast leap in both educational and income levels of American-born Jews. It would be quite difficult, if not impossible, today to distinguish among the descendants of the previous generations of Jewish immigrants. In terms of life style, occupation, and income the overwhelming majority of

Jewish families are in the middle and upper middle class and their breadwinners occupy professional, technical, and managerial positions.

CAUSES FOR EMIGRATION

The Jews left Eastern Europe for much the same reason that most other peoples left their states—grinding poverty at home made them yearn for a decent life elsewhere. In Russia 94 percent of the Jews lived in the "pale of settlement," a huge belt of land in Western and Southwestern Russia and the Ukraine stretching from the Baltic to the Black Sea. Jews could live outside of this area only by special permission. Within the pale their population increased from 1,000,000 in 1800 to 4,000,000 in 1880 and this expansion constricted the possibilities of economic opportunities. In Rumania they were regarded as aliens, while in Galicia Jews suffered from economic boycotts and other manifestations of hostility.

During the 1870s the industrial revolution began to make a significant impact in Russia. That impact was greatest within the pale, where industrialization took place most rapidly. The Russian government, which had earlier set numerous restrictions on Jews, feared their influence, especially after industrialization began. Jews actively engaged in trade and commerce, which attracted many of the gentiles once they were forced off the land. Competition for positions in a tight economy heightened Christian-Jewish tensions. Industrialization also stimulated the movements of Jews and gentiles from rural to urban areas to seek employment. The city of Lodz, which had eleven Jews in 1797, counted 98,677 one hundred years later and 166,628 in 1910. Warsaw's Jewish population leaped from 3,521 in 1781, to 219,141 in 1891. Industrial expansion also led to a major flight of people to the west. Many Jews went to Germany, France, and England in Europe, and to Argentina, Canada, South Africa, and Palestine. More than 90 percent of the Jewish migrants, however, wound up in the United States.

Other factors also propelled the Jewish exodus. As in the case of emigrants from other nations, flight was impelled by specific items like the unsuccessful Polish uprising of 1863, the Lithuanian famine of 1867–69, the Polish cholera epidemic of 1869, and by the predisposition of young people to try their fortunes in a new world, and the developing political ideologies of Zionism and socialism which made traditional modes of thought and behavior too confining. Many Jews were outspoken socialists. They envisioned a new democratic social order with a more equitable distribution of the nation's wealth and resources. Anti-Semitism, which rose in intensity as Pan-Slavism gripped the Eastern Europeans, however, provided a unique reason for the Jewish migration. Jews were not Slavs and therefore stood as an impediment toward nationalistic unity. The assassination of Tsar Alexander II of Russia in 1881 by a group of socialists spawned a wave of pogroms against the Jews which continued intermittently until the First World War. Major pogroms occurred in 1881, 1882, 1903, and 1906, and hundreds of others have been recorded. These pogroms, often inspired by government officials, resulted in wanton and brutal assaults upon Jews and their property. Russia also codified and curtailed Jewish rights after Tsar Alexander's assassination. The May Laws of 1882 restricted the numbers of Jews that might attend Russian universities and the kinds of occupations Jews might pursue. They could not rent or own land outside of the towns and cities nor could they keep their shops open on the Christian sabbath or on Christian holidays.

American letters and money sent by earlier immigrants, along with the advertisements from railroad and steamship lines anxious to transport emigrants, further stimulated migration from Eastern Europe to the New World. Promising economic conditions in the United States, combined with increased persecutions and deprivations in Russia, Galicia, and Rumania, expanded the exodus to the West, as revealed in the following figures:

> 1870s: 40,000
> 1880s: 200,000+
> 1890s: 300,000+
> 1900-14: 1,500,000+

PATTERNS OF SETTLEMENT

Over 90 percent of the more than 2,000,000 Jews who left Eastern Europe between 1870 and 1924 went to the United States. Unlike many other immigrant groups, the Jews mostly traveled with their families. During the years 1899 to 1910, females made up 43.4 percent of the total number of Jewish immigrants and children 24.7 percent, the highest figure for any arriving peoples. During the same period males constituted 95.1 percent of the Greek immigrants and 78.6 percent of the southern Italians. Only the Irish had a larger percentage of females than the Jews (52.1 percent), but it is believed that many of them came alone to work as domestics. Statistical estimates indicate that 71.6 percent of the Jews came from the Russian empire, including Latvia, Lithuania, and Poland; 17.6 percent from Galicia in the Polish area of the Austro-Hungarian empire; and 4.3 percent from Rumania.

Most of these people landed, and remained, in New York City. In 1870 the city's Jewish population had been estimated at 80,000; in 1915 almost 1,400,000 Jews lived there. The newcomers found friends, relatives, jobs, and educational opportunities in New York City, and, in any case, few had the money to travel elsewhere. Moreover, the Orthodox knew that they could find *kosher* butchers which would allow them to maintain Jewish dietary laws, and jobs where they would not have to work on the sabbath. To be sure, those who landed in Boston, Philadelphia, or Baltimore, or even those who made their way to Chicago and other cities, found small Jewish communities in which they could settle. Chicago, in fact, had 200,000 Jews by 1912. But the major center, by far, for East European Jews was New York.

Most of the immigrants who chose to live in New York City settled originally in a small section of Manhattan Island known as the Lower East Side. The boundaries of this ghetto lay roughly within the blocks bordered by Fourteenth Street, Third Avenue and the Bowery, Canal Street, and the East River. The heart of the district, the tenth ward, housed 523.6 people per acre at the beginning of the twentieth century. In the 1890s Jacob Riis, an enterprising reporter, observed that "nowhere in the world are so many people crowded together on a square mile" as in the Jewish quarter. Within the Lower East Side numerous subdivisions could be identified as streets housing primarily Russian, Galician, Rumanian, or Hungarian Jews. The area contained 75 percent of New York City's Jews in 1892, 50 percent in 1903, and 23 percent in 1916.

The tenements where the Jews lived can best be described as dark, dank, and unhealthful. One magazine described the dwellings in 1888 as

great prison-like structures of brick, with narrow doors and windows, cramped passages and steep rickety stairs. They are built
through from one street to the other with a somewhat narrower
building connecting them. . . . The narrow courtyard . . . in
the middle is a damp foul-smelling place, supposed to do duty
as an airshaft; had the foul fiend designed these great barracks
they could not have been more villainously arranged to avoid any
chance of ventilation. . . . In case of fire they would be perfect
death-traps, for it would be impossible for the occupants of the
crowded rooms to escape by the narrow stairways, and the flimsy
fire-escapes which the owners of the tenements were compelled
to put up a few years ago are so laden with broken furniture,
bales and boxes that they would be worse than useless. In the
hot summer months . . . these fire-escape balconies are used as
sleeping-rooms by the poor wretches who are fortunate enough
to have windows opening upon them. The drainage is horrible,
and even the Croton as it flows from the tap in the noisome
courtyard, seemed to be contaminated by its surroundings and
have a fetid smell.

Two families on each tenement floor shared a toilet. In the summer
months the heat and stench in these places were unbearable and the
stagnant air outside provided little relief.

The first Jewish immigrants, despite their toil, earned barely enough
to subsist on. As a result it was not uncommon to find parents, children, other relatives, and some boarders in a two-, three-, or four-room
apartment. The boarder may have paid three dollars a month for his
room and free coffee, but that came to 30 percent of the family's ten-
dollars-a-month rent. Looking back, the prices of four cents for a quart
of milk, two cents for a loaf of bread, and twelve cents for a pound of
kosher meat may look ridiculously cheap, but when one reckons this
on an average weekly income of less than eight dollars, the picture is
quite different.

Fortunately for the Jews, their earnings increased sufficiently after a
few years in this country so that they did not have to rot in the slums
for an interminable period. "It was judged to be a ten-year trek,"
Moses Rischin tells us, from Hester Street, on the Lower East Side, to
Lexington Avenue, in the more fashionable uptown area. The tenements, of course, did not disappear, but their inhabitants continually
changed.

Most of the immigrant Jews from Eastern Europe resided first on the Lower East Side and the Hebrew population in that area of the city peaked at more than half a million in 1910; by the 1920s fewer than ten percent of New York's Jews still lived there. The completion of the subways in the early part of the century opened up vast tracts for settlement in upper Manhattan, Brooklyn, and the Bronx (other boroughs of New York City), and the Jewish working class, anxious and able to take up residence in better neighborhoods, moved away.

Jewish immigrants in Boston, Chicago, and other large cities had initial experiences similar to those who remained in New York. In most other places where Jews went, the tenement areas were smaller or nonexistent, the neighborhoods less congested, and the opportunities to live in more healthful surroundings considerably better. East European Jews who went south or west had experiences considerably different from their brethren who went to the urban areas of the Northeast and Chicago, but they constituted fewer than five percent of the entire migration.

Over the years the children and grandchildren of the newcomers moved out of these cities to surrounding suburban areas or flourishing new communities where economic opportunities beckoned. Most of the subsequent growth in the American Jewish population took place in the states closest to New York: Pennsylvania, New Jersey, and Connecticut, with two major and a few minor exceptions. After World War II job opportunities and a pleasant year-round climate drew hundreds of thousands of Jews to California, especially the Los Angeles area, and many older people first visited and then retired in Miami Beach, Florida. The growth of the Jewish population in California and Florida is primarily a phenomenon of the past thirty years.

LABOR AND BUSINESS

East European Jewish immigrants differed from most of the other foreign-born arrivals in the late nineteenth and early twentieth centuries in that 95 percent of them came from urban rather than rural areas. Their urban origins resulted in the development of skills and talents which would aid them greatly in the United States. An 1898 survey of the Russian pale of settlement found that Jews owned one third of all the factories in the area and that Jewish workers concentrated in the clothing (254,384), metal-working (43,499), wood-working

(42,525), building (39,019), textile (34,612), and tobacco (7,856) industries. The skills they acquired there were also in demand when they reached the United States.

An American survey of the occupations of immigrants entering the United States between 1899 and 1910 listed 67.1 percent of the Jewish workers as skilled compared with a general figure of 20.2 percent for all newcomers. In his study *The Promised City*, Moses Rischin indicates that

> Jews ranked first in 26 out of 47 trades tabulated by the Immigration Commission, comprising an absolute majority in 8. They constituted 80 per cent of the hat and cap makers, 75 per cent of the furriers, 68 per cent of the watchmakers and milliners and 55 per cent of the cigarmakers and tinsmiths. They totaled 30 to 50 per cent of the immigrants classified as tanners, turners, undergarment makers, jewelers, painters, glaziers, dressmakers, photographers, saddle-makers, locksmiths, butchers, and metal workers in other than iron and steel. They ranked first among immigrant printers, bakers, carpenters, cigar-packers, blacksmiths, and building trades workmen.

In the United States the Jewish immigrants found jobs in distilleries or printing, tobacco, and building trades, while significant numbers of others started out as butchers, grocers, newspaper dealers, or candy store operators.

The majority of the Jewish immigrants, however, found work in the needle trades, which were—because of the increasingly efficient methods of mass production and the existence of a mass market—undergoing rapid expansion. The arrival of the East Europeans with their particular talents coincided with this vast growth. By the end of the nineteenth century Jews had just about displaced the Germans and Irish from the industry. In New York City the development of the clothing industry transformed the economy. In 1880 major clothing manufacturers numbered only 1,081, or 10 percent of the city's factories, and employed 64,669 people, or 28 percent of the city's work force. By 1910 the borough of Manhattan (which before the consolidation of the five boroughs in 1898 had been New York City) had 11,172 clothing establishments, which constituted 47 percent of the city's factories. The industry employed 214,428 people, slightly more than 46 percent of Manhattan's workers. In 1890, 60 percent of the employed immigrant Jews worked in the garment industry and on the eve of the First World War more than half of all Jewish workers, and two thirds of Jewish wage earners, were still to be found in the industry. The Jewish influence was so great that the manufacturing of wearing apparel in the United States came to be regarded as a Jewish endeavor. Hebrews not only labored in the garment factories; they also worked their way up to supervisory positions and the bolder ones opened their own establishments. Before the Second World War it was estimated that Jews controlled 95 percent of the women's dress industry, 85 percent of the manufacturing of men's clothing, and 75 percent of the fur industry.

Initially, the owners were German Jews who at first looked down on their East European coreligionists and exploited their labor. Many of the early twentieth-century factories were nothing more than reconverted lofts and tenements or else small areas of workers' apartments. Many garments were actually finished in home sweatshops. Workdays lasting from 4:00 a.m. to 10:00 p.m. in these hovels were not uncommon, and wages averaged $6.00 to $10.00 a week for men and $3.00 to $5.00 for women. (Children also worked on these garments and in other industrial areas as well. Naturally, they earned lower wages than adults.) Because of the seasonal nature of the work, few had a steady yearly income. The annual wage of the average garment worker came to $376.23 in 1900, $1,222 in 1921, and $873.85 in 1930.

Low wages, appalling working conditions, and the insecurity of workers' positions prompted many to think about union organization. Among the Jewish immigrants were many socialists and members of the Russian Jewish Bund who had tried to improve social conditions in Europe. Many of these men also provided the backbone for unionization in the garment trades in the United States. The International Ladies' Garment Workers Union was founded in 1900 but not until the major strikes of clothing workers in 1909 and 1910 were significant victories won and the union firmly established. In Chicago 40,000 garment workers struck in 1910 and in New York 20,000 waist and dressmakers went out from November 1909 through February 1910. In July 1910 as many as 60,000 cloakmakers struck. The strikes attracted wide attention in the press, among social workers, and throughout the Jewish community. The workers won a victory when in July 1910 a

"Protocols of Peace" set up a Board of Arbitration, a Board of Grievances, and a Board of Sanitary Control. Four years later the cloakmakers formed the core of the new Amalgamated Clothing Workers of America, a union which had its origins in Chicago with a less effective group, the United Garment Workers of America.

The International Ladies' Garment Workers and the Amalgamated were the two major Jewish unions in the United States. Because of the socialist heritage of so many of their participants, the two unions were concerned not only with improving labor conditions but with a vast program for improving the living conditions of all of their members. The unions were responsible for ending sweatshops, raising wages, and improving working conditions. They also pioneered in the development of a large number of auxiliary services for members. They built housing developments, established educational programs, maintained health centers, provided pensions, set up vacation resorts, developed a system of unemployment insurance benefits long before the state and federal governments assumed this responsibility, and opened banks giving services at significantly lower cost than other financial institutions. The Jewish unions, in sum, initiated social reforms which other labor organizations adopted. Aside from the ILGWU and the Amalgamated, the only other powerful labor union made up primarily of Jewish workers and leaders was the United Federation of Teachers (now the American Federation of Teachers) which galvanized New York City's schoolteachers in the 1960s and propelled its president, Albert Shanker, to the forefront of labor leadership in America.

EDUCATION AND SOCIAL MOBILITY

Despite the benefits obtained by and from the labor unions, Jews had no desire to remain in the working class. Their ambition to "get ahead" knew no bounds and as soon as possible they, and/or their children, strove to move up to more lucrative and prestigious occupations. As early as 1900, American-born sons of Russian Jews constituted six times as many lawyers and seven times as many accountants as were to be found in their parents' generation but only one third the number of garment workers. As the years passed, this tendency became even more pronounced. Jewish workers also tried to become manufacturers. Many of those who started out as peddlers eventually moved into small retail outlets and some of the latter then expanded into larger emporiums. It was the rare community, in fact, that did not have some Jewish storekeepers. Random samplings in different decades through the 1940s showed anywhere from 31 to 63 percent of the Jews engaged in trade. In one study of the South the author noted, "It is said, 'If there is a Jewish holiday, you cannot buy a pair of socks in this whole country,' a remark which illustrates how complete the control of the retail dry-goods trade by Jews is supposed to be."

The entertainment industry also provided an avenue of advancement for some immigrant Jews. In 1905 it was estimated that half of the actors, popular songwriters, and song publishers in New York City were Jewish. Within a few years Jews also pioneered in the motion picture industry.

The Jews made great economic and social advances because educational and business opportunities were available to the more enterprising and because the masses of East European Jewish immigrants considered it necessary to "Americanize" their children and have them learn the language and customs of the new country as quickly as possible. From their beginnings in this country, the East European Jews also showed a passion for education and professional advancement unique in American history. Members of other immigrant groups, before or since, have not been as zealous in their quest for knowledge. The newcomers themselves were forced to do manual work, but whenever possible they encouraged their children to remain in school, attain an education, and move up in the world. As Samuel Gompers, leader of the American Federation of Labor, observed, "The Jews were fairly ravenous for education and eager for personal development. . . . All industrial work was merely a steppingstone to professional and managerial positions." Jewish parents wanted their children in high-status positions where they could operate on their own and not be subject to the bigotry of employers. Jewish boys strove to become doctors, lawyers, dentists, accountants, and teachers. They also opened pharmacies and other retail businesses. In these occupations Jewish parents felt their children would be both prosperous and independent at the same time. In 1903 it was estimated that Jews comprised about half of New York City's 5,000 to 6,000 physicians and thirty-four years later 65.7 percent of the city's lawyers and judges, 55.7 percent of its physicians, and 64 percent of its dentists. In the 1960s Jews still made up a majority of these professions in New York City.

Statistics of Jewish occupational categories for other cities are similar. By the 1930s only one third of all Jewish workers were still engaged in manual jobs while two thirds were in white-collar positions. The figures for non-Jews were just the reverse: two thirds in manual occupations, one third in white-collar jobs. Jews also moved into professional positions at a much faster rate and in much higher percentages than non-Jews. In the 1930s eighteen out of every 1,000 Jews in San Francisco were lawyers and judges, while sixteen were physicians. For every 1,000 gentiles the figures were five and five, respectively. Similarly, in Pittsburgh fourteen of every 1,000 Jews were lawyers and judges, thirteen were physicians, while the corresponding figures for non-Jews were five and four, respectively.

The tendency for Jews to seek and obtain the highest status positions in American society has not diminished in recent decades. In 1955, some 55 percent of all gainfully employed Jews, compared with 23 percent of non-Jews, had professional, technical, managerial, executive, or proprietary positions while in 1967, 51 percent of the Jews, compared to 23 percent of the Catholics and 21 percent of the Protestants in the United States were classified as professionals. Among younger Jewish adults the figures for professional occupations were even higher. With higher status occupations came higher incomes. In 1967 the Gallup Poll found that 69 percent of the Jews had incomes over $7,000 a year but only 47 percent of the Catholics and 38 percent of the Protestants claimed earnings of that level or higher. By 1971, 60 percent of the Jewish families where the head of the household was between thirty and fifty-nine years old had annual incomes exceeding $16,000.

But money alone does not tell the whole story. Since the end of World War II not only has there been an almost complete disappearance of Jewish young men in blue-collar jobs, but Jews in increasingly larger numbers have shunned retail businesses—frequently owned by their fathers—to seek careers and greater personal satisfaction as journalists, writers, scientists, architects, engineers, and academics, as well as the traditional favorites of the Jewish immigrants: lawyers and physicians. Discouraged earlier by family preferences and gentile bigotry from seeking careers where they would have to be employed by others, the enormous expansion of opportunities in the 1950s and '60s made previously unheralded vocations or fields formerly difficult to enter more attractive and more accessible.

CULTURAL AND RELIGIOUS LIFE

The East European Jews, despite their poverty, arrived in this country with certain advantages. They had a strong commitment to a religion which rigidly dictated much of their daily behavior and gave their lives a structure and continuity which helped them to overcome problems of displacement in a new society. Moreover, unlike other immigrants to the United States who may have been poor at home but who otherwise "belonged," the Jews had been minorities wherever they had dwelled in Europe. As a result they had acquired a knowledge of how to move deftly among the dominant groups who, at best, tolerated them or, at worst, despised them. They had learned how to survive under a variety of hostile conditions and this experience served them well in the United States where they also had to struggle with adversity. Another important advantage that the Jews had brought with them can best be described as a middle-class view of life. They were ambitious, self-disciplined, and intellectually curious. A number of them had been socialists and participants in the revolutionary movement in Russia and Poland. Most had lived in small towns and villages and were attuned to what might now be considered the urban style of life.

The culture that the Jews brought with them to the United States survived in New York City. In recent decades attempts have been made to transplant it, as well, to Miami Beach and Los Angeles. In Boston, Chicago, and other cities where the Jews initially dwelled, they composed too small a percentage of the population to make much impact on the community. They may have had their own food stores and shared an affinity for literature, music, art, and religious observances, and perhaps even were more socialistically inclined than their neighbors, but in time their tastes and views blended with the dominant values of their respective communities, and today outside of the strongholds of the remnants of East European Jewish orthodoxy in New York, Chicago, Cleveland, Pittsburgh, Los Angeles, and Miami Beach, about the only thing left to distinguish Jews from everyone else in the United States is the Reform Temple.

In New York City, however, an East European Jewish culture flowered for decades and still lends a distinctive tone to the life in this vast metropolis. Cafés abounded where Jews would sit around and *shmooze* (talk) for hours over cups of coffee or glasses of hot tea. "For immigrant Jews," one chronicler reminds us, "talk was the breath of life itself." Discussions during these get-togethers ranged over a wide spectrum of topics and no one ever felt the necessity to refrain from participation because of a limited knowledge of the topic under consideration. The cafés gave the Jewish East Side a flavor—"a Yiddish Bohemia, poor and picturesque"—and their patrons included the most intellectual and articulate Jewish actors, poets, playwrights, journalists, and politicians of the day.

Jews also relaxed in the theater. The coming of the East European Jews not only spawned a Yiddish theater in the ghetto but also stimulated vaudeville and the Broadway stage. They also pioneered in the radio industry and virtually founded the motion picture industry.

Jews throughout the United States have been known for their patronage of the arts and their interest in literary endeavors. Between 1885 and 1914, for example, over 150 Yiddish daily, weekly, monthly, quarterly, and festival journals and yearbooks appeared in New York City, including the daily *Forward* which is still published today. Cultural centers were established wherever sufficient numbers of Jews congregated. Typically, the Cleveland Jewish Center had a gym, a roof garden, a library, classes in Hebrew language and literature, a scouting program, art classes, political forums, sewing and baking clubs, etc.

Owners of art galleries and concert halls (about one third of whom in New York City are Jewish) know that the larger a community's Jewish population the more likely it will be that their showings and musicales will be rewarded with large audiences. Jews are also heavily represented in every aspect of radio and television production. They purchase more books and attend more poetry readings than non-Jews and have also been among the major book publishers in New York City.

For the recent arrivals, however, the single most important cultural institution was the synagogue. Unlike the German Jews who came before them and worshiped, for the most part, in Reform temples barely distinguishable from Unitarian churches, the overwhelming proportion of the East Europeans maintained a devout orthodoxy during their first years in the United States. The numbers of synagogues proliferated in geometric proportion. In 1870 there were 189 Jewish congregations in the United States, the majority peopled by German Jews. By 1906 there were 1,769 and twenty years after that 3,118. In New York City alone the number of synagogues increased from 300 at the turn of the century to 1,200 in 1942. Usually these places of worship were no more than converted store fronts or private homes which came into being because one group of men had an argument with another group and then stormed out to find someplace else to pray. Since the end of World War II Americanized Jews have tended to worship in distinguished and substantial edifices but, aside from New York, Miami, and the four or five other cities in the country with large Jewish populations, it would be rare to find a community with even half a dozen Jewish temples or synagogues.

In the Jewish ghettos early in the twentieth century, shops closed on the Sabbath and the men and women, separated by curtains, prayed in the neighborhood synagogues. On the most holy days of the Jewish year, generally in September, 95 percent of the East European Jewish families went to the synagogue. As the Jewish immigrants and their children assimilated and Americanized, this percentage dwindled considerably. Although no statistics on high holy day attendance are available, it would be a safe guess to say that today the figure is at best 50 percent. All we can assert with accuracy, however, is that "all surveys of religious commitment, belief, and practice in the United States indicate that Jews are much less involved in religious activities than Protestants, who are in turn less active than Catholics." Nevertheless, it is still true today that the New York City public schools are closed for the major Jewish holidays because Jews constitute a majority of the teachers and their absence would create severe administrative headaches. Furthermore, on the Jewish holidays many of the city's businesses are closed, restaurants in commercial areas are nearly empty, and the mass transportation system has no more than half, if that many, of its usual patrons.

GERMAN VS. EAST EUROPEAN JEWS

The East European Jews who arrived in the United States in the late nineteenth and early twentieth centuries encountered an unreceptive American Jewry. The American Jews, descended mostly from the German migrations of the middle of the nineteenth century, had achieved a secure middle-class position in the United States. They were doctors, lawyers, bankers, manufacturers, and merchants. They had established or developed some of the leading department stores in the country like Macy's and Sears Roebuck. In addition, they had made every effort to appear indistinguishable from the more prosperous gentile Americans.

The coming of the East European Jews threatened the security of the German Jews. One of them wrote, in 1893, that the experience of the United Jewish Charities in Rochester, New York, "teaches that organized immigration from Russia, Rumania, and other semibarbarous countries is a mistake and has proved a failure. It is no relief to the Jews of Russia, Poland, etc., and it jeopardizes the well being of American Jews." The Americanized Jews felt little kinship with the newcomers and also feared that their presence would constitute a burden on society and stimulate an outburst of anti-Semitism. When the *Hebrew Standard* declared, on June 15, 1894, that "the thoroughly acclimated American Jew . . . is closer to the Christian sentiment around him than to the Judaism of these miserable darkened Hebrews," it probably expressed the dominant sentiment of American Jewry at the time.

Despite their antipathy, the Americanized Jews realized that the gentiles in the United States lumped all Jews together and that the behavior of the Orthodox would reflect on everyone. As Louis D. Brandeis later phrased it,

> a single though inconspicuous instance of dishonorable conduct on the part of a Jew in any trade or profession has far-reaching evil effects extending to the many innocent members of the race. Large as this country is, no Jew can behave badly without injuring each of us in the end. . . . Since the act of each becomes thus the concern of all, we are perforce our brothers' keepers.

One should not minimize, however, the fact that the American Jews also had a paternalistic sympathy for their East European brethren and therefore, since they could not contain the stampede from Russia, Galicia, and Rumania, they set about, after an initial display of coldness, to improve the "moral, mental and physical conditions" of the immigrants.

Once they decided to facilitate assimilation by assisting the newcomers, the American Jews spared no efforts and "few human needs were overlooked." Of all immigrant groups none proved so generous to "their own kind" as did the Jews. Money and organizational talent combined to provide hospitals, orphan asylums, recreational facilities, and homes for unwed mothers as well as for the deaf, the blind, the old, and the crippled. Educational institutions were also established and the "zeal to Americanize underlay all educational endeavor." Part of this Americanizing process also resulted in the building up of the Jewish Theological Seminary in New York City to train Conservative rabbis. The American Jewish establishment could not tolerate orthodoxy but recognized that the East European immigrants would not come around to Reform Judaism. Conservatism provided an acceptable compromise since it preached American values while retaining the most important orthodox traditions.

Another of the projects resulted in an attempt to disperse the immigrants throughout the United States. The Americanized Jews did not want the newcomers to congregate in one massive ghetto. Between 1901 and 1917 the Industrial Removal Office dispatched 72,482 East European Jews to 1,670 communities in forty-eight states. Nevertheless, many of those transplanted eventually returned to New York. In fact, of the 1,334, 627 Jews who did arrive in New York City between 1881 and 1911, 73.5 percent remained there.

The most important and lasting agency set up by the Americanized Jews to help—and lead—their brethren was the American Jewish Committee. Ostensibly formed as a result of the outrageous pogroms in Russia between 1903 and 1905 and dedicated to protecting the civil rights of Jews wherever they were threatened, the American Jewish Committee came into being in 1906 primarily because the established Jewish community in the United States wanted "to assert some control over existing Jewish institutions and mass movements." As Louis

Marshall, one of the American Jewish Committee's leading members and its president from 1912 to 1929, put it in 1908, the purpose of those who formed the organization was "to devise a simple and efficient instrument which might deal quickly, and at the same time deliberately, and with an understanding based on experience, with the problems that might present themselves from time to time."

The American Jewish Committee, composed of wealthy Jews, exercised great influence politically "through private contacts with men in power." Since Jacob Schiff, Cyrus Adler, Louis Marshall, Felix Warburg, Oscar Strauss, Julius Rosenwald, Mayer Sulzberger, and others of their stature dealt regularly with the most prominent Americans of their generation, the Committee "on the whole, acted effectively in the interests of American Jewry." The American Jewish Committee, as one scholar has pointed out, "offered American Jewry a vigorous, disciplined and highly paternalistic leadership as well as a program of Americanization," but its members looked down upon the East Europeans and expected them to follow its leadership. This did not occur. Perhaps if the Committee had been more democratically organized it might have served as a bridge to the newcomers and won them over. But as one of the group said, "let us get away from the idea that the American Jewish Committee must be representative and that its members must be chosen in some way by the vote of the Jews in this country. No great moral movement has been undertaken and carried through except in just such a manner in which we are doing our work."

The enormous assistance provided by the Americanized Jews to the immigrants was accepted with reservations. The established Jews showed disdain for the East Europeans and their culture and the recipients of their largesse felt like beggars and poor relations. The charity may have been given out of a sense of obligation but it did not come with warmth and kindness. And the leadership provided by the American Jewish Committee definitely smacked of elitism which the immigrants would not tolerate. As soon as the East Europeans could provide their own network of charitable and welfare organizations they did so. It would be a long time before they would look upon their "benefactors" without a jaundiced eye.

ANTI-SEMITISM

The German and East European Jews in the United States recognized the vast gulf that separated them socially, economically, and culturally but gentiles did not. The coming of the new Jews intensified latent anti-Semitic feelings among gentile Americans and, as the German Jews had originally feared, this hostility erupted in public. The German Jews felt the sting first. In 1877 a prominent Jewish banker was barred as a guest from a resort hotel that had previously accepted his patronage. As the nineteenth century came to a close, German Jews also found themselves excluded from private schools, prominent social clubs, and other resorts. In 1890 the editors of *The American Hebrew* sent around a questionnaire to prominent Americans inquiring why gentiles were so hostile to Jews and one university president responded that "All intelligent Christians deplore the fact that the historical evidences for Christianity have so little weight with your people."

The East European Jews were not affected at first by social anti-Semitism but in the early years of the twentieth century the bigotry became acute. In rapid succession crude slurs, journalistic reports, and supposedly learned commentaries lambasted the Jews. A letter to the editor of the *New York Herald* complained that "these United States are becoming rapidly so Jew ridden . . . ," while a faculty member at Teacher's College in New York wrote to a colleague and asked him to "please do me the favor of not coming to the banquet tomorrow night, as I have invited a friend who does not like Jews." A magazine writer asked of the Russian Jew, "is he assimilable? Has he in himself the stuff of which Americans are made?" University of Wisconsin sociologist E. A. Ross claimed that "the lower class of Hebrews of eastern Europe reach here moral cripples, their souls warped and dwarfed by iron circumstance . . . many of them have developed a monstrous and repulsive love of gain." Finally, University of Berlin Professor Werner Sombart's prediction "that in another hundred years the United States will be peopled chiefly by Slavs, negroes and Jews," was prominently featured in one of the leading American periodicals of the day.

In view of these prejudices it is no wonder that outside of the garment district and other Jewish-owned establishments Jews had little chance for obtaining decent jobs. Many help-wanted advertisements specified "Christian only," and real estate agents preferred gentile clients. To combat this discrimination one of the older American Jewish fraternal organizations, B'nai B'rith, which had been founded in 1843, established its Anti-Defamation League in 1913. The League over the years has proved quite successful in combating anti-Semitism.

Despite the efforts of the Anti-Defamation League, schools and employers continued discriminating against Jews. Quotas in higher education began in the 1920s and became more rigid during the depression years of the 1930s. As late as 1945 the president of Dartmouth College defended regulations which kept Jewish students out of his school, but he was probably the last outspoken advocate of an already waning policy. Beginning with World War II more opportunities opened to practically all skilled white people and the growth of the economy, the passage of state laws forbidding discrimination in employment and entry into universities, and a generally more tolerant spirit in the land led to widened economic and occupational opportunities for Jews. Law firms, scientific organizations, universities, and businesses needing the very best talent available hired goodly numbers of Jews who were among their few qualified applicants.

Bigotry did not disappear completely. The executive suites of America's largest corporations contain relatively few Jews and one still reads of prominent Jews being denied admission to country clubs. On December 14, 1973, *The Wall Street Journal* ran a story on Irving Shapiro, the new chairman and chief executive of Du Pont and Company, the world's largest chemical concern. Well into the article the author noted that being a lawyer, a Jew, and a Democrat were not helpful to Mr. Shapiro in his rise to prominence within the firm (although his talents, of course, overrode these "handicaps") and then tellingly, "Mr. Shapiro's official biography is noticeably lacking in the kind of club affiliations that adorn those of his colleagues."

LEGISLATION AND POLITICS

There were never any specific laws in the United States regarding East European Jews, but their arrival contributed to the movement for immigration restriction. The major American laws keeping out aliens passed Congress in 1921 and 1924 and these set quotas for groups based on a percentage of their population in the United States in 1910 and 1890, respectively. Such laws were designed to drastically curtail southern and eastern European migration to this country. The Jews, being the second largest immigrant group in the early twentieth century, were obviously one of the major targets of this legislation. As early as 1906 an Italian American had been told by a member of President Theodore Roosevelt's immigration commission that the "movement toward restriction in all of its phases is directed against Jewish immigration. . . ." The Irish, the English, and the Germans who constituted the majority of nineteenth-century immigrants to the United States received the largest quotas. No religious test was allowed by this legislation. Consequently, Jews born in Germany were counted under the German quota and Jews born in England came in under the English quota even though their parents might have come from Russia or Rumania. Subsequent legislation affecting the East European Jews came in 1948 and 1950 when some of the persons displaced by the German policies of the 1930s and the Second World War were allowed to come into the United States under special provisions. Current immigration regulations in the United States make no statement about religion and have done away with quotas based on national origins. Present legislation gives preference to immigrants with close relatives in the United States and to those who have occupational skills in demand in this country.

Jews in the United States have never been legally restrained from pursuing any social or economic interests that struck their fancy. Many states originally restricted voting rights to adult males who believed in the divinity of Jesus Christ, but these were abolished in all but a few states by the beginning of the nineteenth century.

The East Europeans, like other whites, voted after becoming citizens (which took only five years after entering the United States), but they registered and voted in much higher proportion to their numbers than did members of other ethnic groups. They took stands on political issues of concern to them and supported candidates for office who appeared to be in harmony with their own views. A number of Jews have been elected to high political office, such as governor of a state or United States senator, but before the Second World War almost all of these people were of German background. In the past score of years, however, Jews of East European background have achieved similar prominence. The best known of these are United States Senators Jacob Javits of New York and Abraham Ribicoff of Connecticut, and Governors Milton J. Schapp and Marvin Mandel of Pennsylvania and Maryland, respectively. Numerous Jews who were born, or whose parents were born, in Russia, Rumania, and Poland have been elected to the United States House of Representatives and the various state legislatures.

Although Jews have supported Republicans, Democrats, and socialists, since the New Deal era the vast majority have been loyal Democrats both with their votes and their financial contributions. In fact, their contributions are so lavish and their votes so important that policies affecting American Jews—and especially Israel—have to be taken into account by the leading Democratic politicos. So devoted to the Democrats are the Jews that in Richard Nixon's overwhelming reelection victory in 1972 they were the only white ethnic group in the nation that gave a majority of its votes to the Democratic nominee for President, George S. McGovern, although not by the overwhelming support usually accorded Democratic candidates. A few Jews, notably Max Fisher of Detroit, also lubricated Republican coffers. As a result, an anti-Israel policy simply would not be politically acceptable to most of the elected officials in Washington.

SUMMARY AND CONCLUSION

The East European Jews have accomplished great things for themselves in the United States. Most of them arrived on the brink of poverty around the turn of the century and their descendants have risen to comfortable and secure middle-class positions in American society. They can live where they like, work almost any place where they have the necessary skills, and worship—or not—in any manner that pleases them. This almost total freedom has resulted in a good deal of interfaith marriage and a slackening of religious and ethnic ties. During the past decade one out of every three Jewish marriages has been with a non-Jew.

Overt anti-Semitism, with the exception of the controversy between blacks and Jews arising out of the 1967 and 1968 schoolteachers' strikes in New York City, has subsided considerably during the past few decades, and recent laws have forbidden discrimination on the basis of race, creed, or national origins in employment and housing. These laws are not always observed, but they do indicate that the state and federal governments are putting up formal barriers against wanton bigotry. Ironically, diminished discrimination loosens the ties that bind ethnic minorities. The educational system, especially at the college and university levels, inculcates a national culture and a national way of thinking and it is the rare individual who, after being subject to such exposure, can be completely comfortable again in a strictly ethnic setting. With each succeeding generation of educated Jews, therefore, the ties to the traditional culture are weakened. Most American Jews today are products of the American education system and work and live in areas with people of varying ethnic backgrounds. Only some of the Jewish immigrants and their children can still be found in ghettos. And with each passing year their numbers fade.

Also on the wane is Orthodox Jewry. The attachment to the traditional faith was strong among the immigrants and their children but later generations found it a burden. Only a tiny fraction of American Jews keep the Sabbath and only a few more observe the dietary restrictions. Outside of New York, Los Angeles, Chicago, and Miami Beach, the Conservative and Reform branches of Judaism hold sway in temple memberships while the way-of-life practiced by practically all American Jews is in the Reform tradition. Thus attendance at religious services is sparse except at the beginning of the Jewish New Year and the Day of Atonement, and a middle-class life style, almost totally devoid of ethnic flavor, is vigorously pursued.

In the early 1960s one American rabbi said, "Today there is little that marks the Jew as a Jew except Jewish self-consciousness and association with fellow Jews." It is difficult to assess the strength and significance of this self-consciousness. If one "feels" Jewish and seeks out other Jews for companionship, the ties are still there. Jewish identity has also been reinforced by the emergence and travails of the State of Israel. It is impossible, of course, to predict for how many generations such sentiments will sustain American Jewry.

As the Jews become Americanized, strains and dissimilarities between the German and Russian elements have disappeared. When Hitler began persecuting Jews in Germany, and especially in the past score of years, when differences in income and life styles have narrowed considerably, there have been few if any clashes between Jews of German and East European ancestry in the United States. In fact, one might say that with each succeeding generation there is less and less difference among all American Jews regardless of their grandfathers' native lands. Class, geographical location, education, occupation, and income would be more appropriate categories for demarcation than German-Russian or Orthodox-Reform background. The only exception to this generalization would be the American Council for Judaism, whose members are primarily of German-Jewish ancestry. It is supported by only a fraction of 1 percent of the American Jews and it differs considerably from other Jewish organizations in its regard of Israel as just another foreign country with which American Jews should have no special relationships.

Still another aspect of the migration and its subsequent impact in the United States is the fantastic influence that East European Jews have had on the academic, intellectual, medical, political, and cultural life in the country, especially since the end of the Second World War. Whereas in the 1930s it was rare to find Jews, let alone those of East European descent, on the faculties of American colleges, in more recent times Jews whose parents or grandparents came from Russia, Poland, and Rumania adorn the most prestigious American universities. It would be difficult to name them all, but even a cursory cataloging would include sociologists Daniel Bell, Nathan Glazer, and Seymour Martin Lipset of Harvard University (all, by the way, graduates of New York City's City College in the 1930s); Harvard historian Oscar Handlin; and Yale Law School Dean Abraham Goldstein. Also on the Harvard faculty is the Russian-born Nobel Prize winner, Simon Kuznets. Herbert Stein, one of President Nixon's chief economic advisers; former United States Supreme Court Justice and Ambassador to the United Nations, Arthur Goldberg; the discoverer of the vaccine to prevent polio, Jonas E. Salk; film-maker Stanley Kubrick; musician Leonard Bernstein; violinist Yehudi Menuhin; playwrights Arthur Miller and Neil Simon; and artist Ben Shahn are only a few of the others of East European Jewish descent who have made their mark in the United States. In fact, the East European Jews and their descendants have made a much greater impact, and in a wider range of activities, than people from any of the other contemporary group of immigrants.

And yet, despite their absorption into American society, it is still true, as Jacob Neusner wrote in 1973, that "to be a Jew in America is to be in some measure different, alien, a minority." The dominant culture in the United States is still intolerant of differences among groups of people and of non-Christians loyal to a foreign state or a different faith. This, of course, presents great difficulties to the various ethnic minorities in the United States. On the one hand "cultural pluralism" is celebrated in song and spirit from every official podium while deviation is regarded as a sign of subversion and inferiority. This schizophrenic conflict affects all American minorities and to be a non-WASP is to be somehow marginal and alien. For most Jews who are prosperous, employed, and ensconced in comfortable homes, these feelings are rarely discussed, but the fierce American-Jewish devotion to the State of Israel suggests that even in the United States Jews do not feel absolutely secure. Somehow they feel that loyalty to a Jewish state is necessary. Whether it is because of an attachment to the heritage and traditions of Jewry or because of a sense of being part of the same group, or even because they fear that someday they or their descendants might have to flee the United States and take refuge in Israel is impossible to say. But we do know that the sense of identification with Israel is strong and this, in a very specific way, differentiates Jews from other Americans.

4

The Tax to End All Taxes

DAVID HAPGOOD

• Henry George's life demonstrates how varied human experience could be in nineteenth-century America. Born in Philadelphia in 1839, he left school at the age of fourteen and went to sea in 1855, sailing to Melbourne and Calcutta. He later participated in a gold rush to British Columbia, clerked in a San Francisco store, and reported for several newspapers. He even served as California inspector of gas meters.

His life's work came in 1869 when he was on a business trip to New York City and noticed "the shocking contrast between monstrous wealth and debasing want." George began to study the paradox between poverty and riches, and in 1879 he published Progress and Poverty, the most influential study of political economy in American history. It sold more than two million copies and had an unprecedented effect on the labor movement around the world.

Henry George fervently believed that labor was the only true generator of wealth, and that rising land values were a product of social evolution rather than the skill or wisdom of landlords. Rent, therefore, was unjust, and "a toll levied upon labor constantly and continuously." George argued that the "unearned increment" which was lining the pockets of the rich should instead revert to the public. Thus was born the idea of the "single tax," a levy on land values that would permit the government to abolish all other forms of taxation. The subject was technical, but George's passionate sincerity and his analogies to commonplace things humanized his message. As David Hapgood notes in the following essay, George became enormously popular (he almost won election as mayor of New York), and numerous single-tax movements

Reprinted by permission from *American Heritage* (April 1978). © 1978 American Heritage Publishing Company, Inc.

sprang up throughout the nation. Indeed, his ideas and theories continue to have many adherents among both conservatives and radicals in the 1980s.

He had the answer—he believed it, and he persuaded millions of others to believe it, too. Even today there are those willing to maintain that if the American people had just listened to him, we would not now be afflicted by a multitude of taxes like barbs in the skin—including the annual stab of the 1040 form.

His name was Henry George, and he was perhaps the most original economic theorist this nation has produced. In his own day he was as well known as, say, Ralph Nader is today, but among the orthodox economic thinkers of modern times, he has long since been dismissed as a curious footnote to nineteenth-century history, one more crackpot among all the anarchists, Populists, and socialists spewed forth by the industrial revolution. He was far more than that; he had something to say still worth listening to, and he put it all down in a book called *Progress and Poverty*, published in 1879 as the pinnacle of what might be called an intellectual success story by Horatio Alger. As he himself once observed, "If I have been enabled to emancipate myself from ideas which have fettered far abler men, it is, doubtless, due to the fact that my study of social problems was in a country like this, where they have been presented with peculiar directness, and perhaps also to the fact that I was led to think a good deal before I had a chance to do much reading."

Henry George was born in 1839 to a middle-class Philadelphia family. His father, a clerk in the customs house who had published religious books for some years, was a strict Low-Church Episcopalian. Young George was rebellious from the start. Just before he turned fourteen, he dropped out of school, where he later said he had only "wasted time," and never went back. A passing interest in phrenology led him to analyze his character by the shape of his skull. (Fifty years after his death, his granddaughter, Agnes De Mille, the choreographer, wrote that elderly people who had known George would ask her to remove her hat so they could observe the formation of her head.) Some of George's self-observation through skull-bump analysis accurately forecast his adult life: "generally takes sides on every contested question. . . . Is inclined . . . to push his projects with so much energy and zeal as to appear rash and nearly destitute of caution . . . has an insatiable desire to roam about and see the world."

At sixteen he shipped out as a foremast boy on the *Hindoo*, an East Indiaman carrying lumber around Cape Horn to Australia. The round trip, which took the *Hindoo* to Calcutta to pick up a cargo of rice and seeds, lasted fourteen months, and George came home with a net of fifteen dollars and a pet monkey. For the next couple of years he worked in Philadelphia as a printer's apprentice, but the pay was low and the work unsteady. He had heard from a friend in Oregon of the high printers' wages in the new lands of the West, and he was finding family discipline increasingly irksome. In 1858, when he was nineteen, George went to sea again, this time on a ship bound for California, with no intention of making the return journey. He jumped ship in San Francisco.

Henry George landed in California just ten years after the great Gold Rush had begun. It was an incredible new country whose wealth in rich farm land, it was already evident, exceeded even the value of its precious minerals. There should have been enough for everybody, and for a brief time in the 1840's and early 1850's there had been; because good land was cheap, employers had to pay higher wages than in the now-old East to attract labor away from farming. But soon power and land and wealth were concentrated in a few hands, wages fell, and the gulf between those who had and those who had not opened up in faithful duplication of humanity's experience elsewhere.

Land was the key to wealth—and poverty. By the end of the 1860's, through massive federal and state grants, railroads, large-scale farmers, and speculators had acquired much of the new state's most valuable property: almost half the land available for agriculture was owned by one five-hundredth of the population. The owners held their land off the market, knowing its price could go nowhere but up, and new settlers, unable to buy land, had to work for lower wages. The drama was in the deposits of California gold and Nevada silver, but in the words of a contemporary account, "chiefly it was the holders of real estate that made the greatest fortunes." The ups and downs were extraordinary, for history in the California of those days unreeled at the demented speed of an early silent movie: what took generations in the East, and centuries in the Old World, happened in California within the span of Henry George's life. George Bernard Shaw later said about George that "only an American could have seen in a single lifetime the growth of the whole tragedy of civilization from the primitive forest clearing."

This California was to be George's home for the next twenty years. Gold was still being discovered around the West, and soon after his arrival George set out for the latest reported strike, on the Fraser River in British Columbia, in the first of three unsuccessful mining ventures. Back in San Francisco, he found work as a printer at sixteen dollars a week, but nine dollars went for room and board at the respectably all-male What Cheer House, which, he wrote home, had a good library. The job was the first of many: the times were restless, and George was a particularly restless man.

In 1860, at twenty-one, he cast his first vote—for Lincoln (but, like Californians in general, he did not take part in the ensuing Civil War). A year later he married Annie Fox, an Australian-born orphan. The marriage was close and lifelong, and they had four children. George evidently enjoyed their respect, since two of them wrote biographies of their father and a third sculpted his bust. In their accounts, Henry George as parent comes through as impatient but affectionate, interested but absent-minded.

The first years of married life were hard. George kept losing or leaving jobs, his ventures in the printing business were all wrecked in the recurring storms that afflicted California's economy, and the family moved so often that, he observed, they seldom had to clean house. One of George's failures, a job-printing firm he started on a shoestring with two partners, left the couple—with one child, and a second on the way—in particularly difficult circumstances. On Christmas Day, 1864, George wrote in the diary he intermittently kept: "Feel that I am in a bad situation, and must use my utmost effort to keep afloat and go ahead. . . . Saw landlady and told her I was not able to pay rent." Mrs. George sold all her jewelry except her wedding ring, and persuaded the milkman to provide milk in exchange for printed cards. George recalled that "I came near starving to death, and at one time I was so close to it that I think I should have done so but for the job of printing a few cards which enabled us to buy a little corn meal. In this darkest time in my life my second child was born." There was no food in the home, and George went out on a desperate search for money. As he described it, "I walked along the street and made up my mind to get money from the first man whose appearance might indicate that he had it to give. I stopped a man—a stranger—and told him I wanted five dollars. He asked what I wanted it for. I told him that my wife was confined and that I had nothing to give her to eat. He gave me the money. If he had not, I think I was desperate enough to have killed him."

George never had to kill anyone, for he soon began picking up enough work as a substitute printer to support the family, though he was in and out of debt for many years. The privation that he had undergone when unable to find work in wealthy California had a profound effect on his thinking, as soon became evident, because around this time George began to write. His first published effort was a letter to the editor of *Journal of the Trades and Workingmen* in which he asked if it were possible to "check the tendency of society to resolve itself into classes who have too much or too little," a question that was to be his lifelong concern. Another piece, a rather feverish editorial on Lincoln's assassination, got George his first reporting assignments. He began attending political meetings, at one of which he spoke out in favor of free trade, the subject of one of his later books. Soon he was a typesetter, then a reporter, and finally a managing editor of the San Francisco *Times*, a job that lasted until August, 1868.

Later that year the San Francisco *Herald* sent George to New York to try to arrange for wire news service. The experience left a deep impression. George got a firsthand lesson in how the game of monopoly was played. The Associated Press, then the only wire service, refused the *Herald*'s application, and when George enterprisingly started an independent news service, the AP arranged for Western Union, also a monopoly, to raise its rates for news transmission high enough to put the interloper out of business. The city taught him other lessons, too: "The contrast of luxury and want that I saw in New York appalled me, and I left for the West feeling that there must be a cause for this, and that if possible I would find out what it was."

Back in California, George found his answer. Out riding in the hills near San Francisco, he "asked a passing teamster . . . what land was worth there. He pointed to some cows grazing off so far that they looked like mice and said: 'I don't know exactly, but there is a man over there who will sell some land for a thousand dollars an acre [then an outlandish price for farm land].' Like a flash it came upon me that there was the reason of advancing poverty with advancing wealth. With the growth of population, land grows in value, and the men who work it must pay more for the privilege. I turned back, amidst quiet thought, to the perception that then came to me and has been with me ever since."

In 1871 George put his "perception" into a forty-eight-page pamphlet, *Our Land and Land Policy, State and National*, which sold a thousand copies locally and added to his modest reputation in California. Shortly thereafter he had his first unhappy brush with the academic world, a harbinger of the low esteem in which each would hold the other in later years. The new University of California at Berkeley had decided to set up a chair in political economy, and George was asked to deliver a lecture with the thought that, despite his lack of proper credentials, he might be chosen for it.

With his usual willingness to do battle against both odds and his own self-interest, George uncorked a lecture that guaranteed he would not get the job. After castigating the professors for having "given to a simple and attractive science an air of repellent abstruseness and uncertainty," he went on to tell the students: "You do not even need textbooks nor teachers, if you will but think for yourselves. . . . Here you may obtain the tools; but they will be useful only to him who can use them. A monkey with a microscope, a mule packing a library, are fit emblems of the men—and unfortunately they are plenty—who pass through the whole educational machinery, and come out but learned fools." Within the family, George disapproved of homework for his children, and years later, when his eldest son had to choose between a Harvard scholarship and a newspaper job, his father advised the latter, on the grounds that Harvard would leave "much that will have to be unlearned."

George now devoted most of two years to writing *Progress and Poverty*, the book that was to make him a world figure. These were the "Terrible Seventies," a time of bank failures and bankruptcies; the family lived hand to mouth on his occasional earnings from fees as a gas-

meter inspector and from a few lecture engagements. (Most of his
lectures were on land or free trade or politics, but one, which he often
repeated in later years, was on Moses.) George went deeply into debt,
and at one point he had to pawn his watch, but he was determined
to complete the book. Later he recalled that "when I had finished the
last page, in the dead of night, when I was entirely alone, I flung myself on my knees and wept like a child." George sent the manuscript
to New York in early 1879 and got two rejections: D. Appleton & Co.
found it "very aggressive" and to Harper's it was "revolutionary."
George decided to publish it first himself; a friendly printer in San
Francisco offered to make the plates, and George himself set some of
the type.

Progress and Poverty is long and rambling, but often soaring in its
eloquence. George's style is more biblical than economical; this was
before economics had to be written in numbers rather than words.
Along the way, George offers his critique of classical economic doctrine, delves into world history, and concludes—eccentrically, by current standards of economic writing—with a theological chapter on
"the problem of individual life." The subject of the book is summarized in the subtitle: "An inquiry into the cause of industrial de-
pressions and of increase of want with increase of wealth . . . the
remedy."

The "cause" lies with the landowner. Man is entitled only to the
fruits of his own labor, but the holder of land, unlike the worker and
the capitalist, makes no contribution to wealth: he simply charges
others for the use of what was made by nature and which he happens
to possess, usually by theft or conquest. Land has value only when it
is scarce. When land is abundant, as in early America and early California, no one has to pay for it, there are no landlords, and each person is rewarded according to his effort and his ability. The value of
land rises, not through any contribution by its owner, but because
more people need more space; because the growth of a community
enhances the value of strategically located property; and because of
speculation.

The parasitic landowner's share, his "economic" rent—not for any
buildings he may put up, but for the bare, natural land itself—can
only increase at the expense of the true producers, labor and capital
(itself the product of past labor), which George saw as common vic-

tims rather than natural antagonists: "When non-producers can claim as rent a portion of the wealth created by producers, the right of the producers to the fruits of their labor is to that extent denied." And when the owner holds his land out of production, waiting for a better price, land use is distorted because people have to move farther out to find space to work and trade and live—sprawl is what we call it today. Poverty comes with progress. Ultimately, the rough equality of pre-landlord times gives way to the extremes of rich and poor, and, in a passage that suddenly jerks us back to today's newspaper: "Upon streets lighted with gas and patrolled by uniformed policemen, beggars wait for the passer-by, and in the shadow of college, and library, and museum, are gathering the more hideous Huns and fiercer Vandals of whom Macaulay prophesied."

In George's view, a landholder had no more right to charge rent for land he did not create than he would to monopolize the air and charge others for the right to breathe. This is how George put it:

> If we are all here by equal permission of the Creator, we are all here with an equal title to the enjoyment of his bounty—with an equal right to the use of all that nature so impartially offers. This is a right which is natural and unalienable; it is a right which vests in every human being as he enters the world, and which during his continuance in the world can be limited only by the equal rights of others. . . . There is on earth no power which can rightfully make a grant of exclusive ownership in land. . . . For what are we but tenants for a day? Have we made the earth, that we should determine the rights of those who after us shall tenant it in their turn? . . . Though the sovereign people of the state of New York consent to the landed possessions of the Astors, the puniest infant that comes wailing into the world in the squalidest room of the most miserable tenement house, becomes at that moment seized of an equal right with the millionaire's. And it is robbed if the right is denied.

The absolute ownership of land and other resources of nature is the equivalent of chattel slavery, and a more common evil. Slavery grows up where, as in the early American South, the land is so abundant that free laborers can have it for themselves instead of working it for others. Whenever land is scarce enough to be monopolized, however, laborers will be forced to "a condition which, though they be mocked with the titles and insignia of freedom, will be virtually that of slavery." In the extreme case (here one thinks of Hawaii after the American missionaries and traders had appropriated all the land): "Place one hundred men on an island from which there is no escape, and whether you make one of these men the absolute owner of the other ninety-nine, or the absolute owner of the soil of the island, will make no difference either to him or to them. In the one case, as in the other, the one will be the absolute master of the ninety-nine."

Henry George's greatest originality lay in his "remedy." He rejected the usual alternatives of dividing up or nationalizing the land. The first was unworkable and superficial. The second violated both George's profound belief in free enterprise (as long as its fruits were earned) and his equally profound distrust of government. The remedy was to allow private ownership of land, but for society to collect the unearned rent on that land through taxation: "It is not necessary to confiscate land; it is only necessary to confiscate rent." The rent to be "confiscated" was the amount the owner could collect by renting out unimproved land, or if he had improved or built on it, the portion of the rent attributable to the land alone; he would not be taxed on the improvements, because those were products of his own effort. Thus society would recapture the land values society itself had created, and the owner would be forced to put his land to its best use or give it up; hoarding land would no longer pay. Furthermore, the rent, or tax, would be enough to pay all the expenses of government so that neither labor nor capital need be taxed on their just earnings. This was the "single tax" that became glued to Henry George's name. George believed it "would enormously increase production; would secure justice in distribution; would benefit all classes; and would make possible an advance to a higher and nobler civilization."

Such was the message Henry George wanted to preach. When the commercial publication of *Progress and Poverty* was finally assured, George boldly moved to New York, without money or job, to launch his book and himself. As a later chronicler of the single-tax movement, the historian Arthur N. Young, observed: "Scarcely anything in the history of social reform movements is more remarkable than the spectacle of this unknown California printer setting foot in New York

City in 1880, poor in pocket, equipped solely with a book and the consciousness of a message, to become the founder of a new world-wide crusade against world-old evils." The author himself professed the utmost confidence, writing to his eighty-one-year-old father in Philadelphia that "it will ultimately be considered a great book, will be published in both hemispheres, and be translated into different languages."

Against all odds, George was right. Within a year *Progress and Poverty* was widely noticed and began to sell as no book on political economy had ever sold before. It was published in England, and eventually it was translated into more than a dozen languages, including Chinese. Unknown on his fortieth birthday, at forty-two the California printer was on his way to world fame. His short, stocky figure, with reddish beard and high balding forehead, became familiar on the lecture platform. In 1881 George went to England and Ireland on the first of many lecture tours; he was also the correspondent of the New York *Irish World*. The Irish, and English radicals opposed to the exploitation of the Irish by English landowners, were particularly receptive to his views on land. Shaw, who dropped in on one of George's lectures by accident, credited the event with making him a socialist, and most of the members of the reform-socialist Fabian Society came there by way of an earlier exposure to Henry George.

By 1884 George was churning out articles, writing his next book, *Protection or Free Trade?*, and lecturing to working-class audiences, many of whom had read the cheap edition of *Progress and Poverty*. His working-class support led to his race for mayor of New York in 1886. Although Samuel Gompers, head of the newly founded American Federation of Labor, was one of his converts, labor was less interested in the single tax than in the idea that George was the only person who had a chance of defeating the dreary offerings of the two-party system. George didn't particularly want to be mayor, but he saw an opportunity to "raise hell." When the union leaders approached him, he said that, as a guarantee against "ignominious failure," he would only run if they could produce thirty thousand signatures on a petition, a huge number at the time. The unions collected thirty-four thousand signatures, and Henry George formally accepted the nomination at the Great Hall of Cooper Union. The Democrats

FOR MAYOR,

HENRY GEORGE

THE DEMOCRACY OF THOMAS JEFFERSON.

Ⓧ

Make your Mark ✗ in the Circle ◯ under the Rooster.

Thomas Jefferson, whose name was taken in vain in this poster for the mayoralty campaign in New York in 1886, might or might not have approved of George's single tax, but he could well have sympathized with this sentiment from *Progress and Poverty:* "In all the great American cities there is today as clearly defined a ruling class as in the most aristocratic countries of the world. Its members carry wards in their pockets, make up the slates for nominating conventions, distribute offices as they bargain together. . . . They are men of power."

coughed up a relatively respectable figure, Abram S. Hewitt, and the Republicans nominated a rising young patrician politician named Theodore Roosevelt.

Now, Henry George in public office, mayor of the nation's leading city, was quite a different matter from Henry George in the bookstores and on the lecture platform. Wealthy and landed interests joined against such a clear and present danger. All the press was against George, except the *Irish World* and the German-language *Volkeszeitung*, a socialist paper, though some reporters on the major papers moonlighted without pay on a pro-George campaign paper called *The Leader*. The Republicans were advised to withdraw Roosevelt in order to prevent George from winning, for if he did, in Hewitt's words, they might as well "go out onto Henry George's unoccupied lands and hang themselves."

George ran vigorously, speaking to enthusiastic street crowds from the tailboards of carts. But in those days when each candidate had to supply his own watch over the vote counting, he suffered from a fatal handicap that had been diagnosed earlier by a Democratic party worker: "How can George win? He has no inspectors of election." On Election Day, the returns showed George second, with 68,110 votes, only twice his number of petition signatures. Hewitt, the Democrat, came in first with 90,552 votes, and Roosevelt was third with 60,435. The consensus was that the election had been stolen, like others in the city's history, and an expert in the field, Tammany boss Richard Croker, later commented: "Of course they could not allow George to win. It would upset all their arrangements."

George's defeat foreshadowed his consistent failure to translate mass support into either political victory or change in the tax system. A year later the nascent Georgist political movement fell apart, with the socialist faction proclaiming that "the burning social question is not a land tax, but the abolition of all private property in instruments of production." The split was inevitable. Both shared a commitment to the ideal of equity, but George the individualist and believer in Adam Smith's free market could never agree with Karl Marx, another contemporary prophet, that state ownership was the way to get from here to there. Certainly the two had little use for each other. Marx dismissed George as "the capitalists' last ditch," while conceding, rather surprisingly, that "he is otherwise a writer of talent (but to have talent is a Yankee characteristic)." George considered Marx "a most superficial thinker, entangled in an inexact and vicious terminology" and "the prince of muddleheads."

George remained active for the eleven years of life left to him after the 1886 election. His lecture tours took him as far as Australia, which, then and now, practices a diluted form of his land-value tax. (The full "confiscation of rent" exist nowhere.) On the way to Australia he stopped off in California, where local observers commented wonderingly on the world renown achieved by their own "little Harry George." His writing was prolific. From 1887 to 1892 he edited the *Standard*, a weekly platform for his opinions. Having become embroiled in dispute with the Catholic Church over its disciplining of Edward McGlynn, a priest who supported him for mayor, George wrote, in 1891, *An Open Letter to the Pope*, a reply to the papal encyclical *Rerum Novarum*, in which he took Pope Leo XIII to task for his support of property rights in land. Whenever George could find a free-trade candidate, he campaigned for him.

George's life and personality do not seem to have been transformed by his sudden rise from obscurity to fame. Since he never held on to money, his family's life-style remained modest, though not impoverished as in the earlier years. Although single-mindedly devoted to his beliefs, George was free of the hatred that disfigures so many true believers; he showed no vindictiveness toward his opponents, and he did not go around preaching "hang the landowners." Always physically active, he learned to ride a bicycle at fifty-two, and thereafter would drag his family and friends out biking in Central Park.

In 1897 George was persuaded to run again for mayor of New York. On October 29—in the middle of the campaign—he died suddenly of apoplexy. He was fifty-eight. His massive funeral called forth tributes from friend and foe: as with most radicals, Henry George became praiseworthy once he was safely buried.

The single-tax movement survived George as a significant political force for about twenty years. In the first two decades of this century, single-taxers fought—and lost—referendum battles in several states and cities. The issue was fought four times in Oregon alone, the single-taxers being financed by Joseph Fels, a soap manufacturer who gave a total of $173,000 to "put the single tax into effect somewhere in the United States within five years."

The massive influence of Henry George and *Progress and Poverty* in awakening interest in social reform was diverted toward targets other than his land tax, for, as George himself noted, most people had other, more pressing goals. George was fated to be a kind of John the Baptist for other prophets preaching different and often contrary messages. Many of the Americans George had inspired backslid into the Progressive and Populist movements, and the goal of removing unearned profit from landholding was lost. The Georgist movement faded away to the margins of history, where it remains today— a sect apart rather than a serious force, dedicated more to preserving his memory than to implementing his beliefs.

Yet interest in the ideas Henry George expounded has been rising in recent years. That interest spans the range from his method of taxing land to his philosophical view of humanity's relation to nature. Many economists and urban experts, though they do not often invoke his name, now believe he was right about taxing land rather than the improvements *on* the land. Shifting the property tax (which now taxes both equally) all or mostly onto the land itself would benefit both the decaying city and the vanishing countryside. The tax would act on the landowner as both stick and carrot. In and around the cities, where vast amounts of potentially valuable land are vacant or underused, a high tax on land value would force the landowner to put it to its most economic use, while less or no tax on buildings would reduce or remove the present penalty he pays for improving the property. This is land that, being strategically located in terms of transportation, *should* be used intensively: that's why a city grew up there in the first place. Since there is only so much demand for factories and stores and homes, the more intensive use of the best-located land would reduce the pressure on outlying areas. Thus, in the country, the land tax would discourage the phenomenon of sprawl, so costly in land and energy and money, and save some of the acres now disappearing under the suburban bulldozer. Some, not all: people have to live and work somewhere, so the most desirable land now farmed (and often in fact held for speculation) would go to other, more intensive uses. But because the high tax on the most valuable land would encourage thrifty use of it, much larger amounts of land would be saved for open space or agriculture.

The patterns of land use, which in large measure shape our lives, would become more varied—more intensive use here, more open space there—in place of the even spread of the usual suburb. Less land would be used, and other great savings would result: fewer highways, fewer utility lines, less fuel spent on auto travel, less air pollution. This sort of human settlement lends itself to mass transit—an obvious goal of any rational energy-saving policy—and a variant of George's land tax would provide the means to pay for it. Any new transportation line causes an increase in land value along its routes that often exceeds the cost of its construction. This windfall is completely unearned by the property owners who receive it; this is, in fact, a dramatic case of community-created land value. A Georgist would look to that windfall, not to taxes imposed on the general public, as the best and fairest source of money to pay for new transportation lines.

In less strictly economic terms, George's vision of assuring both freedom and fairness in access to natural resources is particularly appealing today. Any reader of *Progress and Poverty* can figure out how George would answer the pressing questions of our times. Instead of trying to prevent pollution by regulation, he would tax polluters heavily enough to motivate them to clean up their messes. He would allow private enterprise to mine minerals and oil and other fossil fuels, but he would tax away that part of the profit due to exclusive access to the gifts of nature. Doubtless he would apply the same principle in the developing debate over mining the ocean floor, taxing in this case for the benefit of all humanity—an attractive alternative to mining for the benefit only of multinational monopolies or authoritarian governments or incompetent international agencies. Beyond that, George's view of the world around us as a trust to be preserved rather than a conquest to be looted is in harmony with our growing awareness of the limits of nature. In this most profound sense—that we are all tenants on this earth, and owe rent for how we use and misuse it—Henry George speaks to the present and the future quite as eloquently as he did to the past.

5

Here Come the Wobblies!

BERNARD A. WEISBERGER

• Throughout the nineteenth century organized labor in the United States never embraced a majority of the industrial working people. In 1901, only one out of every fourteen non-agricultural workers belonged to any union, about half the proportion in Great Britain. The pattern of organizing only specialized craftsmen resulted partly from the exclusionary policy of the American Federation of Labor and partly from public antipathy for the aspirations and organizations of the unskilled working class. The Knights of Labor championed industrial unionism in the 1870s and attempted to unite the nation into one big cooperative enterprise. But it dwindled in effectiveness after the public's false association of it with the Haymarket Riot and anarchism in 1886.

An even more spectacular effort to broaden the base of organized labor was the formation in Chicago, in 1905, of the Industrial Workers of the World. Led by "Big Bill" Haywood of the Western Federation of Miners, the "Wobblies" wanted to abolish the wage system. They hoped to gain their objectives by violent abolition of the state and the formation of a nationwide industrial syndicate governed by the workers themselves. The Wobblies were strongest among unskilled migratory workers in the West, but they had a hand in a number of strikes in the East. During World War I the Wobblies suffered from the patriotic fervor of the government and several vigilante groups, and they waned as a force in the labor movement. Bernard A. Weisberger's essay catches the tragedy and the persecution of the International Workers of the World as they sought to protect the welfare of the American worker.

Reprinted by permission from *American Heritage* (June 1967). © 1967 American Heritage Publishing Co., Inc.

On a hot June day in 1905 William D. Haywood, a thirty-six-year-old miner, homesteader, horsebreaker, surveyor, union organizer, and Socialist, out of Salt Lake City, stood up before a large crowd in a Chicago auditorium. He gazed down at the audience with his one good eye and, taking up a loose board from the platform, impatiently banged for silence.

"Fellow workers," he shouted, "this is the continental congress of the working class. We are here to confederate the workers of this country into a working-class movement that shall have for its purpose the emancipation of the working class from the slave bondage of capitalism."

Thus, in manifesto, the working-class crusade known as Industrial Workers of the World came to birth. It grew amid storms of dissent, lived always in the blast furnace of conflict, and was battered into helplessness over forty years ago. It is still alive, but as a "church of old men" in one author's words, old men still muttering "No" to the status quo. The *Industrial Worker*, the official newspaper of the "One Big Union," still appears, still carries as its masthead motto "An injury to one is an injury to all," still valiantly runs on its editorial page the uncompromising preamble to the constitution adopted at that Chicago convention in 1905:

> The working class and the employing class have nothing in common. There can be no peace so long as hunger and want are found among millions of working people and the few, who make up the employing class, have all the good things of life. . . .
>
> It is the historic mission of the working class to do away with capitalism. The army of production must be organized, not only for the everyday struggle with capitalists, but also to carry on production when capitalism shall have been overthrown. By organizing industrially we are forming the structure of the new society within the shell of the old.

But the old society is still here, thriving more vigorously than ever; the workers have late-model cars, and the struggle of the I.W.W.'s young radicals to burst its bonds is history now—good history, full of poets and tramps, bloodshed and cruelty, and roads not taken by American labor. The history not merely of an organization but of an impulse that stirred men from the lower depths of the economy—vagrants, lumberjacks, harvest hands, immigrant millworkers—and set them to marching in step with Greenwich Village literary radicals to the tune of gospel hymns and innocent ballads fitted with new, class-conscious verses.

But it was not all ballads and broadsides. The I.W.W. was radical in the word's truest sense. When it denied that the working and employing classes had anything in common, it meant precisely what it said. The I.W.W. put no faith in the promises of bourgeois politicians or in the fairness of bourgeois courts. It made no contracts with employers, and it spurned other unions—like those enrolled in the American Federation of Labor—that did. It was composed of hard, hard-working men, little known to respectability. As a result, it badly frightened millions of middle-class Americans, and it meant to.

Yet it must be understood that the I.W.W. did not grow in a vacuum. It arose out of an industrial situation for which the adjective "grim" is pallid. In the America that moved to productive maturity between 1880 and 1920, there was little room or time to care about the worker at the base of it all. It was an America in which children of ten to fourteen could and did work sixty-hour weeks in mine and factory; in which safety and sanitation regulations for those in dangerous trades were virtually unknown—and in which industrial accidents took a horrible toll each year; in which wages were set by "the market place" and some grown men with families worked ten to twelve hours for a dollar and stayed alive only by cramming their families into sickening tenements or company-town shacks; in which such things as pensions or paid holidays were unknown; lastly, it was an America in which those who did protest were often locked out, replaced by scabs, and prevented from picketing by injunction and by naked force. At Homestead, Pullman, Coeur d'Alene, Cripple Creek, Ludlow, and other places where strikers clashed with troops or police between 1892 and 1914, the record of labor's frustrations was marked with bloody palm prints. And at the bottom of the scale was the vast army of migrant workers who beat their way by rail from job to job—not only unskilled, unprotected, and underpaid but unnoticed and unremembered.

Out of such a situation grew the I.W.W. It gained much not only from the horror of its surroundings, but from the spirit of an infant century when the emancipation of almost everyone—women, workers, artists, children—from the dragons of the past seemed to be a live possibility, and "new" was a catchword on every tongue.

The opening years of the organization's life were not promising. Its founding fathers were numerous and diverse—discontented trade unionists, Socialists like Eugene V. Debs and the whiskered, professorial Daniel De Leon, and veterans of almost every other left-wing crusade of the preceding twenty years. There was among them all, a recent I.W.W. historian has written, "such a warfare as can be found only between competing radicals." They were, however, united in objecting to the craft-union principles of A.F.L. chieftain Samuel Gompers, whom Haywood described as "a squat specimen of humanity" with "small snapping eyes, a hard cruel mouth," and "a personality vain, conceited, petulant and vindictive."

Gompers' plan of organizing only skilled craftsmen and negotiating contracts aimed only at securing a better life from day to day struck the I.W.W.'s founders not only as a damper upon whatever militancy the labor movement might generate to challenge capitalism, but also as a betrayal of the unskilled laborers, who would be left to shift for themselves. The new leaders therefore created a "single industrial union," as far removed from craft divisions as possible.

All industrial labor was to be divided into thirteen great, centrally administered divisions—building, manufacturing, mining, transportation, public service, etc. Within each of these would be subgroups. But each such group would take in all employees contributing to that industry's product or service. On the steam railroads, as an instance, clerks, telegraphers, and trackwalkers would share power and glory with engineers, brakemen, and conductors. A grievance of one lowly set of workers in a single shop could bring on a strike that would paralyze a whole industry. And some day, on signal from the One Big Union, all workers in all industries would throw the "Off" switch, and the wage system would come tumbling down.

Much of the scheme came from the brain and pen of a priest, Father Thomas Hagerty, who while serving mining parishes in the Rockies had come to believe in Marx as well as Christ. He had the scheme of industrial unionism all worked out in a wheel-shaped chart, with the rim divided into the major industries and the hub labelled "General Administration." Gompers looked at a copy of it in a magazine and snarled: "Father Hagerty's Wheel of Fortune!" He did not expect it to spin very long.

Nor, during the I.W.W.'s first three years of existence, did it seem likely to. Factional quarrels wracked national headquarters and the

Western Federation of Miners, the biggest single block in the entire I.W.W. structure, pulled out. By spring of 1908 the organization, whose paper strength was perhaps 5,000 but whose actual roster was probably much thinner, was broke and apparently heading toward the graveyard that seems to await all clique-ridden American radical bodies.

But the death notices were premature. The headquarters brawls were among and between trade unionists and Socialists, and the I.W.W.'s future was, as it turned out, linked to neither group. It belonged to a rank-and-file membership that was already formulating surprise tactics and showing plenty of vigor. In Schenectady, New York, for example, I.W.W.-led strikers in a General Electric plant protested the firing of three draftsmen by staying at their machines for sixty-five hours, a use of the sit-down strike thirty years before it was introduced by the auto workers as a radical measure during the Great Depression. In Goldfield, Nevada, the I.W.W. under thirty-one-year-old Vincent St. John organized the town's hotel and restaurant workers into a unit with the local silver and gold miners. This unlikely combination of hash-slingers and miners, an extreme example of industrial unionism, forced the town's employers to boost wage scales, temporarily at least, to levels of five dollars per eight-hour day for skilled underground workers, down to three dollars and board for eight hours of dishwashing by the lowly "pearl divers." It seemed to be clear proof that "revolutionary industrial unionism" could work. The fiery St. John was even able to close down the mines one January day in 1907 for a protest parade—on behalf of Haywood, Charles Moyer, and George Pettibone, three officers of the miners' union who had been arrested (they were later acquitted) in the bomb-killing of former Governor Frank Steunenberg of Idaho. St. John's parade brought three thousand unionists into the small-town streets "all wearing tiny red flags."

The real turning point came at the organization's fourth convention, in 1908. The believers in "direct action at the point of production" forced a change in the I.W.W.'s holy writ, the preamble. It had originally contained the sentence: "A struggle must go on until all the toilers come together *on the political, as well as the industrial field*, and take and hold that which they produce" (italics added). Now this "political clause" was scuttled, over the violent protests of Socialist De Leon, who helplessly denounced the change as an exaltation of "physical force." The shock troops of the direct-action group were twenty lumber workers known as the Overalls Brigade. Gathered in Portland by an organizer named Jack Walsh, they had bummed their way to Chicago in boxcars, raising grubstakes along the way at street meetings in which they sang, harangued, peddled pamphlets, and passed the hat. One of their favorite tunes, with which they regaled the convention, was "Hallelujah, I'm a Bum," set to the old hymn tune "Revive Us Again":

> O, why don't you work
> Like other men do?
> How in hell can I work
> When there's no work to do?

> Hallelujah, I'm a bum,
> Hallelujah, bum again,
> Hallelujah, give us a handout—
> To revive us again.

Sourly, De Leon dubbed Walsh's men The Bummery, but the day was theirs. The veteran Socialist leader retreated and organized a splinter I.W.W., which dwindled away in seven years.

It was the I.W.W.'s second split in a short history, but its most important. It gave the organization over to soapbox singers and bums, brothers in idealism who were poor in all things save "long experience in the struggle with the employer." They were to break from past labor practices and give the I.W.W. its true inwardness and dynamism; to fit it with its unique costume and role in history.

They gave it, first, a musical voice. Walsh's crusaders sang because when they sought the workers' attention on street corners they were challenged by those competing sidewalk hot-gospellers, the Salvation Army. By 1909, the press of the organization's newspaper, the *Industrial Worker*, was able to put out the first edition of *Songs of the Workers to Fan the Flames of Discontent*. More succinctly known as the "Little Red Songbook," it has gone through over thirty subsequent editions—all scarlet-covered and fitted to the size of an overalls pocket. The songbook and the preamble were to the I.W.W. membership what the hymnbook and the *Discipline of the Methodist Church* had been to frontier preachers—the sum and touchstone of faith, the pearl of revelation, the coal of fire touching their lips with eloquence. Most of the songs were the work of men like Richard Brazier, an English-born construction worker who joined up in Spokane in 1908; or Ralph Chaplin, a struggling young Chicago commercial artist who wanted to chant "hymns of hope and hatred" at the shrine of rebellion; or Joe Hill, born Joel Haaglund in Sweden, who wrote not parodies alone but also original compositions, which Chaplin described as "coarse as home-spun and as fine as silk"; or bards known simply as T-Bone Slim or Dublin Dan. The I.W.W. members soared on those songs, enjoying them as much for their mockery as anything.

To the patriotic cadences of "The Battle Hymn of the Republic" they sang "Solidarity forever, for the Union makes us strong" (a version which Ralph Chaplin had given them and which the entire labor movement took over without credit). To the sentimental notes that enfolded Darling Nelly Gray they sang of "the Commonwealth of Toil that is to be," and to the strains that had taken pretty Red Wing through ribald adventures in every barroom in the country, they roared that "the earth of right belongs to toilers, and not to spoilers of liberty." They raided the hymnbook of Moody-and-Sankey revivalism for "Hold the fort for we are coming, union men be strong," and for "There is power, there is power, in a working band" (instead of "in the blood of the Lamb"). They laughed in sharps and flats at Casey Jones, of the craft-proud Brotherhood of Railway Engineers, as a union scab who "kept his junk pile running" and "got a wooden medal for being good and faithful on the S.P. line." They sang in the hobo jungles, on the picket line, and in the jailhouse, and it was their singing especially that separated them from the A.F.L. by an abyss of spirit.

The "new" I.W.W. soon had a nickname, as derisive and defiant as its songs: the Wobblies. It is not certain how the name was born, though a popular legend declares that a Chinese restaurant owner in the Northwest was persuaded to grubstake I.W.W. members drifting through his town. His identification test was a simple question, "Are you I.W.W.?" but it emerged in Cantonese-flavored English as "Ah loo eye wobble wobble?" Whatever its origin, the name was a badge of pride.

The I.W.W.'s new leadership provided halls in the towns where a wandering Wobbly could find a warm stove, a pot of coffee, a corner in which to spread a blanket for the night, and literature: the *Industrial Worker* and *Solidarity*, leaflets by St. John or Haywood, and books like Jack London's *The Iron Heel*, Edward Bellamy's *Looking Back-ward*, Laurence Gronlund's *Co-operative Commonwealth*. All of them furnished material for arguments with the unorganized, and also such stuff as dreams were made on.

In 1909 the I.W.W. attracted national attention through the first of its spectacular clashes with civic authority. In Spokane a campaign was launched urging loggers to boycott the "job sharks," employment agents who hired men for work in lumber and construction camps deep in the woods, charging them a fee for the "service." Many a lumberjack who "bought a job" in this way was swindled—sent to a nonexistent camp or quickly fired by a foreman in cahoots with the shark to provide fast turnover and larger shared profits. At street meet-ings, the Wobblies preached direct hiring by the lumber companies. Spokane's thirty-one agencies retaliated by getting the city council to ban such meetings. The *Industrial Worker* promptly declared Novem-ber 2, 1909, Free Speech Day and urged every man in the vicinity to "fill the jails of Spokane."

From hundreds of miles around, Wobblies poured in by boxcar, mounted soapboxes, and were immediately wrestled into patrol wagons. In a matter of weeks, the jail and a quickly converted schoolhouse were overflowing with five or six hundred prisoners. They came into court bloody from beatings; they were put to hard labor on bread and water, jammed into cells like sardines, and in the name of sanitation hosed with ice water and returned to unheated confinement. Three died of pneumonia. Among the prisoners was a dark-haired Irish girl from New York, Elizabeth Gurley Flynn. Eighteen years old and pregnant, she complicated her arrest by chaining herself to a lamp post. "Gurley," a proletarian Joan of Arc, was lodged with a woman cellmate who kept receiving mysterious calls to the front office. It turned out that she was a prostitute, serving customers provided by the sheriff "for good and valuable consideration." This fact was trumpeted by the I.W.W. as soon as Gurley figured it out.

Fresh trainloads of Wobblies poured relentlessly into town, while those already in jail kept the night alive with selections from the Little Red Songbook roared at full volume, staged hunger strikes, refused to touch their hammers on the rock pile, and generally discomfited their captors. In March of 1910 the taxpayers of Spokane threw in the towel, released the prisoners, and restored the right of free speech to the I.W.W. Other free-speech fights in the next few years carried the Wobbly message throughout the Far West and helped in organizing new locals among the militant.

Two years after the end of the Spokane campaign, the I.W.W. made headlines in the East. In the textile-manufacturing town of Lawrence, Massachusetts, on January 11, 1912, more than 20,000 workers struck against a wage cut that took thirty cents—the price of three loaves of bread—out of pay envelopes averaging only six to eight dollars for a fifty-four-hour week. It was an unskilled work force that hit the bitter-cold streets, and a polyglot one, too. Some twenty-five nationalities, speaking forty-five languages or dialects, were represented, including French Canadians, Belgians, Poles, Italians, Syrians, Lithuanians, Greeks, Russians, and Turks.

There was only a small I.W.W. local in Lawrence, but the tactics of One Big Union under the slogan "An injury to one is an injury to all" had never been more appropriate. I.W.W. pamphlets and newspapers in several languages had already appeared. Now the leadership deployed its best veterans in the field—Haywood, William Trautmann, Elizabeth Gurley Flynn—and in addition a big, jovial-looking Italian organizer of steelworkers, Joe Ettor, whose usual costume was a black shirt and a red tie.

For over two months, something akin to social revolution went on in Lawrence. A strike committee of fifty-six members, representing all nationalities, filled days and nights with meetings and parades. Haywood stood out like a giant. He hurdled the linguistic barrier by speeches partly in sign language (waving fingers to show the weakness of separate craft unions; balled-up fist to demonstrate solidarity), visited workers' homes, and won the women's hearts by joshing the children or smacking his lips over shashlik or spaghetti. He also shrewdly exploited the publicity that bathed Lawrence, which was near the nation's journalistic capitals. Demonstrations were called with an eye not only to working-class morale but to public opinion. It was an education for many Americans to read about "ignorant, foreign" mill girls carrying signs that said: "We Want Bread and Roses, Too."

The employers played into Haywood's hands. National Guardsmen were called out. Police arrested more than three hundred workers and, in a climax of stupidity, clubbed a group of mothers and children preparing to leave town by railroad for foster homes. In defiance of the evidence, Ettor and Arturo Giovannitti, another Italian organizer, were arrested as accessories in the shooting of a woman striker. Authorities held them for seven months before a trial. When it came, it not only let the two men go free but gave Giovannitti a chance to spellbind jury and reporters with an oration on behalf of "this mighty army of the working class of the world, which . . . is striving towards the destined goal, which is the emancipation of human kind, which is the establishment of love and brotherhood and justice for every man and every woman in this earth."

Long before that speech, in March of 1912, the bosses had given up and agreed to the strikers' terms. It was the I.W.W.'s finest hour up to then. Flushed with success, the One Big Union next answered the call of silk workers at Paterson, New Jersey, to lead them in a strike that began in February, 1913. The pattern of Lawrence seemed at first to be repeating. There were nearly fifteen hundred arrests, and in addition police and private detectives killed two workers by random gunfire. One of these, Valentino Modesto, was given a funeral at which twenty thousand workers filed by to drop red carnations on the coffin. But after five months even relief funds and singing rallies could not prevail over hunger. The strike was broken.

Not, however, before it produced a unique project and a strange alliance. One of the reporters who came to Paterson on an April day was John Reed—talented, charming, Harvard '10—who was enjoying life to the hilt in the Bohemian surroundings of Greenwich Village, then in its heyday. When Reed stopped to talk to a striker, a Paterson policeman on the lookout for "agitators" hustled him off to jail. There he stayed for four days, sharing smokes and food with the strikers and amiably teaching them college fight songs and French ballads in return for instruction in the arts of survival in prison. On his release he became an enthusiastic supporter of the embattled workers and brought such friends as Mabel Dodge, Hutchins Hapgood, Walter Lippmann, Lincoln Steffens, and others to hear Haywood and other Wobbly leaders speak.

Between the individualistic rebelliousness of the young artists and writers escaping their bourgeois backgrounds and the hard-shelled but dream-drenched radicalism of the I.W.W. leaders, there was instinctive connection. Reed conceived the idea of a giant fund-raising pageant to present the strikers' case. On June 7, thousands of silk workers came into New York by special train and ferry and marched to Madison Square Garden. There they watched hundreds of fellow strikers reenact the walkout, the shooting of Modesto, his funeral, and the mass meetings that followed. Staged by Reed's Harvard friend Robert Edmund Jones against a backdrop created by the artist John Sloan, the pageant was described by *Outlook* as having "a directness, an intensity, and a power seldom seen on the professional stage." Since it ran for only one night, it failed to earn any money beyond expenses, despite a full house. Yet as a moment of convergence in the currents of radicalism vitalizing American life and letters in the last days of prewar innocence, it has a historic place of its own.

The Lawrence and Paterson affairs were only forays, however. The I.W.W. ran strikes and kept footholds in the East—the dockworkers of Philadelphia were firmly organized in the I.W.W.-affiliated Marine Transport Workers Union, for example—but it lacked staying power in the settled industrial areas. As it moved into its peak years, the future of the One Big Union was in the West, where its message and tactics were suited to the style of migrant workers, and to the violent tempo of what Elizabeth Flynn recalled as "a wild and rugged country where both nature and greed snuffed out human life."

Here, in the mountains and forests, were men who needed protection even more than the unskilled rubber, textile, steel, and clothing workers receiving I.W.W. attention—men like the "timber beasts," who worked in the freezing woods from dawn to dusk and then "retired" to vermin-ridden bunkhouses, without washing facilities, where they were stacked in double tiers like their own logs. The companies did not even furnish bedding, and a lumberjack between jobs was recognizable by his roll of blankets—his "bundle," "bindle," or "balloon" —slung on his back. The bindle stiff who "played the woods," however, was only one member of an army of migrant workers, as many as a half million strong, who as the cycle of each year turned followed the harvests, the construction jobs, the logging operations, and the opening of new mines. Sometimes they got a spell of sea life in the forecastle of a merchant ship; often they wintered in the flophouses of

Chicago or San Francisco; and not infrequently they spent the out-of-season months in jail on charges of vagrancy. The public mind blurred them together, and made no distinction among hoboes, bums, and tramps, assuming them all to be thieves, drunkards, and pan-handlers. But the true migrant was none of these. He was a "working stiff," emphasis on the first word, and thus ripe for the tidings of class war.

The I.W.W. reached him where he lived: in the hobo "jungles" outside the rail junction points, where he boiled stew in empty tin cans, slept on the ground come wind, come weather, and waited to hop a freight bound in any direction where jobs were rumored to be. The Wobblies sent in full-time organizers, dressed in the same caps and windbreakers, but with pockets full of red membership cards, dues books and stamps, subscription blanks, song sheets, pamphlets. These job delegates signed up their men around the campfires or in the box-cars ("side-door Pullmans" the migrants called them), mailed the money to headquarters, and then followed their recruits to the woods, or to the tents in the open fields where the harvest stiffs unrolled *their* bindles after twelve hours of work in hundred-degree heat without water, shade, or toilets. But there were some whom the organizers could not reach, and the I.W.W. sent them messages in the form of "stickerettes." These "silent agitators" were illustrated slogans on label-sized pieces of gummed paper, many of them drawn by Ralph Chaplin. They sold for as little as a dollar a thousand, and Chaplin believed that in a few weeks a good "Wob" on the road could plaster them on "every son-of-a-bitch of a boxcar, watertank, pick handle and pitchfork" within a radius of hundreds of miles.

The stickers were simple and caught the eye. "What Time Is It? Time to Organize!" shouted a clock. "Solidarity Takes the Whole Works" explained a Bunyan-sized workingman with an armload of trains and factories. The three stars of the One Big Union (Organization, Education, Emancipation) winked bright red over a black and yellow earth. A "scissorbill"—a workingman without class loyalty—knelt on bony knees and snuffled to the sky, "Now I get me up to work, I pray the Lord I may not shirk." But the most fateful stickers to appear between 1915 and 1917, as the nation moved toward war, were those that urged: "SLOW DOWN. The hours are long, the pay is small, so take your time and buck 'em all"; and those on which appeared two portentous symbols: the wooden shoe of sabotage, and the black cat, which, as everybody knew, meant trouble.

A tough problem for the I.W.W. was how to achieve "direct action" in the migrant workers' spread-eagle world. A factory or a mine could be struck. But how could the I.W.W.'s farmhands' union, the Agricultural Workers' Organization, "strike" a thousand square miles of wheatfield divided among hundreds of farmer-employers? How could the Forest and Lumber Workers' Industrial Union tie up a logging operation spread among dozens of camps separated by lonely miles?

The answer was, as the Wobblies put it, "to bring the strike to the job," or, more bluntly, sabotage. To the average American, sabotage conjured up nightmares of violence to property: barns blazing in the night, crowbars twisting the steel and wire guts out of a machine. The word itself suggested a European tradition of radical workers' dropping their *sabots*, or wooden shoes, into the works. But the I.W.W. leaders insisted that they had something less destructive in mind—merely the slowdown, the "conscientious withdrawal of efficiency," or, in working-stiff terms, "poor pay, poor work." To "put on the wooden shoe," or to "turn loose the black kitty" or "sab-cat," meant only to misplace and misfile order slips, to "forget" to oil motors, to "accidentally" let furnaces go out. Or simply to dawdle on the job and let fruit rot on the ground or let threshing or logging machinery with steam up stand idle while farmers and foremen fumed.

I.W.W. headquarters was vague about where the limits to direct action lay. Nor did it help matters when it printed dim, oracular pronouncements like Bill Haywood's "Sabotage means to push back, pull out or break off the fangs of Capitalism." Such phrases were enough to frighten not only the capitalists, but the Socialists, who in their 1912 convention denied the red sacraments to any who advocated "crime, sabotage or other methods of violence as a weapon of the working class to aid in its emancipation." (The next year, the Socialists fired Haywood from the party's executive board, completing the divorce between the Wobblies and politics.) Still the I.W.W. leaders in the field pushed ahead with their tactics. The Agricultural Workers, to strengthen the threat of mass quittings by harvest hands, organized a "thousand-mile picket line" of tough Wobblies who worked their way through freight trains in the farm belt, signing up new members and unceremoniously dumping off any "scissorbills" or "wicks" who refused a red card. The Lumber Workers forced the camp owners to furnish clean bedding by encouraging thousands of lumberjacks to celebrate May Day, 1918, by soaking their bindles with kerosene and making huge bonfires of them.

Potentially such tactics were loaded with danger, but from 1913 to 1919 they worked. Ralph Chaplin estimated that in early spring of 1917, when the A.W.O. was signing up members at the rate of 5,000 a month, the going wage in the grain belt had jumped from two dollars for a twelve-to-sixteen-hour day to five dollars for a ten-hour day. Two years later northwestern loggers were averaging twenty-five to fifty dollars a month plus board. These facts meant more to the average reader of *Solidarity* and the *Industrial Worker* than I.W.W. theories about the overthrow of capitalism. If he thought about the shape of society after the final general strike, it was only in the vague way of a church deacon who knew there was a celestial crown reserved for him, but did not trouble his mind about it from day to day. Yet the very success of the organization anywhere stirred not only the anger of its enemies but the fears of unsophisticated Americans who were ready to believe that the Wobblies were already putting the torch to the foundations of government and justice. With war hysteria actively feeding the fires of public hostility, the I.W.W. became the victim of new and spectacular persecutions.

Perhaps it was inevitable that the blood of martyrs would splash the pages of the I.W.W.'s book of chronicles. The mine owners, lumber-camp operators, and ranchers whom the Wobblies fought were themselves hard, resourceful men who had mastered a demanding environment. They knew a challenge when they saw one, and the West, in 1915, was not too far past Indian, stagecoach, and vigilante days. Sheriffs and their deputies were ready to use any method to rid their communities of "agitators"—especially those described in the press as "America's cancer sore." The Los Angeles *Times*, for example, said that

A vast number of I.W.W.'s are non-producers. I.W.W. stands for I won't work, and I want whisky. . . . The average Wobbly, it must be remembered, is a sort of half wild animal. He lives on the road, cooks his food in rusty tin cans . . . and sleeps in "jungles," barns, outhouses, freight cars. . . . They are all in all a lot of homeless men wandering about the country without fixed destination or purpose, other than destruction.

"When a Wobbly comes to town," one sheriff told a visitor, "I just knock him over the head with a night stick and throw him in the river. When he comes up he beats it out of town." Lawmen furnished similar treatment to any hobo or "undesirable" stranger, particularly if he showed a tendency to complain about local working conditions or if, after April 6, 1917, he did not glow with the proper enthusiasm for the war to end wars. Hundreds of suspected and genuine Wobblies were jailed, beaten, shot, and tortured between 1914 and 1919, but some names and episodes earned, by excess of horror or myth-creating power, a special framing among dark memories.

There was the case of Joe Hill. He was the most prolific of the Wobbly bards; the dozens of numbers he composed while drifting from job to job after his emigration from Sweden to America (where his name transformed itself from Haaglund into Hillstrom and then into plain Hill) had done much to make the I.W.W. a singing movement. His songs had, a recent Wobbly folklorist has written, "tough, humorous, skeptical words which raked American morality over the coals." They were known and sung wherever Wobblies fought cops and bosses.

In January, 1914, Salt Lake City police arrested Hill on the charge of murdering a grocer and his son in a holdup. Circumstantial evidence was strongly against him, but Hill went through trial and conviction stoutly insisting that he had been framed. Though a popular ballad written many years afterward intones, "The copper bosses killed you, Joe," Hill was not definitely linked to any strike activity in Utah, and had been in the I.W.W. for only four years. But his songs had made him a hero to the entire radical labor movement, and he had a sure sense of drama. Through months of appeals and protest demonstrations he played—or lived—the role of Pilate's victim magnificently. On November 18, 1915, the day before a five-man firing squad shot him dead, he sent to Bill Haywood, in Chicago, a classic telegram: "Goodbye, Bill. I die like a true blue rebel. Don't waste any time mourning. Organize!" Thirty thousand people wept at his funeral. At his own request, his ashes were put in small envelopes and distributed to be scattered, the following May Day, in every state of the Union.

And there was the "Everett massacre." On October 30, 1916, forty-one Wobblies had travelled from Seattle to Everett, Washington, some forty miles away, to speak on behalf of striking sawmill workers. Vigilantes under Sheriff Donald McRae arrested them, took them to the edge of town, and forced them to run the gantlet between rows of deputies armed with clubs, pick handles, and bats. Next morning the grass was stiff with dried blood. Five days later, two steamer loads of I.W.W. members sailed up Puget Sound from Seattle for a meeting of protest. As they approached the Everett docks singing "Hold the Fort for We Are Coming," the sheriff and his men were waiting. They opened up with a hail of gunfire, and five Wobblies were killed, thirty-one wounded; in the confused firing, two vigilantes were also killed. Seventy-four Wobblies were arrested and tried for these two deaths but were acquitted. No one was tried for killing the I.W.W. men.

The following summer Frank Little, a member of the I.W.W. executive board, died violently in Butte, Montana. Little was a dark-haired man, with only one good eye and a crooked grin. He was part Indian, and liked to josh friends like Elizabeth Gurley Flynn and Bill Haywood by saying: "I am a real Red. The rest of you are immigrants." In June, with his leg in a cast from a recent auto accident, he left Chicago headquarters for Butte to take command of the copper miners' strike, denounced by the mine owners as a pro-German uprising. On the night of August 1, 1917, six armed and masked men broke into his hotel room and dragged him at a rope's end behind an automobile to a railroad trestle, from which he was hanged, cast and all. No arrests were made by Butte police.

As a final gruesome example, there was what happened in Centralia, Washington, on Armistice Day, 1919. An American Legion parade halted before the town's I.W.W. hall, long denounced as a center of seditious efforts to stir lumberjacks to wartime strikes and already once raided and wrecked by townsmen. Now, again, a group of men broke from the line of march and swarmed toward the building. The Wobblies inside were waiting. Simultaneous shots from several directions shattered the air; three legionnaires fell dead. The marchers broke in, seized five men, and pursued a sixth. He was Wesley Everest, a young logger and war veteran. He killed another legionnaire before they captured him and dragged him, with his teeth knocked out, to jail. That night a mob broke in and took Everest to a bridge over the Chehalis

River. There he allegedly was castrated with a razor and then hanged from the bridge in the glare of automobile headlights.

The hand of history struck the I.W.W. its hardest blow, however, in September of 1917. The United States government moved to cripple the One Big Union, not because it was a threat to capitalism (the government insisted, without convincing the Wobblies) but because it was impeding the prosecution of the war. Whereas Samuel Gompers had moved skillfully to entrench the A.F.L. deeper in the hearts of the middle class by pledging it fully to Wilson's crusade, the I.W.W. remained hostile. In its eyes, the only war that meant anything to a working stiff was that foretold in the preamble, between the millions who toiled and the few who had the good things of life. Wobblies had seen too many strikes broken by troops to warm to the sight of uniforms. "Don't be a soldier," said one popular stickerette, "be a man."

The General Executive Board knew the dangers of that position once war was declared. The members hedged on expressing any formal attitude toward America's entry, and when the draft was enacted, the board advised them to register as "I.W.W. opposed to war" and thereafter to consult their own consciences. (Wesley Everest had been one of many Wobblies who chose uniformed service.) But the militant I.W.W. campaigns were frank challenges to the official drive for production. Five months after the declaration of war, federal agents, under emergency legislation, suddenly descended on I.W.W. offices all over the country. They confiscated tons of books, newspapers, letters, and pamphlets—as well as wall decorations, mimeograph machines, and spittoons—as evidence, then returned to remove Wobbly officials handcuffed in pairs.

The biggest trial of Wobblies on various counts of obstructing the war effort took place in federal district court in Chicago in the summer of 1918. Relentlessly the prosecutors drew around one hundred defendants a net of rumors and accusations charging them with conspiring to burn crops, drive spikes in logs, derail trains, dynamite factories. Judge Kenesaw Mountain Landis (later to be famous as professional baseball's "czar") presided in shirt-sleeved informality over the hot courtroom as, day after day, government attorneys read into the record every savory piece of I.W.W. prose or verse from which such phrases as "direct action" and "class war" could be speared and held up for horrified scrutiny. The jury took less than an hour to consider thousands of pages of evidence and hundreds of separate alleged offenses, and returned against all but a handful of the defendants a predictable wartime verdict of "guilty" on all counts. The white-thatched Judge Landis handed out sentences running as high as twenty years, as if he were in magistrate's court consigning the morning quota of drunks to thirty days each.

The 1918 federal trials (which were followed by similar episodes in a number of states that hastily enacted laws against "criminal syndicalism") were a downward turning point for the I.W.W. In theory, the One Big Union was wholly responsive to its rank and file, and invulnerable to the destruction of its bureaucracy.[1] But democratic enthusiasm could not override the fact that the veteran officers and keenest minds of the I.W.W. were behind bars, and their replacements were almost totally absorbed in legal maneuvers to get them out. A pathetic Wobbly fund-raising poster compressed the truth into a single line under a picture of a face behind bars: "We are in here for you; you are out there for us." In 1920 there might still have been fifty thousand on the I.W.W. rolls, but they were riding a rudderless craft.

Other troubles beset the One Big Union. The Communist party rose on the scene and sucked into its orbit some respected veterans, including Elizabeth Gurley Flynn (though she had left the I.W.W. in 1916) and William D. Haywood himself. Released from Leavenworth while his case was on appeal, Big Bill jumped bail and early in 1921 fled to the Soviet Union. Forgivably and understandably, perhaps, his courage had at last been shaken. He was fifty-one years old, seriously ill, and certain that he would die—with profit to no cause—if he had to spend any more time in jail. He was briefly publicized in Russia as a refugee from capitalism. He married a Russian woman, and for a time held a job as one of the managers of an industrial colony in the Kuznetsk Basin. But soon there was silence, and rumors of disillusionment. In May of 1928 he died. Half his ashes were sent to Chicago for burial. The other half lie under the Kremlin wall—like those of his old friend of Paterson days, John Reed. By and large, however, Bolshevik

---

1. The fact was that it made valorous efforts to keep its officialdom humble. As general secretary-treasurer, Bill Haywood received thirty-five dollars a week—just twice what a field organizer took home.

politicians had as little appeal for old-time Wobblies as any other kind. (Yet in 1948 the leadership of what was left of the organization refused to sign Taft-Hartley non-Communist affidavits. No contract, and no deals with bourgeois governments. Principle was principle still.)

More cracks crisscrossed the surface of solidarity. Some of the more successful I.W.W. unions experienced a yearning for larger initiation fees, and for just a taste of the financial stability of the A.F.L. internationals—the stability which had never been a Wobbly strong point. They quarrelled with the General Executive Board. A few locals chafed under what they thought was too much centralization. And finally, in 1924, there was an open split and a secession of part of the organization, taking precious funds and property with it. The last great schism, in 1908, had freed the I.W.W. for vigorous growth. Now it was sixteen years later, and time and chance were playing cruel games.

Middle age was overtaking the young lions, dulling their teeth—especially those who, one by one, accepted individual offers of clemency and emerged from prison, blinking, to find a changed world. The harvest stiff no longer took the side-door Pullman. He was a "gas tramp" now, or a "flivver hobo," riding his battered Model T to the job, and beyond the reach of the thousand-mile picket line. The logger, too, was apt to be a "home-guard," living with his family and driving through the dawn hours to where the saws whined and the big ones toppled. The children of the sweated immigrants of Paterson and Lawrence were clutching their high school diplomas, forgetting their working-class background, becoming salesmen and stenographers. Even the worker who stayed in the mill or the mine was sometimes lulled into passivity by the squealing crystal set or the weekly dream-feast of the picture-show. The ferment in the unskilled labor pool was hissing out. A new society *was* being built; but Ford and the installment plan had more to do with it than the visionaries who had hotly conceived and lustily adopted the I.W.W. preamble of 1905.

There was some fight left in the old outfit. It could run a free-speech fight in San Pedro in 1923, a coal strike in Colorado in 1927–28. But it was dwindling and aging. When the Depression came, labor's dynamism was reawakened by hardship. The C.I.O. was created, and fought its battles under the pennons of "industrial unionism," the heart of the Wobbly plan for organizing the army of production. The C.I.O. used singing picket lines, too, and sit-down strikes—techniques pioneered by such men as Haywood and Vincent St. John when labor's new leaders were in knickers. The old-timers who had known Big Bill and The Saint could only look on from the sidelines as the younger generation took over. Moreover, the success of organizing drives in the thirties, and the programs of the New Deal, vastly improved the lot of millions of working people. The agony that had nourished the I.W.W.'s revolutionary temper was now abating. Ironically, the very success of labor in uplifting itself through collective bargaining and politics drove one more nail into the I.W.W.'s coffin.

But "coffin" is perhaps the wrong word. Like Joe Hill, the I.W.W. never died. In its offices scattered across the country, old-timers still sit and smoke under pictures of Frank Little and Wesley Everest, or leaf through copies of the *Industrial Worker* like the great readers they always were. They do not give up; they expect that history will knock some sense into the workers soon, and that then the cry of "One Union, One Label, One Enemy" will rise again from thousands of throats. But meanwhile, their offices are, in the words of a recent observer, haunted halls, "full of memories and empty of men."

By contrast, the steel and glass office buildings of the bigtime A.F.L.-C.I.O. unions are alive with the ring of telephones, the hum of presses, the clatter of typewriters, and the clicking of secretaries' heels hurrying through the doors behind which sit organized labor's well-dressed statisticians, economists, lawyers, accountants, editors, co-ordinators, and educators. They have given much to their workers, these unions—good wages, decent hours, vacations, benefits, pensions, insurance. But they may be incapable of duplicating two gifts that the I.W.W. gave its apostles, its knights, its lovers—gifts that shine through a pair of stories. One is of the sheriff who shouted to a group of Wobblies, "Who's yer leader?" and got back a bellowed answer, "We don't got no leader, we're all leaders." The other is a recollection by an unidentified witness at the Chicago trial:

> Well, they grabbed us. And the deputy says, "Are you a member of the I.W.W.?" I says, "Yes," so he asked me for my card, and I gave it to him, and he tore it up. He tore up the other cards that the fellow members along with me had. So this fellow member says, "There is no use tearing that card up. We can get duplicates." "Well," the deputy says, "We can tear the duplicates too." And this fellow worker says, he says, "Yes, but you can't tear it out of my heart."

6

The Politics of Reform in Municipal Government in the Progressive Era

SAMUEL P. HAYS

• The period between 1900 and the entrance of the United States into World War I is usually regarded as the Progressive Era. A fervor for change and reform affected every section of the country and both major political parties. Although the movement had its origins in various urban crises of the 1880s and 1890s and although it took in an extraordinarily complex and diverse group of proponents, writers agree that the reform impulse had three major thrusts: (1) new laws and programs to ease the lives of the poor and the underprivileged (for example, workmen's compensation, unemployment insurance, and the abolition of child labor); (2) new attempts at establishing more democracy (for example, the direct primary, the initiative, referendum, and recall, and the direct election of senators); and (3) new efforts to reduce the power of large businesses (for example, antitrust regulations, the Pure Food and Drug Act, and the Interstate Commerce Commission).

Since 1955, when Richard Hofstadter of Columbia University published The Age of Reform: From Bryan to F.D.R. and argued that the movement was led by well-born, well-educated individuals who were concerned about their personal loss of status to the "robber baron" millionaires of an industrial revolution, historians have increasingly doubted that either the intention or the result of Progressive measures was benevolent. Samuel P. Hays of the University of Pittsburgh has been an especially severe critic and has suggested that reformers were typically well-heeled urban businessmen seeking to bring efficiency and honesty to municipal government

Reprinted from *Pacific Northwest Quarterly*, 55 (October, 1964), 157–169, by permission of the author.

at the expense of the poor. Noting that the rhetoric of reform often masked nefarious intentions, Hays argues that there was a profound difference between what Progressives said and what they did. Thus, they spoke of good government and honesty when in fact they advocated elitist measures with decidedly anti-democratic overtones. Schools were centralized to take decision-making power away from immigrant neighborhoods, while commission and city-manager administrative systems were put in as a means of reducing the patronage and the power of political machines. Not everyone agrees with Hays's harsh judgments, but the article reprinted here has had a profound influence on Progressive historiography.

In order to achieve a more complete understanding of social change in the Progressive Era, historians must now undertake a deeper analysis of the practices of economic, political, and social groups. Political ideology alone is no longer satisfactory evidence to describe social patterns because generalizations based upon it, which tend to divide political groups into the moral and the immoral, the rational and the irrational, the efficient and the inefficient, do not square with political practice. Behind this contemporary rhetoric concerning the nature of reform lay patterns of political behavior which were at variance with it. Since an extensive gap separated ideology and practice, we can no longer take the former as an accurate description of the latter, but must reconstruct social behavior from other types of evidence.

Reform in urban government provides one of the most striking examples of this problem of analysis. The demand for change in municipal affairs, whether in terms of over-all reform, such as the commission and city-manager plans, or of more piecemeal modifications, such as the development of city-wide school boards, deeply involved reform ideology. Reformers loudly proclaimed a new structure of municipal government as more moral, more rational, and more efficient and, because it was so, self-evidently more desirable. But precisely because of this emphasis, there seemed to be no need to analyze the political forces behind change. Because the goals of reform were good, its causes were obvious; rather than being the product of particular people and particular ideas in particular situations, they were deeply imbedded in the universal impulses and truths of "progress." Consequently, historians have rarely tried to determine precisely who the municipal reformers were or what they did, but instead have relied on reform ideology as an accurate description of reform practice.

The reform ideology which became the basis of historical analysis is well known. It appears in classic form in Lincoln Steffens' *Shame of the Cities*. The urban political struggle of the Progressive Era, so the argument goes, involved a conflict between public impulses for "good government" against a corrupt alliance of "machine politicians" and "special interests."

During the rapid urbanization of the late 19th century, the latter had been free to aggrandize themselves, especially through franchise grants, at the expense of the public. Their power lay primarily in their ability to manipulate the political process, by bribery and corruption, for their own ends. Against such arrangements there gradually arose a public protest, a demand by the public for honest government, for officials who would act for the public rather than for themselves. To accomplish their goals, reformers sought basic modifications in the political system, both in the structure of government and in the manner of selecting public officials. These changes, successful in city after city, enabled the "public interest" to triumph.

Recently, George Mowry, Alfred Chandler, Jr., and Richard Hofstadter have modified this analysis by emphasizing the fact that the impulse for reform did not come from the working class. This might have been suspected from the rather strained efforts of National Municipal League writers in the "Era of Reform" to go out of their way to demonstrate working-class support for commission and city-manager governments. We now know that they clutched at straws, and often erroneously, in order to prove to themselves as well as to the public that municipal reform was a mass movement.

The Mowry-Chandler-Hofstadter writings have further modified older views by asserting that reform in general and municipal reform in particular sprang from a distinctively middle-class movement. This has now become the prevailing view. Its popularity is surprising not only because it is based upon faulty logic and extremely limited evidence, but also because it, too, emphasizes the analysis of ideology rather than practice and fails to contribute much to the understanding of who distinctively were involved in reform and why.

Ostensibly, the "middle-class" theory of reform is based upon a new type of behavioral evidence, the collective biography, in studies by Mowry of California Progressive party leaders, by Chandler of a nationwide group of that party's leading figures, and by Hofstadter of four professions—ministers, lawyers, teachers, editors. These studies demonstrate the middle-class nature of reform, but they fail to determine if reformers were distinctively middle class, specifically if they differed from their opponents. One study of 300 political leaders in the state of Iowa, for example, discovered that Progressive party, Old Guard, and Cummins Republicans were all substantially alike, the Progressives differing only in that they were slightly younger than the others and had less political experience. If its opponents were also middle class, then one cannot describe Progressive reform as a phenomenon, the special nature of which can be explained in terms of middle-class characteristics. One cannot explain the distinctive behavior of people in terms of characteristics which are not distinctive to them.

Hofstadter's evidence concerning professional men fails in yet another way to determine the peculiar characteristics of reformers. For he describes ministers, lawyers, teachers, and editors without determining who within these professions became reformers and who did not. Two analytical distinctions might be made. Ministers involved in municipal reform, it appears, came not from all segments of religion, but peculiarly from upper-class churches. They enjoyed the highest prestige and salaries in the religious community and had no reason to feel a loss of "status," as Hofstadter argues. Their role in reform arose from the class character of their religious organizations rather than from the mere fact of their occupation as ministers. Professional men involved in reform (many of whom—engineers, architects, and doctors—Hofstadter did not examine at all) seem to have come especially from the more advanced segments of their professions, from those who sought to apply their specialized knowledge to a wider

range of public affairs. Their role in reform is related not to their
attempt to defend earlier patterns of culture, but to the working out
of the inner dynamics of professionalization in modern society.

The weakness of the "middle-class" theory of reform stems from
the fact that it rests primarily upon ideological evidence, not on a
thorough-going description of political practice. Although the studies
of Mowry, Chandler, and Hofstadter ostensibly derive from behavioral
evidence, they actually derive largely from the extensive expressions
of middle-ground ideological position, of the reformers' own descriptions of their contemporary society, and of their expressed fears of
both the lower and the upper classes, of the fright of being ground
between the millstones of labor and capital.

Such evidence, though it acurately portrays what people thought,
does not accurately describe what they did. The great majority of
Americans look upon themselves as "middle class" and subscribe to a
middle-ground ideology, even though in practice they belong to a
great variety of distinct social classes. Such ideologies are not rational-
izations or deliberate attempts to deceive. They are natural phenomena of human behavior. But the historian should be especially
sensitive to their role so that he will not take evidence of political
ideology as an accurate representation of political practice.

In the following account I will summarize evidence in both secondary and primary works concerning the political practices in which
municipal reformers were involved. Such an analysis logically can be
broken down into three parts, each one corresponding to a step in the
traditional argument. First, what was the source of reform? Did it lie
in the general public rather than in particular groups? Was it middle
class, working class, or perhaps of other composition? Second, what
was the reform target of attack? Were reformers primarily interested in
ousting the corrupt individual, the political or business leader who
made private arrangements at the expense of the public, or were they
interested in something else? Third, what political innovations did
reformers bring about? Did they seek to expand popular participation
in the governmental process?

There is now sufficient evidence to determine the validity of these
specific elements of the more general argument. Some of it has been
available for several decades; some has appeared more recently; some
is presented here for the first time. All of it adds up to the conclu-

sion that reform in municipal government involved a political development far different from what we have assumed in the past.

Available evidence indicates that the source of support for reform in municipal government did not come from the lower or middle classes, but from the upper class. The leading business groups in each city and professional men closely allied with them initiated and dominated municipal movements. Leonard White, in his study of the city manager published in 1927, wrote:

> The opposition to bad government usually comes to a head in the local chamber of commerce. Business men finally acquire the conviction that the growth of their city is being seriously impaired by the failures of city officials to perform their duties efficiently. Looking about for a remedy, they are captivated by the resemblance of the city-manager plan to their corporate form of business organization.

In the 1930's White directed a number of studies of the origin of city-manager government. The resulting reports invariably begin with such statements as, "the Chamber of Commerce spearheaded the movement," or commission government in this city was a "businessmen's government." Of thirty-two cases of city-manager government in Oklahoma examined by Jewell C. Phillips, twenty-nine were initiated either by chambers of commerce or by community committees dominated by businessmen. More recently James Weinstein has presented almost irrefutable evidence that the business community, represented largely by chambers of commerce, was the overwhelming force behind both commission and city-manager movements.

Dominant elements of the business community played a prominent role in another crucial aspect of municipal reform: the Municipal Research Bureau movement. Especially in the larger cities, where they had less success in shaping the structure of government, reformers established centers to conduct research in municipal affairs as a springboard for influence.

The first such organization, the Bureau of Municipal Research of New York City, was founded in 1906; it was financed largely through the efforts of Andrew Carnegie and John D. Rockefeller. An investment banker provided the crucial support in Philadelphia, where a Bureau was founded in 1908. A group of wealthy Chicagoans in 1910 established the Bureau of Public Efficiency, a research agency. John H. Patterson of the National Cash Register Company, the leading figure in Dayton municipal reform, financed the Dayton Bureau, founded in 1912. And George Eastman was the driving force behind both the Bureau of Municipal Research and city-manager government in Rochester. In smaller cities data about city government was collected by interested individuals in a more informal way or by chambers of commerce, but in larger cities the task required special support, and prominent businessmen supplied it.

The character of municipal reform is demonstrated more precisely by a brief examination of the movements in Des Moines and Pittsburgh. The Des Moines Commercial Club inaugurated and carefully controlled the drive for the commission form of government. In January, 1906, the Club held a so-called "mass meeting" of business and professional men to secure an enabling act from the state legislature. P. C. Kenyon, president of the Club, selected a Committee of 300, composed principally of business and professional men, to draw up a specific proposal. After the legislature approved their plan, the same committee managed the campaign which persuaded the electorate to accept the commission form of government by a narrow margin in June, 1907.

In this election the lower-income wards of the city opposed the change, the upper-income wards supported it strongly, and the middle-income wards were more evenly divided. In order to control the new government, the Committee 300, now expanded to 530, sought to determine the nomination and election of the five new commissioners, and to this end they selected an avowedly businessman's slate. Their plans backfired when the voters swept into office a slate of anticommission candidates who now controlled the new commission government.

Proponents of the commission form of government in Des Moines spoke frequently in the name of the "people." But their more explicit statements emphasized their intent that the new plan be a "business system" of government, run by businessmen. The slate of candidates for commissioner endorsed by advocates of the plan was known as the "businessman's ticket." J. W. Hill, president of the committees of 300 and 530, bluntly declared: "The professional politician must be ousted and in his place capable business men chosen to conduct the affairs of the city." I. M. Earle, general counsel of the Bankers Life Association and a prominent figure in the movement, put the point more precisely: "When the plan was adopted it was the intention to get businessmen to run it."

Although reformers used the ideology of popular government, they in no sense meant that all segments of society should be involved equally in municipal decision-making. They meant that their concept of the city's welfare would be best achieved if the business community controlled city government. As one businessman told a labor audience, the businessman's slate represented labor "better than you do yourself."

The composition of the municipal reform movement in Pittsburgh demonstrates its upper-class and professional as well as its business sources. Here the two principal reform organizations were the Civic Club and the Voters' League. The 745 members of these two organizations came primarily from the upper class. Sixty-five percent appeared in upper-class directories which contained the names of only 2 percent of the city's families. Furthermore, many who were not listed in these directories lived in upper-class areas. These reformers, it should be stressed, comprised not an old but a new upper class. Few came from earlier industrial and mercantile families. Most of them had risen to social position from wealth created after 1870 in the iron, steel, electrical equipment, and other industries, and they lived in the newer rather than the older fashionable areas.

Almost half (48 percent) of the reformers were professional men: doctors, lawyers, ministers, directors of libraries and museums, engineers, architects, private and public school teachers, and college professors. Some of these belonged to the upper class as well, especially the lawyers, ministers, and private school teachers. But for the most part their interest in reform stemmed from the inherent dynamics of their professions rather than from their class connections. They came from the more advanced segments of their organizations, from those in the forefront of the acquisition and application of knowledge. They were not the older professional men, seeking to preserve the past against change; they were in the vanguard of professional life, actively seeking to apply expertise more widely to public affairs.

Pittsburgh reformers included a large segment of businessmen; 52 percent were bankers and corporation officials or their wives. Among them were the presidents of fourteen large banks and officials of Westinghouse, Pittsburgh Plate Glass, U.S. Steel and its component parts (such as Carnegie Steel, American Bridge, and National Tube), Jones and Laughlin, lesser steel companies (such as Crucible, Pittsburgh, Superior, Lockhart, and H. K. Porter), the H. J. Heinz Company, and the Pittsburgh Coal Company, as well as officials of the Pennsylvania Railroad and the Pittsburgh and Lake Erie. These men were not small businessmen; they directed the most powerful banking and industrial organizations of the city. They represented not the old business community, but industries which had developed and grown primarily within the past fifty years and which had come to dominate the city's economic life.

These business, professional, and upper-class groups who dominated municipal reform movements were all involved in the rationalization and systematization of modern life; they wished a form of government which would be more consistent with the objectives inherent in those developments. The most important single feature of their perspective was the rapid expansion of the geographical scope of affairs which they wished to influence and manipulate, a scope which was no longer limited and narrow, no longer within the confines of pedestrian communities, but was now broad and city-wide, covering the whole range of activities of the metropolitan area.

The migration of the upper class from central to outlying areas created a geographical distance between its residential communities and its economic institutions. To protect the latter required involvement both in local ward affairs and in the larger city government as well. Moreover, upper-class cultural institutions, such as museums, libraries, and symphony orchestras, required an active interest in the larger municipal context from which these institutions drew much of their clientele.

Professional groups, broadening the scope of affairs which they sought to study, measure, or manipulate, also sought to influence the public health, the educational system, or the physical arrangements of the entire city. Their concerns were limitless, not bounded by geography, but as expansive as the professional imagination. Finally, the new industrial community greatly broadened its perspective in governmental affairs because of its new recognition of the way in which factors throughout the city affected business growth. The increasing size and scope of industry, the greater stake in more varied and geographically dispersed facets of city life, the effect of floods on many business concerns, the need to promote traffic flows to and from work for both blue-collar and managerial employees—all contributed to this larger interest. The geographically larger private perspectives of upper-class, professional, and business groups gave rise to a geographically larger public perspective.

These reformers were dissatisfied with existing systems of municipal government. They did not oppose corruption per se—although there was plenty of that. They objected to the structure of government which enabled local and particularistic interests to dominate. Prior to the reforms of the Progressive Era, city government consisted primarily of confederations of local wards, each of which was represented on the city's legislative body. Each ward frequently had its own elementary schools and ward-elected school boards which administered them.

These particularistic interests were the focus of a decentralized political life. City councilmen were local leaders. They spoke for their local areas, the economic interests of their inhabitants, their residential concerns, their educational, recreational, and religious interests —i.e., for those aspects of community life which mattered most to those they represented. They rolled logs in the city council to provide streets, sewers, and other public works for their local areas. They defended the community's cultural practices, its distinctive languages or national customs, its liberal attitude toward liquor, and its saloons and dance halls which served as centers of community life. One observer described this process of representation in Seattle:

> The residents of the hill-tops and the suburbs may not fully appreciate the faithfulness of certain downtown ward councilmen to the interests of their constituents. . . . The people of a state

would rise in arms against a senator or representative in Congress who deliberately misrepresented their wishes and imperilled their interests, though he might plead a higher regard for national good. Yet people in other parts of the city seem to forget that under the old system the ward elected councilmen with the idea of procuring service of special benefit to that ward.

In short, pre-reform officials spoke for their constituencies, inevitably their own wards which had elected them, rather than for other sections or groups of the city.

The ward system of government especially gave representation in city affairs to lower- and middle-class groups. Most elected ward officials were from these groups, and they, in turn, constituted the major opposition to reforms in municipal government. In Pittsburgh, for example, immediately prior to the changes in both the city council and the school board in 1911 in which city-wide representation replaced ward representation, only 24 percent of the 387 members of those bodies represented the same managerial, professional, and banker occupations which dominated the membership of the Civic Club and the Voters' League. The great majority (67 percent) were small businessmen—grocers, saloonkeepers, livery-stable proprietors, owners of small hotels, druggists—white-collar workers such as clerks and bookkeepers, and skilled and unskilled workmen.

This decentralized system of urban growth and the institutions which arose from it reformers now opposed. Social, professional, and economic life had developed not only in the local wards in a small community context, but also on a larger scale had become highly integrated and organized, giving rise to a superstructure of social organization which lay far above that of ward life and which was sharply divorced from it in both personal contacts and perspective.

By the late 19th century, those involved in these larger institutions found that the decentralized system of political life limited their larger objectives. The movement for reform in municipal government, therefore, constituted an attempt by upper-class, advanced professional, and large business groups to take formal political power from the previously dominant lower- and middle-class elements so that they might advance their own conceptions of desirable public policy. These two groups came from entirely different urban worlds, and the political system fashioned by one was no longer acceptable to the other.

Lower- and middle-class groups not only dominated the pre-reform governments, but vigorously opposed reform. It is significant that none of the occupational groups among them, for example, small business-men or white-collar workers, skilled or unskilled artisans, had important representation in reform organizations thus far examined. The case studies of city-manager government undertaken in the 1930's under the direction of Leonard White detailed in city after city the particular opposition of labor. In their analysis of Jackson, Michigan, the authors of these studies wrote:

> The *Square Deal*, oldest Labor paper in the state, has been consistently against manager government, perhaps largely because labor has felt that with a decentralized government elected on a ward basis it was more likely to have some voice and to receive its share of privileges.

In Janesville, Wisconsin, the small shopkeepers and workingmen on the west and south sides, heavily Catholic and often Irish, opposed the commission plan in 1911 and in 1912 and the city-manager plan when adopted in 1923. "In Dallas there is hardly a trace of class consciousness in the Marxian sense," one investigator declared, "yet in city elections the division has been to a great extent along class lines." The commission and city-manager elections were no exceptions. To these authors it seemed a logical reaction, rather than an embarrassing fact that had to be swept away, that workingmen should have opposed municipal reform.

In Des Moines working-class representatives, who in previous years might have been council members, were conspicuously absent from the "businessman's slate." Workingmen acceptable to reformers could not be found. A workingman's slate of candidates, therefore, appeared to challenge the reform slate. Organized labor, and especially the mine-workers, took the lead; one of their number, Wesley Ash, a deputy sheriff and union member, made "an astonishing run" in the primary, coming in second among a field of more than twenty candidates. In fact, the strength of anticommission candidates in the primary so alarmed reformers that they frantically sought to appease labor.

The day before the final election they modified their platform to pledge both an eight-hour day and an "American standard of wages." They attempted to persuade the voters that their slate consisted of men who represented labor because they had "begun at the bottom of the ladder and made a good climb toward success by their own unaided efforts." But their tactics failed. In the election on March 30, 1908, voters swept into office the entire "opposition" slate. The business and professional community had succeeded in changing the form of government, but not in securing its control. A cartoon in the leading reform newspaper illustrated their disappointment; John Q. Public sat dejectedly and muttered, "Aw, What's the Use?"

The most visible opposition to reform and the most readily available target of reform attack was the so-called "machine," for through the "machine" many different ward communities as well as lower- and middle-income groups joined effectively to influence the central city government. Their private occupational and social life did not naturally involve these groups in larger city-wide activities in the same way as the upper class was involved; hence they lacked access to privately organized economic and social power on which they could construct political power. The "machine" filled this organizational gap.

Yet it should never be forgotten that the social and economic institutions in the wards themselves provided the "machine's" sustaining support and gave it larger significance. When reformers attacked the "machine" as the most visible institutional element of the ward system, they attacked the entire ward form of political organization and the political power of lower- and middle-income groups which lay behind it.

Reformers often gave the impression that they opposed merely the corrupt politician and his "machine." But in a more fundamental way they looked upon the deficiencies of pre-reform political leaders in terms not of their personal shortcomings, but of the limitations inherent in their occupational, institutional, and class positions. In 1911 the Voters' League of Pittsburgh wrote in its pamphlet analyzing the qualifications of candidates that "a man's occupation ought to give a strong indication of his qualifications for membership on a school board." Certain occupations inherently disqualified a man from serving:

> Employment as ordinary laborer and in the lowest class of mill work would naturally lead to the conclusion that such men did not have sufficient education or business training to act as school

directors. . . . Objection might also be made to small shop-keepers, clerks, workmen at many trades, who by lack of educational advantages and business training, could not, no matter how honest, be expected to administer properly the affairs of an educational system, requiring special knowledge, and where millions are spent each year.

These, of course, were precisely the groups which did dominate Pittsburgh government prior to reform. The League deplored the fact that school boards contained only a small number of "men prominent throughout the city in business life . . . in professional occupations . . . holding positions as managers, secretaries, auditors, superintendents and foremen" and exhorted these classes to participate more actively as candidates for office.

Reformers, therefore, wished not simply to replace bad men with good; they proposed to change the occupational and class origins of decision-makers. Toward this end they sought innovations in the formal machinery of government which would concentrate political power by sharply centralizing the processes of decision-making rather than distribute it through more popular participation in public affairs. According to the liberal view of the Progressive Era, the major political innovations of reform involved the equalization of political power through the primary, the direct election of public officials, and the initiative, referendum, and recall. These measures played a large role in the political ideology of the time and were frequently incorporated into new municipal charters. But they provided at best only an occasional and often incidental process of decision-making. Far more important in continuous, sustained, day-to-day processes of government were those innovations which centralized decision-making in the hands of fewer and fewer people.

The systematization of municipal government took place on both the executive and the legislative levels. The strong-mayor and city-manager types became the most widely used examples of the former. In the first decade of the 20th century, the commission plan had considerable appeal, but its distribution of administrative responsibility among five people gave rise to a demand for a form with more centralized executive power; consequently, the city-manager or the commission-manager variant often replaced it.

A far more pervasive and significant change, however, lay in the centralization of the system of representation, the shift from ward to city-wide election of councils and school boards. Governing bodies so selected, reformers argued, would give less attention to local and particularistic matters and more to affairs of city-wide scope. This shift, an invariable feature of both commission and city-manager plans, was often adopted by itself. In Pittsburgh, for example, the new charter of 1911 provided as the major innovation that a council of twenty-seven, each member elected from a separate ward, be replaced by a council of nine, each elected by the city as a whole.

Cities displayed wide variations in this innovation. Some regrouped wards into larger units but kept the principle of areas of representation smaller than the entire city. Some combined a majority of councilmen elected by wards with additional ones elected at large. All such innovations, however, constituted steps toward the centralization of the system of representation.

Liberal historians have not appreciated the extent to which municipal reform in the Progressive Era involved a debate over the system of representation. The ward form of representation was universally condemned on the grounds that it gave too much influence to the separate units and not enough attention to the larger problems of the city. Harry A. Houlmin, whose book, *The City Manager*, was published by the National Municipal League, stated the case:

> The spirit of sectionalism had dominated the political life of every city. Ward pitted against ward, alderman against alderman, and legislation only effected by "log-rolling" extravagant measures into operation, mulching the city, but gratifying the greed of constituents, has too long stung the conscience of decent citizenship. This constant treaty-making of factionalism has been no less than a curse. The city manager plan proposes the commendable thing of abolishing wards. The plan is not unique in this for it has been common to many forms of commission government.

Such a system should be supplanted, the argument usually went, with city-wide representation in which elected officials could consider the city "as a unit." "The new officers are elected," wrote Toulmin, "each to represent all the people. Their duties are so defined that they must administer the corporate business in its entirety, not as a hodge-podge of associated localities."

Behind the debate over the method of representation, however, lay a debate over who should be represented, over whose views of public policy should prevail. Many reform leaders often explicitly, if not implicitly, expressed fear that lower- and middle-income groups had too much influence in decision-making. One Galveston leader, for example, complained about the movement for initiative, referendum, and recall:

> We have in our city a very large number of negroes employed on the docks; we also have a very large number of unskilled white laborers; this city also has more barrooms, according to its population, than any other city in Texas. Under these circumstances it would be extremely difficult to maintain a satisfactory city government where all ordinances must be submitted back to the voters of the city for their ratification and approval.

At the National Municipal League convention of 1907, Rear Admiral F. E. Chadwick (USN Ret.), a leader in the Newport, Rhode Island, movement for municipal reform, spoke to this question even more directly:

> Our present system has excluded in large degree the representation of those who have the city's well-being most at heart. It has brought, in municipalities . . . a government established by the least educated, the least interested class of citizens.
>
> It stands to reason that a man paying $5,000 taxes in a town is more interested in the well-being and development of his town than the man who pays no taxes. . . . It equally stands to reason that the man of the $5,000 tax should be assured a representation in the committee which lays the tax and spends the money which he contributes. . . . Shall we be truly democratic and give the property owner a fair show or shall we develop a tyranny of ignorance which shall crush him.

Municipal reformers thus debated frequently the question of who should be represented as well as the question of what method of representation should be employed.

That these two questions were intimately connected was revealed in other reform proposals for representation, proposals which were rarely taken seriously. One suggestion was that a class system of representation be substituted for ward representation. For example, in 1908 one of the prominent candidates for commissioner in Des Moines proposed that the city council be composed of representatives of five classes: educational and ministerial organizations, manufacturers and jobbers, public utility corporations, retail merchants including liquor men, and the Des Moines Trades and Labor Assembly. Such a system would have greatly reduced the influence in the council of both middle- and lower-class groups. The proposal revealed the basic problem confronting business and professional leaders: how to reduce the influence in government of the majority of voters among middle- and lower-income groups.

A growing imbalance between population and representation sharpened the desire of reformers to change from ward to city-wide elections. Despite shifts in population within most cities, neither ward district lines nor the apportionment of city council and school board seats changed frequently. Consequently, older areas of the city, with wards that were small in geographical size and held declining populations (usually lower and middle class in composition), continued to be overrepresented, and newer upper-class areas, where population was growing, became increasingly underrepresented. This intensified the reformers' conviction that the structure of government must be changed to give them the voice they needed to make their views on public policy prevail.

It is not insignificant that in some cities (by no means a majority) municipal reform came about outside of the urban electoral process. The original commission government in Galveston was appointed rather than elected. "The failure of previous attempts to secure an efficient city government through the local electorate made the business men of Galveston willing to put the conduct of the city's affairs in the hands of a commission dominated by state-appointed officials." Only in 1903 did the courts force Galveston to elect the members of the commission, an innovation which one writer described as "an abandonment of the commission idea," and which led to the decline of the influence of the business community in the commission government.

In 1911 Pittsburgh voters were not permitted to approve either the new city charter or the new school board plan, both of which provided for city-wide representation; they were a result of state legislative enactment. The governor appointed the first members of the new city council, but thereafter they were elected. The judges of the court of common pleas, however, and not the voters, selected members of the new school board.

The composition of the new city council and new school board in Pittsburgh, both of which were inaugurated in 1911, revealed the degree to which the shift from ward to city-wide representation produced a change in group representation. Members of the upper class, the advanced professional men, and the large business groups dominated both. Of the fifteen members of the Pittsburgh Board of Education appointed in 1911 and the nine members of the new city council, none were small businessmen or white-collar workers. Each body contained only one person who could remotely be classified as a blue-collar worker; each of these men filled a position specifically but unofficially designed as reserved for a "representative of labor," and each was an official of the Amalgamated Association of Iron, Steel, and Tin Workers. Six of the nine members of the new city council were prominent businessmen, and all six were listed in upper-class directories. Two others were doctors closely associated with the upper class in both professional and social life. The fifteen members of the Board of Education included ten businessmen with city-wide interests, one doctor associated with the upper class, and three women previously active in upper-class public welfare.

Lower- and middle-class elements felt that the new city governments did not represent them. The studies carried out under the direction of Leonard White contain numerous expressions of the way in which the change in the structure of government produced not only a change in the geographical scope of representation, but also in the groups represented. "It is not the policies of the manager or the council they oppose," one researcher declared, "as much as the lack of representation for their economic level and social groups." And another wrote:

> There had been nothing unapproachable about the old ward aldermen. Every voter had a neighbor on the common council who was interested in serving him. The new councilmen, however,

made an unfavorable impression on the less well-to-do voters.
. . . Election at large made a change that, however desirable in
other ways, left the voters in the poorer wards with a feeling
that they had been deprived of their share of political importance.

The success of the drive for centralization of administration and
representation varied with the size of the city. In the smaller cities,
business, professional, and elite groups could easily exercise a dominant
influence. Their close ties readily enabled them to shape informal political power which they could transform into formal political power.
After the mid-1890's the widespread organization of chambers of commerce provided a base for political action to reform municipal government, resulting in a host of small-city commission and city-manager
innovations. In the larger, more heterogeneous cities, whose subcom-
munities were more dispersed, such community-wide action was extremely difficult. Few commission or city-manager proposals material-
ized here. Mayors became stronger, and steps were taken toward
centralization of representation, but the ward system or some modified
version usually persisted. Reformers in large cities often had to rest
content with their Municipal Research Bureaus through which they
could exert political influence from outside the municipal government.

A central element in the analysis of municipal reform in the Progressive Era is governmental corruption. Should it be understood in moral
or political terms? Was it a product of evil men or of particular socio-
political circumstances? Reform historians have adopted the former
view. Selfish and evil men arose to take advantage of a political arrangement whereby unsystematic government offered many opportunities for personal gain at public expense. The system thrived until
the "better elements," "men of intelligence and civic responsibility,"
or "right-thinking people" ousted the culprits and fashioned a political force which produced decisions in the "public interest." In this
scheme of things, corruption in public affairs grew out of individual
personal failings and a deficient governmental structure which could
not hold those predispositions in check, rather than from the peculiar
nature of social forces. The contestants involved were morally de-

fined: evil men who must be driven from power, and good men who must be activated politically to secure control of municipal affairs.

Public corruption, however, involves political even more than moral considerations. It arises more out of the particular distribution of political power than of personal morality. For corruption is a device to exercise control and influence outside the legal channels of decision-making when those channels are not readily responsive. Most generally, corruption stems from an inconsistency between control of the instruments of formal governmental power and the exercise of informal influence in the community. If powerful groups are denied access to formal power in legitimate ways, they seek access through procedures which the community considers illegitimate. Corrupt government, therefore, does not reflect the genius of evil men, but rather the lack of acceptable means for those who exercise power in the private community to wield the same influence in governmental affairs. It can be understood in the Progressive Era not simply by the preponderance of evil men over good, but by the peculiar nature of the distribution of political power.

The political corruption of the "Era of Reform" arose from the inaccessibility of municipal government to those who were rising in power and influence. Municipal government in the United States developed in the 19th century within a context of universal manhood suffrage which decentralized political control. Because all men, whatever their economic, social, or cultural conditions, could vote, leaders who reflected a wide variety of community interests and who represented the views of people of every circumstance arose to guide and direct municipal affairs. Since the majority of urban voters were workingmen or immigrants, the views of those groups carried great and often decisive weight in governmental affairs. Thus, as Herbert Gutman has shown, during strikes in the 1870's city officials were usually friendly to workingmen and refused to use police power to protect strikebreakers.

Ward representation on city councils was an integral part of grassroots influence, for it enabled diverse urban communities, invariably identified with particular geographical areas of the city, to express their views more clearly through councilmen peculiarly receptive to their concerns. There was a direct, reciprocal flow of power between wards and the center of city affairs in which voters felt a relatively close connection with public matters and city leaders gave special attention to their needs.

Within this political system the community's business leaders grew in influence and power as industrialism advanced, only to find that their economic position did not readily admit them to the formal machinery of government. Thus, during strikes, they had to rely on either their own private police, Pinkertons, or the state militia to enforce their use of strikebreakers. They frequently found that city officials did not accept their views of what was best for the city and what direction municipal policies should take. They had developed a common outlook, closely related to their economic activities, that the city's economic expansion should become the prime concern of municipal government, and yet they found that this view had to compete with even more influential views of public policy. They found that political tendencies which arose from universal manhood suffrage and ward representation were not always friendly to their political conceptions and goals and had produced a political system over which they had little control, despite the fact that their economic ventures were the core of the city's prosperity and the hope for future urban growth.

Under such circumstances, businessmen sought other methods of influencing municipal affairs. They did not restrict themselves to the channels of popular election and representation, but frequently applied direct influence—if not verbal persuasion, then bribery and corruption. Thereby arose the graft which Lincoln Steffens recounted in his *Shame of the Cities*. Utilities were only the largest of those business groups and individuals who requested special favors, and the franchises they sought were only the most sensational of the prizes which included such items as favorable tax assessments and rates, the vacating of streets wanted for factory expansion, or permission to operate amid antiliquor and other laws regulating personal behavior. The relationships between business and formal government became a maze of accommodations, a set of political arrangements which grew up because effective power had few legitimate means of accomplishing its ends.

Steffens and subsequent liberal historians, however, misread the significance of these arrangements, emphasizing their personal rather than their more fundamental institutional elements. To them corruption involved personal arrangements between powerful business leaders and powerful "machine" politicians. Just as they did not fully appreciate the significance of the search for political influence by the rising business community as a whole, so they did not see fully the role of the "ward politician." They stressed the argument that the political leader manipulated voters to his own personal ends, that he used constituents rather than reflected their views.

A different approach is now taking root, namely, that the urban political organization was an integral part of community life, expressing its needs and its goals. As Oscar Handlin has said, for example, the "machine" not only fulfilled specific wants, but provided one of the few avenues to success and public recognition available to the immigrant. The political leader's arrangements with businessmen, therefore, were not simply personal agreements between conniving individuals; they were far-reaching accommodations between powerful sets of institutions in industrial America.

These accommodations, however, proved to be burdensome and unsatisfactory to the business community and to the upper third of socioeconomic groups in general. They were expensive; they were wasteful; they were uncertain. Toward the end of the 19th century, therefore, business and professional men sought more direct control over municipal government in order to exercise political influence more effectively. They realized their goals in the early 20th century in the new commission and city-manager forms of government and in the shift from ward to city-wide representation.

These innovations did not always accomplish the objectives that the business community desired because other forces could and often did adjust to the change in governmental structure and reëstablish their influence. But businessmen hoped that reform would enable them to increase their political power, and most frequently it did. In most cases the innovations which were introduced between 1901, when Galveston adopted a commission form of government, and the Great Depression, and especially the city-manager form which reached a height of popularity in the mid-1920's, served as vehicles whereby business and professional leaders moved directly into the inner circles of government, brought into one political system their own power and the formal machinery of government, and dominated municipal affairs for two decades.

Municipal reform in the early 20th century involves a paradox: the ideology of an extension of political control and the practice of its concentration. While reformers maintained that their movement rested on a wave of popular demands, called their gatherings of business and professional leaders "mass meetings," described their reforms as "part of a world-wide trend toward popular government," and proclaimed an ideology of a popular upheaval against a selfish few, they were in practice shaping the structure of municipal government so that political power would no longer be broadly distributed, but would in fact be more centralized in the hands of a relatively small segment of the population. The paradox became even sharper when new city charters included provisions for the initiative, referendum, and recall. How does the historian cope with this paradox? Does it represent deliberate deception or simply political strategy? Or does it reflect a phenomenon which should be understood rather than explained away?

The expansion of popular involvement in decision-making was frequently a political tactic, not a political system to be established permanently, but a device to secure immediate political victory. The prohibitionist advocacy of the referendum, one of the most extensive sources of support for such a measure, came from the belief that the referendum would provide the opportunity to outlaw liquor more rapidly. The Anti-Saloon League, therefore, urged local option. But the League was not consistent. Towns which were wet, when faced with a county-wide local-option decision to outlaw liquor, demanded town or township local option to reinstate it. The League objected to this as not the proper application of the referendum idea.

Again, "Progressive" reformers often espoused the direct primary when fighting for nominations for their candidates within the party, but once in control they often became cool to it because it might result in their own defeat. By the same token, many municipal reformers attached the initiative, referendum, and recall to municipal charters often as a device to appease voters who opposed the centralization of representation and executive authority. But, by requiring a high percentage of voters to sign petitions—often 25 to 30 percent—these innovations could be and were rendered relatively harmless.

More fundamentally, however, the distinction between ideology and practice in municipal reform arose from the different roles which each played. The ideology of democratization of decision-making was negative rather than positive; it served as an instrument of attack against the existing political system rather than as a guide to alternative action. Those who wished to destroy the "machine" and to eliminate party competition in local government widely utilized the theory that these political instruments thwarted public impulses, and thereby shaped the tone of their attack.

But there is little evidence that the ideology represented a faith in a purely democratic system of decision-making or that reformers actually wished, in practice, to substitute direct democracy as a continuing system of sustained decision-making in place of the old. It was used to destroy the political institutions of the lower and middle classes and the political power which those institutions gave rise to, rather than to provide a clear-cut guide for alternative action.

The guide to alternative action lay in the model of the business enterprise. In describing new conditions which they wished to create, reformers drew on the analogy of the "efficient business enterprise," criticizing current practices with the argument that "no business could conduct its affairs that way and remain in business," and calling upon business practices as the guides to improvement. As one student remarked:

> The folklore of the business elite came by gradual transition to be the symbols of governmental reformers. Efficiency, system, orderliness, budgets, economy, saving, were all injected into the efforts of reformers who sought to remodel municipal government in terms of the great impersonality of corporate enterprise.

Clinton Rodgers Woodruff of the National Municipal League explained that the commission form was "a simple, direct, businesslike way of administering the business affairs of the city . . . an application to city administration of that type of business organization which has been so common and so successful in the field of commerce and industry." The centralization of decision-making which developed in the business corporation was now applied in municipal reform.

The model of the efficient business enterprise, then, rather than the New England town meeting, provided the positive inspiration for the municipal reformer. In giving concrete shape to this model in the strong-mayor, commission, and city-manager plans, reformers engaged in the elaboration of the processes of rationalization and systematization inherent in modern science and technology. For in many areas of society, industrialization brought a gradual shift upward in the location of decision-making and the geographical extension of the scope of the area affected by decisions.

Experts in business, in government, and in the professions measured, studied, analyzed, and manipulated ever wider realms of human life, and devices which they used to control such affairs constituted the most fundamental and far-reaching innovations in decision-making in modern America, whether in formal government or in the informal exercise of power in private life. Reformers in the Progressive Era played a major role in shaping this new system. While they expressed an ideology of restoring a previous order, they in fact helped to bring forth a system drastically new.

The drama of reform lay in the competition for supremacy between two systems of decision-making. One system, based upon ward representation and growing out of the practices and ideas of representative government, involved wide latitude for the expression of grass-roots impulses and their involvement in the political process. The other grew out of the rationalization of life which came with science and technology, in which decisions arose from expert analysis and flowed from fewer and smaller centers outward to the rest of society. Those who espoused the former looked with fear upon the loss of influence which the latter involved, and those who espoused the latter looked only with disdain upon the wastefulness and inefficiency of the former.

The Progressive Era witnessed rapid strides toward a more centralized system and a relative decline for a more decentralized system. This development constituted an accommodation of forces outside the business community to the political trends within business and professional life rather than vice versa. It involved a tendency for the decision-making processes inherent in science and technology to prevail over those inherent in representative government.

Reformers in the Progressive Era and liberal historians since then misread the nature of the movement to change municipal government because they concentrated upon dramatic and sensational episodes and ignored the analysis of more fundamental political structure, of the persistent relationships of influence and power which grew out of the community's social, ideological, economic, and cultural activities. The reconstruction of these patterns of human relationships and of the changes in them is the historian's most crucial task, for they constitute the central context of historical development. History consists not of erratic and spasmodic fluctuations, of a series of random thoughts and actions, but of patterns of activity and change in which people hold thoughts and actions in common and in which there are close connections between sequences of events. These contexts give rise to a structure of human relationships which pervade all areas of life: for the political historian the most important of these is the structure of the distribution of power and influence.

The structure of political relationships, however, cannot be adequately understood if we concentrate on evidence concerning ideology rather than practice. For it is becoming increasingly clear that ideological evidence is no safe guide to the understanding of practice, that what people thought and said about their society is not necessarily an accurate representation of what they did. The current task of the historian of the Progressive Era is to quit taking the reformers' own description of political practice at its face value and to utilize a wide variety of new types of evidence to reconstruct political practice in its own terms. This is not to argue that ideology is either important or unimportant. It is merely to state that ideological evidence is not appropriate to the discovery of the nature of political practice.

Only by maintaining this clear distinction can the historian successfully investigate the structure of political life in the Progressive Era. And only then can he begin to cope with the most fundamental problem of all: the relationship between political ideology and political practice. For each of these facets of political life must be understood in its own terms, through its own historical record. Each involves a distinct set of historical phenomena. The relationship between them for the Progressive Era is not now clear; it has not been investigated. But it cannot be explored until the conceptual distinction is made clear and evidence tapped which is pertinent to each. Because the nature of political practice has so long been distorted by the use of ideological evidence, the most pressing task is for its investigation through new types of evidence appropriate to it. The reconstruction of the movement for municipal reform can constitute a major step forward toward that goal.

7

World War I: European Origins and American Intervention

JOHN MILTON COOPER, JR.

• World War I is the central event of the twentieth century. The first truly global conflict, it caused the deaths of at least ten million people, including practically an entire generation of the young manhood of Russia, Germany, France, and Great Britain, and it led directly to the Russian Revolution of 1917. Had Germany won the conflict, which seemed entirely possible as late as May 1918, or at least achieved a stalemate, the dislocations which led to the rise of Adolf Hitler and ultimately to World War II would not have been likely.

Although Americans played a relatively minor role in World War I, arriving in force only eight months before the Armistice, their participation was crucial to Allied success. The great German offensive of 1918, which carried virtually to the suburbs of Paris, was halted because of the presence and tenacity of American reserves who were thrown into the gap. Exhausted after four years of horrible trench warfare, the Kaiser's soldiers were demoralized by the appearance of fresh troops from across the ocean.

Because World War I was so momentous and because American intervention tipped the balance against Germany and thus changed the course of history, President Woodrow Wilson's attitudes and actions have understandably attracted considerable attention. Having won reelection in 1916 on his record of keeping the United States neutral, he decided on April 2, 1917, to shift his course. In the following essay, John Milton Cooper, Jr., recounts the pivotal events which determined that boys from Iowa and Brooklyn would fight and

Reprinted with permission from *Virginia Quarterly Review* 56 (Winter 1980), 1–18. © *The Virginia Quarterly Review*.

*sometimes die in the tiny villages and devastated fields of
northern France.*

One day in July 1955 the ground around the town of Messines, Belgium, trembled from an underground shock. It was not an earthquake.
It was the explosion of a cache of munitions buried nearly 40 years
before. For eleven months, during 1916 and 1917, British troops had
dug 21 mineshafts deep under the German lines in that part of Flan-
ders and had filled them with five hundred tons of explosives. Early
in the morning of June 7, 1917, the British had detonated the charges,
causing a blast that had awakened people as far away as London, 130
miles distant. Only 19 of the loaded mineshafts had blown up, however. The rumbling in 1955 signaled the explosion of one of the two
remaining charges. The other lies somewhere in the Flemish earth,
still unexploded but practically certain to go off someday.

That incident of the explosives planted deep and their continuing
after-effects is emblematic of the impact of World War I both on its
own time and on the subsequent history of the 20th century. The
war appeared to many contemporaries as a gigantic explosion or earthquake; those were two of the most popular terms used to describe the
conflict. In longer perspective, too, the war looks like an explosion or
earthquake in a metaphorical sense. It undermined an international
dispensation under which European nations dominated among the
world's major powers and ruled over much of the globe through their
colonial empires. Likewise, the war shattered the domestic stability of
those nations, sapping the authority of traditionally dominant groups
and giving rise to violent extremism at both ends of the political spectrum. The shocks generated by the crumbling of that international
and domestic order have precipitated the greatest events of the last
60 years, since the end of the war, and their final tremors are yet to
be felt.

From its outbreak, nearly everyone recognized the momentousness
of World War I. The suddenness and magnitude of the conflict that
erupted in August 1914 tended to throw imaginations out of kilter.
Observers instinctively grasped for non-human terms to describe it.
Natural catastrophes, like an explosion or earthquake, came readily to
mind. Henry James called the war "the plunge of civilization into this

abyss of blood and darkness." Theodore Roosevelt believed that it was "on a giant scale like the disaster to the Titanic." Others resorted to supernatural terms. In the United States, which was so strongly influenced by Bible-reading Protestantism, the most widely used name for the war came to be "Armageddon," the nation-shattering miracle preceding the Last Judgment in the book of Revelation. "Now Armageddon has a real meaning," announced one American magazine. "If this be not Armageddon, we shall never suffer the final death grip of nations." Those who have witnessed later occurrences in this century may balk at that assertion, but no one can doubt that people at the time of World War I knew that they were living through one of history's greatest events.

Such knowledge was not an unalloyed advantage to the participants. The ready comparison of the war to events that did not have human origins betokened an attitude that the war was also beyond human control. That attitude, not the destruction and carnage, was what made World War I so profoundly disheartening. World War II claimed more lives, laid waste more land and cities, and introduced more terrible weapons. Yet that later war has legitimately exciting, hopeful, and noble aspects. The difference between the world wars involved more than the fixity of the first versus the movement of the second. Rather it is a question of why they differed in that way, and the answer lies less in the technology or art of war and more in the imagination and grasp of the civilian and military leaders of the belligerent powers.

"The Second World War in some ways gave birth to less novelty and genius than the First," writes Sir Isaiah Berlin, who compares the literary production of the two wars. "Yet," Berlin adds, "perhaps there is one respect in which the Second World War did outshine its predecessor: the leaders of the nations involved in it were, with the significant exception of France, men of greater stature, psychologically more interesting than their prototypes." One does not have to agree with all of Berlin's judgments of individual leaders to concede the truth of his observation. H. H. Asquith, Sir Douglas Haig, Erich Ludendorff, and Kaiser Wilhelm, for example, contrast so hollowly with Winston Churchill, George S. Patton, Erwin Rommel, and even Adolf Hitler, because those earlier figures made themselves captives rather than masters of events. World War I produced only two

authentic world leaders, Woodrow Wilson and Vladimir Lenin, because they alone of all the national leaders grappled with the task of
controlling the war itself. In their conflicting ways, Wilson and Lenin
offered the only lights in the drab field of leadership in World War I.

What really made the war so staggering to people's sensibilities was
its human origin: for the first time in history the deeds of men seemed
to match the accidents of nature and the acts of God. World War I
sprang from two related breakdowns in mankind's proudest creations
at the beginning of the 20th century—the highly civilized nation-states
of Europe. One breakdown, which was immediate and obvious, lay in
relations among those nation-states. Although Europe had not experienced a general conflict for a hundred years before 1914, its state
system had shown unmistakable signs of instability for at least a generation. All the main European powers except Great Britain held
grudges against each other, and their grudges involved such intractable
matters as control of territories and populations and assertions of political and economic influence that were considered vital. The relative detachment of the British afforded no safety, either, since the
general instability also threatened them. Imperial expansion during
the generation before the war had sometimes deflected rivalries from
European concerns, but in the end controversies over colonies and
spheres of influence in Africa and Asia had exacerbated tensions
among the home countries. Moreover, the colonial and naval dimensions of the European rivalries had alarmed the British and drawn
them into the struggle in ways that strictly continental controversies
probably would not have done.

It seems clear now that of all the instigators of the war which broke
out in 1914 Germany bore the heaviest responsibility. During the
preceding ten years Europe had witnessed a series of crises initially
occasioned by conflicts in the Far East, North Africa, or the Balkans.
The Germans had either fomented those crises or rushed into them,
each time in hopes of sowing discord among their rivals and reaping
gains for themselves and their client states. Those German actions
had reflected more than a normal but reckless desire to get ahead at
the expense of adversaries. As Fritz Fischer and other German historians have shown, an expansionist consensus had grown up since the
1890's behind the proposition that Germany must become a "world
state" with a "world mission." Further, a number of German leaders

had become convinced that their nation's destiny could be fulfilled only through what the Foreign Minister in 1913 called "the coming world war." By 1914, diplomatic setbacks in the Balkans and the Near East and foreign economic uncertainties had created what Fischer terms a "crisis of German imperialism." The government in Berlin therefore greeted the dispute following the Austrian Archduke's assassination at Sarajevo in a mood of desperate hope. The Germans not only gave the Austrians a "blank check" in their dealings with Serbia, but they encouraged their ally to go to war. As Fischer concludes, "It is impossible to speak seriously either of Germany's being 'towed in Austria's wake' or of her being 'coerced.' "

Laying such responsibility at the Germans' door does not mean that they should once more be arraigned for "war guilt," as the victorious Allies did in 1919 in the Treaty of Versailles. No one has yet examined British, French, or Russian moves with the same access and assiduity that Fischer has studied the German role in the coming of the war. It seems likely that closer examination of French or, if it were possible, Russian sources might uncover at least a few comparable actions in goading Germany toward confrontation. Some elements in France did seek and welcome war in 1914. There, too, a nationalist revival had been flourishing, with increasingly shrill assertions of French destiny and revanchism toward Alsace and Lorraine. Even Britain, which was the last and most reluctant major power to enter the war in 1914, does not appear entirely blameless. For a number of years the British Foreign Secretary, Sir Edward Grey, had been giving assurances to the French of backing in the event of war. Grey had kept those assurances secret not only from Parliament but also from the full Cabinet, and though he had never explicitly promised British intervention, he had made commitments to the French that could not realistically be honored without fighting at their side. As events transpired, the German violation of Belgian neutrality averted a political crisis over Britain's entry into World War I. Defending "brave little Belgium" forestalled debate and rallied people to the colors in Britain in 1914 much as Pearl Harbor did in America in 1941.

Responsibility for the war was also generalized among the European nations in another way besides their diplomatic conduct. The second breakdown that contributed to the outbreak of World War I lay in the internal affairs of the countries involved. Foreign policy never exists in a vacuum, and in 1914 the actions of all the nations that became belligerents reflected domestic conditions. The Kaiser's regime ruled Germany in a mood of constant, though often exaggerated, insecurity. A plethora of proscriptions and legal disadvantages had not availed to prevent the Social Democrats from emerging as the strongest single party, and in 1913 and 1914 some conservative spokesmen had advocated war as a means of curbing rising Socialist strength. In France socialism and nationalism had competed for the allegiance of the working classes, and only the fortuitous assassination of the eloquent Jean Jaurès in July 1914 had removed a potential rallying point for Socialist opposition to the war. British internal discord stemmed not only from the growing strength and militancy of the Labour Party but also from woman suffrage agitation and, most gravely, from incipient civil war over autonomy for Ireland. Ironically, of all the major European powers, only backward, despotic, chronically troubled Russia seemed to be gaining in internal stability, thanks to massive industrialization and sweeping land reform.

By 1914, the breakdown that became so evident in Europe after World War I was already well advanced. The war undoubtedly accelerated the process, and in the case of Russia it may well have paved the way for a revolution that might not otherwise have occurred. But the war did not cause that internal breakdown. Instead, the breakdown contributed to the war. The dominant mood of the leaders of the nations that took up arms in 1914 was relief. British, French, and German leaders all seemed glad to lay aside their troubles at home and fight a foreign foe. David Lloyd George, the strongest figure in the British government, told one friend in August 1914, "In a week or two it might be good fun to be the advance guard of an expeditionary force to the coast of France, and run the risk of capture by a German ship!" The masses of men who went to war briefly shared such summer holiday sentiments, but their euphoria soon gave way to gloom and despair. Among thoughtful European observers, World War I almost at once instilled doubts about human nature and the progress of civilization. For men in the trenches and reflective onlookers, it was understandable that the war might seem beyond human control. For their leaders, however, the abdication of responsibility seems to have stemmed from their original relief at having escaped upleasant domestic conditions. It would seem that European leaders did not try harder to control the war because they did not want to. They evidently preferred the carnage of the war to the upheavals which they knew would meet its end if they did not emerge somehow triumphant.

II

Viewed from America, many aspects of World War I appeared different. Observers in the United States also immediately marveled at the immensity of the conflict, and they used the same nonhuman descriptions and bemoaned the setback to human progress. But other elements entered into reactions on this side of the Atlantic. Where Europeans initially thrilled to the adventure of war, Americans expressed relief at not being in it. Later, when the United States did enter the war, the most popular description for it would be "over there"; that phrase also expressed the basic American attitude toward World War I at its outbreak. From the American standpoint, the war was a terrible catastrophe that had befallen somebody else, far away. "Again and ever I thank Heaven for the Atlantic Ocean," wrote the American ambassador in London at the end of July 1914. People in the United States felt not only geographically but also morally removed from the war. It appeared to offer spectacular confirmation of longstanding notions about New World innocence and purity in opposition to Old World sin and decadence. In August 1914, the *New York Times,* usually a sober newspaper, contrasted the opening of the Panama Canal with the outbreak of the war by gloating, "The European ideal bears its full fruit of ruin and savagery just at the moment when the American ideal lays before the world a great work of peace, goodwill, and fair play." In short, many Americans reacted to the outbreak of World War I by figuratively repeating the Pharisee's prayer, "Thank God I am not as other men are."

That pervasive sense of removal from the war presented the most formidable barrier to eventual American intervention. But any thoughts of intervention lay well in the future. When President Wilson admonished his countrymen in August 1914 to remain "neutral in fact as well as in name," he simply seemed to be voicing the prevailing popular attitude. The following December he reiterated such sentiments when he dubbed the European conflict "a war with which we have nothing to do, whose causes can not touch us." Actually, Wilson meant to do more than convey soothing reassurance, since he had early come to fear the potential impact of the conflict on the United States. The mood of detachment lasted for the better part of the first year of the war. By the spring of 1915—despite some expressions of sympathy for the Allies, despite frictions with the British over their blockade of the Central Powers, and despite jitters at the German submarine proclamation—people appeared less concerned than ever about World War I. "Americans regard the war either as a bore," reported the British ambassador in Washington in April 1915, "or as an immensely interesting spectacle provided for their entertainment, of which they are commencing to be rather tired."

The great majority of Americans' attitudes toward World War I changed suddenly and dramatically on the afternoon of May 7, 1915. That was when the news reached the United States that a German submarine had sunk the British liner *Lusitania*, the world's largest passenger ship, killing 1,198 men, women, and children, 198 of whom were Americans. Ten years later the journalist Mark Sullivan discovered that all the people he interviewed could remember exactly where they had been when they had learned of the sinking of the *Lusitania*, what they had thought and felt, and what they had done for the rest of the day. The event left an indelible memory not only because it was another great catastrophe but also because it raised the threat of involvement in the war. Although many spokesmen fumed with outrage over the *Lusitania*, few raised cries for war. Out of 1,000 newspaper editors asked to telegraph their views to New York newspapers, six called for war. President Wilson caught the dominant public reaction when he stated a month after the sinking of the *Lusitania*, "I wish with all my heart I saw a way to carry out the double wish of our people, to maintain a firm front in respect of what we demand of Germany and yet do nothing that might by any possibility involve us in the war."

That statement defined the diplomatic dilemma that persisted until the United States entered World War I in April 1917. German-American relations did not begin a long slide toward war. A grave but polite diplomatic duel persisted between the two countries for nearly a year, until an American ultimatum forced the Germans to restrain their submarines in the spring of 1916. Thereafter, the threat of war receded for several months, and most of the friction between the United States and European belligerents involved the Allies, particularly Britain. Only Germany's launching of an expanded submarine offensive at the end of January 1917 brought the final crisis that plunged America into the war. Yet behind the ebb and flow of German-American relations lay the same conditions that Wilson had described after the sinking of the *Lusitania*. From mid-1915 onward two basic requisites existed for American intervention. Those requisites were the German use of the submarine and the presence of Woodrow Wilson in the White House.

For the last 40 years nearly all American interpreters have portrayed their nation's entry into World War I as a well-nigh inevitable event. Deploring "revisionists" and applauding "realists" have alike viewed intervention in 1917 as an outcome virtually foreordained by the machinations of great political, economic, and strategic forces. By contrast, most British interpreters and Arthur S. Link in this country have emphasized the twists and turns of specific events and the roles of individual actors. Although the two perspectives can be complementary, whether to stress the weight of overarching forces or the actions of contemporaries poses an inescapable choice in assessing American entry into World War I. Of the two perspectives, the second—the stress on specific men and events—is the correct one. When due account has been given to the influences of culture, trade, political sympathies, and strategic reckoning that may have affected the course of American policy, two incontrovertible facts remain. First, the United States would almost certainly never have entered World War I if Germany had not resorted to submarine warfare. Second, the vehicle through which the United States did enter the war was Woodrow Wilson.

The German decision to use the submarine represented one of the most fateful moves of the war. It also involved two great blunders. The first blunder occurred with the initial submarine proclamation in February 1915, when Germany threatened to sink without warning all merchant shipping in a zone surrounding the British and French coasts. By issuing that proclamation, the Germans were, as Ernest May has pointed out, doing the only thing that could have caused meaningful hostility with the Americans. British control of the seas had curtailed contacts between the United States and Germany so thoroughly that no other occasion for war or even much diplomatic friction could have arisen without the submarine. Worse, the Germans were risking a wider war for doubtful military advantage. Not only were Germany's World War I submarines small, vulnerable craft which carried few torpedoes and had a short cruising range, but in 1915 there were so few of them that they could inflict at most minimal shipping losses. Why the Germans took such a bad risk and then clung stubbornly to their intentions in the face of American protests sprang in part from tense, complicated civil-military relations within the Kaiser's regime. But the submarine policy also reflected a new and disheartening development in the history of warfare. The German submarine advocates' claims in 1915 offered the earliest example of what has become a familiar 20th-century faith in military "hardware"—the notion that some new piece of technology will bring victory that is both quick and cheap in one's own expenditure of manpower and resources. Air power and nuclear weapons would offer later fields for this faith which the submarine had first occasioned.

The second even greater submarine blunder was the decision in January 1917 to resume and widen the undersea war. The German government made that decision in full knowledge and expectation of likely American intervention. They were taking the calculated risk that their submarines could knock the Allies out of the war by cutting off their overseas supplies of munitions and food long before any American contribution could swing the balance against them. This risk in 1917 seemed considerably better than the earlier one, inasmuch as German shipyards had by then built enough submarines to make serious inroads in Allied shipping. The rate of tonnage losses inflicted in the spring of 1917 nearly crippled the British war effort. Only the timely adoption of the convoy system cut those losses to an acceptable level by providing an effective defense against the submarine.

III

The German error in 1917 lay in believing that the submarine offered the sole means to victory. By the beginning of that year, the Allies had fallen into desperate financial straits. The impending collapse of their credit in the United States was about to accomplish the same result as the German submarine offensive—cutting the Allies' overseas supply lifeline—with no risk of American intervention. In fact, the Allied financial position had deteriorated so badly that nothing could save them short of the rapid, massive infusion of money that would require American co-belligerency as a precondition. By resuming and broadening submarine warfare in January 1917 the Germans were doing the one thing that could save the Allies from collapse. To use a recent phrase, Germany was snatching defeat from the jaws of victory. Why the Germans made this blunder evidently stemmed from two considerations. One was a simple, though inexcusable failure of intelligence. "So far as I know the Germans were totally unaware of our financial difficulty," wrote the British Treasury expert John Maynard Keynes, who talked with his German opposite numbers after the war. Such ignorance seems incredible, particularly because much of the information about the Allied financial predicament was public knowledge and a few hours of simple intelligence gathering in New York and Washington would have yielded further, convincing evidence.

A second, deeper consideration also underlay the German blunder. As the German historian Gerhard Ritter has observed, indications abounded in Berlin not only that the best chance to win the war lay in waiting to let Allied troubles mount but also that a more cautious submarine policy might keep the United States neutral. Despite those signs, the Germans went ahead with the submarine campaign because nothing less than swift, decisive military victory seemed acceptable to the men in power. That decision sprang in part, as Ritter suggests, from the ascendancy of the military, which had transformed the Kaiser's government into a dictatorship by General Ludendorff behind the figurehead of Field Marshal Paul von Hindenburg. Even more, the decision reflected the abdication by both military and civilian leaders to what they regarded as the larger than human requirements of the World War. They were simply unable to conceive of any course except riding the war through to total victory. It seems likely, therefore, as the British historian Patrick, Lord Devlin has speculated, that the German leaders would have chosen to unleash their submarines even if they had known more about the Allies' financial peril. If that were so, then the German choice of the submarine campaign was, as Edmund Burke described the French Revolution, "a fond election of evil."

The second incontrovertible fact about American intervention in World War I is what Winston Churchill recognized more than 50 years ago when he wrote of Woodrow Wilson, "It seems no exaggeration to pronounce that the actions of the world depended, during the awful period Armageddon, upon the workings of this man's mind and spirit to the exclusion of almost every other factor; and that he played a part in the fate of nations incomparably more direct and personal than any other man." Wilson's role was the opposite of that of the German submarine. If the United States would not have entered World War I except for the submarine, no one besides Wilson would have done so much to keep the country out of the war. No major American statesman of the time equaled Wilson either in representing majority opinion or in grasping basic problems. His principal rivals and critics all leaned too far toward the belligerent half of the people's "double wish," as with Theodore Roosevelt, Elihu Root, and Henry Cabot Lodge, or toward the pacific half, as with William Jennings Bryan and Robert M. La Follette. William Howard Taft and Charles Evans Hughes came closer to Wilson's middle ground, and Taft also looked beyond the immediate controversies, but they lacked Wilson's boldness and perception.

From the war's outbreak, Wilson had apprehended that his fundamental task lay in attempting to end the conflict and prevent the recurrence of anything like it. His early admonitions about neutrality and remoteness from the war had also contained urgings to remain self-controlled in order to be ready to perform great international services. That vision of service owed less to any Presbyterian idealism of Wilson's than to his convictions about the indivisibility of world peace and security. In this regard, he resembled his fellow, deeply religious Southerner, Jimmy Carter, with whom he has been compared, rather than a more worldly operator like Franklin Roosevelt. In his handling of the submarine troubles with Germany in 1915 and 1916, Wilson proved highly resourceful in hewing to the middle way between war and submission when so many others were falling away, including his successive Secretaries of State, Bryan and Robert M. Lansing, and his main confidant, Colonel Edward M. House. Moreover, all the while he was preparing for an effort to end the war and lay the basis for a new international order.

Wilson's finest hour during World War I came in the two-

and-a-half months following his re-election in November 1916, when he moved simultaneously on several fronts to mediate the conflict and create a structure for peace. Shortly after the election, Wilson exercised America's financial leverage over the Allies by backing and strengthening a Federal Reserve Board warning against excessive foreign loans. Then in December 1916 he dispatched a circular note to the belligerent powers, asking them to state their peace terms and pledging American participation in a future international body empowered to maintain peace. The note went first through diplomatic channels and was made public two days afterward. Finally, on January 22, 1917, after receiving various replies from the warring nations, Wilson delivered a speech to the Senate in which he called for "a peace without victory. . . . Only a peace among equals can last. Only a peace the very principle of which is equality and a common benefit." In that speech he also laid down the specific principles for the war's settlement which he reiterated a year later in the Fourteen Points, and he again pledged American participation in an international concert to keep the peace.

Wilson gave an extraordinary performance. He moved deftly and calmly amid suspicions, jealousies, and recriminations abroad and at home. The Germans and the Allies responded to the American initiative by executing labyrinthine, often deceitful, maneuvers which reflected internal strains as well as mutual enmity. The mediation effort drew fire in the United States from pro-Allied stalwarts like Lodge and Roosevelt, who charged Wilson with playing Germany's game. His proposal for American membership in an international peacekeeping organization earned denunciations both from pacific isolationists, who feared involvement in foreign conflicts, and from nationalists, who rejected any abridgment of sovereignty and self-interest. Those attacks in December 1916 and January 1917, which were spearheaded by Senators Henry Cabot Lodge and William E. Borah, offered a foretaste of the postwar debate over joining the League of Nations. Besides outright opposition, Wilson also had to brook disloyalty from his top lieutenants as Secretary Lansing and Colonel House each in his own way tried to sabotage the mediation venture. Whether Wilson's attempt to gain control of the international situation at the beginning of 1917 would have succeeded if Germany had not reopened submarine warfare is doubtful. Too many factors seem to have been working against it. Yet, merely by making the attempt, Wilson had staked his claim to world leadership.

The German submarine decision transformed Wilson's task from guiding other nations toward peace to wrestling with his own country's likely involvement in war. The two months from the unleashing of the submarines to American intervention formed what Arthur Link has called Wilson's "Gethsemane." Alone of the nation's leaders, he apprehended that no quick, simple choice could be made between going into and staying out of World War I. Curiously, this most solitary of modern Presidents found himself perfectly attuned to the sentiments of the great majority of his countrymen. Studies of public opinion have shown that even after the mounting submarine sinkings and the publication of the Zimmermann telegram in February and March 1917, relatively few people favored intervention. Likewise, a number of contemporary observers noted that most members in both Houses of Congress remained undecided about entering the war right down to the night of April 2, 1917, when the President finally disclosed his decision. As it was, Wilson convinced large majorities in the House and Senate to go in, but he could almost certainly have persuaded equally large majorities to stay out.

Why Wilson chose war has remained a puzzle ever since. In recent years some doubt has been cast on the reliability of his eleventh-hour outpouring to Frank Cobb of the *New York World* about making Americans "go war-mad, quit thinking and devote their energies to destruction." But even if Wilson did not say those exact words to Cobb, he gave plenty of other indications between February and April 1917 that he hated to plunge the United States into World War I. Even more than possible hysteria at home Wilson recoiled from the loss of control abroad. To Cobb he reportedly said that intervention "means an attempt to reconstruct a peace-time civilization with war standards, and at the end of the war there will be no bystanders with sufficient power to influence the terms. There won't be any peace standards left to work with." Earlier, in his second inaugural address, on March 5, 1917, Wilson had reviewed America's relations with the war, emphasizing that "all the while we're not part of it." Americans had "grown more and more aware and more and more certain that the part we wished to play was the part of those who mean to vindicate and fortify peace." No matter what trials lay ahead, he had vowed, "nothing will alter our thought or purpose." At bottom, the problem remained how to keep Americans from surrendering to the war.

IV

Wilson made it clear in his war address on April 2, 1917, that he wanted American belligerency to serve the same ends as his peace initiative. "I have exactly the same things in mind now," he asserted, "that I had in mind when I addressed the Senate on the twenty-second of January last. . . . Our object now, as then, is to vindicate the principles of peace and justice as against selfish and autocratic power and to set up amongst the really free and self-governed peoples of the world such a concert of purpose and of action as will henceforth insure the observance of those principles." Wilson was not sounding the trumpet for a holy war. The tone of the war address was somber and low-keyed. Wilson alluded to the "solemn and even tragical character of the step I am taking," and he prefaced his conclusion by conceding, "It is a fearful thing to lead this great peaceful people into war, into the most terrible and disastrous of all wars, civilization itself seeming to be in the balance." The Allies soon painfully discovered that Wilson had not enlisted America on their side in a crusade. Rather he was still seeking to control the war. Only now he believed that he could not avoid belligerency, and he was gambling that he could make belligerency serve the same ends of reaching a just settlement and maintaining a lasting peace.

Wilson knew that the gamble might fail. He feared that belligerent means might subvert his pacific goal, but he believed that he had no choice. Interestingly, Wilson's last words in the war address, which followed his declaration that America would fight to achieve a new international order, were "God helping her, she can do no other." The phrase was, as some observers recognized, a paraphrase of Martin Luther's declaration to the Diet of Worms: "God helping me, I can do no other." The phrase had probably occurred to Wilson by chance, but it did express both his own Christian philosophy and the role in which he was casting the United States. Like Luther, he was acknowledging that men and nations could not avoid sin but must, in seeking to do God's will, "sin boldly." He was asking his countrymen to "sin boldly" in seeking to control the war and in striving to make the world better, freer, and more peaceful.

American intervention revolutionized World War I. It saved the Allies from financial collapse, which, together with the other reverses they suffered in 1917, would have insured their defeat. It gave the British and French the morale boost that allowed them to hold out on the Western Front in the spring of 1918 against the last great German offensive. It supplied fresh manpower for the counteroffensive that ended the war on November 11, 1918. Moreover, American intervention made the war for the first time a global conflict. Before April 1917, it had involved mostly European nations and had had ramifications elsewhere largely through their colonial possessions. The entry of the United States drew in the Western Hemisphere and extended connections into the Pacific. Also, because of Wilson's efforts, the war came to be about more than territorial appetites and imperial designs. Now it involved world-wide aspirations to self-government, new ways of conducting relations among nations, and attempts to create a different international order. Without Wilson and without the United States, it would have been a far different war.

Woodrow Wilson never forgot that he might be making a tragic mistake by entering World War I, and he may have. Certainly his justification for intervention helped implant the habits of glib globalizing and facile homogenizing of disparate parts of the world which have been besetting sins of American foreign policy since World War I. Similarly, despite Wilson's intentions, the war did turn into a self-righteous crusade for many Americans, thereby confirming another dangerous predilection in the nation's conduct in world affairs. The international and the domestic orders of Europe lay in ruins, and instability was going to reign there no matter who won the war. Perhaps, as the isolationists always insisted, America might have done better to have left that unhappy continent alone and might have done more for the world by setting an example of restraint. But that was not what Woodrow Wilson chose to do, and that has not been America's role in the 20th-century world. Thanks to him and to the long-running aftereffects of World War I, the United States has tried again and again to shape events that have seemed to others beyond human control. That has been America's glory and tragedy.

II MATURE NATION, 1920 TO PRESENT

8

Al Capone: "I Give the Public What the Public Wants"

JOHN G. MITCHELL

• Long before the Civil War, temperance enthusiasts had
sought to make the country safe from demon rum. In 1880,
Neil Dow labeled the liquor traffic "the most important political question facing the nation," and thereafter two generations of religious fundamentalists, Anti-Saloon Leaguers,
and Women's Christian Temperance Union members carried
on the fight. Enthusiasm for prohibition swept across the
United States in the early years of the twentieth century, and
it became law finally in 1919 by riding the patriotic fervor of
World War I. As Frederick Lewis Allen wrote: "If a sober
soldier was a good soldier and a sober factory hand was a productive factory hand, then the argument for prohibition was
for the moment unanswerable."

At best, the moral amendment to the Constitution was a
mixed blessing. In part it represented the attempt of the
middle class to impose its values upon inner-city residents
who found that drinking eased the drabness of their daily
lives. The strong desire for spirits felt by many people was not
quenched by legislation. Some legitimate businesses folded
and alcoholism may have declined, but much of the liquor
trade simply went underground. Speakeasies replaced saloons,
and underworld entrepreneurs built illegal empires out of the
liquor trade.

No city was more troubled by gangster violence than Chicago, and no underworld figure was more notorious than
"Scarface" Al Capone. Born in a tough neighborhood near
the Brooklyn Navy Yard, Capone gained a reputation as a
fighter as a youth and moved to Chicago to escape a possible

From "Said Chicago's Al Capone," *American Heritage* (February/March
1979). Reprinted by permission of International Creative Management. Copyright © 1979 by American Heritage.

New York murder indictment. Gaining the confidence and support of the famous Johnny Torrio, Capone operated initially on Chicago's South Side before gradually expanding his influence, usually via the gun, throughout the metropolitan area. As John G. Mitchell notes in the following essay, Capone simply gave the public what it wanted, thus demonstrating the difficulty of altering standards of personal morality by constitutional dictums.

The newspapers called him Scarface, but the sobriquet did not safely bear repeating in his presence. It was *Mister* Capone instead, or Big Al; or, among trusted lieutenants of his palace guard, "Snorky," a street word connoting a certain princely elegance. The elegance was mostly in cloth, in expensive suits from Marshall Field, silk pajamas from Sulka, the upholstery of the custom Cadillac that was said to have cost more than twenty grand in 1920's dollars. In his pockets, it was rumored, he carried cash enough to buy two such limousines; he tipped lavishly, and showered his friends with gold-plate gifts. To hide the furrows of the scars on his left cheek, he powdered his face with talcum and explained that the wounds were inflicted by shrapnel while he was fighting in France with the "Lost Battalion." He believed in the sanctity of the American family. "A woman's home and her children are her real happiness," he once told a reporter. "If she would stay there, the world would have less to worry about."

For a time, a good part of the world worried about Alphonse Capone of Chicago, Illinois. He was a prince, all right. Beneath the elegant veneer he was prince of the bootleggers, baron of the brothels, and vicar of assorted vices that for more than a decade scrambled the innards of the Second City, its labor, its industry, its law enforcement, its municipal officialdom. He ruled an empire of corruption the likes of which had never before and have not since been witnessed by any American city. He commanded an army of emissaries and assassins whose numbers at peak approached one thousand. He sat at the pinnacle of a society so grotesque the newspapers felt obliged to give both its principals and its understudies nicknames: Mike de Pike, Bathhouse John, Greasy Thumb Guzik, Hinky Dink Kenna, Two-

Gun Alterie, and Bloody Angelo; Ecola the Eagle and Izzy the Rat and Lupo the Wolf and Duffy the Goat; Hop Toad Giunta and Blubber Bob, among dozens of others.

In Capone's supreme snorkiness there was always some wrinkle. Though the tailoring was splendid, it never quite seemed to conceal the bulge in his jacket beneath the left armpit. The Cadillac was custom-made not just for the plush upholstery but for a half a ton of armor plate, the steel visor over the gas tank, the thick, bulletproof glass, the removable rear window that converted the back seat into a machine-gun emplacement. The generous tipping was not limited to newsboys and hatcheck girls; he also tipped the eccentric William Hale Thompson a quarter-million dollars to help elect him mayor of Chicago, and Thompson later rewarded his benefactor by dismissing the city's official obeisance to gangsters as "newspaper talk." For Capone, a quarter-million was merely a fractional gratuity. His syndicate's net profits in the late 1920's were estimated by the Chicago Crime Commission at sixty million dollars a year.

There was even a wrinkle in his story about the scars, for he had never been to France in military uniform, had never felt shrapnel. He had felt instead the cutting edge of a pocketknife in a Brooklyn saloon, his reward for insulting a woman. Of which, in Capone's view of the species, there were two distinct kinds—the ones who stayed home, and the ones who didn't. "When a guy don't fall for a broad," said Big Al years later, "he's through." There was a bit of self-fulfilling prophecy in the remark. In his time, Capone no doubt dodged—and dispensed in kind—more flying metal than any doughboy who served in France. Yet it was to be his fate to die not with his spats on but in his silk pajamas, *through* at the age of forty-eight, from neurosyphilitic complications.

He was of an era that today seems more romantic than grotesque, more imagined than real. He brought to the third decade of this century much of its celebrated roar; and for that, in the minds of many Americans born too late to have heard the harsh authentic decibels, he looms as something of a folk hero, a Robin Hood of the Loop, a grand desperado much closer in style to the flamboyant two-gun type of the Old West than to today's furtive *capo* who, in stressful moments, is more likely to reach for a pocket calculator than a snubnosed Smith & Wesson. In a society vicariously fascinated with crime and violence, it is not surprising that Alphonse Capone should be accorded such retrospective honors. He was the last of the Great American Gunslingers.

After Big Al—notwithstanding the subsequent rise of Lucky Luciano and Vito Genovese and Frank Costello and other latter-day godfathers—everything changed. To be sure, the violence did not end with Capone; it simply became more sophisticated—ice picks through the eardrum instead of baseball bats about the head and shoulders, corpses consolidated with scrap metal rather than abandoned in the gutter. After Capone, the rackets diversified, dope preempted illicit booze, the crime families intermarried, and the profits proliferated. But no one ever quite managed to fill Snorky's shoes. And no other name again became synonymous with Chicago.

According to all accounts, Chicago had always been special, the distinctively American town. It was the Queen of the Lake, the Wonder of the Wonderful West. Sarah Bernhardt found in it "the pulse of America." Carl Sandburg praised it as hog butcher for the world. For a time, however, part of the city's distinction was its capacity to inspire the pejorative phrase. Strangers turned away appalled by its open display of raw vice and spectacular mayhem. "It is inhabited by savages," wrote Rudyard Kipling. "A grotesque nightmare," said Don Marquis. One of its own, the alderman Robert Merriam, observed that Chicago was unique because it "is the only completely corrupt city in America." The English writer Kenneth Allsop noted in his book *The Bootleggers and Their Era* that Chicago during the 1920's "was effectively a city without a police force, for [the police] operated partially as a private army for the gangs." And in his informal history of the city's underworld, *Gem of the Prairie*, Herbert Asbury described the decade as a time when "banks all over Chicago were robbed in broad daylight by bandits who scorned to wear masks. . . . Burglars marked out sections of the city as their own. . . . Fences accompanied thieves into stores and appraised stocks of merchandise before they were stolen."

After one especially noisy series of intergang bombings, a newspaper pundit wryly remarked that "the rockets' red glare, the bombs bursting in air / Gave proof through the night that Chicago's still there." In the United States Congress, a Midwestern senator suggested that President Calvin Coolidge recall the Marine expeditionary force then in Nicaragua and dispatch it to a place more worthy of armed intervention—Chicago.

The city's pernicious reputation was well established long before the arrival of Al Capone. By the turn of the century the Queen of the Lake had become the hussy of America. Its red-light district—outshining even those of New York, New Orleans, and San Francisco—sprawled for block after block across the seamy South Side. The district, according to one chronicler, swarmed with "harlots, footpads, pimps, and pickpockets" operating in and out of "brothels, saloons, and dives of every description." Within the area were a number of subdistricts affectionately known as the Bad Lands, Coon Hollow, Satan's Mile, Hell's Half-Acre, and Dead Man's Alley; later these quaint neighborhoods became known collectively as the "Levee."

Among the city's most notorious whoremasters was one James Colosimo. Son of an immigrant from Calabria, Italy, Big Jim Colosimo had learned all the ropes that the Levee had to offer. He had been a bootblack, pickpocket, pimp, and bagman for the aldermen who controlled the district's votes and vices. In 1902 he met and married the brothelkeeper Victoria Moresco. Soon Big Jim was managing scores of bordellos and ancillary saloons; and from every dollar earned by a prostitute, more than half went to Colosimo. Colosimo's Café, on South Wabash Avenue, had green velvet walls and crystal chandeliers. It had the best entertainers, the most beautiful chorus girls, the largest selection of imported wines in Chicago. It established Colosimo as a man of considerable means. Inevitably, too, it marked him as a target for extortion.

Extortion was then the specialty of the Black Hand, the secret Sicilian underworld society. Colosimo, being Calabrian, was fair game. If he could afford to pay off the South Side aldermen and the police, surely he could afford some modest tribute to the society. Say, for starters, about five thousand dollars? Colosimo agreed. Then the Black Handers upped the ante. On the second scheduled payoff, Colosimo contrived to ambush the extortionists and left three of them dead under a South Side bridge. But the threats and demands continued. Colosimo needed help. He sent for his nephew in New York, Johnny Torrio, a veteran of the notorious Five Points gang. Several years later Johnny Torrio in turn would send for Al Capone.

He was the fourth of nine children born to Gabriel and Teresa Capone, who in 1893 had emigrated from Naples to the slums of the Brooklyn Navy Yard district. Gabriel was a barber. The family lived in a dingy flat heated by a potbellied stove. Dodging vegetable carts and ice wagons, the children played stickball in the streets. Nearby, according to Capone's most definitive biographer, John Kobler, were the fleshpots of Sands Street where "sailors piled ashore, clamoring for liquor and women." Alphonse attended P.S. 7 on Adams Street. One of his closest friends was a boy named Salvatore Luciana, later known as Lucky Luciano. When Al was eight, the family moved a mile south to Garfield Place. There was a new social club in the neighborhood. Gilt letters in a window identified it as the John Torrio Association.

To what extent Torrio figured in the early underworld education of Al Capone is not altogether clear. Kobler quotes Capone as having said, from the perspective of middle age, that he "looked on Johnny like my adviser and father and the party who made it possible for me to get my start." No doubt it was Torrio who steered both Capone and Luciano to apprenticeship with the Five Points gang while they were still in their mid-teens. Torrio was a man of eclectic connections and alliances. He commanded the respect of Frankie Uale (alias Yale), who specialized in murder contracts and who for ten years was national boss of the *Unione Siciliane*, a sort of institutional missing link between the Black Hand of the Old World and the Mafioso of the New. Yale hired Capone as a bouncer-bartender at his Harvard Inn at Coney Island. There, according to Kobler, young Al's "huge fists, unarmed or clutching a club, struck [obstreperous carousers] with the impact of a pile driver." In 1918 Capone married Mae Coughlin of Brooklyn. The following year, facing a murder indictment should a man he had pile-driven in a barroom brawl die, he received word from Torrio that his huge fists were needed in Chicago. Though the brawl victim survived, Big Al was already a murder suspect in two other New York cases. To Chicago he went.

It was a good time to be going to Chicago. His mentor, Torrio, was beginning to eclipse Colosimo for control of the South Side rackets. William Hale Thompson, the laissez-faire mayor, was soon to be reelected. And Congress was preparing to make the nation dry with passage of the Volstead Act. One hour after Prohibition became the law, at midnight January 17, 1920, a whisky shipment stamped "for medicinal purposes" was hijacked on Chicago's South Side. The Anti-Saloon League had promised "an era of clear thinking and clean living." But it had misjudged the prodigious thirst of the American people. By 1929 the bootleg liquor industry was reaping an annual income of three billion dollars—a sum more than three times greater than the amount paid that year by individual taxpayers to the Internal Revenue Service. By 1930 Chicago had ten thousand speak-easies. Each speak-easy, on a weekly average, purchased two cases of liquor (at ninety dollars the case) and six barrels of beer (at fifty-five dollars the barrel). Estimated bootleg revenues each week came to $5,300,000. And sooner than later every dollar passed through the hands of one or another of Chicago's multitudinous gangs. Increasingly each year, the largest share found its way to the gang that was headed by Johnny Torrio and Scarface Al Capone.

Torrio had seized control of the South Side as early as 1920. On May 11 he had arranged for a shipment of whisky to be delivered to Colosimo's Café, and Colosimo himself was to be there to receive it. The whisky never arrived. Waiting in the café vestibule, Colosimo instead received a fatal bullet in the back of his head. Police suspected, but could never prove, that the assassin was Frankie Yale, imported from New York under contract to Johnny Torrio.

With Colosimo gone, Torrio promoted Capone to the unofficial rank of chief field general, installed him as manager of Torrio headquarters at the Four Deuces on South Wabash Avenue, cut him in for 25 percent of all brothel profits, and promised him half the net from bootleg operations. As Kobler reconstructs it: "They complemented each other, the slight older man, cool, taciturn, reserved, condoning violence only when guile failed; the beefy younger one, gregarious, pleasure-loving, physically fearless, hot-tempered. By the second year they no longer stood in the relationship of boss and hireling; they were partners."

Among Torrio's many schemes for extending his operations beyond the South Side was a dream of ruling the nearby suburb of Cicero. Cicero traditionally had been the turf of the O'Donnell brothers and their West Side gang; but Torrio, a master of crafty diplomacy, had managed to secure a beachhead in the community and soon installed Capone in new headquarters there at the Hawthorne Inn.

The final siege of Cicero began in the spring of 1924. It was election time. Joseph Klenha, the corrupt incumbent president of the village board, was facing a challenge from a slate of Democratic reformers. To counter the threat of a reform victory, the Klenha machine made an offer that Torrio and Capone could hardly afford to refuse: Ensure a Klenha landslide, the gangsters were told, and Cicero is yours. It was a task tailor-made for Al Capone.

In his detailed account of crime and politics, *Barbarians in Our Midst*, Virgil W. Peterson, director of the Chicago Crime Commission, described the Cicero election as "one of the most disgraceful episodes in American municipal history." Armed with machine guns, Capone mobsters (some two hundred by Kobler's count) "manned the polls. Automobiles filled with gunmen patrolled the streets. Polling places were raided and ballots stolen at gunpoint. Voters were kidnapped and transported to Chicago where they were held captive until after the polls closed." Apprised of the reign of terror, a Cook County judge dispatched over a hundred patrolmen and detectives from Chicago to Cicero, and gun battles between gangsters and police raged through the afternoon. Among the several fatal casualties was Big Al's brother, Frank Capone. President Klenha was handily reelected. "And Cicero," observed Virgil Peterson, "became known throughout the nation as one of the toughest places in America, a reputation it was to retain for many years."

Capone's stunning conquest of Cicero left little doubt in the minds of rival mobsters that a new and formidable leader had arrived in their midst. From Torrio he had acquired the organizational skills to put together a tightly disciplined army of thugs, hit men, and specialists in assorted vices; and with them—after the retirement of Torrio in 1925—he proceeded to wrest from his rivals a large piece of virtually any racket he fancied.

Directly under Capone on the organizational flow chart was his good friend and business manager, Jake "Greasy Thumb" Guzik. For liaison with the *Unione Siciliane*, there was Frank "The Enforcer" Nitti. His departmental chieftains included, for bootlegging operations, Capone's brother Ralph (nicknamed "Bottles") and his cousin, Charlie Fischetti; for brothels, Mike de Pike Heitler; and for gambling, Frank Pope. Farther down on the chart were Capone's musclemen: Jim Belcastro, the bomber of breweries; Phil D'Andrea, the sharpshooting bodyguard; and Samuel Hunt, alias "Golf Bag," so-called for the luggage in which he preferred to carry his shotgun. (Golf Bag's first intended victim survived the buckshot, Kobler notes, and was thereafter known as "Hunt's hole in one.") Other torpedoes of importance included Anthony Accardo (alias Joe Batters), Sam Giancana, Paul "The Waiter" Ricca, Murray "The Camel" Humphreys, and Jack "Machine Gun" McGurn, whose real name was De-Mora and to whom police over the years attributed no fewer than twenty-two murders.

For the most part, Capone's lieutenants enjoyed an *esprit de corps* unlike that of any other mob in Chicago. There was no place in the organization for men who would not adhere to a code of unfaltering loyalty and rigid discipline. Despite the predilection of some associates for booze and cigars, Capone insisted on keeping his troops in fine fighting shape. In one headquarters spread, at the Hotel Metropole, two rooms were set aside as a gymnasium and equipped with punching bags and rowing machines.

A subsequent command post was established in the Lexington Hotel. Capone occupied a corner suite, presiding at the head of a long mahogany conference table. Framed on the wall behind him were portraits of George Washington, Abraham Lincoln, and Mayor William Hale Thompson. Two floors below, in a maids' changing room, a hinged full-length mirror concealed a secret door leading to an adjacent office building. Capone used it frequently to frustrate those who tried to pry into the pattern of his daily itinerary.

He lived constantly within a shield of armed guards. When he dined in public, the bar of the chosen restaurant would be crowded—in advance—by his trusted henchmen. When he went to the theater, twelve seats were reserved for him and his entourage in the rear of the house, where vigilance was easy. In transit, the custom-built Cadillac was always preceded by a scout car, and followed by a touring car filled with his most proficient marksmen. His headquarters swivel chair had an armor-plate back. He crossed sidewalks and hotel lobbies in a huddle of bodies three deep. Yet for all these precautions, no life insurance company would write him a policy. Capone and his kind had been going to too many funerals, and too many rivals were planning a funeral for Capone.

On the North Side, for example, there was Dion O'Banion, the choir-boy-turned-safecracker, and now ostensibly a florist, who had supplied twenty thousand dollars in wreaths and arrangements for the funeral of the slain Frank Capone. "A most unusual florist," observed Virgil Peterson, for O'Banion "not only furnished flowers . . . but also provided the corpses." Chicago police said he was responsible for twenty-five murders. O'Banion detested Capone. Among the choirboy's chief lieutenants was George "Bugs" Moran, whom history remembers not only as the inspiration for a memorable Valentine's greeting from Al Capone, but as the man who first produced and directed murder-by-motorcade, a system whereby, if all went well, the victim was rapidly riddled from a slow procession of passing cars.

Swinging counterclockwise from O'Banion's North Side, one presently arrived on the turf of Roger "The Terrible" Touhy, whose headquarters were in Des Plaines and who had little traffic—or trouble, for that matter—with the mob of Capone. At nine o'clock—west lay the precincts of the aforementioned O'Donnell gang, perennial foes of the South Side Italians. At eight o'clock, in the valley between Cicero and Chicago's own Little Italy, one entered the fiefdom of Terry Druggan and Frankie Lake, pious Irishmen both. Once, hijacking a beer truck parked in front of a Catholic church, Druggan was said to have ordered the bootleggers out of the cab of the truck at gunpoint. "Hats off when you're passing the House of God," said Druggan, "or I'll shoot 'em off."

On the Southwest Side, at seven o'clock, near the site of today's Midway Airport, yet another gang skulked under the leadership of Joe Saltis and Frank McErlane, the latter being regarded by the Illinois Association for Criminal Justice as "the most brutal gunman who ever pulled a trigger in Chicago." Like Bugs Moran, McErlane was an innovator, the first gangster in America to demonstrate the superior firepower of the Thompson submachine gun.

Virtually all these mobs, at one time or another in the 1920's, were aligned against the army of Capone. In fact, there was only one independent organization with which Capone had any strong ties whatsoever, and that was the Sicilian community ruled by the six Genna brothers. Through political connections, the Gennas had obtained a license to process industrial alcohol. They processed it, all right—into bootleg whisky; and soon, under their direction, alky cooking (as Kobler recounts it) "became the cottage industry of Little Italy." The mash was powerful, the denaturing process resulted in a product capable of blinding the consumer, and in a single lot of one hundred confiscated barrels of the liquor, police were said to have found dead rats in every one. For hit men, the Gennas relied on John Scalise and Albert Anselmi, who, in the mistaken belief that garlic in the bloodstream could cause gangrene, anointed all their bullets against the possibility of a slightly misplaced shot.

Thus were the territories staked out and the players positioned when the great Chicago beer wars broke out in the fall of 1924. Sometimes the action was difficult to follow. As Virgil Peterson perceived it, "The lines of battle were constantly shifting." No matter. The florists and undertakers had never had it so good.

O'Banion was the first to go. There had been a confrontation with Torrio over sharing profits from saloons. There had been much bad blood between North Siders and the Gennas. O'Banion had ordered the hijacking of one of the Gennas' alky trucks. He had told the Sicilians to go to hell, and had boasted of outwitting Johnny Torrio. At noon on November 10, 1924, three men (two later identified as Scalise and Anselmi) called at O'Banion's flower shop while the Irishman was clipping chrysanthemum stems. Six shots were fired. None were misplaced.

On January 12, outside a restaurant at State and Fifty-fifth streets, a limousine with Hymie Weiss and Bugs Moran at the curbside windows pulled abreast of a parked vehicle. A moment earlier, Al Capone had stepped from that vehicle into the restaurant. Weiss and Moran raked the car with buckshot, wounding Al's chauffeur. The unscathed Capone later surveyed the damage, then put in a call to General Motors with specifications for a bulletproof Cadillac.

It was Torrio's turn twelve days later. Standing on the sidewalk near his apartment, he was hit in the jaw, the right arm, and the groin by buckshot and bullets from a passing limousine. At Jackson Park Hospital, Capone came and sat at his bedside, weeping. But

Torrio was tough. He survived, and eagerly accepted a sentence of nine months in the Lake County Jail. It was safe there. Having served his time, he announced that he would retire and leave everything to Capone. Then he departed for Italy.

Meanwhile, in May of 1925, the O'Banionites had resumed their reprisals. They struck down Angelo Genna. He was buried in unconsecrated ground at Mt. Carmel Cemetery, within shotgun range of the grave of Dion O'Banion. Capone may have sent flowers, but he shed no tears. The lines had been shifting. He wanted control of the Gennas' alky industry. Within six weeks, two more Gennas, Michael and Anthony, were ambushed and killed. Scalise and Anselmi defected to Capone's camp. Both were captured by the police and charged with murder. There were many suspects, but no convictions.

Then the lines shifted again, to Cicero and the West Side. In the first four months of 1926, police recorded twenty-nine gangland slayings. Among the last of that group to die was the assistant state's attorney, William McSwiggin. He was cut down by gunfire in front of the Red Pony Inn, not far from Capone's Cicero command post. Capone went into hiding for three months.

It was a relatively quiet summer—a few desultory killings here and there, a gun battle on Michigan Avenue. Capone reappeared in his old haunts. On September 20 he lunched at a restaurant next door to the Hawthorne Inn. Suddenly there was a burst of machine-gun fire. Capone dove for the floor. Outside, on Twenty-second Street, an eleven-car motorcade slowly passed in review. Guns protruded from every window. The inn, the restaurant, storefronts on either side were raked by tommy guns, shotguns, and revolvers. Slugs ripped through twenty-five autos parked at the curb, and the sidewalk glittered with shards of broken glass. As the eleventh car sped away, up from the floor rose Capone, unhurt, but paler than the talc on his otherwise ruddy jowls. There is no record of what he was thinking then, but very possibly he was thinking only—and darkly—of Hymie Weiss and Bugs Moran.

And within a month, Weiss was dead, shot down from ambush in the shadow of Holy Name Cathedral, near the flower shop where O'Banion had died barely two years before. "It's a real goddamn crazy place," New Yorker Lucky Luciano was reported to have said of Chicago after a visit. "Nobody's safe in the streets."

Throughout all the vicious years, Al Capone no doubt held himself in high personal esteem. After all, he was merely providing services, the supply of which, like his brothel whores, could never quite meet the demand. "I give the public what the public wants," he told a reporter during one of his many "frank" interviews. "I've given people the light pleasures . . . and all I get is abuse."

Surprisingly, a large segment of the public seemed to share Capone's view of himself as the pleasurable benefactor. Though on one day Chicagoans might read with horror of the latest atrocity linked to his mob, on the next they might cheer his waving arrival at Charlestown Racetrack. In Evanston once, during a Northwestern University football game, an entire troop of Boy Scouts startled the crowd with the rousing cry "Yea, Al!" (He had bought them their tickets.) His fan mail was heavy. By some accounts, he was Chicago's greatest philanthropist. At the pit of the Depression, he was said to have financed a South Side soup kitchen dispensing 20,000 free meals a week. People liked to remember things like that—and liked to forget just exactly what it was the big fellow did to afford such beneficence.

But not everyone was impressed by the good-guy image. On a visit with his wife to Los Angeles, his presence came to the attention of the police; they gave him twenty-four hours to clear out of town. In Miami he was *persona nongrata* until he discovered that the mayor was a realtor. So Capone bought a house, a fourteen-room villa on Palm Island in Biscayne Bay. He promptly improved it with an encircling wall of concrete blocks and a thick, oaken portcullis. Capone liked to swim and fish and bask in the sun; the sun helped him forget all the troubles of Chicago. In fact, he was doing just that on Februray 14, 1929. It was Valentine's Day.

The infamous massacre of seven Bugs Moran associates in a warehouse on Chicago's North Clark Street bears no detailed recounting here (having been the focus of numerous books and movies), except to note that quite by accident Moran was not among the machine-gunned victims, and that the triggermen were the garlic anointers, Scalise and Anselmi. For these two thugs, it should further be noted, there was a strange reward. On May 7, at the Hawthorne Inn, Capone assembled a roomful of mobsters ostensibly to honor Scalise and Anselmi for their recent deeds. It was a jovial occasion until, shortly after midnight, Capone announced to the guests of honor that he was privy to their part in a budding conspiracy to dethrone him. Having passed sentence on the Sicilians, Capone signaled his bodyguards to bind and gag them; and then, according to witnesses, the good guy who gave people so many simple pleasures proceeded to club his lieutenants to death with a baseball bat.

The following week Capone was in Atlantic City, attending a business convention. Guzik and Nitti flanked him at the conference table. Joe Saltis was there, and Frankie McErlane. There was "Boo Boo" Hoff from Philadelphia. From New York there were Lucky Luciano, Frank Costello, and Dutch Schultz. Torrio had returned from Italy to preside as the elder statesman. The purpose of the conference was peace. There was to be an end to the killing. The nation henceforth was to be redistricted; the *Unione Siciliane* was to be reorganized, and the Chicagoans were to stop this petty quarreling among themselves and merge under the leadership of Capone. Big Al was delighted, except for one catch: Bugs Moran had declined an invitation to the meeting. Back in Chicago, Moran would still be after him. Back in Chicago, a dozen Sicilian gunmen were awaiting their chance to avenge the clubbing of Scalise and Anselmi.

And the risks were by no means limited to Chicago. According to crime reporter Edward Dean Sullivan, who wrote the following in 1930, "The effort to 'get' Capone became virtually nationwide. Killers in every town that Capone might reach were assigned to the job. . . . When he got to Philadelphia from Atlantic City, having failed to arrange a peace with the Moran outfit on any terms, Capone, charged with having a concealed weapon, was soon in prison and untroubled."

Released from Eastern Penitentiary in March, 1930, Capone returned to Chicago with a bodyguard, wrote Sullivan, "the size of which indicated his state of mind." But the climate of the windy city was such that "he left for Florida within ten days and as this is written, six months later, he has just returned to Chicago. Twenty of his enemies died in his absence."

Sullivan further noted that Capone's most frequently repeated statement was: "We don't want no trouble." As it turned out, he was about to get a large measure of trouble. By 1931 the troubles had piled up on two fronts. There were frequent raids against the Capone breweries and distilleries; G-men with sledgehammers were wrecking the old alky stills and pouring the contraband booze into the gutters. Meanwhile, as if this were not enough for Capone to contend with, agents of the Internal Revenue Service began making discreet inquiries about town as to why, after so many extravagant years of big spending, he had never once filed a tax return. In a kind of dress rehearsal for their biggest act, the IRS agents won tax-evasion indictments against Ralph Capone and Frank Nitti. Then Big Al himself was charged with twenty-two counts of failing to render unto Uncle Sam what was Uncle Sam's; and in October, 1931, in federal court, he was found guilty by jury trial, fined fifty thousand dollars, and sentenced to eleven years in prison. Capone was stunned. It would never have turned out like this in the good old days.

But the good old days were long gone. Pending an appeal, Capone was held in the Cook County Jail, where the amenable warden David Moneypenny provided his celebrated prisoner with all the comforts of home, including unlimited visitations by the likes of Jake Guzik and Murray Humphreys and Lucky Luciano and Dutch Schultz. For all such audiences, Capone insisted on absolute privacy; and Moneypenny obliged by allowing Big Al to use the most secure suite in the entire jail—the death chamber.

The appeal was denied. In the spring of 1932, handcuffed to a fellow prisoner, Capone was transferred to the federal penitentiary at Atlanta, Georgia. There he was given the identifying number 40,822 and assigned to work eight hours daily cobbling shoes. For the most part he stayed out of trouble; but his old reputation belied to authorities his new good behavior. In the retributive penal spirit of the times, he was considered an "incorrigible." And by 1934 the government had a special place for people like that. They called it Alcatraz.

Capone was among the first of the incorrigibles confined on the skullcap rock in San Francisco Bay. His new number was 85. He was assigned to Cellblock B and the laundry-room detail. He was conceded no favors. Feisty young inmates, looking for ways to enhance their own reputations for toughness, insulted Capone to his face. They called him "wop with the mop." A thug from Texas shoved a pair of barber's scissors into his back. He was jumped in a hallway and almost strangled before he managed to flatten his assailant. Capone somehow endured. But his health was failing. The syphilis which had gone so long untreated was beginning to erode his central nervous system. There were periods when lucidity escaped him. He could respond to treatment, but the disease was too advanced to hope for a cure.

In January, 1939 (with time off the original sentence for good behavior and working credits), Capone left Alcatraz for the less dismal precincts of a federal correctional institution near Los Angeles; and in November, at Lewisburg, Pennsylvania, he was released into the custody of his wife Mae and brother Ralph. In Chicago, according to Kobler, "reporters asked Jake Guzik if Capone was likely to return and take command again." Whereupon Guzik "replied in language harsher than he intended, for his loyalty had never wavered." Al, said Guzik, was "nutty as a fruitcake."

Capone lingered on in Miami, his mind confused, his sleep haunted by dreams of assassins. Finally, in January, 1947, he suffered a brain hemorrhage. The hemorrhage was soon followed by pneumonia. The body was taken to Chicago for burial. The funeral was modest; the Church had forbidden a requiem mass.

There are those who say that Scarface Al Capone bequeathed to America a legacy of corruption that prevails to this day. In 1963 Senator John L. McClellan's Subcommittee on Investigations elicited from Chicago police superintendent Orlando Wilson a remarkable statistic. Since 1919, Wilson reported, there had been 976 gangland murders in his city, but only two of the killers had ever been convicted. Wilson's choice of 1919, not being round numbered, may have seemed arbitrary to most of his listeners; but to seasoned observers of organized crime it was clearly Chicago's watershed year. For in 1919 a young man from New York had come to Chicago—an unsingular happenstance at the time, yet one that seems to have made all the difference ever since.

9

Race, Ethnicity, and Real Estate Appraisal

KENNETH T. JACKSON

• Relentlessly, almost unconsciously, the United States has become the world's first suburban nation. Since 1950, millions of acres of brush, shrub oak, pine, and prairie have given way to crabgrass and concrete, and the suburban total of 85 million now represents the largest single element of the national population. Indeed, suburbia has become the most quintessential aesthetic achievement of the United States and has come to symbolize the fullest, most unadulterated embodiment of the American present, a manifestation of some of the most fundamental characteristics of modern society, among them conspicuous consumption, a reliance upon the private automobile, upward mobility, the breakdown of the extended family into nuclear units, the widening division between work and leisure, and a tendency toward racial and economic exclusiveness.

Despite certain common human attitudes about "home," any residential comparison of the United States with the rest of the world will reveal that America is unusual in terms of its preference for the free-standing house on its own plot, its high degree of home ownership (about 66 percent of all households in 1981), its use of wood as the predominant building

Reprinted from *Journal of Urban History*, August 1980, © Sage Publications, Beverly Hills, by permission of the publisher.

AUTHOR'S NOTE: I wish to express my appreciation to Herbert J. Gans, Robert Kolodny, Peter Marcuse, William E. Leuchtenburg, and John A. Garraty of Columbia University; to Joseph B. Howerton, Jerry N. Hess, and Jerome Finster of the National Archives; to Frederick J. Eggers, Mary A. Grey, and William A. Rolfe of the Department of Housing and Urban Development; to Joel A. Tarr of Carnegie-Mellon University; to John Modell of the University of Minnesota; to Mark Gelfand of Boston College; to Joan Gilbert of Yale University; and to Margaret Kurth Weinberg of the Connecticut Governor's Office.

*material, and its pattern of wealthy suburbs and poor inner-
city neighborhoods.*

*Why have the metropolitan areas of the United States sub-
urbanized so quickly? One might think of the plentiful land
around most cities, of the relative wealth of the nation, of the
heterogeneity of the American people, of the cheap energy
and its inducement to decentralization, of the attractiveness
of the domestic ideal, and of rapid technological advances like
streetcars and automobiles which made long-distance com-
muting feasible. But government has not been an impartial
observer in the contest between cities and their suburbs. Fed-
erally financed interstate highways have undermined the lo-
cational advantages of inner-city neighborhoods, while in-
come-tax deductions have encouraged families to buy houses
rather than rent apartments. In the following essay, Professor
Kenneth T. Jackson focuses on the much-praised mortgage
policies of Uncle Sam and points out the extraordinarily fla-
grant discrimination that was built into them from the beginning.*

If a healthy race is to be reared, it can be reared only in healthy
homes; if infant mortality is to be reduced and tuberculosis to be
stamped out, the first essential is the improvement of housing
conditions; if drink and crime are to be successfully combated,
decent sanitary houses must be provided. If "unrest" is to be converted into contentment, the provision of good houses may prove
one of the most potent agents in that conversion.

King George V, 1919

A nation of homeowners, of people who own a real share in their
own land, is unconquerable.

President Franklin D. Roosevelt, 1933

The appeal of low-density living for more than a century in the United
States and across regional, class, and ethnic lines has led some observers to regard it as natural and inevitable, a trend "that no amount
of government interference can reverse." Or, as a senior Federal Housing Administration (FHA) official told the 1939 convention of the
American Institute of Planners: "Decentralization is taking place. It

is not a policy, it is a reality—and it is as impossible for us to change this trend as it is to change the desire of birds to migrate to a more suitable location."

Despite such protestations, there are many ways in which government largesse can affect where people live. For example, the federal tax code encourages businesses to abandon old structures before their useful life is at an end by permitting greater tax benefits for new construction than for the improvement of existing buildings. Thus, the government subsidizes an acceleration in the rate at which economic activity is dispersed to new locations. Similarly, Roger Lotchin has recently begun important research on the importance of defense spending to the growth of Sunbelt cities since 1920. Military expenditures have meanwhile worked to the detriment of other areas. Estimates were common in the late 1970s that Washington was annually collecting between $6 billion and $11 billion more than it was returning to the New York metropolitan area.

On the urban-suburban level, the potential for federal influence is also enormous. For example, the Federal Highway Act of 1916 and the Interstate Highway Act of 1956 moved the government toward a transportation policy emphasizing and benefiting the road, the truck, and the private motor car. In conjunction with cheap fuel and mass-produced automobiles, the urban expressways led to lower marginal transport costs and greatly stimulated deconcentration. Equally important to most families is the incentive to detached-home living provided by the deduction of mortgage interest and real estate taxes from their gross income. Even the reimbursement formulas for water line and sewer construction have had an impact on the spatial patterns of metropolitan areas.

The purpose of this article, which is part of a much larger analysis of the process of suburbanization in the United States between 1815 and 1980, is to examine the impact of two innovations of the New Deal on the older, industrial cities of the nation.

THE HOME OWNERS LOAN CORPORATION

On April 13, 1933, President Roosevelt urged the House and the Senate to pass a law that would (1) protect small homeowners from foreclosure, (2) relieve them of part of the burden of excessive interest and principal payments incurred during a period of higher values and higher earning power, and (3) declare that it was national policy to protect home ownership. The measure received bipartisan support. As Republican Congressman Rich of Pennsylvania, a banker himself, remarked during the floor debate:

> I am opposed to the Government in business, but here is where I am going to do a little talking for the Government in business, because if aid is going to be extended to these owners of small homes, the Government will have to get into this business of trying to save their homes. The banker dares not loan for fear the depositor will draw out his deposit; then he must close his bank or the Comptroller of the Currency will close it for him.

The resulting Home Owners Loan Corporation (HOLC), signed into law by the President on June 13, 1933, was designed to serve urban needs; the Emergency Farm Mortgage Act, passed almost a month earlier, was intended to reduce rural foreclosure.

The HOLC replaced the unworkable direct loan provisions of the Hoover administration's Federal Home Loan Bank Act and refinanced tens of thousands of mortgages in danger of default or foreclosure. It even granted loans at low interest rates to permit owners to recover homes lost through forced sale. Between July 1933 and June 1935 alone, the HOLC supplied more than $3 billion for over a million mortgages, or loans for one-tenth of all owner-occupied, nonfarm residences in the United States. Although applications varied widely by state—in Mississippi, 99 percent of the eligible owner-occupants applied for loans while in Maine only 18 percent did so—nationally about 40 percent of eligible Americans sought HOLC assistance.

The HOLC is important to housing history because it introduced, perfected, and proved in practice the feasibility of the long-term, self-amortizing mortgage with uniform payments spread over the whole life of the debt. Prior to the 1930s, the typical length of a mortgage was between 5 and 10 years, and the loan itself was not paid off when the final settlement was due. Thus, the homeowner was periodically at the mercy of the arbitrary and unpredictable forces in the money market. When money was easy, renewal every five or seven years was no problem. But if a mortgage expired at a time when money was tight, it might be impossible for the homeowner to secure a renewal, and foreclosure would ensue. Under the HOLC program, the loans were fully amortized, and the repayment period was extended to about 20 years.

Aside from the large number of mortgages which it helped to refinance on a long-term, low-interest basis, the HOLC systematized appraisal methods across the nation. Because it was dealing with problem mortgages—in some states over 40 percent of all HOLC loans were foreclosed even after refinancing—the HOLC had to make predictions and assumptions regarding the useful or productive life of housing it financed. Unlike refrigerators or shoes, dwellings were expected to be durable—how durable was the purpose of the investigation.

With care and extraordinary attention to detail, HOLC appraisers divided cities into neighborhoods and developed elaborate questionnaires relating to the occupation, income, and ethnicity of the inhabitants and the age, type of construction, price range, sales demand, and general state of repair of the housing stock. The element of novelty did not lie in the appraisal requirement itself—that had long been standard real estate practice. Rather, it lay in the creation of a formal and uniform system of appraisal, reduced to writing, structured in defined procedures, and implemented by individuals only after intensive training. The ultimate aim was that one appraiser's judgment of value would have meaning to an investor located somewhere else. In evaluating such efforts, the distinguished economist C. Lowell Harriss has credited the HOLC training and evaluation procedures "with having helped raise the general level of American real estate appraisal methods." A less favorable judgment would be that the HOLC initiated the practice of "redlining."

This occurred because HOLC devised a rating system which undervalued neighborhoods that were dense, mixed, or aging. Four categories of quality—imaginatively entitled First, Second, Third, and Fourth, with corresponding code letters of A, B, C, and D and colors of green, blue, yellow, and red—were established. The First grade (also A and green) areas were described as new, homogeneous, and "in demand as residential locations in good times and bad." Homogeneous meant "American business and professional men"; Jewish neighborhoods or even those with an "infiltration of Jews" could not possibly be considered "Best."

The Second security grade (blue) went to "still desirable" areas that had "reached their peak," but were expected to remain stable for many years. The Third grade (yellow) or "C" neighborhoods were usually described as "definitely declining," while the Fourth grade (red) or "D" neighborhoods were defined as areas "in which things taking place in C areas have already happened."

The HOLC's assumptions about urban neighborhoods were based on both an ecological conception of change and a socioeconomic one. Adopting a dynamic view of the city and assuming that change was inevitable, its appraisers accepted as given the proposition that the natural tendency of any area was to decline—in part because of the increasing age and obsolescence of the physical structures and in part because of the filtering down of the housing stock to families of lower income and different ethnicity. Thus physical deterioration was both a cause and an effect of population change, and HOLC officials made no real attempt to sort them out. They were part and parcel of the same process. Thus, black neighborhoods were invariably rated as Fourth grade, but so were any areas characterized by poor maintenance or vandalism. Similarly, those "definitely declining" sections that were marked Third grade or yellow received such a low rating in part because of age and in part because they were "within such a low price or rent range as to attract an undesirable element."

The HOLC did not initiate the idea of considering race and ethnicity in real estate appraising. As Calvin Bradford has demonstrated, models developed at the University of Chicago in the 1920s and early 1930s by Homer Hoyt and Robert Park became the dominant explanation of neighborhood change. They suggested that different groups of people "infiltrated" or "invaded" territory held by others through a process of competition. These interpretations were then adopted by prominent appraising texts, such as Frederick Babcock's *The Valuation of Real Estate* (1932) and *McMichael's Appraising Manual* (1931). Both advised appraisers to pay particular attention to "undesirable" or "least desirable" elements and suggested that the influx of certain ethnic groups was likely to precipitate price declines.

The HOLC simply applied these notions of ethnic and racial worth to real estate appraising on an unprecedented scale. With the assistance of local realtors and banks, it assigned one of its four ratings to every block in every city. The resulting information was then translated into the appropriate color and duly recorded on secret "Residential Security Maps" in local HOLC offices. The maps themselves were placed in elaborate "City Survey Files," which consisted of reports, questionnaires, and workpapers relating to current and future values of real estate.

Because the two federal agencies under analysis here did not normally report data on anything other than a county basis, the St. Louis area was selected as a case study. There, the city and county were legally separated in 1876 so that there was no alternative to individual reporting. In addition, an even older industrial city, Newark, New Jersey, was selected because of the availability of an unusual FHA study.

The residential security map for the St. Louis area in 1937 gave the highest ratings to the newer, affluent suburbs that were strung out along curvilinear streets well away from the problems of the city. Three years later, in 1940, the advantage of the periphery over the center was even more marked. In both evaluations, the top of the scale was dominated by Ladue, a largely undeveloped section of high, rolling land, heavily wooded estates, and dozens of houses in the $20,000 to $50,000 range. In 1940, HOLC appraisers noted approvingly that the area was "highly restricted" and occupied by "capitalists and other wealthy families." Reportedly not the home of "a single foreigner or Negro," Ladue received an "A" rating. Other affluent suburbs like Clayton and University City were also marked with green and blue on the 1937 and 1940 maps, indicating that they, too, were characterized by attractive homes on well-maintained plots and that the appraisers felt confident about mortgages insured there. And well they might have been; in University City almost 40 percent of the homes had been valued at more than $15,000 in 1930, while in Clayton the comparable figure was an astounding 72.3 percent (see Table 1).

At the other end of the scale in St. Louis County were the rare Fourth grade areas. A few such neighborhoods were occupied by white laborers, such as "Ridgeview" in Kirkwood, where the garagelike shacks typically cost less than $1,500. But the "D" regions in the county were usually black. One such place in 1937 was Lincoln Terrace, a small enclave of four- and five-room bungalows built about

TABLE 1

Home Values, HOLC Ratings, and Population Growth in Selected St. Louis Area Communities

Community	Percentage of Homes Owner-Occupied in 1930	Value of Owned Homes, 1930, in thousands of dollars				Predominant HOLC Rating in 1940	Population in 1940	Population in 1970
		Below 3	3-7.5	7.5-15	Above 15			
St. Louis City	31.6%	11.6%	49.6%	30.1%	7.7%	C	816,048	622,236
University City	50.1	4.8	19.9	23.2	37.5	A	33,023	46,309
Webster Groves	78.5	7.3	29.5	39.2	23.2	A	18,394	27,455
Maplewood	56.3	7.0	60.9	28.2	12.0	C	12,875	12,785
Kirkwood	68.3	13.0	41.9	32.1	11.2		12,132	31,769
Richmond Heights	57.2	6.5	28.3	50.6	13.8	B	12,802	13,802
Clayton	49.8	2.5	7.5	17.4	72.3	A	13,069	16,222
Ferguson	72.7	9.7	52.2	29.6	7.4	B	5,724	28,759
Brentwood	66.3	14.6	70.5	13.2	1.5	C	4,383	11,248
Ladue	84.6	1.2	4.8	14.9	79.1	A	3,981	10,591

SOURCE: 1930 United States Census Tracts for St. Louis; HOLC City Survey Files in National Archives, and National Resources Committee, *Regional Planning, Part II–St. Louis Region* (Washington: Government Printing Office, 1936), p. 52.

1927. Originally intended for middle-class white families, the venture was unsuccessful, and the district quickly developed into a black neighborhood. But even though the homes were relatively new and of good quality, the HOLC gave the section (D-12 in 1937, D-8 in 1940) the lowest possible grade, asserting that the houses had "little or no value today, having suffered a tremendous decline in values due to the colored element now controlling the district."

In contrast to the gently rolling terrain and sparse settlement of St. Louis County, the city had proportionately many more Third and Fourth grade neighborhoods, and more than twice as many renters as homeowners. Virtually all the residential sections along the Mississippi River or adjacent to the central business district received the lowest two ratings. This harsh judgment was in part a reflection of their badly deteriorated physical character. Just a few years earlier, the City Plan Commission of St. Louis had made a survey of 44 acres surrounding the business section. Only about 40 percent of the 8,447 living units had indoor toilets, and the tuberculosis morbidity rate was three times that of the city as a whole. As the St. Louis Regional Planning report pessimistically concluded in 1936:

> The older residential districts which are depreciating in value and in character constitute one of the most serious problems in this region. They can never be absorbed by commercial and industrial uses. Even if owners wished to build new homes within them, it would be inadvisable because of the present character of the districts.

But the HOLC appraisers marked other inner-city areas down not because of the true slum conditions but because of negative attitudes toward city living in general. The evaluation of a white, working-class neighborhood near Fairgrounds Park was typical. According to the description, "Lots are small, houses are only slightly set back from the sidewalks, and there is a general appearance of congestion." Although an urban individual might have found this collection of cottages and abundant shade trees rather charming, the HOLC thought otherwise: "Age of properties, general mixture of type, proximity to industrial section on northeast and much less desirable areas to the south make this a good fourth grade area."

As was the case in every city, any Afro-American presence was a source of substantial concern to the HOLC. In a confidential and generally pessimistic 1941 survey of the economic and real estate prospects of the St. Louis metropolitan area, the Federal Home Loan Bank Board (the parent agency of HOLC) repeatedly commented on the "rapidly increasing Negro population" and the resulting "problem in the maintenance of real estate values." The officials evinced a keen interest in the movement of black families and included maps of the density of Negro settlement with every analysis. Not surprisingly, even those neighborhoods with small proportions of black inhabitants were typically rated "D," or hazardous.

Like St. Louis, Newark has long symbolized the most extreme features of the urban crisis. In that troubled city, federal appraisers took note in the 1930s of the high tax rate, the heavy relief load, the per-capita bonded debt, and the "strong tendency for years for people of larger incomes to move their homes outside the city." The 1939 Newark area residential security map did not designate a single neighborhood in that city of more than 400,000 as worthy of an "A" rating. "High class Jewish" sections like Weequahic and Clinton Hill, as well as Gentile areas like Vailsburg and Forest Hill all received "B" or the Second grade. Typical Newark neighborhoods were rated even lower. The well-maintained and attractive working class sections of Roseville, Woodside, and East Vailsburg were given Third grade or "C" ratings; the remainder of the city, including immigrant Ironbound and every black neighborhood, was written off as "hazardous."

Immediately adjacent to Newark is New Jersey's Hudson County, which is among the half-dozen most densely settled and ethnically diverse political jurisdictions in the United States. Predictably, HOLC appraisers had decided by 1940 that Hudson County was a lost cause. In the communities of Bayonne, Hoboken, Secaucus, Kearny, Union City, Weehawken, Harrison, and Jersey City, taken together, they designated only two very small "B" areas and no "A" sections.

The HOLC insisted that "there is no implication that good mortgages do not exist or cannot be made in Third and Fourth grade areas." And, there is some evidence to indicate that HOLC did in fact make the majority of its obligations in "definitely declining" or "hazardous" neighborhoods. This seeming liberality was actually good business because the residents of poorer sections generally maintained a better pay back record than did their more affluent cousins. As the Federal Home Loan Bank Board explained:

> The rate of foreclosure per 1000 non-farm dwellings during 1939 was greater in St. Louis County than in St. Louis City by about 2½ to 1. A partial explanation or causation of this situation is the fact that County properties consist of a greater proportion of units in the higher priced brackets.

The damage caused by the HOLC came not through its own actions, but through the influence of its appraisal system on the financial decision of other institutions. During the late 1930s, the Federal Home Loan Bank Board circulated questionnaires to banks asking about their mortgage practices. Those returned by savings and loan associations and banks in Essex County (Newark), New Jersey, indicated a clear relationship between public and private redlining practices. One specific question asked: "What are the most desirable lending areas?" The answers were often "A and B" or "Blue" or "FHA only." Similarly, to the inquiry, "Are there any areas in which loans will not be made?" the responses included, "Red and most yellow," "C and D," "Newark," "Not in red," and "D areas." Obviously, private banking institutions were privy to and influenced by the government's Residential Security Maps.

THE FEDERAL HOUSING ADMINISTRATION

Direct, large-scale Washington intervention in the American housing market dates from the adoption of the National Housing Act on June 27, 1934. Although intended "to encourage improvement in housing standards and conditions, to facilitate sound home financing on reasonable terms, and to exert a stabilizing influence on the mortgage market," the primary purpose of the legislation was the alleviation of unemployment in the construction industry. As the Federal Emergency Relief Administrator testified before the House Banking and Currency Committee on May 18, 1934:

> The building trades in America represent by all odds the largest single unit of our unemployment. Probably more than one-third of all the unemployed are identified, directly and indirectly, with the building trades. . . . Now, a purpose of this bill, a fundamental purpose of this bill, is an effort to get the people back to work.

Between 1934 and 1968, the FHA had a remarkable record of accomplishment. Essentially, it insured long-term mortgage loans made by private lenders for home construction and sale. To this end, it collected premiums, set up reserves for losses, and in the event of a default on a mortgage, indemnified the lender. It did not build houses or lend money. Instead, it induced leaders who had money to invest it in residential mortgages by insuring them against loss on such investments, with the full weight of the U.S. Treasury behind the contract. And it revolutionized the home finance industry in the following ways.

First, before FHA began operations, first mortgages typically were limited to one-half or two-thirds of the appraised value of the property. During the 1920s, for example, savings and loan associations held one-half of America's outstanding mortgage debt. Those mortgages averaged 58 percent of estimated property value. Thus, prospective home-buyers needed a down payment of at least 30 percent to close a deal. By contrast, the fraction of the collateral that the lender was able to lend for a FHA-secured loan was about 93 percent. Thus, large down payments were unnecessary.

Second, continuing a trend begun by the HOLC, the FHA extended the repayment period for its guaranteed mortgages to 25 or 30 years and insisted that all loans be fully amortized. The effect was to reduce both the average monthly payment and the national rate of mortgage foreclosure. The latter declined from 250,000 nonfarm units in 1932 to only 18,000 in 1951.

Third, FHA established minimum standards for home construction that became almost universal in the industry. These regulations were not intended to make any particular structure fault-free, or even to assure the owner's satisfaction with the purchase. But they were designed to assure with at least statistical accuracy that the dwelling would be free of gross structural or mechanical deficiencies. Although there was nothing innovative in considering the quality of a house in relation to the debt placed against it, two features of the system were new; first, that the standards were objective, uniform, and in writing; second, that they were to be enforced by actual, on-site inspection—prior to insurance commitment in the case of an existing property and at various fixed stages in the course of construction in the case of new housing. Since World War II, the largest private contractors have built all their new houses to meet FHA standards, even though financing has often been arranged without FHA aid. This has occurred because many potential purchasers will not consider a home that cannot get FHA approval.

Fourth, in the 1920s, the interest rate for first mortgages averaged between 6 and 8 percent. If a second mortgage was necessary, as it usually was for families of moderate incomes, the purchaser could obtain one by paying a discount to the lender, a higher interest rate on the loan, and perhaps a commission to a broker. Together, these charges added about 15 percent to the purchase price. Under the FHA and Veterans Administration (VA) programs, by contrast, there was very little risk to the banker if a loan turned sour. Reflecting this government guarantee, interest rates fell by two or three percentage points.

These four changes substantially increased the number of American families who could reasonably expect to purchase homes. By the end of 1972, FHA had helped nearly 11 million families to own houses and another 22 million families to improve their properties. It had also insured 1.8 million dwellings in multiunit projects. And in those same years between 1934 and 1972, the percentage of American families living in owner-occupied dwellings rose from 44 percent to 63 percent.

Quite simply, it often became cheaper to buy than to rent. Long Island builder Martin Winter recently recalled that in the early 1950s, families living in the Kew Gardens section of Queens were paying almost $100 per month for small two-bedroom apartments. For less money they could, and often did, move to the new Levittown-type developments springing up along the highways from the city. Even the working classes could aspire to home ownership. As one person who left New York for suburban Dumont, New Jersey, remembered: "We had been paying $50 a month rent, and here we come up and live for $29 a month. That paid everything—taxes, principal, insurance on your mortgage, and interest." Not surprisingly, the middle-class suburban family with the new house and the long-term, fixed-rate FHA-insured mortgage became a symbol, and perhaps a stereotype, of "the American way of life."

Unfortunately, the corrollary to this achievement was the fact that FHA programs hastened the decay of inner-city neighborhoods by stripping them of much of the middle-class constituency. This occurred for two reasons. First, although the legislation nowhere mentioned an antiurban bias, it favored the construction of single-family and discouraged construction of multifamily projects through unpopular terms. Historically, single-family housing programs have been the heart of FHA's insured loan activities. Between 1941 and 1950, FHA-insured single-family starts exceeded FHA multifamily starts by a ratio of almost four to one (see Table 2). In the next decade, the margin exceeded seven to one. Even in 1971, when FHA insured the largest number of multifamily units in its history, single-family houses were more numerous by 27 percent.

Similarly, loans for the repair of existing structures were small and for short duration, which meant that a family could more easily purchase a new home than modernize an old one. Finally, the only part of the 1934 act relating to low-income families was the embryonic authorization for mortgage insurance with respect to rental housing in regulated projects of public bodies or limited dividend corporations. Almost nothing was insured until 1938, and even thereafter, the total insurance for rental housing exceeded $1 billion only once between 1934 and 1962.

The second and more important variety of suburban, middle-class favoritism had to do with the so-called unbiased professional estimate that was a prerequisite for any loan guarantee. This mandatory appraisal included a rating of the property itself, a rating of the mortgagor or borrower, and a rating of the neighborhood. The lower the valuation placed on properties, the less government risk and the less generous the aid to the potential buyers (and sellers). The purpose of the neighborhood evaluation was "to determine the degree of mortgage risk introduced in a mortgage insurance transaction because of the location of the property at a specific site." And unlike the HOLC, which used an essentially similar procedure, the FHA allowed personal and agency bias in favor of all-white subdivisions in the suburbs to affect the kinds of loans it guaranteed—or, equally important, refused to guarantee. In this way the bureaucracy influenced the character of housing at least as much as the 1934 enabling legislation did.

The FHA was quite precise in teaching its underwriters how to

TABLE 2

New Housing Starts in the United States, 1935–1968
(in thousands)

Year	Total Starts	FHA Starts	VA Starts	Public Housing
1935	216	14	0	5
1936	304	49	0	15
1937	332	60	0	4
1938	399	119	0	7
1939	458	158	0	57
1940	530	180	0	73
1941	619	220	0	87
1942	301	166	0	55
1943	184	146	0	7
1944	139	93	NA	3
1945	325	41	9	1
1946	1015	69	92	8
1947	1265	229	160	3
1948	1344	294	71	18
1949	1430	364	91	36
1950	1408	487	191	44
1951	1420	264	149	71
1952	1446	280	141	59
1953	1402	252	157	36
1954	1532	276	307	19
1955	1627	277	393	20
1956	1325	192	271	24
1957	1175	168	128	49
1958	1314	295	102	68
1959	1495	332	109	37
1960	1230	261	75	44
1961	1285	244	83	52
1962	1439	259	78	30
1963	1582	221	71	32
1964	1502	205	59	32
1965	1451	196	49	37
1966	1142	158	37	31
1967	1268	180	52	30
1968	1484	220	56	38

SOURCE: U.S. Bureau of the Census, *Housing Construction Statistics, 1889–1964* (Washington: GPO, 1966), TABLE A-2; and U.S. Department of Housing and Urban Development, *HUD Trends: Annual Summary* (Washington: HUD, 1970).

measure the quality of residential area. Eight criteria were established (the numbers in parentheses reflect the percentage weight given to each):

(1) relative economic stability (40 percent)
(2) protection from adverse influences (20 percent)
(3) freedom from special hazards (5 percent)
(4) adequacy of civic, social, and commercial centers (5 percent)
(5) adequacy of transportation (10 percent)
(6) sufficiency of utilities and conveniences (5 percent)
(7) level of taxes and special assessments (5 percent)
(8) appeal (10 percent).

Although FHA directives insisted that no project should be insured that involved a high degree of risk with regard to any of the eight categories, "economic stability" and "protection from adverse influences" together counted for more than the other six combined. Both were interpreted in ways that were prejudicial against heterogeneous environments. The 1939 *Underwriting Manual* taught that "crowded neighborhoods lessen desirability" and "older properties in a neighborhood have a tendency to accelerate the transition to lower class occupancy." Smoke and odor were considered "adverse influences," and appraisers were told to look carefully for any "inferior and nonproductive characteristics of the areas surrounding the site."

Obviously, prospective buyers could avoid many of these so-called undesirable features by locating in peripheral sections. In 1939, the Washington headquarters asked each of the 50-odd regional FHA offices to send in the plans for six "typical American houses." The photographs and dimensions were then used for a National Archives exhibit. An analysis of the submissions clearly indicates that the ideal home was a bungalow or a colonial on an ample lot with a driveway and a garage.

In an attempt to standardize such ideal homes, FHA set up minimum requirements for lot size, for setback from the street, for separation from adjacent structures, and even for the width of the house itself. While such requirements did provide air and light for new structures, they effectively eliminated whole sections of cities, such as the traditional 16-foot-wide row houses of Baltimore, Philadelphia, and New York from eligibility for loan guarantees. Even apartment owners were encouraged to look to suburbia: "Under the best of conditions a rental development under the FHA program is a project set in what amounts to a privately owned and privately controlled park area."

Reflecting the broad segregationist attitudes of a majority of the American people, the FHA was extraordinarily concerned with "inharmonious racial or nationality groups." Homeowners and financial institutions alike feared that an entire area could lose its investment value if rigid white-black separation was not maintained. Bluntly warning, "If a neighborhood is to retain stability, it is necessary that properties shall continue to be occupied by the same social and racial classes," the *Underwriting Manual* openly recommended "enforced zoning, subdivision regulations, and suitable restrictive covenants" that would be "superior to any mortgage." Such covenants were a common method of prohibiting black occupancy until the U.S. Supreme Court ruled in 1948 (*Shelley v. Kraemer*) that they were "unenforceable as law and contrary to public policy." Even then, it was not until late 1949 that FHA announced that as of February 15, 1950, it would not insure mortgages on real estate subject to covenants. Although the press treated the FHA announcement as a major advancement in the field of racial justice, former housing official Nathan Straus noted that "the new policy in fact served only to warn speculative builders who had not filed covenants of their rights to do so, and it gave them a convenient respite in which to file."

In addition to recommending covenants. FHA compiled detailed reports and maps charting the present and most likely future residential locations of black families. In a March 1939 map of Brooklyn, for example, the presence of a single, nonwhite family on any block was sufficient to mark that entire block as black. Similarly, very extensive maps of the District of Columbia depicted the spread of the black population and the percentage of dwelling units occupied by persons other than white. As late as November 19, 1948, Assistant FHA Commissioner W. J. Lockwood could write that FHA "has never insured a housing project of mixed occupancy" because of the expectation that "such projects would probably in a short period of time become all-Negro or all-white."

Occasionally, FHA racial decisions were particularly bizarre and capricious. In the late 1930s, for example, as Detroit grew outward, white families began to settle near a black enclave near Eight Mile Road. By 1940, the blacks were surrounded, but neither they nor the whites could get FHA insurance because of the presence of an adjacent "inharmonious" racial group. So in 1941, an enterprising white developer built a concrete wall between the white and black areas. The FHA then took another look and approved mortgages on the white properties.

One of the first persons to point a finger at FHA for discriminatory practices was Professor Charles Abrams. Writing in 1955, he said:

> A government offering such bounty to builders and lenders could have required compliance with a nondiscrimination policy. Or the agency could at least have pursued a course of evasion, or hidden behind the screen of local autonomy. Instead, FHA adopted a racial policy that could well have been culled from the Nuremberg laws. From its inception FHA set itself up as the protector of the all white neighborhood. It sent its agents into the field to keep Negroes and other minorities from buying houses in white neighborhoods.

The precise extent to which the agency discriminated against blacks and other minority groups is difficult to determine. Although the FHA has always collected reams of data regarding the price, floor area, lot size, number of bathrooms, type of roof, and structural characteristics of the single-family homes it has insured, it has been quite secretive about the spatial distribution of these loans. For the period between 1942 and 1968, the most detailed FHA statistics cannot be disaggregated below the county level.

Such data as are available indicate that neighborhood appraisals were very influential in determining for FHA "where it would be reasonably safe to insure mortgages." Indeed, the Preliminary Examiner was specifically instructed to refer to the Residential Security Maps in order "to segregate for rejection many of the applications involving locations not suitable for amortized mortgages." The result was a degree of suburban favoritism even greater than documentary analysis would have indicated. Of a sample of 241 new homes insured by FHA throughout metropolitan St. Louis between 1935 and 1939 a full 220 or 91 percent were located in the suburbs. Moreover, more than half of these home buyers (135 of 241) had lived in the city immediately prior to their new home purchase. Clearly, the FHA was helping to denude St. Louis of its middle-class residents. As might be expected, the new suburbanites were not being drawn from the slums or from rural areas, but from the "B" areas of the central city.

A detailed analysis of two individual subdivisions in St. Louis County—Normandy and Affton—confirms the same point. Located just northwest of the city limits, Normandy was made up in 1937 of new five- and six-room houses costing between $4,000 and $7,500. In 1937 and 1938, exactly 127 of these houses were sold under FHA-guaranteed mortgages. Of the purchasers, 100 (78 percent) moved out from the city, mostly from the solid, well-established blocks between West Florrissant and Easton Streets.

On the opposite, or southwest, edge of St. Louis, Affton was also the scene of considerable residential construction in 1938 and 1939. Of 62 families purchasing FHA-insured homes in Affton during these years, 55 were from the city of St. Louis. Most of them simply came out the four-lane Gravois Road from the southern part of the city to their new plots in the suburbs.

For the period since 1942, detailed analyses of FHA spatial patterns are difficult. But a reconstruction of FHA unpublished statistics for the St. Louis area over the course of a third of a century reveals the broad patterns of city-suburban activity. As Table 3 indicates, in the first 27 years of FHA operation (through Decmber 31, 1960), when tens of thousands of tract homes were built west of the city limits, the county of St. Louis was the beneficiary of more than five times as much mortgage insurance as the city of St. Louis, whether measured in number of mortgages, amount of mortgage insurance, or per capita assistance.

One possible explanation for the city-county disparities in these figures is that the city had very little room for development, that the populace wanted to move to the suburbs, and that the periphery was where new housing could be most easily built. But in the 1930s, many more single-family homes were constructed in the city than in the county. Moreover, more than half of the FHA policies traditionally went to *existing* rather than *new* homes, and the city of course had a much larger inventory of existing housing than did the county in the period before 1960. Even in terms of home improvement loans, a category in which the aging city was obviously more

TABLE 3

Cumulative Total of FHA Home Mortgage Activities and Per Capita
Figures for Ten Selected United States Counties, 1934–1960

Jurisdiction	Cumulative Number of Home Mortgages, 1934–1960	Cumulative Amount of Home Mortgages, 1934–1960	Per Capita Amount of Home Mortgages, as of January 1961
St. Louis County, Mo.	62,772	$558,913,633	$794
Fairfax County, Va.	14,687	190,718,799	730
Nassau County, N.Y.	87,183	781,378,559	601
Montgomery County, Md.	14,702	159,246,550	467
Prince Georges County, Md.	15,043	144,481,817	404
St. Louis City	12,166	94,173,422	126
District of Columbia	8,038	66,144,612	87
Kings County (Brooklyn), N.Y.	15,438	140,330,137	53
Hudson County, N.J.	1,056	7,263,320	12
Bronx County, N.Y.	1,641	14,279,243	10

SOURCE: These calculations are based upon unpublished statistics available
in the Single Family Insured Branch of the Management Information Systems
Division of the Federal Housing Administration.
a. The per capita amount was derived by dividing the cumulative amount of
home mortgages by the 1960 population.

needy, only $43,844,500 went to the city, while about three times
that much, or $112,315,798, went to the county through 1960. In
the late 1960s and early 1970s, when the federal government attempted to redirect moneys to the central cities, the previous imbalance was not corrected. Figures available through 1976 show a
total of well over $1.1 billion for the county and only $314 million
for the city. Thus, the suburbs have continued their dominance.

Although St. Louis County apparently has done very well in terms
of per capita mortgage insurance in comparison with other areas of
the nation, the Mississippi River was not an isolated case of FHA
suburban favoritism. In Essex County, New Jersey, FHA commitments went in overwhelming proportion to Newark's suburbs. And

in neighboring Hudson County, residents received only $12 of mortgage insurance per capita through 1960, the second lowest county total in the nation after the Bronx (Table 3).

The New Jersey data reveal that the most favored areas for FHA mortgage insurance were not the wealthiest towns. Rather, the most likely areas for FHA activity were those rated "B" on the Residential Security Maps. In 1936, 65 percent of new housing units in suburban Livingston were accepted for insurance; for Caldwell and Irvington, also solidly middle-class, the percentages were 59 and 42, respectively. In elite districts like South Orange, Glen Ridge, Milburn, and Maplewood, however, the FHA assistance rates were about as low as they were for Newark, or less than 25 percent. Presumably this occurred because the housing available in the so-called "Best" sections was beyond the allowable price limits for FHA mortgage insurance, and also because persons who could afford to live in such posh neighborhoods did not require government financing.

Even in the nation's capital, the outlying areas were considered more appropriate for federal assistance than older neighborhoods. FHA commitments at the beginning of 1937 in the District of Columbia were heavily concentrated in two peripheral areas; (1) between the U.S. Soldiers Home and Walter Reed Hospital in white and prosperous Northwest Washington and (2) between Rock Creek Park and Connecticut Avenue, also in Northwest Washington. Very few mortgage guarantees were issued in the predominantly black central and southeastern sections of the district. More important, at least two-thirds of the FHA commitments in the metropolitan area were located in the suburbs—especially in Arlington and Alexandria in Virginia and in Silver Spring, Takoma Park, Bethesda, Chevy Chase, University Park, Westmoreland Hills, and West Haven in Maryland. Perhaps this was but a reflection of the 1939 FHA prediction that:

> It should be noted in this connection that the "filtering-up" process, and the tendency of Negroes to congregate in the District, taken together, logically point to a situation where eventually the District will be populated by Negroes and the suburban areas in Maryland and Virginia by white families.

Following a segregationist policy for at least the next 20 years, the FHA did its part to see that the prophecy came true; through the end of 1960, as Table 3 indicates, the suburban counties had received more than seven times as much mortgage insurance as the District of Columbia.

For its part, the FHA usually responded that it was not created to help cities, but to revive homebuilding and to stimulate homeownership. And it concentrated on convincing both Congress and the public that it was, as its first Administrator, James Moffett, remarked, "a conservative business operation." The agency emphasized its concern over sound loans, no higher than the value of the assets and the repayment ability of the borrower would support, and its ability to make a small profit for the federal government.

But FHA also helped to turn the building industry against the minority and inner-city housing market, and its policies supported the income and racial segregation of most suburbs. Whole areas of cities were declared ineligible for loan guarantees; as late as 1966, for example, FHA did not have a mortgage on a single home in Camden, New Jersey, a declining industrial city.

Despite the fact that the government's leading housing agency was openly exhorting segregation, throughout the first 30 years of its operation, very few voices were raised against FHA's redlining practices. Between 1943 and 1945, Harland Bartholomew and Associates prepared a series of reports as a master plan for Dallas. The firm criticized FHA for building "nearly all housing" in the suburbs and argued that "this policy has hastened the process of urban decentralization immeasurably." And Columbia Professor Charles Abrams wrote in 1955 against FHA policies that had "succeeded in modifying legal practice so that the common form of deed included the racial covenant."

Not until the civil rights movement of the 1960s did community groups and scholars become convinced that redlining and disinvestment were a major cause of neighborhood decline and that home improvement loans were the "lifeblood of housing." In 1967, Martin Nolan summed up the indictment against FHA by asserting, "The imbalance against poor people and in favor of middle-income homeowners is so staggering that it makes all inquiries into the pathology of slums seem redundant." In the following year, Senator Paul Douglas of Illinois reported for the National Commission on Urban Problems on the role of the federal government in home finance:

The poor and those on the fringes of poverty have been almost completely excluded. These and the lower middle class, together constituting the 40 per cent of the population whose housing needs are greatest, received only 11 per cent of the FHA mortgages. . . . Even middle-class residential districts in the central cities were suspect, since there was always the prospect that they, too, might turn as Negroes and poor whites continued to pour into the cities, and as middle and upper-middle-income whites continued to move out.

Moreover, as Jane Jacobs has said, "Credit blacklisting maps are accurate prophecies because they are self-fulfilling prophecies."

The main beneficiary of the $119 billion in FHA mortgage insurance issued in the first four decades of FHA operation was suburbia, where approximately half of all housing could claim FHA or VA financing in the 1950s and 1960s. In the process, the American suburb was transformed from a rich person's preserve into the normal expectation of the middle class.

CONCLUSION

The HOLC was created in the midst of the Great Depression to refinance mortgages in danger of default or foreclosure. In the course of accomplishing its mission, the HOLC developed real estate appraisal systems that discriminated against racial and ethnic minorities and against older, industrial cities. But HOLC apparently extended aid without regard for its own ratings and evaluations and met the needs of a variety of families and neighborhoods.

The FHA cooperated with HOLC and followed HOLC appraisal practices. But unlike the HOLC, the FHA acted on the information in its files and clearly favored suburban areas over industrial cities. It is conceivable that the heavy disparity demonstrated in this article was the result not of prejudicial intent, but of other factors, such as family size, attitudes toward child rearing, or stages in the life cycle. In my judgment, however, the evidence is clear; both FHA guidelines and actual FHA assistance favored new construction over existing dwellings, open land over developed areas, businessmen over blue-collar workers, whites over blacks, and native-born Americans over immigrants.

10

A Klansman Joins the Court:
The Appointment of Hugo L. Black

WILLIAM E. LEUCHTENBURG

• Fear of blacks and foreigners was largely responsible for the enormous popularity of the Ku Klux Klan in the early 1920s. The secret order got its start in 1915 when "Colonel" (the title was honorary in the "Woodmen of the World") William Joseph Simmons, a tall, clean-shaven, two-hundred-pound fraternal organizer, persuaded fifteen fellow Atlantans to motor out to nearby Stone Mountain to burn a cross, raise an American flag, and read a few biblical verses. The small group swore allegiance to the Invisible Empire, Knights of the Ku Klux Klan.

For almost five years, the Invisible Empire remained confined to the Peachtree State and neighboring Alabama, and could best be described as just another indolent Southern fraternal group. In the spring of 1920, however, two enterprising promoters took a long, interested look at the Klan, recognizing its financial, as well as patriotic, possibilities. Edward Young Clarke, an unimposing dark-haired man in his early thirties, and Mrs. Elizabeth Tyler, a crafty, voluptuous divorcee, noticed the secret order's floundering condition and reasoned correctly that it could greatly broaden its appeal by exploiting the fears and prejudices of uncritical minds against the Catholic, the Jew, the Negro, the Oriental, and the recent immigrant. They formed the Southern Publicity Association and entered into negotiations with Simmons, who despite his title as Imperial Wizard, was richly endowed with neither character nor ability. According to the contract, Clarke would be appointed Imperial Kleagle and receive two dollars and fifty cents for each new recruit. It was a tidy arrangement

From the *University of Chicago Law Review*. © 1973 by the University of Chicago.

and would occasionally yield him thirty thousand dollars per week.

Once free to put their booster techniques into practice, Clarke and Tyler quickly transformed the little society into the militant, uncompromising instrument that soon scourged the nation. By 1925 about two million persons had paid the ten-dollar initiation fee to become a citizen of the Invisible Empire, which by that time was being described by Stanley Frost as "the most vigorous, active and effective organization in American life outside business." Strongest in Indiana, Ohio, Texas, and in such big cities as Chicago, Portland, Denver, Indianapolis, and Dallas, the Klan was particularly successful in the political arena and for a time claimed a half dozen governorships, including those of Oregon, Indiana, and Colorado. It had only a minor impact upon presidential politics, but its divisiveness as a national issue was well illustrated by the appointment of Hugo L. Black to the United States Supreme Court. Soon after President Franklin D. Roosevelt announced the nomination, Black's involvement with the Birmingham chapter of the Invisible Empire became known. In the article below, one of the nation's most eminent historians, William E. Leuchtenburg of University of North Carolina, Chapel Hill, discusses the ironies involved in the selection of a Klansman who was to become one of the country's leading exponents of civil liberties.

I. THE NOMINATION

On August 12, 1937, Franklin Delano Roosevelt, rebounding from the worst setback of his long Presidency, took the first of a series of steps toward creating what historians would one day call "the Roosevelt Court." Galling defeat had come less than a month before when the Senate had killed his scheme to add a Justice to the Supreme Court for every member aged seventy or over who did not resign or retire. The original plan would have allowed the President to name as many as six new Justices, but after a bitter 168-day fight, the measure was buried, amid loud rejoicing from FDR's opponents. Roosevelt was not finished yet, however, for one legacy of the protracted struggle was the creation of a vacancy on the Supreme Court, and it was the President's prerogative to nominate a successor. The choice he finally made would trigger an acrimonious controversy and would have a momentous impact on the disposition of the Court.

The vacancy resulted, at least indirectly, from Roosevelt's "Court-packing" plan. The President had advanced his bold proposal in February because he was frustrated by the performance of the Supreme Court, particularly the conservative "Four Horsemen"—Willis Van Devanter, Pierce Butler, James McReynolds, and George Sutherland. In May, during the congressional battle, Van Devanter announced his retirement in what some thought was a well-timed move to dispose of the plan. Roosevelt was urged to drop the Court bill, since replacing Van Devanter with a liberal would give the Administration a decisive margin in most cases. As soon as Van Devanter's communication was made known on the Senate floor, however, the senators crowded around their colleague, Joseph T. Robinson, to congratulate him on his impending nomination for Van Devanter's seat. They all but usurped the power of appointment from Roosevelt, who knew that he could not avoid honoring the Majority Leader without inciting an uprising. Unfortunately for the New Dealers, Robinson was a 65-year-old conservative who had close connections to private utility interests. So the fight went on into June and July with tempers growing short in the brutal Washington heat. In July, at a critical point in the Great Debate, Robinson died. His death doomed the President's Court-packing scheme, but it left Roosevelt with an opportunity that his opponents had hoped to deny him—naming the first Justice of his own choosing to the Supreme Court.

The battle over the Court plan, Joseph Alsop and Turner Catledge have written, "conferred a strange, almost a lurid importance on the President's choice for the Supeme Court vacancy." As he had done in February while preparing his Court-packing message, Roosevelt moved in a covert manner that put Washington on edge. Each day it was expected that he would send a name to the Senate, but July ran its course without a decision and Congress, which had hoped to go home in June, found itself in the sultry capital in August with adjournment near and still no word from the White House.

In early August, a *New York Times* correspondent noted that "an unusually fierce attack of nervous irritability has seized the 529 legislators." "You have to see the shaking hands and the quivering facial muscles, hear the rage-quavers of the voices" of Congressmen as they spoke to appreciate "the violence of the nerve tension." They "snap at each other over trifles in floor debates" and were biting the heads off secretaries, prompting the correspondent to report "a new high in headless . . . secretaries." One secretary remarked, "Yesterday morning I had to phone six Senators, all of them my friends, and remind them of a subcommittee meeting. Five of them bawled me out for it, and the sixth hung up on me." Another secretary said: "The boss came back from a subcommittee row over a technicality the other day so ill that I had to nurse him and dose him for an hour and then call a doctor. It's the first time I've ever known him to be sick without a hangover for eleven years."

Roosevelt had added to this anxiety when, at a press conference on July 27, he said that he was exploring the possibility of making the appointment after the Senate had adjourned. Mutinous legislators were incensed at the prospect of not having a chance to act on Roosevelt's selection until after the nominee had donned the black robes of a Justice and taken part in the Court's decisions. The President's declaration also indicated that he might be contemplating a particularly offensive nomination, making it desirable for him to bypass the Senate. Attorney General Homer Cummings assured Roosevelt that he could fill a vacancy at any time, even when the Senate was not in session, although, of course, any designee would ultimately have to be confirmed. The historical record on this point, however, did not give the President as much comfort as he wanted, and the Senate was kicking up a storm. By early August he had resolved to settle on a nominee before the Senate adjourned.

Although Roosevelt may have been needling the senators with his talk of a recess appointment, he did have a valid reason for his inquiry. On August 4 Stephen Early, the White House press secretary, reviewed the situation for a Scripps-Howard columnist, Raymond Clapper. Early explained that the President did not know how long Congress would remain in session, and he needed two to four more weeks to make up his mind. It had not been clear until the Senate killed the Court bill in late July that he would have only one seat to fill. It might be supposed, Early said, that Roosevelt could easily come up with one name since he had originally sought to choose six, but in fact it was harder to pick one, because he could not submit a balanced group and had to "make it a bull's eye." Clapper summarized the President's position in his diary: "been sixty to 75 names recommended since Robinson died. All have to be carefully investigated. Is serious matter and Rvt [Roosevelt] would be in bad spot if he sent up a name and then the opposition dug out some dumb chapter in his record. . . . Opposition which has been complaining that Rvt is slapdash would leap on him and say this is the kind of dumb[b]ell or bad actor he would have given us six of."

As the tension mounted, congressmen and reporters made book on whom the President would pick, but they had little to go on. Although it was expected that Roosevelt would try to heal the breaches within his party and the Senate by making an especially judicious choice, he gave no sign of where his favor might light. Even veteran Administration senators like James F. Byrnes remained in the dark. "I haven't the slightest idea who will be appointed to the Supreme Court, nor has anybody in Washington other than the President," Byrnes wrote a South Carolina friend on August 10. "The President certainly has not consulted anybody in the Senate about it. The only information we have is that contained in the Press; namely, that Sam Bratton of New Mexico, now a Judge of the Circuit Court of Appeals and formerly a member of the Senate, is receiving serious consideration. It may be that it is because the Senators have such a high opinion of Bratton that they think he has a good chance."

When Roosevelt finally made his decision, he moved in the same furtive manner he had used in preparing the Court plan. On the night of August 11 the President startled the man he had finally chosen by summoning him to the White House after dinner and, upon informing him of the honor in store for him, pledged him to silence. Not even the White House staff knew what had transpired. The next morning Stephen Early indicated that Roosevelt was still considering a list of sixty or seventy names and that a selection might not be made during the current congressional session. Two hours later the President sent a courier to Capitol Hill with a notice of appointment that Roosevelt had written in his own hand. The President kept the secret almost to the very end, but it had become too much for him. Like "a small boy waiting for his surprise to be revealed," as Virginia

Hamilton has written, he had to blurt out the news to someone. Before the messenger reached the door of the Senate chamber, Roosevelt told Early the name of the nominee. "Jesus Christ!" Early exploded. FDR grinned.

II. THE SENATE CONSENTS

The words "I nominate Hugo L. Black . . . ." sent the Senate into a state of shock. Senator Black, who had not let on at any point that he knew what the message contained, now slumped in his seat, white-faced and wordless, and nervously shredded a sheaf of papers. A few liberal colleagues came over to congratulate the Alabama senator, but other legislators did not try to hide their unhappiness. The House of Representatives responded more volubly. One reporter noted, "From the House press gallery it was quite a show to watch the reactions of the Congressmen as the news swept across the floor. A great buzzing as the name of Black was passed from lip to lip."

If Roosevelt anticipated immediate acquiescence from the Senate, he was reckoning without the diehards. Henry Fountain Ashurst, the eloquent chairman of the Judiciary Committee, rose on behalf of the administration and asked the senators to confirm instantly the appointment of this "lawyer of transcendent ability, great, industrious and courteous in debate, young, vigorous, of splendid character and attainments." Ashurst contended that there was "an immemorial rule of the Senate that whenever the Executive honors this body by nominating a member thereof, that nomination by immemorial usage is confirmed without reference to a committee for the obvious reason that no amount of investigation or consideration by a committee could disclose any new light on the character or attainments and ability of the nominee, because if we do not know him after long service with the nominee no one will ever know him." When Hiram Johnson of California and Edward Burke of Nebraska objected, however, Ashurst was compelled to name a subcommittee to consider the nomination. Not since 1888, when President Grover Cleveland nominated Lucius Quintus Cincinnatus Lamar to the Supreme Court, had a proposed appointment of a senator or former senator been sent to committee.

Roosevelt could hardly have made a choice that would have discomforted his opponents more. Black was an ardent New Dealer and had been a strong supporter of Court-packing; indeed, it was said that he was one of the few senators who actually believed in the plan. Most people had expected that Roosevelt would take pains to name someone like a federal judge, but Black's only judicial experience consisted of eighteen months as a police court judge in Birmingham. Little about him suggested the judicial temperament, and he had especially incensed conservatives by his performance as an exceptionally vigorous prosecutor on Senate committees. As one biographer described it, "The paths of his investigations had been lurid with charges and countercharges, *subpoenas duces tecum,* searches and seizures, and contempt proceedings," and the political scientist Earl Latham has noted that "Senator Black in 1936 was the kind of legislator Justice Black had no use for twenty years later."

A year before the nomination Newton D. Baker, a onetime progressive leader who had become a prominent corporation attorney, had written a friend: "I heard last week that the incredible Senator Black with his eavesdropping, peeping-Tom committee had secured from the Western Union Telegraph Company all the telegrams sent out of my office in a year. As I run a law office and not a criminal conspiracy, I am entirely indifferent as to what he discovered from the telegrams, but the oftener I permit myself to reflect on this outrage, the more violent I become. Man of peace as I am, I am quite sure I could not keep my hand off the rope if I accidentally happened to stumble upon a party bent on hanging him."

Conservatives outdid themselves in expressions of indignation. "If the President had searched the country for the worst man to appoint, he couldn't possibly have found anyone to fill the bill so well," grumbled one senator. "Mr. Roosevelt could not have made a worse appointment if he had named John L. Lewis," wrote the columnist David Lawrence, and Herbert Hoover protested that the court was now "one-ninth packed." The most devastating critique appeared on the editorial page of the *Washington Post*:

> Men deficient in the necessary professional qualifications have occasionally been named for the Supreme Court. And qualified men have sometimes been put forward primarily because they were also politically agreeable to a President. But until yesterday students of American history would have found it difficult to refer to any Supreme Court nomination which combined lack of train-

ing on the one hand and extreme partisanship. In this one respect the choice of Senator Black must be called outstanding.

. . . .

If Senator Black has given any study or thought to any aspect of constitutional law in a way which would entitle him to this preferment, his labors in that direction have been skillfully concealed. If he has ever shown himself exceptionally qualified in either the knowledge or the temperament essential for exercise of the highest judicial function, the occasion escapes recollection.

Although Black came from Alabama, no group was unhappier about his nomination than the Southern congressmen. A sharp-tongued, unrelenting partisan who kept too much to himself, Black had never been a member of "the club." More important, he was a Southern liberal, and his selection signaled Roosevelt's determination to back those who were attempting to transform the conservative structure of Southern politics, an inclination that was later manifested in the 1938 purge. A Georgia congressman called the nomination of Black "the worst insult that has yet been given to the nation"; a Texas congressman said, "I wouldn't appeal a case with him there." Black had particularly antagonized Southern conservatives by sponsoring the wages and hours bill, which they claimed was denying their constituencies a competitive advantage granted by God. When reporters asked the veteran Virginia Senator Carter Glass for a comment on Black, he replied, "Don't start me off again."

Yet Roosevelt knew very well that there was not a thing they could, or would, do about it. Black was a senator, and the sense of collegiality was so strong that it was inconceivable that the Senate would fail to confirm one of its members. As the President told Democratic Chairman James A. Farley, "They'll have to take him."

The Senate proved unwilling to entertain the real objections many felt to Black's nomination. It would not consider the assertion that Black was too liberal, because ideological differences were not regarded as proper grounds for refusing to confirm a fellow senator; nor was Black's lack of judicial background explored, since it could not be conceded that any member of the Senate might be unqualified to sit on the Supreme Court. The little consideration given the appointment therefore focused on technical matters. Senator William E. Borah of Idaho claimed that since Van Devanter had taken advantage of legislation passed earlier in the session allowing retirement rather than resignation, he was still a member of the Court, and there was no vacancy for Black to fill. Ashurst retorted that if all nine Justices retired or went mad, according to Borah's reasoning, there would be no Court; even Van Devanter thought the argument was nonsense, since he had no intention of ever returning to the bench. Others speculated that Black was ineligible for another reason: since the retirement legislation also guaranteed the pensions of retiring Justices, Congress had increased their emoluments, and the Constitution forbade any member of Congress to accept a post under such circumstances. Few people thought much of that argument either.

Two days after the nomination, a more explosive consideration arose—it was said that Black, at the outset of his career, had been associated with the Ku Klux Klan. The National Association for the Advancement of Colored People and the Socialist Party each urged the Senate to explore Black's racial attitudes. The Socialist leader Norman Thomas also asked the Judiciary Committee to investigate Black's opposition during the Hoover administration to proposals to equalize relief between Whites and Negroes, his hostility to antilynching legislation, and his silence about the "Scottsboro boys," a group of Negroes convicted in Alabama in what appeared to be an outrageous miscarriage of justice. "We fully appreciate Senator Black's championship of labor legislation," Thomas said, but "no other excellence can fit a man for the Supreme Court whose record is marred by race prejudice."

Despite these reservations the nomination moved quickly through committee, but not without occasioning some animosity. Matthew Neely of West Virginia, an Administration stalwart, allotted the matter only two hours in a meeting of his subcommittee on Friday, August 13, the day after the nomination; the subcommittee then reported the recommendation by a vote of 5–1, with only Warren Austin of Vermont dissenting on constitutional grounds. On the following Monday, as the Judiciary Committee convened behind closed doors, William Dieterich of Illinois accused certain committee members of trying to "besmirch" their colleague by linking him to the Ku Klux Klan. Dieterich's tirade nearly resulted in a fist fight with a fellow Democrat when Senator Burke charged at him. Although "tempers flared to white heat," the committee approved the nomination 13–4.

When the full Senate took up the Black appointment on August

17, Senator Royal S. Copeland of New York opened the debate by asserting that his Alabama colleague's first election to the Senate in 1926 had been supported by the Klan. Before crowded public galleries, Copeland read a *New York Times* report on Black's exploitation of anti-Catholic sentiment in attacking the Presidential ambitions of Alfred E. Smith. Copeland asserted, "We are free because we are guarded by the Supreme Court. Catholics, Protestants, Negroes, Jews, Gentiles, all of us, are guarded by the Supreme Court. But what will happen if a half dozen men of the mental bias of the nominee should be seated on the bench? . . . Does the leopard change his spots? Will Mr. Justice Black be any different from Candidate Black? . . . Naturally we wonder what Mr. Justice Black would do were another Scottsboro case appealed to the Supreme Court."

Copeland made no headway with his charges, because they were regarded as blatantly political and because the Senate received reassurances. Many believed that Copeland, an anti-New Deal Democrat who was running for Mayor of New York City, was exploiting the Klan issue to curry ethnic voters. Although Black left the question unresolved when cornered by some of his supporters during the debate, the unpredictable Borah came to his aid. The Idaho maverick, who eventually voted against confirmation on the technical ground of ineligibility, conceded that senators had received thousands of telegrams about Black and the Klan, but insisted, "There has never been at any time one iota of evidence that Senator Black was a member of the Klan. . . . We know that Senator Black has said in private conversation, not since this matter came up but at other times, that he was not a member of the Klan." When Copeland asked Borah how he would vote if he knew that Black was or had been a Klansman, the Idaho senator replied, "If I knew that a man was a member of a secret association organized to spread racial antipathies and religious intolerance through the country, I should certainly vote against him for any position."

Late in the afternoon of August 17, just five days after the Black nomination was made and after only six hours of debate, the Senate confirmed the appointment by the lopsided margin of sixty-three to sixteen. Of the Republicans present all but three voted "nay," as did six Democrats, including Burke and Copeland. However, some of the most reactionary Southern Democrats, who had bitterly fought the Court plan, ended up supporting the administration. Ickes recorded,

"Even 'Cotton Ed' Smith, of South Carolina, who 'God-damned' the nomination all over the place when it was first announced, didn't have the courage to stand up and vote against a fellow Senator from the Deep South." The Klan issue had fizzled, but it left some uneasiness. In Washington, a one-liner went from mouth to mouth: "Hugo won't have to buy a robe; he can dye his white one black." Despite the rumbling about the KKK, Roosevelt and the New Dealers had apparently won a stunning victory, less than a month after the opposition thought FDR was on the ropes. Ickes concluded: "So Hugo Black becomes a member of the Supreme Court of the United States, while the economic royalists fume and squirm, and the President rolls his tongue around in his cheek."

The outcome left conservatives disconsolate. When Carter Glass heard the nomination called a triumph for the common man, he snapped, "They must be Goddam common!" Senator Peter Gerry of Rhode Island explained to Canada's prime minister, "His legal experience was not considered sufficient and he hasn't a judicial attitude of mind. He is a prosecutor and not a judge." An Oregon editor went even further: "His appointment of Black was the grossest insult to the Supreme Court and the American people that we have ever been called upon to accept." Roosevelt's former adviser Raymond Moley commented, "There have been worse appointments to high judicial offices; but . . . I can't remember where or when."

After Congress adjourned, Hiram Johnson wrote a confidant in California: "This was a most unsatisfactory session. We wound up by confirming Black, who is unfit to be a Supreme Court Justice. . . . Had it not been for me, Black's nomination would have gone through with a 'Hurrah!' . . . Borah and other distinguished patriots wished it so, but I had 'guts' enough to stop it. I accomplished nothing —save that sixteen men in the Senate showed their feeling of his unfitness. I understand he was a member of the Ku Klux Klan when first elected to the Senate. He never dared say anything about it subsequently, and Borah and his other friends, saw to it that he was not called as a witness."

Once Black was confirmed, the hubbub died down. Congressmen left the capital, and Black sailed with his wife to Europe for a vacation. His name soon disappeared from the newspapers, and the controversy appeared to be at an end.

III. THE REVELATION

On September 13 the Pittsburgh *Post-Gazette* detonated a bombshell. It published the first of six articles by Ray Sprigle, an enterprising reporter who had dug up original materials, including the transcript of a Klan meeting, conclusively connecting Hugo Black to the Ku Klux Klan. The series grabbed front page headlines in newspapers throughout the country.

Sprigle began, "Hugo Lafayette Black, Associate Justice of the United States Supreme Court, is a member of the hooded brotherhood that for ten long blood-drenched years ruled the Southland with lash and noose and torch, the Invisible Empire, Knights of the Ku Klux Klan." Since it was generally suspected that Black had once had a KKK relationship, that allegation hardly constituted news. Sprigle developed three points in his series, however, that were very damaging. First, he demonstrated that Black had not merely run with Klan backing, but had actually been a member of the organization. He gave an account of the night of September 11, 1923, when Black pledged that he would never divulge, even under threat of death, the secrets of the Klan; surrounded by white-robed members of the Robert E. Lee Klan No. 1 in Birmingham, Black had vowed, "I swear that I will most zealously and valiantly shield and preserve by any and all justifiable means and methods . . . white supremacy."

Second, Sprigle recounted vivid examples of the views held by the Klansmen with whom Black had associated. In a meeting on September 2, 1926, the Imperial Wizard Hiram Wesley Evans said, "We find that America up to now has done all that has been worthwhile under the leadership of native-born, white, gentile, Protestant men. . . . There isn't a Negro in Alabama that dares open his mouth and says he believes in social equality of the black man. . . . I mean to tell you any time they propose to produce equality between me and a certain said Negro they are simply going to have to hold a funeral for the Negro." The Imperial Wizard added that Northern Negroes "will be murdered by the Yankees that have gotten all the sass from the Negroes that they want." On that same occasion the KKK's Imperial Legal Adviser in Washington observed, "To come down here now and find that you have given us a man named Black who wears 'white'—do you get that boys—to occupy a seat in the Senate of the United States is like getting an inspiration before baptism." Turning to Bibb Graves, who had just won the Democratic nomination for Governor, tantamount to election, he added, "I am so glad that you have a man, all but elected Governor, who comes from a town that, prior to his advent as Exalted Cyclops of the local Klan, I am told was owned by the Jews, controlled by the Catholics and loved by Negroes [Laughter and applause]. Now he tells me that the Jews have a foreclosure sale at bankruptcy, selling out, the Catholics are on the run, and the Negroes are in hiding [Applause]."

Most of Black's own remarks that afternoon were unexceptionable. In fact he spoke of the "principles of liberty which were written in the Constitution of this country" and the ideal of loving one's enemies. But he also assured the assembled Klansmen, "I realize that I was elected by men who believe in the principles that I have sought to advocate and which are the principles of this organization," and said to them and to the Grand Dragon, "I thank you from the bottom of a heart that is yours."

Finally, Sprigle made a third and critical contribution—he established that, on the same afternoon in 1926, Black, who had resigned from the Klan in the summer of 1925 for reasons of political expediency, had been awarded a special life membership, a gold "grand passport." Black had thanked the Klan for this honor, which only a half dozen men in the United States had received. Most important, the card was presumably still valid because there was no evidence in the Klan archives that it had been returned. In short, Sprigle was saying not merely that Black had been elected with Klan backing, not merely that Black had thanked the Klan leaders for their aid, but that Black was *still* a member of the Ku Klux Klan.

Sprigle's articles prompted denunciations of Black and Roosevelt that far exceeded, in both volume and vehemence, the protests that had greeted the nomination. Cartoonists had a field day depicting the members of the Supreme Court assembled in their silk, eight in black and the ninth in the white robe and hood of the KKK. In the pages of the *American Mercury* the mordant critic Albert Jay Nock called Black "a vulgar dog" and wrote that Roosevelt's appointment "was the act of a man who conceives himself challenged to do his very filthiest."

Several senators who had voted to confirm Black hastened to declare that if they had known of his Klan connection they would have opposed his elevation to the Court. Some thought they had been duped, since Black had temporized when the KKK rumors surfaced in August, and others had given assurances that there was no foundation to the allegations. Democratic senators from New Jersey and South Dakota charged that John Bankhead of Alabama had deliberately misled them by stating that Black had not been a member of the Klan. "I feel that not only I but the rest of the Senators were deceived and imposed upon," complained Clyde Herring, and his Iowa colleague, Guy Gillette, added, "I hope something is done to keep Black from the high court bench."

The issue hit directly at the core of Roosevelt's urban coalition since the main targets of the KKK had been Catholics and Negroes. The revelations also embarrassed Northern Democratic senators with large ethnic constituencies who had voted for Black. Groups like the Ancient Order of Hibernians demanded that Black resign or be removed; the Catholic Club of the City of New York deemed the appointment "a direct affront to the more than 20,000,000 Catholic citizens of the United States as well as to countless numbers of other citizens." In New Hampshire the Knights of Columbus adopted resolutions castigating Senator Fred Brown for supporting confirmation, and a member of the staff of Senator Theodore Green of Rhode Island noted, "At a very large meeting of the Hibernian County Convention last night a great many Democrats were denouncing Roosevelt. Very severe criticism among the Democrats."

Irish Catholic politicians played a numerically disproportionate role in the campaign to get rid of Black. Representative John J. O'Connor, chairman of the House Rules Committee, reported he had been canvassing congressmen about instituting impeachment proceedings and had found no one opposed to such a move. "If Mr. Justice Black was a member of the Klan when nominated and confirmed, his silence constituted a moral fraud upon the American people," said Representative Edward L. O'Neill, a New Jersey Democrat. Lieutenant Governor Francis E. Kelly of Massachusetts drafted a resolution asking the President to insist upon Black's resignation, and Senator David I. Walsh, who favored the same course, declared, "There are two counts against him, one that Black, for political advantage joined the Klan and took the oath of a Klansman and subscribed to its creeds; two, that Black obtained his nomination and confirmation by concealment and thereby deceived the President and his fellow-Senators, especially the latter."

Sprigle's articles appeared just as the campaign for the mayoralty in New York City was reaching a climax, and Senator Copeland took full advantage of the opportunity. He told a Carnegie Hall audience: "I never expected to see the day when a member of that organization, sworn to bigotry and intolerance, should become a member of the court. Shame upon him that he did not have the courage and decency to tell his colleagues in the Senate that the suspicion of his affiliation was a reality." Copeland accused his rival, Jeremiah T. Mahoney, of approving Roosevelt's action in the "placing upon the court of a Klansman who wears a black robe of court by day and a white robe of the Klan by night." "Imagine a man named Mahoney being mixed up with the Klan," his opponent spluttered. "Show me a Ku Klux Klanner and I promise he won't be alive a minute after I see him!"

Negro spokesmen joined in the hue and cry. The National Association for the Advancement of Colored People urged the President to call upon Black "to resign his post in the absence of repudiation and disproof of charges" that he held life membership in the KKK. Robert L. Vann, who was the Negro editor of the *Pittsburgh Courier*, a special assistant United States attorney general, and also credited with playing the largest role in swinging Pennsylvania Negroes to the Democratic Party, wired Roosevelt to remove Black. "Your friends are on the spot," Vann said. "You must save your friends or you must release them."

Despite this widespread feeling, even Roosevelt's conservative critics in the Senate conceded that nothing could be done if Black decided to stick it out. The President could not oust a Justice, and since he had been lambasted month after month for trying to tamper with the Court, Roosevelt and his supporters surmised that any attempt to coerce Black into resigning would not be well received. People would be led to conclude "that, if the President should request Justice Black's resignation, he might also attempt to drive Justice McReynolds, Sutherland and Butler from the bench." Nor did there appear to be grounds for impeachment. The civil liberties attorney Osmond K.

Fraenkel observed, "I don't believe a judge can be impeached for something that happened before his appointment, but even if that were so, I do not see how he could be impeached for membership in an organization. Membership in the Klan, however politically inadvisable, is not a crime."

The electrifying disclosures exasperated the President. Washington, which so recently had been the self-confident capital of the New Deal, was now jeered at as "Ku-Kluxville-on-the-Potomac." The situation was especially embarrassing to the New Dealers because Roosevelt had taken a firm stand for religious liberty in 1928 while campaigning for Al Smith, a Catholic, and had been severely criticized for having too many Jews in his administration and for giving too many benefits to Negroes. Despite this record the President now bore the onus of having brought the main battle of his second term to a climax by naming a Klansman to the Supreme Court.

In an editorial in the *Emporia Gazette* William Allen White wrote:

> When Franklin Roosevelt is dead and buried and all his bones are rotted, the fact that he played around with Black and appointed to the highest honorable office in American life a man who was a member of the Ku Klux Klan, as Black was charged when Roosevelt named him, well, as we started to say, when Roosevelt is dead and gone he will be remembered in the history of this day and time by the fact that he was not above dishonoring the Supreme Court by putting a Klansman there.
>
> Why could not a man as smart as Franklin Roosevelt, as brave and as benevolent, also be wise in a day of crisis?

IV. "I DID JOIN THE KLAN"

While Roosevelt's prospects were imperiled by the unexpected turn of events, Black's life had become all but unendurable. The clamor followed the new Justice to Europe, where he was still vacationing when the Sprigle series broke. Journalists hounded him, first in Paris, then in London. "A dreadfully worried United States judge hid himself away in a palatial hotel suite in London yesterday while all his fellow countrymen were asking for a straight answer to a straight question," reported the British *Daily Herald*. One newspaperman jumped out of a darkened corridor scaring Black's wife, and another seized his arm as he emerged from a London theater. "I don't see you; I don't know you; I don't answer you," Black told him. The columnist Dorothy Thompson wrote, "In London tonight a Justice of the United States Supreme Court is barricaded behind locked doors. His telephone rings but he does not answer it. Reporters try to interview him but in vain. This man . . . sees only the waiters who bring him food, the maids who tidy his rooms and the traffic of London moving in the streets below. . . . He is front page news in England, where the British are taking revenge for the Simpson case." After letting it be known that he would sail back to America on a large transatlantic liner, on which one of his fellow passengers would have been Mr. Justice McReynolds, Black escaped from his hotel by a service entrance and drove to Southampton where he boarded a small mail steamer, *The City of Norfolk*. He left England, said the *Sun*, "Klandestinely."

No longer would Black be permitted to remain silent. Senator Walsh said that he had to speak out to be fair to the Catholic senators, and to those with Catholic and Jewish constituents, who had voted for his confirmation and who might suffer the consequences in the next election. Democratic Senator Bennett Champ Clark of Missouri commented, "I do not wish to be in the position of concluding as to the authenticity of the charges contained in the newspapers against Justice Black, but it does seem to me that he has had ample opportunity to answer a simple statement of fact." As Black's vessel headed westward across the Atlantic toward Norfolk, a Gallup Poll revealed that 59 percent of those interviewed believed that he should resign if he were proven to have been a member of the Klan. At Felix Frankfurter's suggestion, the young *Nation* editor Max Lerner flew to Norfolk, made his way through throngs of newspapermen, and at breakfast with Black aboard ship argued that he should issue an explanation. That night, Lerner spent four more hours with Black in Alexandria. Under all of this pressure, Black finally decided to accept an invitation to speak over the radio on October 1, but he now had less than two days to draft his speech.

The address, carried over three national networks with three hundred stations, attracted the largest American audience of the decade, except for that tuned in to the abdication of Edward VIII. (The huge audience, however, did lack one prominent listener—Franklin Roosevelt contrived to be in the Pacific Northwest in an automobile without a radio as Black spoke.) The fact of Black's speech was a sensation because of the cardinal rule that Justices do not make statements on public matters, and the dramatic nature of the occasion was enhanced when fiery crosses lit the hillsides in different parts of the country.

In his talk, Black admitted having belonged to the Klan—he could hardly do anything else—but said that he had resigned before entering the Senate and never rejoined. He minimized the grand passport as an "unsolicited card" which he did not view as membership in the Klan, had never used, and had not kept. He also voiced his disdain, without naming the KKK, for "any organization or group which, anywhere or at any time, arrogates to itself the un-American power to interfere in the slightest degree with complete religious freedom."

Black's speech is remembered today as a courageous denunciation of the Klan that foreshadowed his future character as a Justice, but in truth it was not. Black neither explained his past Klan membership nor offered any apology for signing up with the KKK; nor did he account for why he had sat through the Senate discussion of his alleged Klan connections without a word to anyone either in the Senate or, apparently, in the administration. He repudiated none of the atrocities perpetrated by the Klan in Alabama while he was in the secret order. In all, he used only eleven of the thirty minutes allotted to him. The most unfortunate aspect of his talk, however, was not what he failed to say but what he did say. He spent the first third of his remarks cautioning against the possibility of a revival of racial and religious hatred, but he warned that this might be brought about not by groups like the Klan but by those who questioned his right to be on the Supreme Court. He went on to affirm that some of his best friends were Jews and Catholics, told the national audience about his longtime Jewish chum in Birmingham, and mentioned that he numbered among his friends "many members of the colored race."

Rarely in the twentieth century has any statement by an American public figure brought down such abuse on him in the press as Black's brief address called forth. The *New York Herald Tribune* branded him a humbug and a coward: "The effort of Senator Black to suggest that he is the real protagonist of tolerance and that his enemies are intolerant is perhaps the greatest item of effrontery in a uniquely brazen utterance. Only a man heedless of the truth and a man afraid of his official skin could fall so low." The *Boston Post* called on him to resign, for "one who associates with bigots, bids for their support, takes the bigots' oath and then is so craven that he allows his friends in a crisis to deny it all, can't clear himself by asserting it was all contrary to his real character." About Black's references to Catholic, Jewish, and Negro friends, the *New York Post* said, "We might reply in kind that one of our best liberal friends was a Klansman but we still don't think he ought to be on the Supreme Court." The *Newark Ledger* added that Black had "resigned from the Klan to maintain an appearance of decency. He should resign from the Supreme Court to attain the substance of decency." Catholic outrage ranged across the political spectrum from the liberal *Commonweal* to periodicals and spokesmen on the right. "Since there was no sign of his being ashamed for himself," wrote the editor of *The Catholic World*, "I was ashamed for him; ashamed too for the Supreme Court, ashamed for the President of the United States."

Roosevelt, however, had no doubt that Black's performance had carried the day. When Jim Farley telephoned him a few days later the President asked, "What d'you think of Hugo's speech of the other night?" "He did the best he could under the circumstances, but I think he should have hit the Klan," Farley answered. "It was a grand job," Roosevelt returned. "It did the trick; you just wait and see."

The President was absolutely right. The address was inevitably applauded, if not altogether convincingly, by Black's supporters in the New Deal. "If you listened to Mr. Justice Black's radio talk," said Senator Green of Rhode Island, "I am sure that you must have felt as I did that he admirably expressed the principles on which Roger Williams founded this State." Elements of Roosevelt's urban coalition also remained loyal. Labor leaders praised Black's speech, and Rabbi Herbert S. Goldstein of Yeshiva College spoke for others in saying, "As a citizen, I do not seek 'the pound of flesh' and as a Jew, I do not seek retaliation." Most important, Black's discourse won the majority of his listeners, albeit not a substantial majority. After the broadcast 56 percent of the people polled by Gallup responded that Black should stay on the bench, which was precisely what he had intended to do all along.

V. MR. JUSTICE BLACK

On the morning of October 4, three days after Black's radio talk, the Supreme Court opened its fall term, and huge crowds gathered to see the former Klansman take his seat. Long lines extended for hundreds of feet in the corridor, and much of the throng was unable to enter the courtroom. When the Justices filed in, it was noted pointedly that Black sat to the "extreme left" of the Chief Justice. For the first time in public, Black wore the silk robes of a Justice, but the occasion was not the hour of triumph the man from Clay County, Alabama, might have hoped for. To the dismay of his supporters, two petitions were filed to challenge his right to be a Justice. For all Black's efforts and those of Roosevelt, the controversy continued to simmer.

The President quickly remedied the situation. The next day in Chicago, he delivered his historic "quarantine" address, and by nightfall the country had turned its attention from Black to foreign affairs and the prospect of a second world war. A distinguished authority on international law, John Bassett Moore, wrote, "The President never was more adroit than in his Chicago speech. All the talk about Black, balancing the budget, the C.I.O., the 'dictatorial drift,' etc. etc., . . . suddenly ceased when the war cry was raised." Critics charged that FDR had deliberately seized the headlines in order to distract attention from the Black furor. "The speech would never have been made if there had been no Black case," Hiram Johnson protested. Actually, the situation was more complex than such conspiracy notions suggested. From Washington, His Majesty's Chargé D'Affaires sent the British Foreign Secretary Anthony Eden a more balanced report:

> I have every reason to believe that the speech had long been contemplated, but the President was prepared to await the psychological moment for its delivery. He had returned from his Western tour fully convinced that, however lukewarm the feeling regarding the Supreme Court might be in those parts, the electors as a whole had not lost confidence in his personal leadership. On the other hand the regrettable "Black and Klan" incident was still front page news and required something more important to remove it to the back page. In fact unkind Wall Street wits are talking of "a red herring drawn across the Black trail." The President's arrival at Chicago coincided with the

decision at Geneva to refer the Far Eastern crisis to the signatories of the Nine-Power Treaty. Here was a good opportunity for Mr. Roosevelt to make his appeal to the nation to abandon a policy of complete isolation.

Although the quarantine address was followed by reduced attention to Black in the press, lawyers and Washington correspondents continued to scrutinize him closely. Even after the Court summarily dismissed the petitions to deny Black a seat, every eye seemed to be inspecting the new Justice. "I went to the Court last week and had the opportunity to see Mr. Justice Black on the bench," Newton D. Baker wrote to the former Supreme Court Justice John H. Clarke. "He is young enough to make a good judge but he has a wavering expression of the eyes which he will have great trouble in straightening out if he wants to be like the judges on that Court usually are—impervious to all considerations except their view of the public good." The veteran *New York Times* columnist Arthur Krock had a different perspective; he observed:

> Mr. Justice Black's court-room demeanor provided material for interesting study. His face had gained color. His manner had acquired content. He looked benign instead of harried. But now and then, as the Chief Justice read the orders and Mr. Justice Black looked out upon the lawyers and spectators from his impregnable fortress of life tenure, an expression touched his face which is common to certain types of martyrs. It was a mixture of forgiveness and satisfaction, of pity for unreconstructed dissenters and sympathy for himself who had borne so much in comparative silence. Charles Dickens, who gave many passages to the description of Mr. Christopher Catesby, would have recognized it at once.

Black might well have nourished such sentiments in his first year on the bench, for he was permitted to forget neither his Klan past nor his limited judicial background. In his first month, Black drew scathing criticism when the conviction of one of the Scottsboro boys came up on appeal and Black disqualified himself. The treatment accorded him by liberal Justices Louis Brandeis and, more particularly, Harlan Fiske Stone caused greater distress. In strolls through Washington with the newspaperman Marquis Childs, Stone abandoned discretion and vented his distress over Black's inexpertise. Childs later said that Stone was "like an old New England wood-carver, and here they suddenly brought someone in the shop who doesn't know a knife from a hoe. This really upset him very greatly." In an article inspired by his chats with Stone, Childs created a hullabaloo by stating that Black's opinions frequently had to be rewritten by his colleagues in order to bring them up to the standards of the Court and that Black's incompetence had caused the other Justices "acute discomfort and embarrassment."

Yet even in these early days Black won admirers for his courage and skill. Rather than meekly accommodating himself as might be expected of a newcomer tarred by scandal, he boldly advanced iconoclastic notions. "Mr. Justice Black, dissenting" became a familiar phrase; indeed, he was said to have set a record for lone dissents. Walton Hamilton expressed his esteem for Black's cleanly written opinions and the independence of a man who "regards the sacred cows as ordinary heifers." By 1939 Erwin D. Canham was observing that "Mr. Justice Black . . . has climbed out of the pit into which the circumstances of his appointment had hurled him, and is on the way to being regarded as another Brandeis."

The allusion to Brandeis suggested both a craftsmanship that demeaning references to the police court judgeship had not prepared critics for and a solicitude for civil liberties that many people had not expected of an ex-Klansman. In 1940 Black was spokesman for the Court in two notable decisions. In *Chambers v. Florida*, generally thought to be his ablest opinion, he spoke for a unanimous Court in holding that the convictions of four Negroes for murder, obtained by using coerced confessions, violated the due process clause of the fourteenth amendment. In *Smith v. Texas*, he again spoke for all nine Justices in setting aside the rape conviction of a Negro based on an indictment handed down by a grand jury from which Negroes were excluded. Black became best known, however, not as the eloquent voice of a unanimous Court, but as a dissenter urging the Court to break new ground on civil liberties, particularly as an advocate of uninhibited application of the first amendment. Justice William O. Douglas observed in 1956, "I dare say that when the critical account is written, none will be rated higher than Justice Black for consistency in construing the laws and the Constitution so as to protect the civil rights of citizens and aliens, whatever the form of repression may be." A decade later Alexander Bickel wrote of "a Hugo Black majority" on the Court, "for in this second half of Justice Black's third decade of service, the Court was overturning many a precedent that had entered the books over his dissent." When he finally left the bench in 1971, Justice Black, who had once been jeered at for his alleged lack of expertise, was praised for his "extraordinary capacity to clarify and make vivid the issues in a case" through "seemingly impregnable logic," and as one of "the court's intellectual pillars" with a reputation for "judicial integrity, dignity and tight reasoning."

Black's subsequent career made the widespread alarm expressed at his appointment seem badly misdirected and gave Roosevelt a sense of vindication. The President had remained rather touchy about the Black affair. In February, 1938, Raymond Clapper related in his diary an episode that took place in the Gridiron Club, the organization of Washington correspondents: "President Geo Holmes told about visit he and Gould Lincoln made to Rvt on Monday after dinner. Rvt said like dinner except thought one skit in bad taste. Said that was Klan skit on Black. . . . Said Harding had an illegitimate child but Gridiron club never use anything on that. . . . Said matter was dying out skit by being printed in newspapers tended to reopen whole thing keep it agitated. Holmes told us he couldn't see analogy of Rvt's unless he meant that Black was like Nan Britton." When the *Chambers* decision was handed down, Roosevelt seized the opportunity at his press conference the next day to tell reporters, "I would put in a general dig that some of the Press should not only give a little praise but also a modicum of apology for things they have said in the last two years. Is that fair?"

VI. "A WONDERFULLY GOOD APPOINTMENT"

Black's emergence as a champion of civil liberties has been offered as proof that Roosevelt knew what he was doing all along, that he perceived potential in Black that others did not. Perhaps he did; it is hard to determine, particularly this long after the fact, what one man sensed in another. It is highly improbable, though, that FDR foresaw Black's ultimate accomplishments, even if he may have supposed that Black, like other men, might show new qualities when given the independence of life tenure.

Other commentators have said that Black's post-1937 conduct accorded with his pre-1937 career, for he had come out of a populist tradition in Alabama and had long been an exponent of civil liberties and individualism and a friend of labor and the Negro. This view acknowledges that he had been a Klansman, but contends that the KKK was a populist, prolabor movement that sponsored liberal, humanitarian measures, such as aid for underprivileged children. Some have also claimed that he joined at the urging of a Jewish friend in order to exercise his benign influence within the Klan.

The evidence for these familiar arguments is, at best, ambiguous. It is true that Black appears never to have been associated with Klan violence, that he was an attorney for unions, and that he was responsible for reforms in court procedure in Alabama. Nevertheless, the link of Black to populism has been too easily assumed, quite apart from the difficulty of showing the connection between populism and modern civil libertarianism. Black did have Negro clients, but he was also reproached for making a blatant appeal to race prejudice while defending the accused murderer of a priest. The strongest statement that Daniel M. Berman could make in his informative article in the *Catholic University Law Review* was that "there is no evidence that Judge Black treated Negroes any more harshly than whites." As late as 1932, Black had opposed a government relief bill because it would, in code language, interfere with "social habits and social customs." Correspondent Paul Y. Anderson reported that Black "became hysterical over the prospect of a federal relief plan which might feed Negroes as well as whites, and gave an exhibition which brought a blush to the face of Tom Heflin, lurking in the rear of the chamber." The one thing known for certain about Black's attitude toward the Negro was that, in the very month Roosevelt appointed him to the Supreme Court, Black was planning to speak in the Senate against the antilynching bill.

At a press conference in September Roosevelt responded "No" to the question: "Prior to the appointment of former Senator Black, had you received any information from any source as to his Klan membership?" The President may not have known about "membership," but it is inconceivable that he had no awareness of a Klan connection. It was widely recognized, at the very least, that the Alabama senator had Klan backing when he was first elected to the U.S. Senate. In fact, as a writer in the *Washington Post* noted, "It is difficult to find a sketch of Senator Black which does not contain some reference to the Ku Klux Klan." In addition, because of his association with the polio center at Warm Springs, Roosevelt regarded himself as much a son of Georgia as of New York, and in his many sojourns in Georgia he would have been likely to have acquired good intelligence about the politics of neighboring Alabama.

It is more likely that civil liberties considerations did not loom large in Roosevelt's mind in choosing a nominee. The central issue in the Court crisis had been the fate of New Deal economic legislation, and the President was looking for someone to legitimate the growth of the State. Concentration on such matters, rather than civil liberties and civil rights, reflected the basic attitudes of 1930s liberalism. It is true that interest in civil liberties and civil rights grew during the Depression, fostered by New Deal activities, particularly in the Justice Department, the inclinations of New Deal administrators like Harold Ickes, the example set by Eleanor Roosevelt, and the spirit of concern that the New Deal conveyed. Not until the 1940s, however, did civil liberties and civil rights come to have a truly prominent place on the agenda of American liberalism.

For many New Deal supporters, Black's Klan affiliation was distressing, but it was not thought to be central, as it would be today. Klan membership was regarded as the entry fee Black had to pay for political advancement in Alabama, nothing more. Senator George Norris, the most respected of all the progressives and father of the TVA, who had fought the Klan and been fought by it, called the naming of Black "a wonderfully good appointment." He added, "Even if he was a member of the Klan, there's no legal objection to that. I've an idea many members of the House and the Senate belong to the Klan also but that is their privilege."

Progressives characterized the outcry against Black as a conservative scheme to discredit the Roosevelt administration and thereby scuttle the New Deal and prospects for reform. They did not attack what was said about Black, but rather who said it; when Sprigle's series appeared, Black's supporters concentrated their fire on his publisher, Paul Block, and other hostile newspaper titans like William Randolph Hearst. They offered the defense, in Heywood Broun's words, that "few justices of the Supreme Court swim up to the high bench as immaculate as Little Eva on the way to Heaven" and contended that the elements opposed to Black would not have shown the same intense concern about the past of a reactionary nominee. The liberal columnist Jay Franklin wrote, "One point only should be made in relation to these charges: If Hugo L. Black had been a labor-baiter, a trust corporation attorney, a man who had amassed a fortune and achieved political prominence as a result of helping the banks, utilities and corporations to loot the State of Alabama and stifle competition by strong-arm monopolies, he could have engaged in devil-worship, he could have practiced polygamy, he could have hunted down run-away share-croppers with blood-hounds, and eaten babies for breakfast, for all that his conservative Northern critics would care."

The New Dealers insisted that Black should be measured by the yardstick of twentieth century social reform and by the imperatives of the Great Depression. *The Progressive,* the organ of the La Follette dynasty in Wisconsin, noting Black's "excellent and long standing record of liberalism," pointed out that Black had fought the big-navy lobby and the power trust. Congressman David Lewis, a Maryland Democrat who had cosponsored the social security bill, asserted, "The real issue is not Black's qualifications, but whether the court is going to keep out of the 'nullification business'—that is quit vetoing acts of Congress." A Providence newspaper observed, "We don't like the idea of a Supreme Court Judge having been at any time or for whatever purpose associated with the Ku Klux Klan, but the issue is not religion, it is not race or creed; the issue is economics."

In its "Topics of The Times" column, the *New York Times* satirized this sentiment in *Alice in Wonderland* style:

> After a while the White Rabbit summed up the debate, nobody dissenting.
> "You see, Alice," he said, "it's all because we have recently discovered that all life is functional. Once upon a time people thought there were definite things like truth, justice, honor, mercy, courage, and so forth. But now we know these things are only functions of the economic system. . . . That is why Liberals in the United States feel it does not matter if a member of the Supreme Court used to belong to the KKK. The only important thing is how does he stand on the question of 1½ cents per kilowatt hour f.o.b. Norris Dam."

This preoccupation with economic and social policy had led the President to choose Black, but it was not the only consideration. Roosevelt certainly sought an enthusiastic New Dealer, but he also wanted someone who was young, came from a section that did not have a Supreme Court Justice, and could readily be confirmed. He and Cummings had reduced a list of sixty names to seven, four of whom were federal judges. None of the judges, however, including the highly touted Bratton, had sufficient liberal ardor to suit the President. "Bratton belongs to a judicial school of thought that ought not to be represented on the bench," he later told Farley. So the candidates were reduced to three: Solicitor General Stanley Reed, Black, and Senator Sherman Minton of Indiana.

Reed was crossed off as "middle-of-the-road . . . a good man but without much force or color," and attention focused on the choice of a senator. Roosevelt found that solution particularly beguiling, especially after the Robinson episode in May, in which the Senate in effect made its own nomination of a Justice. If he named a senator, even one regarded as a radical, the Senate would be trapped into going along, a circumstance that appealed to FDR's love of surprise and of turning the tables on his opponents with a clever move. He was initially inclined toward the fiery Shay Minton, but the Hoosier senator recognized that during the recent struggle over the Court bill he had made too many harsh comments about the Justices who would be his colleagues. Moreover, he was needed in the Senate. The President therefore settled on Black, who was young enough at 51, from a large unrepresented circuit in the Deep South, and, most important, a true believer in expanding governmental power.

Far from seeking to placate Congress by picking a moderate like Bratton, Roosevelt wanted to make clear that he was as committed to the New Deal as ever, and his selection of Black was a symbolic and defiant act. FDR's original plan seems to have been motivated by a desire not only to reform the Court, but also to punish the Justices for wronging him in the past. The appointment afforded Roosevelt another opportunity to express his contempt for the illusion that the Court was a body that lived on Mt. Olympus and his conviction that it was essentially a political agency. The Senate was even more of a target for revenge, for it had just humiliated him in the Court-packing battle. Donald Richberg, a prominent New Dealer, confided, as Clapper noted, that "Roosevelt was mad and was determined to give Senate the name which would be most disagreeable to it yet which it could not reject."

The President's faith in Black's liberal proclivities proved well founded. "Although Black's appointment did not mark the precise chronological point from which the Court's philosophy began its deviation from its previous path," Charlotte Williams has written, "it was this event which made it plain beyond all doubt that the Court was about to be reconstituted in the image of the New Deal." Black immediately gave the Administration a 6-3 majority on the Court, and his lone dissents indicated that he favored even more advanced stands than Justices like Brandeis, Cardozo, and Stone. Wallace Mendelson has calculated that in sixty cases involving the Federal Employer's Liability Act from 1938 through 1958, Black sustained workingmen's claims in every case but one, and that in the decade beginning 1949, in nineteen Sherman Act conflicts between business and consumer interests, "only Mr. Justice Black found a violation of the law in every instance."

In nominating Black, the President set the pattern that most of the other selections for "the Roosevelt Court" would follow. To the Supreme Court would go progressives, like Frank Murphy and William O. Douglas, who shared Black's zeal for the New Deal. The typical appointee would, like Black, be several years younger than William Howard Taft's representative choice. Only once would FDR pick a man with prior experience in the federal judiciary; indeed, Black was exceptional in that, except for Wiley Rutledge, the former police court magistrate was the only Roosevelt appointee who had ever served as a judge prior to joining the Court.

Black's appointment turned out to be only the first of many for the President. Roosevelt, who was unable to designate anyone for the Supreme Court in his first term, named eight Justices, including the Chief Justice, in the six years from 1937 to 1943. So rapidly did the composition of the Court change under Roosevelt and Truman that by the late 1940s Black, whose tenure seemed so precarious in 1937, was the senior member. Black remained on the bench through the thirties, forties, fifties, sixties and into the seventies, and would fall only months short of establishing a new record for length of service as a Justice.

The Black controversy is rich in paradox and irony—a former Klansman becoming one of the century's leading exponents of civil liberties, a Justice chosen for one set of reasons winning fame for accomplishments that had hardly been anticipated, an Alabaman who created alarm among Negro groups when he was nominated but who lived to be denounced as a foe of the white South—but not least of the many ironies is the fact that the President's bitterly fought campaign to rejuvenate the Court by terminating tenure at the age of seventy would end in his naming, as his first appointment, a man who would still be on the bench on his eighty-fifth birthday and whose lengthy and brilliant career would be seen as a testament to Roosevelt's perspicacity.

II

Germany's Declaration of War on the United States: A New Look

GERHARD L. WEINBERG

• The United States officially entered World War II on December 8, 1941, when President Franklin D. Roosevelt asked Congress for a declaration of war against the empire of Japan. Americans were enraged by the "sneak attack" on Pearl Harbor the previous day and were determined to gain revenge against anybody and anything Japanese.

The United States did not then declare war against Germany, which at that time was engaged in a titanic land struggle against the Soviet Union in the east and a lesser contest with Great Britain in North Africa. American planners, President Roosevelt included, realized that Germany was a far more serious threat than either Japan or Italy, but the anger of Americans was aimed at the "Rising Sun." For most people in the United States, Germany was not the major concern.

Inexplicably, Adolf Hitler took the initiative and declared war on the United States on December 11. Why? The German army was generally regarded as the best-trained, best-led, and the most formidable fighting force in the world, and the German people had a reputation for efficiency, industriousness, and technological proficiency. But Germany was a relatively small nation, and it was already engaged in a two-front war. What could have been the advantage in adding the

AUTHOR'S NOTE: The author's work on this topic has been assisted by the National Endowment for the Humanities and the Bellagio Study and Conference Center of the Rockefeller Foundation.

United States and its vast industrial potential to the list of opponents? In the following essay, Gerhard L. Weinberg offers a fresh perspective on one of the vital decisions of the twentieth century.

The German government's decision to declare war on the United States in December 1941 has puzzled some historians. The decision was made by Hitler personally, but anticipated as likely by German Foreign Minister Joachim von Ribbentrop, greeted with relief—even joy—by the German navy, and so far as is known, *not* advised against by a single figure in the German government. It is thus unique among German decisions to start or dramatically to expand the war. This unusual unanimity on a decision many have often seen as suicidal, or at least stupid, offers room for a reexamination. This reexamination will focus on the perceptions of those who made or knew of the choices on peace and war, perceptions into which war with the United States fitted considerably more easily than the literature on the subject might otherwise lead one to expect.

Hitler himself had begun with an image of a strong United States, an image drawn from the supposed racial advantages of selective immigration and the economic potential of a huge domestic market. Under the impact of the depression, Hitler had reassessed the racial development of America. He combined the resulting negative view of a racial melting pot—in which the scum naturally floated to the top—with his antipathy for cultural influences emanating from the United States—reflected in the developments of Weimar Germany he most detested—into a view of the United States that was to remain constant until his suicide. This view of the United States saw potential strength, and therefore danger, and actual weakness and disarray. The industrial potential of a large country might some day threaten Germany's effort at world domination, but the country's internal divisions and incompetent leadership assured German triumph. In the long run, Germany would have to fight the United States, and it was therefore necessary to make an early start on appropriate measures in the field of naval construction, since these required the longest lead-time for completion. Yet, there was no need for great concern in the interim because the weakness of the disarmed and depressed United States precluded any serious American steps that might interfere with Germany's initial foreign policy adventures.

In the years before the war, therefore, Hitler moved with little interest in, or concern for, American reactions; except for Fritz Wiedemann, his military adjutant, no one in the higher levels of the German government suggested otherwise to him. As Hans Luther had been elegantly removed from the presidency of the Reichsbank in 1933 by being shipped off to the insignificant post of ambassador to the United States, so Wiedemann was exiled to the even less significant—if more scenic—San Francisco. Some cautionary dispatches from the German embassy in Washington were easily waved aside. When the German military attaché to the United States had an opportunity to talk with Hitler in February 1939, the only subject which interested the Führer was the discovery of an alleged Jewish ancestor of Roosevelt about whom the German government was to launch a great propaganda campaign. The contemptuous dismissal of FDR's peace appeal of April 14, 1939, reflects in both tone and substance the assumption that nothing the United States was likely to do could have a major impact on German plans, which already included war that year.

The neutrality policy of the United States undoubtedly reinforced Berlin's picture of America. Convinced that entry into World War I had been a terrible mistake, the United States had adopted a policy designed to remove what were perceived to be the causes of that error. The legislation prohibiting the sale of weapons to belligerents reinforced Germany's head start in rearmament as Berlin—like London and Paris—well knew, and also deterred the use of foreign orders to rebuild American defense industry. President Roosevelt's attempt to aid the rebuilding of the French air force crashed quite literally in an incident on January 23, 1939; the administration's hopes for revision of the neutrality law failed in a Congress determined to stay out of Kaiser Willie's war. The German government ignored the last-minute peace appeals of President Roosevelt and responded to his call for conducting air warfare humanely by dropping a bomb in the garden of the villa that Ambassador Francis Biddle had rented as a refuge for the secretaries of the United States legation in Warsaw.

Hitler had hoped to keep his eastern front quiet by the subordination of Poland and Hungary during a war against England and France as the necessary preliminary to the later conquest of European Russia. The refusal of Poland to yield her independence had led him to reverse the sequence. He hoped for war against an isolated Poland but willingly risked a war with France and England since such a war was next on his program in any case. Hence, the entrance of the Western powers into the conflict in September 1939 led to only minor readjustments in German policies. A massive program for the construction of the two-engined Ju-88 dive-bomber would make possible a "deadly blow" at England after an invasion of the Low Countries had enabled the German army to crush France. How did the German government perceive the role of the United States during this stage of the conflict?

The United States was a neutral, and it appeared inclined to provide some help to Germany's enemies. Neutrality merely confirmed Hitler's negative assessment of the United States. In his second book he had set forth at considerable length a view that he appears to have adhered to thereafter: neutrality was the policy of the weak, the stupid, and the indecisive; nations with clear purpose and farsighted leadership took advantage of wars started elsewhere either by participating or by starting other wars of their own. A country led less brilliantly might demonstrate at least a modicum of good sense by assisting one side or the other in return for appropriate concessions, and all who were so inclined were invited to do just that for Germany. Both the Soviet Union and Spain could provide secret bases for German naval warfare. Sweden and Japan could provide critically needed raw materials. Any others willing to join the charmed circle of those benevolently neutral to Germany and malevolently neutral to her enemies could be confident of Berlin's very temporary good will. There would even be reciprocity, with Germany prepared to assist the Soviet Union in its blockade of Finland just as the Russians would assist the Germans in their attack on Narvik. From time to time, the German government expatiated on the legal aspects of neutrality, but such rules were always assumed to be binding only on those neutrals outside the charmed circle.

As for American inclination to assist Germany's enemies in the war, the German government naturally thought this as evil as it held Soviet aid to itself wise. Hitler hoped to keep his future war with the United States separate from his current one with Poland and the

Western powers; hence he would not heed the leaders of the German navy, advisors prepared to risk war with the United States in 1939 and urging steps in that direction ever more insistently thereafter. Since World War II was to see a rerun of sorts of the World War I German internal dispute over unrestricted submarine warfare, a word needs to be said about this issue as seen by the German navy and by Hitler when it first came up in the fall of 1939.

The German naval leadership thought the war against England had begun too early. Their own naval construction program was not far enough advanced—the construction programs of others were generally ignored in these calculations. Accordingly, Germany must make the most of whatever she did have. With England perceived as the main enemy, the navy, since 1918, had seen Britain's transatlantic shipping as the main target of German arms. The very inadequacy of the available means at sea seemed to make it all the more important to use the surface ships and submarines Germany did have without restrictions and cautions. Whatever floated—wherever it was bound— should be sent to the bottom as quickly as possible. All else ought to be subordinated to this concept since Germany had no possible alternative strategy for victory over its major foe. This view, eloquently and continuously advanced by Admiral Erich Raeder, was occasionally countered by former Ambassador Hans Dieckhoff, but on the whole met *no* objections from *other* German military and diplomatic figures at the highest levels of the Third Reich.

Hitler himself, however, was by no means certain that the portion of the navy's program likely to bring the United States into the war was, at this early stage of the war, either necessary or wise. Why alarm the United States and stimulate it toward rearmament if a slow tightening of the naval blockade of England would accomplish most of what Germany's small fleet could do anyway? Japan was still an uncertain quantity; having been affronted by the German pact with Russia, it might relieve the United States of worry in the Pacific and enable America to concentrate on the Atlantic. If Japan and Russia could be reconciled, this might change; in the meantime, why take steps that would alarm American opinion and strengthen Roosevelt's hand at home, yet lead to only a minimal increment in sinkings? So each time Raeder requested new measures in the naval war, Hitler allowed some but not all of what had been asked. And as long as the war simmered quietly in the winter of 1933–40, this procedure appeared to serve Germany's purposes.

Hitler, of course, did not intend that the war simmer quietly forever. The longer an offensive in the West was postponed, the more time his enemies would have to perfect their armaments. Eventually they might even draw on the productive capacity of the United States. The sooner Germany moved, the better; only bad weather forced repeated postponements of the attack from November 1939 to May 1940.

At first, that attack appeared to accomplish its purpose. France was crushed; Britain was driven off the Continent; the new air and naval bases acquired on the coast facing England and the Atlantic seemed to guarantee Britain's defeat. Slow thinkers that they were, the English might take a few weeks to recognize the new reality, but in the meantime Germany could look ahead to the campaigns that would *follow* England's acceptance of the German victory. In the plans and projects of June and July 1940 for the direction of German efforts *after* the end of war in Western Europe, we can see more precisely how Hitler and his immediate advisors intended to handle German policy toward the United States.

Once again the critical element would be time. The outbreak of general as opposed to local war in September 1939 had forced a halt on those construction projects of the German navy that looked to a great blue-water fleet. Work had been stopped on all battleships scheduled beyond the *Tirpitz* as well as on the whole aircraft carrier program. With France and England defeated, those time- and materiel-consuming projects could be resumed. It seems to me a key indication of German plans that the immediate deduction from the assumption of victory in the West was a plan to reduce the German army combined with return to a huge program of battleship construction. No doubt a school of revisionist historians will seek to prove that this was only Hitler's way of coping with the threat Liechtenstein posed for the Third Reich, but it is more likely that Hitler and his advisors were looking not up the Rhine but across the Atlantic.

This interpretation is supported by the simultaneous development of plans for the bases at which the huge new fleet would be stationed, serviced, and if necessary, repaired. To the previously projected great new base at Trondheim on the Norwegian coast were now added not only bases on the northern and western coasts of France but also a whole string of bases on and off the coast of northwest Africa. A noteworthy sign of the priority which Hitler and his naval advisors placed on these bases is their readiness—when he was confident of victory in Western Europe—to sacrifice to this concept the participation of Spain in the war on Germany's side. So long as he was sure that England was beaten, he did not need Spain; what he did need was bases in French and Spanish Morocco and on the Spanish islands off the African coast for the fleet required by his future policy toward the Western Hemisphere.

All these glorious prospects suffered sharp modification as the war Hitler thought to be over failed to end. British determination to continue the war puzzled and angered him. The anger could be relieved by ordering devastating air raids and gearing up for an invasion of the United Kingdom. The puzzle of England's continued fighting bothered him for some weeks and greatly influenced the decision of late July 1940 to attack the Soviet Union.

War with the United States formed part of Hitler's long-term conception of Germany's role in the world; war with the Soviet Union had always been a part of his plan for expanding Germany's living space eastward. Timing and circumstance had been left open questions, and if the timing of the decision to attack Russia is no longer in serious dispute, the circumstances are surely worth noting. In the contemporary situation, invading Russia and conquering most or all of its European territory looked easier to Hitler and most of his military advisors than invading England. If the Russian operation was to occur sooner or later, this looked like a particularly auspicious moment. If launched immediately—and we must recall that Hitler originally hoped to strike in the fall of 1940—the attack would offer great incidental benefits for the war against England. With the loss of its major Continental ally, England must be fighting on in the expectation of substitutes for France, and for such a role the Soviet Union and the United States were the obvious candidates. An attack on the Soviet Union—and its removal as a hope for Britain—was not only easier than an attack on the United States, given the readier accessibility of Russia to German military power, but Germany's anticipated success against the Soviet Union would have the further effect of immobilizing the United States as a possible supporter of England. Destruction of Soviet military power would free Japan to move forward in Southeast Asia, and thereby pull the attention, energy, and resources of the United States away from the Atlantic and leave Britain without hope of support from anywhere.

To be sure, the decision to attack Russia meant another change in German armaments policy. Now the army had to be made bigger, not smaller. Plans for super-battleships had to go back into the files, but submarines could be built quickly to cope with the English. The Americans would first be diverted to the Pacific by an unleashed Japan and their subsequent fate postponed until the release of German resources *after* the quick defeat of Russia allowed a return to naval adventures.

The apparently necessary postponement of an attack on Russia until the spring of 1941 meant that a slow but steady increase in American aid to Britain ran parallel to the equally steady increase of Soviet shipments of supplies to Germany. Berlin frowned on the one as it smiled on the other; it was not easy, however, to decide what to do other than frown. Various German efforts to influence American opinion during and after the 1940 election proved ineffective. Hope that the Tripartite Pact with Japan might spur Tokyo to a more adventurous course was only partially realized; the United States was alerted rather than deterred by this more formal association of Berlin and Tokyo. The German navy as usual had its answer at hand—sink anything that floated. Hitler still favored limited increments in naval action: increments to reduce the flow of supplies to England, but limits in order to postpone a clash with the United States at a time when the German armaments effort had just had to be directed toward a major increase in land power at the expense of the massive naval program needed to cope with the United States. A study of the effects of a German surprise attack by U-boats on the American navy in port which Hitler had ordered—a sort of underwater Pearl Harbor—was not sufficiently encouraging; and his projects for seizing the Azores and other islands in the Atlantic to use as bases for bombers to attack American cities were far short of realization. In the interim, that is, until Germany could turn her military power directly against the United States, the indirect approach would have to do.

Even before the German attack on Russia opened the road south for Japan, therefore, the Germans tried very hard to encourage the Japanese to move in that direction. The German navy in particular was concerned about Tokyo's delays and constantly urged an attack on Singapore. Raeder's advice to Hitler that Japanese Foreign Minister Matsuoka Yosuke be told of the forthcoming attack on Russia during his visit to Germany in March and April 1941 belongs in this context: if the Japanese knew that the Soviet Union would soon be attacked by Germany, they would be less reluctant to move in the direction Germany wanted, against Singapore. Hitler shared Raeder's hope, but he would not share his own secret: though giving priority to a Japanese attack against England, he reassured Matsuoka about any complications with the United States. If a Japanese move in Southeast Asia, or anywhere else, did lead to war with America, Germany would side with Japan. Whatever his preference for postponing war with the United States, Hitler was quite willing to take part in such a war earlier if that was what was needed to involve Japan in war against England. Hitler never read the Tripartite Pact as narrowly as some of its postwar American interpreters. Quite the contrary, having tried to turn the Japanese against the Western powers since 1938, he was happy to give the pact the broadest and most aggressive interpretation.

The Japanese government as a whole did not share the German hurry. Its assessment of the risks induced greater caution among at least some elements in Tokyo. Even the nonaggression pact with Russia that Matsuoka signed on his return trip failed to remove all the worries in the Japanese capital. An attack on the exposed colonial possessions of France, Great Britain, and the Netherlands in Southeast Asia looked so inviting as to be almost irresistible, but what about the United States? Guam, tiny, undefended, and indefensible, could be ignored, but the Philippines could not. The Americans were to leave in 1946, and it is hardly a coincidence that, during 1941, the Japanese repeatedly cited that year to the Germans as the one in which they would be ready to move. Even without the Germans' pointing it out to them, however, the Japanese knew perfectly well that by then the European war was likely to be over, and that, whatever the outcome, the United States would be able to devote full attention to Southeast Asia. If Germany won, would it allow Japan to reap the colonial harvest made available by the exertions of German might? If Germany lost, would not the owners of the lands Japan coveted recover their strength? If there were a compromise peace, could Japan risk starting a new war? Surely the time to move—if ever—was now.

These puzzles, and the internal rifts over alternative policies in Tokyo, led to the long exploration of a possible accommodation between Japan and the United States. The aspect of the Japanese-American negotiations of 1941 which needs to be examined here is the relationship of the negotiations to Germany's policy toward the two powers, one a half-ally, the other a half-enemy. The Germans observed the talks with extreme anxiety. Unlike the Americans, they could not read the main Japanese diplomatic code; by this time, they were having much less luck than earlier with the American codes, and the Japanese told them very little. German suspicions were quickly, and not unjustifiably, aroused. Twice before, in the summer of 1938 and in the winter of 1938–39, the Germans had failed to secure a firm Japanese commitment against the Western powers. Now that the Germans were at war, they were not getting from Japan the sort of economic or naval aid they wanted—a particularly galling situation when Berlin compared what Japan was doing for its Tripartite Pact partner with what America was doing for Britain. And now it looked as if the Japanese might reach a real accommodation with the United States which would have the double effect of lessening the chances of a Japanese attack on Britain and relieving American concern in the Pacific. The obverse of an unleashed Japan's drawing the United States into the Pacific was obviously a quiescent Japan's allowing the United States to increase its support of Britain in the Atlantic.

The Germans' anxiety was raised to a very high level by almost simultaneous developments during May 1941. On the one hand, there appeared to be a real chance of progress in the United States–Japanese negotiations. The Japanese refusal at one point to oblige the Germans by waiting a few days for German comment on a new proposal in early May led the German authorities to suspect the worst. In repeated conferences, Hitler and von Ribbentrop reviewed the situation. But they could only wave frantically from the sidelines, warning Japan of American perfidy and emphasizing the golden opportunity of the moment. Soon after, the sinking of the *Bismarck* struck a major blow at German hopes in the Battle of the Atlantic. The approaching deadline for the attack on Russia reinforced Hitler's concern about the defense of Norway and combined with British bombing of Brest to produce his decision to station the remaining large German surface ships in Norwegian waters. Although this resolve was not finally implemented by a reluctant navy until February 1942, Hitler's thinking, as Raeder well knew, had long been moving in this direction. Combined with other naval losses and the sinking of the *Bismarck*, this trend effectively dashed all remaining hopes for a resumption of surface raiding by German fleet units in the Atlantic. The obvious deduction was that the increasing stream of American supplies to England should be cut by submarines.

Believing that the United States was doing as much as it could under any circumstances, the naval leaders saw little sense in avoiding formal American entrance into the war. Although Hitler shared the assessment of America's limited potential in spite of contrary advice from former Ambassador Dieckhoff, he still preferred to postpone formal American participation. A quick triumph over Russia might, as he had calculated originally, end the war for the time being—thus giving him time to build a real surface navy—by depriving England of all its potential allies. With Russia eliminated, the Japanese would surely keep America preoccupied, and in any case, until 1942 the United States would not be able to do much. The days just before and after the invasion of Russia were therefore a time to avoid incidents in the Atlantic.

The first weeks of the attack on Russia gave many leaders of the Third Reich the impression that the campaign would soon be over. Accordingly they promptly began to plan for the period *after* victory in the East had been achieved. Some of these plans were extensions of the eastern campaign itself; for example, the expansion of the program to murder the Jews of occupied Russia to include those of all Europe, and the projects for using the newly occupied areas as bases for an assault on the British position in the Near East. Our interest must focus on the project pointing in the opposite direction. In the late summer of 1940 the projected blue-water fleet had been pushed aside by the higher immediate priority of the planned campaign against Russia. In July 1941, however, as in June and July 1940, German "postwar planning" once again included a huge surface fleet. Projected at 25 battleships, 8 aircraft carriers, 50 cruisers, 400 submarines, 150 destroyers, and miscellaneous other ships, it provides important insight into German long-term aims in the Western Hemisphere—unless you are prepared to assume that the big ships were to be sent down the Danube or hauled by rail to the Caspian Sea.

As the fighting in Russia continued, the program for murdering Jews went forward. The plan to attack the Near East had to be postponed a year, but the plan to reorder armaments priorities to favor the navy once again evaporated. For a moment, it seemed that, as a substitute, Japan might be lured into the war by the back door of having her join in crushing Russia, but that project was soon abandoned, at least by Hitler. American aid to Russia as well as Britain, however, suggested other views: how much more than helping England and Russia could America do? If very little, why spare her ships and shipping lanes?

On the other side of the globe, the Japanese were now relieved of the danger they felt at their own back door. Japan's main concern now was what it saw, quite correctly, as a British-American strategy of stalling for time in East Asia while defeating Germany and then confronting Japan with overwhelming power in the Pacific. Having had their own very sad experiences with the Red Army in 1938 and 1939, the Japanese expected the survival of the Soviet Union and the likelihood of a new German-Soviet accommodation rather than a collapse of Russia, so that the developments on the Eastern Front suggested to them that the time for Japan to move south might well be at hand. And this was certainly what they heard from the Germans.

When the Japanese decided to go forward, they did so on the assumption that Germany and Italy would be their allies while the Soviet Union would remain neutral. Their own attack would be directed against the United States and Great Britain, and they certainly wanted those countries denied bases in the Soviet Far East, a subject on which they appear to have sounded the Russians beforehand. Their question to Berlin and Rome—whether those countries would join them in war on the United States—was put with the thought that should their Tripartite Pact partners respond with a request for a declaration of war on Russia, Japan would decline. What would be the answer from Berlin?

When the Japanese ambassador to Germany raised this question with von Ribbentrop on November 30, 1941, Hitler was preoccupied with the crisis on the Eastern Front. Von Ribbentrop said that Germany would immediately join in the war with America—he had said about the same thing spontaneously a few days earlier—but he would need Hitler's official approval to make the statement authoritative. Surely von Ribbentrop had discussed the matter with Hitler earlier and was confident he was accurately reflecting his master's views, for we know he had heard Hitler express them to Matsuoka. Hitler's views had indeed remained unchanged, and von Ribbentrop could reassure Hiroshi Oshima on the point early on December 5. The Germans believed Japanese-American relations to be at the breaking point, but we must remember that they did not know Japan intended to strike in a few days—any more than they had known when they gave similar assurances in April that Tokyo would wait for several months.

Why was Hitler, who had been trying to avoid incidents in the Atlantic, willing to go to war now? A series of reasons emerges from his previous policies. With Great Britain still perceived as a key, if not the key, enemy of Germany, if this were what it took to get Japan to move against that country, so be it. Especially if the alternative might be a *modus vivendi* between Japan and United States which would release America from concern in the Pacific and enable it to concentrate on the Atlantic. The alternative of war with the United States, rather than confronting Germany with greater difficulty in the Atlantic, offered the hope—daily stressed by naval leaders —of massive successes by German U-boats in that very theater. Hitler was convinced that Germany had lost World War I because of the "stab-in-the-back" by a home front beguiled by the promises of President Wilson; he was certain that would not be repeated; the German people would never fall for such tricks again, and any so inclined would be crushed if still at large. Since Hitler did not believe that American military might, as opposed to its propaganda, had played any significant part in the Entente's victory over Germany, he saw no reason to fear such might now, or at least during the coming war when he anticipated major victories on the Eastern Front. If he must ultimately fight the United States anyway—as he had believed for years and as he had so often tried to factor into his armaments program—then this, if not the ideal moment, was surely an acceptable time. In 1939 he had made the same calculation in regard to England; though preferring to postpone war in the West and to deal only with Poland, he had accepted the likelihood of war with England then rather than later. Now an analogous choice vis-à-vis the United States was before him, not with an Italy dithering on the sidelines but a Japan prepared to commit herself against Britain and the United States first. The earlier premium on delay was now much smaller.

Since the Japanese were as careful not to reveal their plans to the Germans as the latter had been to conceal their own, the attack on Pearl Harbor came as a most pleasant surprise for Berlin. The idea of a Sunday morning attack in peacetime had been tried out by the Germans themselves on Belgrade earlier that year, and the Japanese imitation evoked nothing but applause. As for the immediate Japanese question about Germany's participation, that would be answered in the affirmative. Again Hitler had to be asked formally, and since he happened to be away from his regular headquarters to deal with a crisis in command and strategy at the southern end of the Eastern Front, there was a short delay in securing an answer; but all speculations about this delay are based on overlooking the practical problems of getting a decision from Hitler at that moment. Hitler himself had no hesitation. His positive views as expressed a few days earlier in response to Oshima's question could only be reinforced by what had happened in the meantime. Here was an ally who obviously knew his business, and the sooner all joined together, the better.

Unlike previous occasions when Germany had taken full initiative, this time the formal arrangements had to be made after action taken by others elsewhere. A few days were needed to set up the propaganda scenery in Berlin. Hitler had to get back to the capital; the Reichstag deputies had to be summoned from all over to acclaim the happy news of war with the United States. December 11 was the earliest practical day for this martial celebration, but to Hitler that did not seem any reason to postpone fighting the Americans. That could start forthwith. In the night of December 8–9, therefore, he gave the German navy orders to proceed at once with sinking American vessels as well as the ships of all those countries that had declared their solidarity with the United States. No one then knew that David Irving would one day prescribe retroactively how Hitler was supposed to give orders, so no one questioned the Führer's oral directives. Long straining at the leash, the German navy could now pounce upon its prey in the Atlantic. The ceremonies of December 11 confirmed rather than initiated the state of war between Germany and the United States.

There is a final question to be dealt with. Why did not the German leaders ask Japan to go to war with Russia when the Japanese asked the Germans to join them in fighting the United States? This looks like an obvious question, given the troubles the Germans were then having in the East. Hitler saw the issue differently. He knew that Japan's power was not unlimited. Tied up in a long war in China, Japan could not be expected to make a major contribution to fighting Great Britain—his major concern—to take on the United States and divert the full attention of that power to the Pacific and also became embroiled in another land war in Asia. Had Germany wanted Japan to attack Russia, what had been the point of urging her to employ her resources in an attack on Singapore? Only in the summer of 1941, when it looked as if there might be a Japanese-American agreement, had Hitler asked for a Japanese attack on Russia as a back door through which to get the ever-hesitating ally into the fray. Now, with Japan willing to move on its own, it was hardly time to raise questions that might lead Tokyo to a total reconsideration of the issue. If the Japanese believed they could attack Great Britain only if they also went to war with the United States, then Germany should make this decision as easy, not as difficult as possible. For years, the Japanese had demonstrated to the Germans that they were all too inclined to delay decisions, and Hitler had no desire to stimulate *that* tendency. On the contrary, a prompt and positive response from Berlin might at last assist those in Japan who favored war. Certainly there was no point in assisting the Tokyo peace faction—if any remained—by qualified answers or additional questions. Especially if you expected to beat the Russians next year, thought little of the war-making capabilities of the United States, and expected to fight that power one day. Like the policy makers in Washington, those in Germany in December as in April 1941 were looking primarily at the expected Japanese move south. With Japan apparently poised on the brink, at last ready to join Germany in a war against Great Britain, Germany ought to provide a quick shove, not a new puzzle.

Few Germans were in any position to bring their views on this matter to the attention of the dictator. Unlike all other major policy choices of the regime, however, this was one on which there appear to have been no dissents, oral or written. Only rarely during the escalation of incidents in the Atlantic, never during the attempt to involve Japan in war with Great Britain, and certainly not in the final crisis did anyone among Hitler's political, diplomatic, or military leaders advocate a more cautious approach. Many had, at one point or another, argued against earlier measures to expand the war. Only this one time was the unanimity of the Reichstag mirrored in the apparatus of government. Hope or resignation, stupidity or wilful ignorance elsewhere, for once enabled the Führer to follow his intuition without contrary advice. There is a curious irony in a situation where the leaders of a country were united on war with the one nation they were least likely and worst equipped to defeat.

12

The Detroit Race Riot of 1943

HARVARD SITKOFF

• *Of all the sources of civil disorder in American history, none has been more persistent than race relationships. Whether in the North or South, whether before or after the Civil War, whether in city or small town, this question has been at the root of more physical violence than any other. But because most forms of prejudice were more blatant and more virulent in the South than in the North, blacks sought for generations to cross the Mason-Dixon Line in search of a new land of equality and opportunity. Unfortunately, the big cities of the East and Middle West provided a fresh set of problems, and the continuing migration away from farm tenancy and share-cropping did not immediately improve the quality of Afro-American life. The pattern of the ghetto—residential segregation, underemployment, substandard housing, disrupted family life, inferior education, filth, and disease—was set even before 1920. Neither was violence left behind in the land of the plantation. In the "red summer of 1919," white-black rioting claimed more than one hundred lives and demonstrated again that the most striking feature of black life was not the existence of slum conditions, but the barriers to residential and occupational mobility.*

Following closely upon earlier conflicts in Mobile, Los Angeles, and Beaumont, the Detroit riot of 1943 illustrates the range of racial disorders that broke out sporadically during World War II. The Negro population of the city had risen sharply from 40,000 to 120,000 in the single decade between 1920 and 1930, and had jumped again by 50,000 in the fifteen months before the riot. Sparked by scattered gang fighting on a hot summer day, the riot ended by taking thirty-four lives. It was particularly notable for its ferocity and duration and for the fact that it began on a recreational spot—Belle Isle—

Permission to reprint Harvard Sitkoff, "The Detroit Race Riot of 1943," from *Michigan History* (Fall 1969) was granted by the Michigan History Division, Lansing, Michigan.

that had previously been used by both races. Professor Harvard Sitkoff's article recreates that tragic event and urges us to question whether the United States has moved very far along the path of racial justice in the last third of a century.

For the American Negro, World War II began a quarter of a century of increasing hope and frustration. After a long decade of depression, the war promised a better deal. Negroes confidently expected a crusade against Nazi racism and for the Four Freedoms, a battle requiring the loyalty and manpower of all Americans, to be the turning point for their race. This war would be "Civil War II," a "Double V" campaign. No Negro leader urged his people to suspend grievances until victory was won, as most did during World War I. Rather, the government's need for full cooperation from the total population, the ideological character of the war, the constant preaching to square American practices with the American Creed, and the beginning of the end of the era of white supremacy in the world intensified Negro demands for equality *now*.

Never before in American history had Negroes been so united and militant. Led by the *Baltimore Afro-American, Chicago Defender, Pittsburgh Courier,* and Adam Clayton Powell's *People's Voice* ("The New Paper for the New Negro"), the Negro press urged civil rights leaders to be more aggressive. It publicized protest movements, headlined atrocity stories of lynched and assaulted Negroes, and developed race solidarity. Every major civil rights organization subscribed to the "Double V" campaign, demanding an end to discrimination in industry and the armed forces. The National Association for the Advancement of Colored People, National Urban League, National Negro Congress, A. Philip Randolph's March-on-Washington Movement, and the newly organized Congress of Racial Equality joined with Negro professional and fraternal organizations, labor unions, and church leaders to insist on "Democracy in Our Time!" These groups organized rallies, formed committees, supported letter and telegram mail-ins, began picketing and boycotting, and threatened unruly demonstrations. This as well as collaboration with sympathetic whites helped exert pressure on government officials.

The combined effects of exhortation and organization made the Negro man-in-the-street increasingly militant. After years of futility, there was now bitter hope. As he slowly gained economic and political power, won victories in the courts, heard his aspirations legitimized by respected whites, and identified his cause with the two-thirds of the world's colored people, the Negro became more impatient with any impediment to first-class citizenship and more determined to assert his new status. Each gain increased his expectations; each improvement in the conditions of whites increased his dissatisfaction. Still forced to fight in a segregated army supplied by a Jim Crow industrial force, still denied his basic rights in the South and imprisoned in rat-and-vermin-infested ghettos in the North, he rejected all pleas to "go slow." At the same time many whites renewed their efforts to keep the Negro in an inferior economic and social position regardless of the changes wrought by the war. Frightened by his new militancy and wartime gains, resenting his competition for jobs, housing, and power, whites sought to retain their cherished status and keep "the nigger in his place." The more Negroes demanded their due, the more white re-sistance stiffened.

American engagement in a world war, as well as the lack of govern-ment action to relieve racial anxiety or even enforce "neutral" police control, made it likely that racial antagonism would erupt into vio-lence. President Roosevelt, preoccupied with international diplomacy and military strategy, and still dependent on Southern support in Congress, ignored the deteriorating domestic situation. Participation in the war increased the prestige of violence and its use as an effective way to accomplish specific aims. The psychological effects of war, the new strains and uncertainty, multiplied hatred and insecurity. Many petty irritations—the rationing, shortages, overcrowding, and high prices—engendered short tempers; the fatigue of long work weeks, little opportunity for recreation, the anxious scanning of casualty lists, the new job and strange city, and the need for the noncombatant to prove his masculinity led to heightened tension and the desire to express it violently.

For three years public officials throughout the nation watched the growth of racial strife. Fights between Negroes and whites became a daily occurrence on public vehicles. Nearly every issue of the Negro press reported clashes between Negro soldiers and white military or civilian police. At least seventeen Negroes were lynched between 1940 and 1943. The accumulation of agitation and violence then burst into an epidemic of race riots in June, 1943. Racial gang fights, or "zoot-suit riots," broke out in several non-Southern cities. The worst of these hit Los Angeles. While the city fathers wrung their hands, white sailors and their civilian allies attacked scores of Negroes and Mexican-Americans. The only action taken by the Los Angeles City Council was to declare the wearing of a zoot suit a misdemeanor. In mid-June, a rumor of rape touched off a twenty-hour riot in Beaumont, Texas. White mobs burned and pillaged the Negro ghetto. War production stopped, businesses closed, thousands of dollars of property were damaged, two persons were killed, and more than seventy were injured. In Mobile, the attempt to upgrade some Negro workers as welders in the yards of the Alabama Dry Dock and Shipbuilders Company caused twenty thousand white workers to walk off their jobs and riot for four days. Only the intervention of federal troops stopped the riot. The President's Committee on Fair Employment Practices then backed down and agreed to let segregation continue in the shipyards.

Nowhere was trouble more expected than in Detroit. In the three years after 1940, more than fifty thousand Southern Negroes and half a million Southern whites migrated to the "Arsenal of Democracy" seeking employment. Negroes were forced to crowd into the already teeming thirty-block ghetto of Paradise Valley and some fifty registered "neighborhood improvement associations" and the Detroit Housing Commission kept them confined there. Although ten percent of the population, Negroes comprised less than 1 percent of the city teachers and police. Over half the workers on relief in 1942 were Negro, and most of those with jobs did menial work. Only three percent of the women employed in defense work were Negro, and these were mainly in custodial positions. The Negro demand for adequate housing, jobs, recreation, and transportation facilities, and the white refusal to give anything up, led to violence. Early in 1942, over a thousand whites armed with clubs, knives, and rifles rioted to stop Negroes from moving into the Sojourner Truth Housing Project. Fiery crosses burned throughout the city. More than a thousand state troopers had to escort two hundred Negro families into the project. Federal investigators warned Washington officials of that city's inability to keep racial peace, and the Office of Facts and Figures warned that "unless strong and quick intervention by some high official, preferably the President, is . . . taken at once, hell is going to be let loose." Nothing was done in Detroit or Washington. Throughout that year Negro and white students clashed in the city's high schools, and the number of outbreaks in factories multiplied.

In 1943, racial violence in Detroit increased in frequency and boldness. The forced close mingling of Negroes with Southern whites on buses and trolleys, crowded with nearly forty percent more passengers than at the start of the war, led to fights and stabbings. White soldiers battled Negroes in suburban Inkster. In April, a racial brawl in a city playground involved more than a hundred teenagers. Early in June, twenty-five thousand Packard employees struck in protest against the upgrading of three Negro workers. More than five hundred Negroes and whites fought at parks in different parts of the city. Negro leaders openly predicted greater violence unless something was done quickly to provide jobs and housing. Walter White of the NAACP told a packed rally in Cadillac Square: "Let us drag out into the open what has been whispered throughout Detroit for months—that a race riot may break out here at any time." Detroit newspaper and national magazines described the city as "a keg of powder with a short fuse." But no one in the city, state, or federal government dared to act. Everyone watched and waited. When the riot exploded, Mayor Edward Jeffries told reporters: "I was taken by surprise only by the day it happened."

The riot began, like those in 1919, with direct clashes between groups of Negroes and whites. Over 100,000 Detroiters crowded onto Belle Isle on Sunday, June 20, 1943, to seek relief from the hot, humid city streets. The temperature was over ninety. Long lines of Negroes and whites pushed and jostled to get into the bath house, rent canoes, and buy refreshments. Police continuously received reports of minor fights. Charles (Little Willie) Lyon, who had been attacked a few days earlier for trying to enter the all-white Eastwood Amusement Park, gathered a group of Negro teenagers to "take care of the Hunkies." They broke up picnics, forced whites to leave the park, beat up some boys, and started a melee on the bridge connecting Belle Isle with the city. Brawls broke out at the park's casino, ferry dock, playground, and bus stops. By evening rumors of a race riot swept the island. Sailors from a nearby armory, angered by a Negro assault on two sailors the previous day, hurried to the bridge to join the fray. Shortly after 11:00 P.M. more than five thousand people were fighting

on the bridge. By 2:00 A.M. the police had arrested twenty-eight Negroes and nineteen whites, quelling the melee without a single gunshot.

As the thousands of rioters and onlookers returned home, stories of
racial violence spread to every section of Detroit. In Paradise Valley,
Leo Tipton jumped on the stage of the Forrest Club, grabbed the
microphone and shouted: "There's a riot at Belle Isle! The whites
have killed a colored lady and her baby. Thrown them over a bridge.
Everybody come on! There's free transportation outside!" Hundreds
rushed out of the nightclub, only to find the bridge barricaded and all
traffic approaches to the Isle blocked. Sullen, the mob returned to the
ghetto, stoning passing white motorists, hurling rocks and bottles at
the police, and stopping streetcars to beat up unsuspecting whites.
The frustrations bottled up by the war burst. Negroes—tired of moving
to find the promised land, tired of finding the North too much like
the South, tired of being Jim-Crowed, scorned, despised, spat upon,
tired of being called "boy"—struck out in blind fury against the white-
owned ghetto. Unlike the riots of 1919, Negroes now began to destroy
the hated white property and symbols of authority. By early morning
every white-owned store window on Hastings Avenue in the ghetto
had been smashed. There was little looting at first, but the temptation
of an open store soon turned Paradise Valley into an open-air market:
liquor bottles, quarters of beef, and whole sides of bacon were freely
carried about, sold, and bartered.

As the police hesitatingly struggled to end the rioting in the ghetto,
rumors of white women being raped at Belle Isle enraged white crowds
forming along Woodward Avenue. Unhampered by the police, the
mobs attacked all Negroes caught outside the ghetto. They stopped,
overturned, and burned cars driven by Negroes. The mob dragged off
and beat Negroes in the all-night movies along the "strip" and those
riding trolleys. When a white instructor at Wayne University asked
the police to help a Negro caught by a white gang, they taunted him
as a "nigger lover." The police would do nothing to help. Throughout
the morning fresh rumors kept refueling the frenzy, and rioting grew.
The excitement of a car burning in the night, the screeching wail of
a police siren, plenty of free liquor, and a feeling of being free to do
whatever one wished without fear of police retaliation, all fed the
appetite of a riot-ready city.

At 4:00 A.M. Detroit Mayor Edward Jeffries met with the Police

Commissioner, the FBI, State Police, and Colonel August Krech, the highest-ranking Army officer stationed in Detroit. With hysteria growing, and the ability of the police to control violence diminishing, most of the meeting involved a discussion of the procedure to be used to obtain federal troops. They agreed that the Mayor should ask the Governor for troops; the Governor would telephone his request to General Henry Aurand, Commander of the Sixth Service in Chicago; and Aurand would call Krech in Detroit to order the troops into the city. Colonel Krech then alerted the 728th Military Police Battalion at River Rouge, and assured the Mayor that the military police would be patrolling Detroit within forty-nine minutes after receiving their orders. Nothing was done to check the plan for acquiring federal troops, and no mention was made of the need for martial law or a presidential proclamation.

When the meeting ended at 7:00 A.M. the Police Commissioner prematurely declared that the situation was now under control, and federal troops would not be needed. The opposite was true. Negro looting became widespread, and white mobs on Woodward Avenue swelled. Two hours later Negro leaders begged the Mayor to get federal troops to stop the riot. Jeffries refused, promising only to talk with them again at a noon meeting of the Detroit Citizens Committee. The Mayor would discuss neither the grievances of the Negro community nor how Negroes could help contain the destruction in the ghetto. A half hour later Jeffries changed his mind, telling those in his City Hall office that only federal troops could restore peace to Detroit.

Harry F. Kelly, the newly elected Republican Governor of Michigan, was enjoying his first session of the Conference of Governors in Ohio when shortly before 10:00 A.M. he was called to the telephone. Mayor Jeffries described the riot situation to the Governor, asserted that the city was out of control, and insisted that he needed more manpower. Kelly responded by ordering the Michigan state police and state troops on alert. An hour later he telephoned Sixth Service Command Headquarters in Chicago. Believing he had done all that was necessary to get federal troops into the city, Kelly hurriedly left for Detroit. But according to the Sixth Service Command, the Governor's call was only about a *possible* request for troops. Thus, the twelve-hour burlesque of deploying federal troops in Detroit began. The War Department and the White House flatly refused to take the initiative.

Army officials in Chicago and Washington kept passing the buck back and forth. And both Kelly and Jeffries feared doing anything that might indicate to the voters their inability to cope with the disorder.

After Kelly's call to Chicago, Aurand dispatched his director of internal security, Brigadier General William Guthner, to Detroit to command federal troops "in the event" the Governor formally requested them. Military police units surrounding Detroit were put on alert but forbidden to enter the city. In Washington the top brass remained busy with conferences on the use of the Army taking over mines in the threatened coal strike. No advice or instructions were given to Aurand. The Washington generals privately agreed that Aurand could send troops into Detroit without involving the President, or waiting for a formal request by the Governor, by acting on the principle of protecting defense production. But the War Department refused to give any orders to Aurand because it might "furnish him with a first class alibi if things go wrong."

While the generals and politicians fiddled, the riot raged. With most of the Detroit police cordoning off the ghetto, white mobs freely roamed the city attacking Negroes. At noon, three police cars escorted the Mayor into Paradise Valley to attend a Detroit Citizens Committee meeting. The interracial committee roundly denounced the Mayor for doing too little but could not agree on what should be done. Some argued for federal troops and others for Negro auxiliary police. Exasperated, Jeffries finally agreed to appoint two hundred Negro auxiliaries. But with no power and little cooperation from the police, the auxiliaries accomplished nothing. Rioters on the streets continued to do as they pleased. At 1:30 P.M. high schools were closed, and many students joined the riot.

Shortly after three, General Guthner arrived in Detroit to tell Kelly and Jeffries that federal martial law, which could only be proclaimed by the President, was necessary before federal troops could be called in. Dumbfounded by this new procedure, the Governor telephoned Aurand for an explanation. Aurand, more determined than ever to escape the responsibility for calling the troops, confirmed Guthner's statement. Despite Jeffries's frantic plea for more men, Kelly refused to ask for martial law: such a request would be taken as an admission of his failure.

Not knowing what else to do, after almost twenty hours of rioting,

Jeffries and Kelly made their first radio appeal to the people of Detroit. The Governor proclaimed a state of emergency, banning the sale of alcoholic beverages, closing amusement places, asking persons not going to or from work to stay home, prohibiting the carrying of weapons, and refusing permission for crowds to assemble. The proclamation cleared the way for the use of state troops but still did not comply with Aurand's prerequisites for the use of federal troops. Mayor Jeffries pleaded for an end to hysteria, arguing that only the Axis benefited from the strife in Detroit.

On the streets neither the proclamation nor the plea had any effect. Negro and white mobs continued their assaults and destruction. The weary police were barely able to restrain whites from entering Paradise Valley or to check the extent of Negro looting. Just as the Mayor finished pleading for sanity, four teen-agers shot an elderly Negro because they "didn't have anything to do." Tired of milling about, they agreed to "go out and kill us a nigger. . . . We didn't know him. He wasn't bothering us. But other people were fighting and killing and we felt like it too." As the city darkened, the violence increased. At 8:00 P.M. Jeffries called for the state troops. The Governor had ordered the force of two thousand mobilized earlier, but now the Mayor learned that only thirty-two men were available. At the same time the Mayor was informed that a direct clash between whites and Negroes was imminent. At Cadillac Square, the police were losing their struggle to hold back a white mob heading for the ghetto. Nineteen different police precincts reported riot activity. Seventy-five percent of the Detroit area was affected. Sixteen transportation lines had to suspend operation. The Detroit Fire Department could no longer control the more than one hundred fires. Detroiters entered Receiving Hospital at the rate of one every other minute.

In Washington, Lieutenant General Brehon Somervell, Commander of all Army Service Forces, directed the Army's Provost Marshal, Major General Allen Guillon, to prepare a Presidential Proclamation. At 8:00 P.M. Guillon and Somervell took the proclamation to the home of Secretary of War Henry Stimson. Sitting in the Secretary's library, the three men laid plans for the use of federal troops; as they discussed the situation they kept in telephone contact with the President at Hyde Park, the Governor in Detroit, and General Aurand in Chicago. Stimson instructed Aurand not to issue the text of the proclamation until the President signed it. Shortly after nine, Kelly telephoned Colonel Krech to request federal troops. At 9:20, the Governor repeated his appeal to General Aurand. Aurand immediately ordered the military police units into Detroit, although federal martial law had not been declared and the President had not signed the proclamation.

As the politicians and generals wrangled over the legality of Aurand's order, three hundred and fifty men of the 701st Military Police Battalion raced into Cadillac Square to disperse a white mob of over ten thousand. In full battle gear, bayonets fixed at high port, the federal troops swept the mob away from Woodward Avenue without firing a shot. The 701st then linked up with the 728th Battalion, which had been on the alert since 4:00 A.M., to clear rioters out of the ghetto. Using tear gas grenades and rifle butts, the military police forced all Negroes and whites off the streets. At 11:30 the riot was over, but the Presidential Proclamation was still to be signed.

After Aurand had transmitted his orders to Guthner, he had called Somervell to get permission to issue the proclamation. Somervell demanded that Aurand follow Stimson's instructions to wait until Governor Kelly contacted the President and Roosevelt signed the official order. Aurand relayed this message to Guthner, but the Governor could not be located until the riot had been quelled. Not until shortly before midnight did Kelly call Hyde Park to request the troops already deployed in the city. President Roosevelt signed the proclamation at 11:55 P.M. The Detroit rioters, now pacified, were commanded "to disperse and retire peaceably to their respective abodes." Twenty-one hours had passed since Army officials in Detroit first planned to use federal troops to end the riot. More than fifteen hours had been wasted since the Mayor first asked for Army manpower. Half a day had been lost between the Governor's first call to Sixth Service Command and Aurand's decision to send the military police into Detroit. General Guthner sat in Detroit for six hours before deploying the troops he had been sent to command. And it was during that time that most of Detroit's riot toll was recorded: thirty-four killed, more than seven hundred injured, over two million dollars in property losses, and a million man-hours lost in war production.

The armed peace in Detroit continued into Tuesday morning. Five thousand soldiers patrolled the streets, and military vehicles escorted buses and trolleys on their usual runs. Although racial tension remained high, firm and impartial action by the federal troops kept the city calm. Following Aurand's recommendations, Guthner instructed his troops to act with extreme restraint. Each field order ended with the admonition: "Under no circumstances will the use of firearms be resorted to unless all other measures fail to control the situation, bearing in mind that the suppression of violence, when accomplished without bloodshed, is a worthy achievement."

Continued hysteria in the city caused most of Guthner's difficulties. Rumors of new violence and repeated instances of police brutality kept the Negro ghetto seething. Most Negroes feared to leave their homes to go to work or buy food. Guthner persistently urged the Commissioner to order the police to ease off in their treatment of Negroes, but Witherspoon refused. Tales of the riot inflamed Negroes in surrounding communities. A group of soldiers at Fort Custer, 140 miles west of Detroit, tried to seize arms and a truck to help their families in the city. In Toledo, police turned back 1,500 Negroes trying to get rail transportation to Detroit. Muskegon, Indiana Harbor, Springfield, East St. Louis, and Chicago reported racial disturbances. Aurand changed his mind about leaving Chicago for Detroit and ordered Sixth Service Command troops in Illinois on the alert.

Unrest and ill-feeling continued throughout the week. The city courts, disregarding the depths of racial hostility in Detroit, employed separate and unequal standards in sentencing Negroes and whites arrested in the riot. With little regard for due process of law, the police carried out systematic raids on Negro rooming houses and apartments. Anxiety increased, isolated racial fights continued, repeated rumors of a new riot on July Fourth poisoned the tense atmosphere. Negroes and whites prepared for "the next one." Workmen in defense plants made knives out of flat files and hacksaw blades. Kelly and Jeffries urged the President to keep the federal troops in Detroit.

While the troops patrolled the streets, the search for answers and scapegoats to give some meaning to the outburst began. Adamant that it really "can't happen here," the same liberals and Negro leaders who had warned that white racism made Detroit ripe for a riot now attributed the violence to Axis agents. Telegrams poured into the White House asking for an FBI investigation of German agents in Detroit who aimed to disrupt war production. When the myth of an organized fifth column behind the riot was quickly shattered, liberals accused domestic reactionaries. The KKK, Gerald L. K. Smith, Father Charles Coughlin, Reverend J. Frank Norris, Southern congressmen, and anti-union demagogues were all singled out for blame. The NAACP aimed its sights at reactionary Poles who led the battle against decent Negro housing. Conservatives were just as anxious to hold liberals and Japanese agents responsible for race conflict. Martin Dies, Chairman of the House Un-American Activities Committee, saw the Japanese-Americans released from internment camps behind the riot. Congressman John Rankin of Mississippi taunted his colleagues in the House who supported the antipoll tax bill by saying "their chickens are coming home to roost" and asserted that the Detroit violence had been caused by the "crazy policies of the so-called fair employment practices committee in attempting to mix the races in all kinds of employment." Many Southerners blamed Negro agitators. Some talked of "Eleanor Clubs" as the source of the riot. "It is blood on your hands, Mrs. Roosevelt," claimed the *Jackson Daily News*. "You have been personally proclaiming and practicing social equality at the White House and wherever you go, Mrs. Roosevelt. In Detroit, a city noted for the growing impudence and insolence of its Negro population, an attempt was made to put your preachments into practice, Mrs. Roosevelt. What followed is now history." A Gallup Poll revealed that most Northerners believed Axis propaganda and sabotage were responsible for the violence, while most Southerners attributed it to lack of segregation in the North. An analysis of two hundred newspapers indicated that Southern editors stressed Negro militancy as the primary cause, while Northern editors accused fifth column subversives and Southern migrants new to city ways.

In Detroit the causes and handling of the riot quickly became the central issue of city politics. The Congress of Industrial Organizations, Negro organizations, and many civil liberties groups formed an alliance to defeat Mayor Edward Jeffries in November, to get rid of Commissioner Witherspoon, and to demand additional housing and jobs for Negroes. Led by United Auto Worker President R. J. Thomas and City Councilman George Edwards, a former UAW organizer, the coalition gained the backing of most CIO locals, the NAACP and Urban League, International Labor Defense, National Lawyers Guild, National Negro Congress, National Federation for Constitutional

Liberties, Catholic Trade Unionists, Socialist Party of Michigan, Inter-Racial Fellowship, Negro Council for Victory and Democracy, Metropolitan Detroit Youth Council, Union for Democratic Action, and March-on-Washington Movement. They were supported editorially by the *Detroit Free Press*, the *Detroit Tribune*, and the Negro *Michigan Chronicle*. Throughout the summer the coalition clamored for a special grand jury to investigate the causes of the riot and the unsolved riot deaths.

Michigan's leading Republicans, the Hearst press, and most real estate and antiunion groups opposed any change in the Negro's status. The Governor, Mayor, and Police Commissioner, abetted by the obliging Common Council, squelched the pleas for better housing and jobs and a grand jury investigation. Unwilling to make any changes in the conditions underlying the riot, the Republicans made meaningless gestures. The Mayor established an interracial committee with no power. After a few sleepy sessions, it adjourned for a long summer vacation. Commissioner Witherspoon refused to allow changes in the regulations to make possible the hiring of more Negro policemen. Instead of a grand jury investigation, the Governor appointed his own Fact-Finding Committee of four Republican law officers involved in the handling of the riot. And the Detroit Council of Churches, nonpartisan but similarly reluctant to face the issue of white racism, called upon the city to observe the following Sunday as a day of humility and penitence.

A week after the riot, Witherspoon appeared before the Common Council to report on his department's actions. He blamed Negroes for starting the riot and Army authorities for prolonging it. The Commissioner pictured white mob violence as only "retaliatory action" and police behavior as a model of "rare courage and efficiency." In fact, Witherspoon concluded, the police had been so fair that "some have accused the Department of having a kid glove policy toward the Negro." No one on the Council bothered to ask the Commissioner why the police failed to give Negroes the adequate protection required by law, or how this policy accounted for seventeen of the twenty-five Negroes killed in the riot having been shot by the police. Two days later, Mayor Jeffries presented his "white paper" to the Common Council. He reiterated the Commissioner's criticism of the Army and praise for the police and added an attack on "those Negro leaders who insist that their people do not and will not trust policemen and the Police Department. After what happened I am certain that some of these leaders are more vocal in their caustic criticism of the Police Department than they are in educating their own people to their responsibilities as citizens." The Common Council heartily approved the two reports. Gus Dorias and William (Billy) Rogell, two Detroit athletic heroes on the Council, advocated a bigger ghetto to solve the racial crisis. Councilman Comstock did not think this or anything should be done. "The racial conflict has been going on in this country since our ancestors made the first mistake of bringing the Negro to the country." The conflict would go on regardless of what was done, added Comstock, so why do anything?

Throughout July the accusations and recriminations intensified. Then, as the city began to tire of the familiar arguments, a fresh controversy erupted. When three Negro leaders asked William Dowling, the Wayne County Prosecutor, to investigate the unsolved riot deaths, Dowling berated them for turning information over to the NAACP that they withheld from him. He charged the NAACP with being "the biggest instigators of the race riot. If a grand jury were called, they would be the first indicted." The NAACP threatened to sue Dowling for libel, and the county prosecutor quickly denied making the charge. "Why, I like Negroes," he said. "I know what it is to be a member of a minority group. I am an Irish Catholic myself." The next day Dowling again charged an "unnamed civil rights group" with causing the riot. Witherspoon endorsed Dowling's allegation, and the battle flared. "It was as if a bomb had been dropped," said one Negro church leader. "The situation is what it was just before June 21."

In the midst of this tense situation, the Governor released the report of his Fact-Finding Committee. Parts I and II, a detailed chronology of the riot and supporting exhibits, placed the blame for the violence squarely on Negroes who had started fights at Belle Isle and spread riot rumors. Content to fix liability on the initial aggressors, the report did not connect the Sunday fights with any of the scores of incidents of violence by whites against Negroes which preceded the fights at Belle Isle. Nor did the report mention any of the elements which permitted some fights to lead to such extensive hysteria and violence, or which allowed rumors to be so instantly efficacious. No whites were accused of contributing to the riot's causes. The sailors responsible for much of the fighting on the bridge, and the nineteen other whites arrested by the police Sunday night, escaped blame. The report emphasized the culpability of the Negro-instigated rumors, especially Leo Tipton's, but let the other rumors remain "lily-white." Although many instances of police brutality were attested and documented, the committee failed to mention them. And while only a court or grand jury in Michigan had the right to classify a homicide as legally "justifiable," the committee, hearing only police testimony, took it upon itself to "justify" all police killings of Negroes.

Part III, an analysis of Detroit's racial problems, completely departed from the committee's aim of avoiding "conclusions of a controversial or conjectural nature." The section on those responsible for racial tensions omitted any mention of the KKK, Black Legion, National Workers League, and the scores of anti-Negro demagogues and organizations openly preaching race hatred in Detroit. Racial tension was totally attributed to Negro agitators who "constantly beat the drums of: 'Racial prejudice, inequality, intolerance, discrimination.' " Repeatedly, the report referred to the Negro's "presumed grievances" and complaints of "alleged Jim Crowism." In the world of the Fact-Finding Committee no real Negro problems existed, or if they did, they were to be endured in silence. Publication of the obviously prejudiced report proved an immediate embarrassment to the Governor. Most newspapers and journals denounced it as a "whitewash," and Kelly's friends wisely buried it. The Common Council then declared the riot a "closed incident."

In Washington, too, politics went on as usual. The administration did nothing to prevent future riots or attempt to solve the American dilemma. The problem of responding to the riots became compounded when the same combination of underlying grievances and war-bred tensions which triggered the Detroit riot led to an orgy of looting and destruction in Harlem. Henry Wallace and Wendell Willkie delivered progressive speeches; leading radio commentators called for a new approach to racial problems; and many prominent Americans signed newspaper advertisements urging the President to condemn segregation and racial violence. But the White House remained silent.

In much the same way it had handled the question of segregation in the armed forces and discrimination in defense production, the Roosevelt administration muddled its way through a summer of violence. The four presidential aides handling race relations problems, all Southerners, determined to go slow, protect the "boss," and keep the shaky Democratic coalition together, fought all proposals for White House action. They politely buried pleas for the President to give a fireside chat on the riots and brushed aside recommendations that would force Roosevelt to acknowledge the gravity of the race problem. The Interior Department's plans for a national race relations commission, and those of Attorney General Francis Biddle for an interdepartmental committee were shelved in favor of Jonathan Daniels' inoffensive suggestion to correlate personally all information on racial problems. Even Marshall Field's proposal to circulate pledges asking people not to spread rumors and to help "win the war at home by combating racial discrimination wherever I meet it," which appealed to Roosevelt, went ignored. The federal government took only two actions: clarification of the procedure by which federal troops could be called, and approval of J. Edgar Hoover's recommendation to defer from the draft members of city police forces. Like the Republicans in Michigan, the Democrats in the capital occupied themselves with the efficient handling of a future riot rather than its prevention.

With a war to win, Detroit and the nation resumed "business as usual." Negroes continued to be brutalized by the police and the "first fired, last hired." In the Senate, the administration killed a proposal to have Congress investigate the riots, and Michigan's Homer Ferguson and Arthur Vandenberg stymied every proposal for Negro housing in Detroit's suburbs. Their constituents continued boasting "the sun never sets on a nigger in Dearborn." Governor Kelly appropriated a million dollars to equip and train special riot troops. Mayor Jeffries, running as a defender of "white supremacy," easily won re-election in 1943 and 1945. The lesson learned from the riot? In the Mayor's words: "We'll know what to do next time." Yet Southern Negroes continued to pour into Detroit looking for the promised land—only to find discrimination, hatred, a world of little opportunity and less dignity. The dream deferred waited to explode. "There ain't no North any more," sighed an old Negro woman. "Everything now is South."

13

Mildred Pierce and Women in Film

JUNE SOCHEN

• From 1896 until the advent of television in the early 1950s, movies were the most popular and influential form of culture in the United States. Newspapers and magazines were read each day by millions of people, and live vaudeville acts and theater groups performed even in small towns. But movies were the first of the modern mass media, and they rose to the surface of cultural consciousness from the bottom up, receiving their principal support from the lowest and most invisible classes of American society.

Movie buffs have long argued whether cinema reflects popular culture or leads it. No one can doubt, however, that motion pictures have served as a primary source of information about society and human behavior for large masses of people. Ordinarily, the media have reflected dominant ideologies and interests and have not sought to transform the nature of human life. But what is remarkable is the way that American movies have occasionally challenged traditional values and thus provided alternative ways of understanding the world. Mildred Pierce was such a film. Rather than depicting the female in a subservient, dependent role, it cast Joan Crawford as an ambitious, competent, and successful businesswoman who is nonetheless constrained by motherhood. The following essay by June Sochen demonstrates the pivotal role of the film and indicates how American culture sought to punish strong, deviant women.

Reprinted by permission of *American Quarterly*, June Sochen, and the University of Pennsylvania. Copyright 1978, Trustees of the University of Pennsylvania.

AUTHOR'S NOTE: I would like to acknowledge the invaluable aid that Joyce S. Schrager gave me in doing this project. I would also like to thank Susan Dalton, Film Archivist for the University of Wisconsin's Center for Theater and Film Research, for her cooperation.

During the 1930s, the opening of any Joan Crawford movie thrilled thousands of fans and assured MGM box office success. But Crawford, frustrated by the predictability of roles offered to her, left Louis B. Mayer's studio early in the forties. For over two years she rejected all screen roles shown to her and then in 1944 read and accepted a part in the script that marked her return to the screen and gave Crawford her only Academy Award. The screenplay was *Mildred Pierce*, a dark, suspenseful movie based upon a James Cain novel. Crawford fans, ever loyal, flocked to New York's Strand Theater on September 28, 1945, when *Mildred Pierce* opened, and continued to attend in record numbers. Warner Brothers, the producers of the film, reported a gross of five million dollars.

Mildred Pierce was both a familiar and novel character for Crawford to play. A drab California divorcee with two daughters to support, Mildred seemed similar to Sadie McKee and other Crawford heroines of the thirties. As Mildred, Crawford began the movie in Sears, Roebuck specials and then succeeded to the fashionable Adrian outfits that had become her trademark. She was after all no stranger to roles that required her to begin a movie as poor but beautiful. Both she and her fans knew that the poverty would be overcome precisely because of her beauty. Mildred Pierce, however, departed from the formula in that the poor but lovely woman not only reached the peaks of success but also experienced the depths of failure; in the end, nothing remained but a flicker of hope. It is the tragedies that befell Mildred and the bleak ending that distinguished *Mildred Pierce* from its innumerable predecessors.

It took six screenwriters to make the Cain novel an acceptable screenplay. Though only Ranald MacDougall received screen credit, the other contributors to the script included novelist William Faulkner and veteran screenwriter Catherine Turney. The cast of characters assembled for this production by Jerry Wald for Warner Brothers was impressive: Joan Crawford as Mildred, Zachary Scott as Monte Berragon, III, Jack Carson as Wally Fay, Eve Arden as Ida, Ann Blyth as Veda Pierce, Butterfly McQueen as Letty, and Bruce Bennett as Bert Pierce.

Mildred Pierce is a rich, multi-layered movie. On one level, it is an effective murder mystery. On another, it gives us a stunning portrayal of a woman trying to live by the cultural rules under difficult circumstances. On still another, it is an indictment of the American family and its values. The movie skillfully interweaves all three themes with Mildred at its center. Her life and thought provide the substance for every essential action in the movie. Director Michael Curtiz, a master of Americana, used the flashback technique to heighten tension and to unravel the parts of the mystery. As critic John Davis has said, the flashback was the favorite fatalistic method of the forties film. The murder, shown first, was the inevitable conclusion to everything that had preceded it.

The movie begins with gunshots and a man falling to the floor muttering "Mildred." The next scene shows the back of a well-dressed woman walking along the wharf. It is nighttime and the streets are rain-drenched. The woman stops by the railing of the wharf and looks pensively into the water. She leans over the railing only to be ordered to stop by a policeman. She walks away, stops outside a nightclub, and goes inside when the owner, Wally Fay (Jack Carson) invites her in. The woman, of course, is Mildred Pierce. Wally is surprised to see her slumming; she invites him to have a drink with her at her beach-house. Delighted by Mildred's invitation (since Wally has been pursuing her for years), he goes with her to the house. As soon as they enter, the viewer recognizes the murder scene. A light from outside illuminates the body of the dead man, though neither Wally nor Mildred sees it.

While Mildred excuses herself to get into something more comfortable, arrogant Wally regales her with small talk. Moments go by and Wally discovers he is alone in the house. He runs furtively from room to room looking for Mildred; when he discovers the dead body, his running becomes more intense. The doors are all locked. Wally smashes an upstairs window and jumps out, only to be discovered by two patrolling policemen and taken in for questioning. Mildred is also brought to headquarters and told that her husband, Monte Berragon, III (Zachary Scott), was found dead at the beachhouse. The police think her first husband, Bert Pierce (Bruce Bennett) was the murderer. Seated in the sergeant's office, Mildred tells her life story to the officer:

> We lived on Corvalis Street where all the houses looked alike. I was always in the kitchen. I felt as though I'd been born in a kitchen and lived there all my life, except for the few hours it

took to get married. I married Bert when I was seventeen. I never knew any other kind of life . . . just cooking, washing, and having children.

When Bert loses his job, their mutual frustration leads to frequent quarreling. Their two daughters, Kay and Veda, often become the subject of their arguments. Mildred insists during one argument that the children come first in her life and "I will do their crying for them too." Bert counters that "you are trying to buy love from those kids." Mildred retorts that they were going to have a better life than she had. Bert ends the argument by saying he is going to visit his friend Mrs. Biederhof. Mildred warns him that if he goes to his girlfriend's house, he should never come back. Bert agrees.

Mildred's daughters, the subject of her continuous bickering with Bert, offer a study in contrasts. Kay, the younger girl, is a sweet tomboy; Veda (played by Ann Blyth) is a selfish, deceitful, snobbish teenager. She is ashamed of their modest home, contemptuous of her mother's housewife image, and disgusted with her ineffectual father. Instead of disciplining her, Mildred spoils her. She scrimps and saves to buy Veda a new dress that Veda tells Kay is common. When her mother tries to kiss her good night the first night after Bert leaves, Veda resists saying, "Let's not be sticky about it."

Mildred accepts the crumbs of love given her by Veda, neglects the sweet-natured Kay, and grimly goes looking for a job. She quickly discovers how hard it is to get a job in Depression America when one is female and unskilled. Finally, she finds work as a waitress in a restaurant. Ida, the hostess (played by Eve Arden), teaches her the ropes, and within a few months Mildred is an excellent waitress. At night, she bakes cakes for neighbors' special occasions and is able to employ a maid, Letty (played by Butterfly McQueen), to help her with the baking and housework. Mildred does not tell her children where she works, fearing Veda's contempt for the proletariat. One day Mildred comes home to discover Letty wearing one of her waitress uniforms. When questioned, Letty says Miss Veda asked her to wear it.

Mildred confronts Veda. "Where did you find the uniform?" Veda cooly says she assumed it was bought for Letty. Mildred gets angry at Veda and slaps her face, immediately regretting the action. "I'd rather have cut off my hand," she says. Mildred quickly explains that she is working as a waitress to learn the restaurant business. Ambitious Veda likes this idea, declaring that then they will become rich and she can have the beautiful clothes and beautiful surroundings she so wants. Mildred goes to see Wally Fay, Bert's former real estate partner, and seeks his help in purchasing a piece of property—an old mansion, now in disrepair and owned by the Berragon family.

The next series of sequences seems inevitable. Mildred meets Berragon, a playboy who makes an art out of doing nothing but whose family money is slowly dwindling away. He sells Mildred the house, begins a love affair with her, and stays around to watch Mildred become a female Horatio Alger. Meanwhile, Bert takes his daughters off to Arrowhead one weekend and returns with sweet Kay suffering from pneumonia. Mildred cannot be reached because she is having a tryst with Monte at his Malibu beachhouse. She returns in time to see her daughter whisper "Mommy" and then expire.

After Kay's death, Mildred concentrates on her restaurant and in a short time turns it into a successful enterprise; within a year, there are other "Mildred's" around town. As she becomes a wealthy businesswoman, her daughter Veda becomes an insatiable devourer of more and more things. Monte escorts Veda around town and educates her into the dissipated life, a life financed by Mildred, as Monte is without funds. Mildred disapproves of Monte's influence upon her daughter and finally writes him a last check, telling him to stop seeing Veda. He complies and Veda proceeds to marry a rich young man whom she then promptly sues for divorce. She insists upon a large settlement claiming that she is pregnant. Mildred is stunned by this turn of events; upon confronting Veda, she realizes that Veda faked the pregnancy claim in order to get the money. Mother and daughter exchange bitter words, and Mildred tears up Veda's check only to have her daughter slap her in the face. "Get out before I kill you," are Mildred's parting words to her daughter.

In a state of desperation, Mildred leaves Ida in charge of her business and travels around the country. She returns many months later, weary, shaky, and grimly aware of the fact that "Veda is a part of me. She is still my daughter and I cannot forget that." Ever the cynical friend, Ida reminds Mildred that alligators had the right idea; they ate their young. Mildred laughs bitterly and discovers that her daughter is singing in Wally Fay's dive on the wharf. In order to win Veda back, Mildred decides to achieve the status desired by Veda by purchasing Berragon's in-town mansion and marrying him in order to acquire his prestigious name. A one-third ownership in her business persuades Monte. "Sold one Berragon," Mildred notes as Monte tries to kiss her to consummate the deal. Whatever feeling Mildred had for Monte has disappeared.

Veda returns and the social whirl and spending sprees resume. A business meeting on the evening of Veda's birthday party reveals the fact that Monte has sold his interest in Mildred's and has gotten Wally, who also has a one-third interest, to sell too. Mildred is wiped out. The lavish expenses of Veda and Monte have broken her. That very night Veda and Monte go to the beachhouse; they quarrel when Veda insists that Monte divorce her mother and marry her; Monte laughs and an enraged, jealous Veda shoots him. It is this scene that Mildred walks in upon; she discovers her second husband on the floor and her daughter pleading with her to save her once again. "It's your fault I am the way I am," Veda shouts at Mildred. Mildred agrees to help Veda, walks to the wharf, contemplates suicide, and after being shooed away by the policeman, sees Wally Fay and invites him to the beachhouse.

The sergeant figures it all out as well and the movie ends with Veda being taken away to jail while Mildred walks out of the police headquarters as dawn breaks. Bert Pierce, her first husband, waits on the steps of the building for her, and together they walk away into the sunrise. So ends *Mildred Pierce*.

While women viewers wiped the tears away from their eyes and thought about ungrateful daughters and self-sacrificing mothers, a few discerning critics noted the movie's absolutely bleak portrait of American family life and its corrupting materialistic values. James Agee commented that *Mildred Pierce* was a "nasty, gratifying version of the James Cain novel about suburban grass-widowhood and the power of the native passion for money and all that money can buy." But most critics agreed with Thomas Pryor of the *New York Times* who found it unrealistic. Pryor wondered, how "a level headed person like Mildred Pierce, who builds a fabulously successful chain of restaurants on practically nothing, could be so completely dominated by a selfish and grasping daughter, who spells trouble in capital letters."

Some critics like John McManus of *PM* complained that the movie would be bad propaganda for the United States abroad. None bothered to probe the connection between *Mildred Pierce* and the rich quantity of women's movies that had preceded it from 1930 to 1945. Mildred Pierce was the culmination of a long series of screen heroines, a subject to which we will return.

More energetic and entrepreneurial than most, Mildred exhibited the all-American (usually male) traits of hard work, self-reliance, and perseverance. Her efforts paid off in the best Horatio Alger tradition. But, and this is a major but, she was also a mother and this role required primary attention. While businessmen may or may not be fathers, businesswomen-mothers must attend to their mothering first. Thus, Mildred Pierce was blamed implicitly (and blamed herself) for her children's behavior. Though Bert was caring for Kay when she took sick, the implication was that Mildred should have been on call, always ready to care for her children. Making love to Monte, rather than sitting home awaiting the return of her children, was an abdication of maternal responsibility. Similarly, Mildred's indulgence of Veda and her unwillingness to discipline her resulted in Veda's behavior. When Mildred slapped Veda's face for her insolence, she regretted her action. After Veda shot Monte, she declared to Mildred: "It's your fault I am the way I am."

What worse series of events could occur to a mother than to have one daughter die while the other one murdered her second husband? Mildred Pierce, a successful businesswoman, failed miserably in her maternal role. Who was to blame? Individualistic American values, reflected in this movie, suggested that the blame belonged upon Mildred's shoulders. Because justice prevailed in Hollywood movies, Mildred lost her business as well as her children. Defeat became her fate: ambitious women beware.

Ineffectual Bert (the inevitable husband to a strong woman?) cannot be blamed for the course of actions. After all, he warned Mildred when they divorced that *she* was spoiling Veda. Strength is an unwomanly trait, always to be punished. How was Mildred to support herself and her daughters after her unemployed husband left? *Mildred Pierce* raised many more questions than it answered, one of its most intriguing features. It was a tragedy, one experienced by women who, understandably, invested a great deal in their children. Joan

Crawford received the empathy of many fans who knew that a woman's lot has always been a hard one and that patience and endurance have been her only course of action.

Mildred's strength was both a blessing and a curse. Surely women viewers admired her ability to care for her daughters, earn a living, and survive psychically intact. But her strength was impotent in the face of a rebellious daughter. While Veda was unimpressed and unaffected by her mother's strength, Bert appeared to be intimidated by the steely Mildred, and corrupt Monte paraded his ineffectuality in public. Was Mildred responsible for the men's inability to cope with life? The implicit message of *Mildred Pierce* was yes: strong women threatened the development of whole men. There has been a long history of women's films that preach female submissiveness and warn strong, independent women that they will be without a man in the last reel unless they learn to submit.

Mildred Pierce acted as a piece of social control for women. Women of America, know your place. Erase any ideas you may have to divorce your husband and/or enter the big, bad business world. (Mildred, remember, was betrayed by men and lost her restaurants as a result.) Women, remain within the domestic sphere, an arena you naturally know and belong to. Attend to the raising of your children, every hour of the day and night; only then can you be assured of their continued obedience and loyalty. Don't spoil your children. Be totally devoted but not possessive.

American women were not revolted by *Mildred Pierce*; neither did they revolt. They did not question a culture that restricted their adult life to mothering, though circumstance and inclination may have led them to other pursuits. Neither did they question the overwhelming burden of motherhood. The message for American women was clear: stay in the preordained domain.

Mildred Pierce was the end of a genre, the culmination of the woman's film of the thirties and early forties. Though there would be many more entries of the same type following it, it signaled the sad and grim ending to a category of film that had rich and exciting features. Specifically, *Mildred Pierce* was the eerie joining together of two subtypes of women's films: the weepie and the Independent Woman film. Each has had a long history with many distinguishable

qualities. The weepies, also known as the melodrama and the soap
opera, always had a heroine who suffered and suffered and suffered.
The Independent Woman film had a heroine who was strong and exciting and often had a full-time career outside of the home. The melodramas of Bette Davis and the professional women films of Katharine
Hepburn ended with Joan Crawford's Mildred. This film became Hollywood's ultimate comment on the fate of all women. Strong women
neglected their family while all women ended up sacrificing, giving up
more than they got on this earth. Bette Davis enjoyed a brief period
of happiness before dying of a brain tumor in *Dark Victory*. Mildred
Pierce experienced no happiness, only sorrow.

Throughout the 1930s and early 1940s, Bette Davis made an art
out of suffering, as did innumerable other actresses of the period. She
was the penultimate self-sacrificer in both *Dark Victory* (1939) and
Now, Voyager (1941). In the former movie, she changed from a
spoiled rich girl to a loving wife who lived heroically knowing she
was going to die. In the latter film, she changed from an ugly duck-
ling to an attractive woman who remained chastely loyal to a married
man with whom she would never consummate her love, for reasons
too complicated to delineate, though audiences accepted it all happily. Unquestioning, a "good" woman remained virginal before marriage and stayed virginal if the man she loved could not marry her.
Her adult fate was in the hands of the male in her life. In *Now, Voyager*, Davis contented herself with caring for her "lover's" neglected
daughter. The handkerchiefs dampened quickly in these movies and
remained wet throughout.

Reviewers continually referred to the weepies as women's films,
films that provided a cathartic effect for women audiences. What
revelation were they touching upon without acknowledging? The commentators seem to have been admitting the despair, emptiness, and
sadness of women's lives. They seemed to recognize the injustice of
continual self-sacrifice. But neither they nor their audiences questioned the exclusivity of sacrifice and tragedy for women. The overwhelming acceptance of woman's lot as one of suffering was so complete, so sure, that Hollywood melodramas merely reinforced that cultural message. Melodrama, the exaggeration of dramatic material, the
bombardment of disaster after disaster in a short period of time,
seemed the stuff of a woman's life. No tragedy was too great, no se-

ries of disasters too many to deter a woman from being sweet, cooperative, and sacrificing. She lived for and through others.

Mildred Pierce was a logical extension of Judith Traherne (*Dark Victory*) and Charlotte Vance (*Now, Voyager*). Though the movie melodrama seemed at an extreme with *Mildred Pierce*, the genre has obviously flourished in other media. Today, daytime television soaps combined with the new, nighttime hit *Soap* continue the tradition. Women's capacity for melodrama seems endless though *Mildred Pierce* could not be bested; no later entry could outdo the horror of a twice-married woman whose daughter killed her second husband after he betrayed the wife in business. Though credibility has never been a criterion in the weepies, the semblance of credibility is generally practiced. If the movie makers had envisioned the Mary Hartman approach of satire, then they could have mined this vein much further. But in 1945, and for the next decade, the melodrama took on darker tones, warning all of the threat of ambitious women and describing in seemingly realistic terms the multiple tragedies that befell them.

The other strain of the women's films, that of the strong, Independent Woman type, also had a long, exciting history in Hollywood filmmaking prior to 1945. This genre included screen characterizations of career women, businesswomen, entertainers, and marginal types such as gangsters' girl friends and whores. Career women films were quite common in the thirties and early forties. Rosalind Russell played 23 different professional woman roles in that period. Hepburn's whole career was based upon that characterization. Bette Davis, Barbara Stanwyck, Kay Francis, Joan Crawford, Myrna Loy, Jean Arthur, Claudette Colbert, and numerous others played newspaper reporters, writers, lawyers, doctors, commercial artists, and nurses in the films of the period. Similarly, many played down-and-out women who had to display strength to survive.

When Adolphe Menjou in *Golden Boy* (1939) called his girlfriend, Barbara Stanwyck, "baby" she retorted: "I'm my mother's baby." Stanwyck may have been a gun moll, but she was also her own person, not the property of her boyfriend. When Stanwyck or Davis, for example, played a whore, they did it without self-pity but rather with resilience and wit. The strong woman film was exciting precisely because of its amazing variety of characterizations. In *A Marked Woman* (1937) Bette Davis played a whore who made the best out of a very difficult set of circumstances. She defied the gangsters only to get her face cut up and her life endangered, but she stuck to her guns and testified against the hoods. When district attorney Humphrey Bogart offered her a life with him at the end of the movie, she turned him down, linked arms with her sister whores, and walked off into the sunset.

Katharine Hepburn as Tess Harding in *Woman of the Year* (1942) epitomized the exciting, brilliant, Independent Woman. In a story modeled after the life of journalist Dorothy Thompson, she bedazzled all around her with her knowledge of multiple languages and foreign policy. She met her match, of course, in the form of the classic American Adam: Spencer Tracy as sportswriter Sam Craig. Contrary to the formula of romantic pursuit until the final reel, Harding and Craig married early in the film and the bulk of the movie concerned itself with the career/marriage struggle that inevitably resulted. With dialogue written by Ruth Gordon, it was a sparkling movie that dealt with so many contemporary themes that audiences today are delighted by it.

The adoption of a child whom Tess quickly relegated to her housekeeper became the crisis point in the movie. After all, Tess had no intention of abandoning her exciting career for full-time mothering. The movie ended with a long, silent scene, considered a classic comic sequence (though from the feminist viewpoint it was a tragic relinquishment of identity) in which Hepburn tried her inexperienced hand in the kitchen in order to be reconciled with her husband. After the coffee sputtered forth and the waffles seeped all over the kitchen—no wonder, she put yeast into the batter—she cried out in desperation. The great journalist was a failure in the kitchen, where it really counted for a woman. Sam consoled her and ended the movie with a speech in which he said that she didn't have to be Mrs. Sam Craig or Tess Harding but she could be Tess Harding Craig. How she would accomplish that task remained unanswered as THE END flashed across the screen.

To some, *Woman of the Year* typified the capitulation of the strong woman to the dominant male. It fit into the long line of women's films in which the women abandoned their careers for love and marriage. Rosalind Russell sacrificed a successful career as advertising executive in *Take a Letter Darling* (1941) to run off to Mexico with

struggling artist Fred MacMurray, while Bette Davis gave up a promising career as a newspaper reporter for marriage to George Brent in
Front Page Woman (1935). To others, the ambiguity of Sam Craig's
last speech suggested that some accommodation would be reached between ambitious, career-oriented Tess and traditionalist Sam. Women
audiences admired the independent Hepburn and the witty repartee
between her and Tracy. The chemistry between them in this film was
so exciting that it became the first of nine collaborations.

Surely part of the power of the Independent Woman genre was its
ability to satisfy both male and female traditionalists and experimenters. Advocates of the status quo delighted in the subjugation of the
woman by the man. The questioners of sex roles focused upon the
battle between the sexes throughout the movie and ignored the ending. During most of the film, Hepburn, Russell, Stanwyck, or Davis
were in commanding positions. This pleased men and women who
wondered what life would be like if and when men and women lived
in the same world and shared the same tasks of working and home-
making.

During the Depression and war years, the Independent Woman image flourished. Hollywood could excite women viewers with the adventures of a Tess Harding; both Hollywood and women moviegoers
knew full well that most women could never duplicate Tess' life. But
women could be strong and courageous; indeed they had to be to
survive. Women audiences positively admired the no-nonsense quality of Davis and Stanwyck. They adored the wit of Hepburn and the
dominance of Crawford. That image also appealed to men, who could
admire these women for their playfulness, their companionship, and
their spunk. Further, men had it both ways; they fantasized about the
fun they could have with a daring woman while watching her final
capitulation at the end of the movie. The men most always emerged
the victors, and the social order remained intact.

Perhaps unintentionally, Hollywood movie producers had successfully fulfilled both fantasy needs and social role expectations in creating this film type. The genius of American movies, after all, has
been their ability to present fantasy simultaneous with the preservation of social roles. No revolution resulted from a viewing of an
American movie. No new life styles have been suggested. The Independent Woman type thrived when women gained vicarious pleasure

from watching the emancipated Tess Harding, all the while knowing that they could not duplicate her lifestyle. Both sexes enjoyed the adventures of their favorite stars.

In *Woman of the Year,* as strong and exciting as Hepburn was, she gave in to Tracy. She yielded to his guidance, she admitted her need for his direction. This need became exaggerated in *Mildred Pierce.* How ironic. A woman needs a man, any man. Even weak Bert became sufficient to comfort and aid strong but defeated Mildred. Mildred Pierce had been humbled by her hubris, by her overarching ambition for herself and Veda, just as Hepburn had been brought down by the traditional values of Tracy. In this context, *Mildred Pierce* appeared as the ultimate message to all strong independent women in film and in life. Women's strength inevitably destroyed others as well as themselves. Tess Harding was a warning while Mildred Pierce became the fulfilled threat. If women did not channel their energies into the properly defined roles of wife and mother, they lost both husband and children, and became masculinized or lonely women. Most of the independent women film stars averted either fate. They flirted with "masculine" roles but realized the error of their ways and fell into the arms of the waiting male.

Mildred Pierce ended the playful admiration of the Independent Woman. She was too dangerous, too suggestive of new, unexpected possibilities. If Mildred had succeeded both personally and in the business world she would have created a new social type: a career wife–mother. This type portended new social arrangements precisely at the time when American society wanted to return to normalcy, to the *status quo antebellum.* Mildred Pierce had to be destroyed to eliminate any troublesome thoughts held by working mothers. Rosie the Riveter and Mildred Pierce had to go home again. In the Depression thirties, a divorced housewife in business may have been portrayed as heroic; in 1945, she had to be reminded of her proper role.

Mildred Pierce appears, then, as the object lesson for all women to learn. The paths of all the screen characterizations of strong women lead inevitably to Mildred Pierce, undesirable role model. It may be exciting to watch Mildred succeed in the business world, but the price she had to pay for that success was too high. Tess Harding conversed with Batista but who kept her company after the adulating crowds left her? Bette Davis' marked woman stands out as an atypical example of the genre. She defied convention and remained with her sister whores at the end, not in the arms of the district attorney. Critics noted this exceptional ending, but the exception only served to prove the rule: most strong women, competing in a male world, gave up that world in order to fulfill their biological—cultural destiny as wife and mother. Rosalind Russell, Katharine Hepburn, and Joan Crawford all did. Only whores, a minority of the strong women in the Independent Woman genre, retained their independence by rejecting mainstream values. But they too paid a price for their independence: they remained outsiders.

After *Mildred Pierce*, the women's movie took an ominous turn. The melodrama and the Independent Woman types combined to produce destructive women, women who were unhappy about their domestic situations and usually expressed their unhappiness in brutal ways. The women's movies of the fifties portrayed restless women who sought escape through murder and adultery. Barbara Stanwyck, as an unhappy housewife in *Double Indemnity* (1944) and *Clash by Night* (1952), took up with another man while she planned her husband's murder. Joan Crawford acted as a ruthless, evil woman in *Queen Bee* (1955) and got her comeuppance at the end. Davis asked in *All About Eve* (1950) where all the parts were for mature actresses and found herself playing a wife in *Payment on Demand* (1951) whose husband sought a divorce.

Joan Crawford went mad in a number of movies in the 1950s while women became destroyers or utter victims in a spate of movies as well. Olivia de Havilland, Joan Caulfield, and Ingrid Bergman were only a few of the women stars who were betrayed by malevolent men and unable to control their fates. Even Barbara Stanwyck could not escape the fifties fate; she played a paralyzed woman tormented by an anonymous telephone caller in *Sorry, Wrong Number* (1948). It is interesting to note the extremes in the film portrayal of women—as evildoers or as passive victims. Women became either lawless or impotent, forces outside normal human behavior. Further, a whole new generation of actresses portraying women as sexual temptresses dominated the new crop of women stars. Movies with women as whores, of course, were not new to Hollywood movies, but in the postwar period the whores semed to lose their strength and their independence.

Ava Gardner, Rita Hayworth, Lana Turner, and Jane Russell played itinerant singers and prostitutes with hearts of gold, but they survived thanks to the largesse of the man in their life, not on their own.

Doris Day, Marilyn Monroe, and Elizabeth Taylor were three of the new generation of women movie stars in the fifties. Their films dramatically illustrate the difference betwen the pre-1945 period of women's movies and the postwar variety. Doris Day played a cafe singer who got beaten up by a gangster in *Love Me or Leave Me* (1955), a frightened wife in Hitchcock's *The Man Who Knew Too Much* (1956), and finally an interior decorator in *Pillow Talk* (1959) with Rock Hudson. Day had finally found her image; she became a career woman who used feminine wiles to catch her man. Both in *Pillow Talk* and *Lover Come Back* (1962), she pursued Rock Hudson until he captured her. Her career in each case seemed to be a temporary activity until she married. These two Day–Hudson movies were enormously popular comedies, a telling symbol of how career women were treated in the 1950s.

Marilyn Monroe, the virgin-temptress of American movies, became stereotyped early in the decade with *How to Marry a Millionaire* (1953) and *Gentlemen Prefer Blondes* (1953). *River of No Return* (1954) did little to alter the image while *The Seven Year Itch* (1955) reinforced it. *Bus Stop* (1956) offered a more sympathetic portrayal of the sexpot who does not understand her own power while *The Prince and the Showgirl* (1957) returned to the type. While Ava Gardner, Rita Hayworth, et al. were knowledgeable though weary, Marilyn Monroe's characterizations emphasized her bewilderment at her own attractiveness. Elizabeth Taylor, in her first decade as an adult star, portrayed an innocent beauty in *Ivanhoe* (1952), but quickly became the tempestuous beauty in *The Last Time I Saw Paris* (1954). In *Giant* (1956) she was a woman with strength who used her beauty intelligently. *Raintree County* (1957) appeared as a return to the image of Taylor as restless, selfish beauty but as Maggie in *Cat on a Hot Tin Roof* (1958) she brought warmth, sincerity, and sympathy to the characterization.

In *Suddenly, Last Summer* (1959) Elizabeth Taylor was a mentally ill woman surrounded by family members anxious to see her become permanently deranged. Finally, in *Butterfield 8* (1960), she won the Academy Award as a desperate mistress who could not extricate herself from the man she both loved and hated. Taylor, like Greta Garbo in the thirties, usually portrayed women who had not come to terms with their beauty. Their intelligence, sensitivity, and ambition could never be reconciled with their physical attractiveness and the problems attendant upon it. Indeed, woman's physicality seemed to be the dominant concern of Hollywood movies in the post-1945 period, whether it was the sultry beauty of Ava Gardner, the lushness of Marilyn Monroe, or the stunning presentation of Elizabeth Taylor. Appearance became woman's only persona.

The few exciting women stars of the fifties who may have developed into Independent Woman types were all mistreated by Hollywood in different ways: Ingrid Bergman was excommunicated for her personal sin of becoming pregnant by a man other than her husband and announcing it; Joanne Woodward was given hackneyed roles; Marilyn Monroe became typecast as the sexy but dumb blond; and Elizabeth Taylor became the captive of her own beauty. The veteran women stars, as already suggested, were given roles as murderers and adulteresses. Rosalind Russell abandoned drama entirely for comedy. Only Hepburn survived, though not entirely. In 1952, she made both *Pat and Mike* and *African Queen,* the former movie being another continuation in the Tracy–Hepburn collaboration in which she played a professional athlete. In *African Queen* with Humphrey Bogart, she became a spinster missionary, tough but dependent as well. After appearing in 1959 as the cold, cruel Mrs. Venable in *Suddenly, Last Summer,* she became fed up with women's roles in the movies. As Charles Higham said in *Kate:* "She wanted to construct. She loved women, believing them to be superior to men. Distressed by the trend that pictures were taking—toward grotesquerie and perversion—she returned to the stage."

The turbulent sixties were no more compatible for the image of strong women than the quiescent fifties. Males' search for sexual freedom and identity became a dominant theme with Mrs. Robinson as the classic Eve initiating Benjamin–Adam into the joys of sex in *The Graduate* (1967), while a cooperative prostitute tried to help Jack Nicholson achieve potency in *Carnal Knowledge* (1969). The titles of some of the Academy Award–winning movies of the decade reflect the male monopoly of films: *Tom Jones, Lawrence of Arabia, A Man for All Seasons, Midnight Cowboy,* and *Patton.* Indeed, there have been few women stars, with musical superstars Barbra Streisand and Liza Minnelli standing out as exceptions. The few women who appeared in films were often whores, the classic Eves. Jane Fonda may consult a psychiatrist in the popular *Klute*, but she is still a whore. Critic Pauline Kael remarked in the early 70s that the romantic duo of the era was Paul Newman and Robert Redford.

At the beginning of the '70s, when films were priding themselves upon their realism and their honest confrontation of human problems, filmmakers admitted their inability to deal with women's liberation by ignoring the subject and omitting women from the screen altogether. Streisand's *Up the Sandbox* (1973), one of the few attempts to deal with the subject, failed miserably. *The Way We Were* (1974) showed us a woman with a political philosophy and a social activistic bent, but her romantic involvement with Robert Redford became the dominant theme with the strong, interesting woman receding into the background. *Alice Doesn't Live Here Anymore* (1975), a bittersweet story about a widow with a young son, was a popular success which treated the subject of female friendships and women alone effectively. Generally, 1975 and 1976 did not produce many successful followers to *Alice*. The economy dipped and moviemakers abandoned realism for the catastrophe films and the sci-fi fantasies.

In 1977–78, advocates of women's movies took heart with the appearance of *Julia* and *The Turning Point*. Both of these movies featured exciting characterizations of women. Each treated women as important, worthy subject matter for contemporary film. Whether these films will be followed by a long line of diverse and vital portraits of women remains to be seen. A successful Mildred Pierce seems as threatening in the 1970s as in 1945. The realistic possibilities of independent women, no longer relegated to the fantasy level, portend serious social changes in sex roles. Perhaps it is the 1970s concern for role models that makes moviemakers uneasy. In the 1930s, movie viewers knew that Hepburn as a lawyer, reporter, athlete, or pilot depicted unusual women, women that could not be easily imitated. If Hollywood showed well-adjusted, witty, fun-loving, and serious women professionals who also happened to be wives and mothers today, they might be accused of advocating women's liberation. The frightening prospect remains zealously avoided.

Hollywood, today, keeps its fantasy movies and realistic movies separated. Science fiction, horror, Westerns, cops and robbers, and catastrophe movies operate as fantasies that are popular with audiences. "Realistic" movies have become the property of artistically minded directors who are less interested in the commercial success of their work and are willing to explore man–woman relationships in bold ways. While women's movies of the thirties were fantasies, be they melodramas or Independent Woman films, the realities of the 1970s seem to preclude a continuation of that genre. With Hollywood concentrating on the catastrophe and adventure fantasies, then, women become subordinate to the central male characters and events or disappear entirely.

Within this context, what kind of female portrayals are possible for the screen? The woman as whore remains the most acceptable type, but even within this image there is less and less variation. Sexual explicitness eliminates the need for Eves to be inventive, interesting, or unique. Eve becomes most frequently seen in pornographic films, the last and now, seemingly, only place for women. A sorry comment, indeed. A young Rita Hayworth or Ava Gardner might find a job as a sex kitten in another version of *Deep Throat* if she were willing to bare all; otherwise, there would be no movie work for her. The rich diversity of Eve characterizations, as performed by Stanwyck, Davis, Claire Trevor, Ida Lupino, Gardner, Hayworth, and others, is absent from the screen today.

Movies no longer provide either fantasy outlets or socially approved roles for women. They ignore them entirely. One major reason Hollywood has been able to effect this Great Disappearance Act against women is that women moviegoers have cooperated. Researchers of audience taste claim that women will watch men on the screen happily and not require the presence of women in the cast. Similarly, men enjoy watching male exploits on the screen. Thus, both sexes patronize men's films and neither laments the absence of women's roles. If *Julia* and *The Turning Point* are extremely profitable, the situation may change.

While Hollywood movies prevailed as the major form of recreation for Americans, they shaped the dreams of their viewers. Movies provided the dream ingredients for young girls and boys; they showed off new fashions in clothes and hair; they gave vicarious pleasure to many devoted fans. Inveterate moviegoers knew that Hollywood adventures were unrealistic; indeed, they reveled in the improbabilities and the adventures they saw portrayed on the silver screen. Women moviegoers, the mainstay of the audiences especially during the war years, knew that Bette Davis' sufferings were more extreme, more unlikely, and more exaggerated than anything that could happen in real life. But they also knew that suffering was a universal female experience and therefore served as the basis for the melodrama. Fans of Joan Crawford knew that there were not too many female Horatio Alger stories in real life, but they also knew that Joan Crawford's personal biography read like an Alger story.

Movie fans separated the fantastic from the real in their movie dreams. Without articulating it, they understood the difference between reality and fantasy. They did not object to the numerous movies about rich people during Depression America. Women loved the long fashion sequences in movies such as *The Women* (1939) precisely because they would never wear such clothes. They enjoyed seeing their favorite star live in a mansion, ride horses across the open plantation, and attend gay parties nightly. None of these activities interfered with the preservation of traditional values. The family, private enterprise, monogamy, fidelity, decency, and love of country remained essential values, undisturbed and unthreatened by Hollywood movies. Evil was always punished and good rewarded.

Fantasy and reality intermingled in a prophetic way in *Mildred Pierce*. More American women worked outside the home than ever before during World War II, but many left their lucrative defense jobs rapidly after the war in order to go home and have babies. Mildred Pierce, as a successful businesswoman, probably would not have returned to the home under normal cricumstances. She had to be removed from her business dramatically and decisively. On the fantasy level, many women moviegoers identified with successful, commanding Mildred but also wondered who cared for her home and family while she worked full time. Indeed, American women resisted the creation of day care centers during the war precisely because they believed that each mother should care for her children in her own home. *Mildred Pierce* was acceptable fantasy but not desired reality. Thus, her ending provided satisfaction: Mildred's independence was ended and traditional values preserved.

Mildred Pierce demonstrated, in the bleakest possible terms, what would happen to the American family if strong women left the home. Women, the mainstay of the family, the raisers of the children, and the preservers of traditional values, determine whether stability or change characterizes family patterns. And since stability is the desired norm, women must be returned to the home and removed from all other domains, thus ending both the Independent Woman and the Eve images in the movies. Hollywood moviemakers, as well as most American tastemakers, have always listened to the conservatives, not the reformers. They have agreed, by their screen portrayals of women, that strong, independent women are potential disruptors of social patterns. They have lauded the sweet Marys and duly punished the naughty Eves. They have put the Hepburns and Davises and Crawfords in their proper places by either marrying them off or killing them at the end of the movie. Creators of popular forms of entertainment have appreciated the sensitive, pivotal role women play in shaping society. And they successfully enforced established patterns rather than experiment with new ones. They responded to the expectations of their audience, to the habitual, the tried and true ways.

Mildred Pierce remains a powerful movie today. Its melodramatic treatment of the universal human struggle between mother and daughter and of thwarted human ambition touches contemporary audiences. Its particular history, its emergence at precisely the point in time when Americans looked forward to a time of peace and hope, suggests an unspoken commitment to keeping women in their place as an essential step in achieving that peaceful time. James Cain, Michael Curtiz, and all of the other participators in the making of *Mildred Pierce* captured the unarticulated American need to punish strong, deviant women, and in so doing, recognized the sensitive and influential role women played in the American family.

The most enduring of American popular cultural genres endure because they continue to express the dreams, wishes, ambitions, and adventures of their audience. The need for new frontiers keeps the Western alive in fiction and film. While melodrama lives again in the medium of television, it had exhausted its cinematic possibilities in *Mildred Pierce*. The Independent Woman genre has not yet found a congenial home in popular cultural forms. Television has not been an eager developer of this genre though *Rhoda, Mary Tyler Moore*, and *Maude* have been exciting beginnings. (*Police Woman* and *Charlie's*

Angels emerge as distortions of the genre.) Women, who have always been the major patronizers of both the melodrama and Independent Woman form of entertainment, remain devoted to the soaps, to the gothic romances with their fragile and dying-for-love heroines, to women's fiction with its neurotic, indecisive heroines, and to the few independent women portrayed on the screen. From the ashes of *Mildred Pierce*, we have *Julia*. One hopes that this important branch of the woman's film will be revivified and will flourish in the future.

14

The Atomic Bomb and the Origins of the Cold War

MARTIN J. SHERWIN

• In early August 1945, Japan was prostrate before the economic and military power of the United States. Its once proud Imperial Fleet and great battleships were at the bottom of the Pacific, its best-trained pilots were dead, its army was decimated by hopeless defenses of isolated islands, its skies were violated with impunity by the bombers of the American army and navy, and its population was practically starving. If that was not enough, the Soviet Union was already shifting its armies from Germany and Europe to the Far East, where they would attack Japanese forces on the Asian mainland.

In such circumstances, was the United States justified in dropping atomic bombs on Hiroshima and Nagasaki? Would the Japanese have realized the hopelessness of their position even without the introduction of nuclear weapons? Could the bombs have had an equivalent psychological impact if they had been dropped in rural areas rather than in the midst of crowded cities? Was the atomic bomb the last shot of World War II or the first shot of the Cold War?

Although such questions have inspired a large and diversified literature, perhaps no one has approached the subject with more care and clarity than Martin J. Sherwin of Tufts University. As you read his article, and especially as you reflect upon the statement by University of Chicago scientists in the final paragraph, you might attempt to imagine yourself as the diplomatic representative of another nation—perhaps France or Russia or Japan. What reasons would they have had for assuming that the ultimate weapon was anything more or less than an instrument for advancing American foreign policy? Do you think that the United States was then,

From the *American Historical Review*, 78 (October 1973). Reprinted by permission of the author. Martin J. Sherwin, Professor of History at Tufts University, is author of *A World Destroyed: The Atomic Bomb and The Grand Alliance* (1975).

> or is now, willing to share its military secrets for the benefit
> of mankind?

During the second World War the atomic bomb was seen and valued
as a potential rather than an actual instrument of policy. Responsible
officials believed that its impact on diplomacy had to await its development and, perhaps, even a demonstration of its power. As Henry L.
Stimson, the secretary of war, observed in his memoirs: "The bomb as
a merely probable weapon had seemed a weak reed on which to rely,
but the bomb as a colossal reality was very different." That policymakers considered this difference before Hiroshima has been well documented, but whether they based wartime diplomatic policies upon an
anticipated successful demonstration of the bomb's power remains a
source of controversy. Two questions delineate the issues in this debate. First, did the development of the atomic bomb affect the way
American policymakers conducted diplomacy with the Soviet Union?
Second, did diplomatic considerations related to the Soviet Union
influence the decision to use the atomic bomb against Japan?

These important questions relating the atomic bomb to American
diplomacy, and ultimately to the origins of the cold war, have been
addressed almost exclusively to the formulation of policy during the
early months of the Truman administration. As a result, two anterior
questions of equal importance, questions with implications for those
already posed, have been overlooked. Did diplomatic considerations
related to Soviet postwar behavior influence the formulation of Roosevelt's atomic-energy policies? What effect did the atomic legacy Truman inherited have on the diplomatic and atomic-energy policies of
his administration?

To comprehend the nature of the relationship between atomic-
energy and diplomatic policies that developed during the war, the
bomb must be seen as policymakers saw it before Hiroshima, as a
weapon that might be used to control postwar diplomacy. For this task
our present view is conceptually inadequate. After more than a quarter century of experience we understand, as wartime policy makers did
not, the bomb's limitations as a diplomatic instrument. To appreciate
the profound influence of the unchallenged wartime assumption about
the bomb's impact on diplomacy we must recognize the postwar purposes for which policymakers and their advisers believed the bomb

could be used. In this effort Churchill's expectations must be scrutinized as carefully as Roosevelt's, and scientists' ideas must be considered along with those of politicians. Truman's decision to use the atomic bomb against Japan must be evaluated in the light of Roosevelt's atomic legacy, and the problems of impending peace must be considered along with the exigencies of war. To isolate the basic atomic-energy policy alternatives that emerged during the war requires that we first ask whether alternatives were, in fact, recognized.

What emerges most clearly from a close examination of wartime formulation of atomic-energy policy is the conclusion that policy makers never seriously questioned the assumption that the atomic bomb should be used against Germany or Japan. From October 9, 1941, the time of the first meeting to organize the atomic-energy project, Stimson, Roosevelt, and other members of the "top policy group" conceived of the development of the atomic bomb as an essential part of the total war effort. Though the suggestion to build the bomb was initially made by scientists who feared that Germany might develop the weapon first, those with political responsibility for prosecuting the war accepted the circumstances of the bomb's creation as sufficient justification for its use against any enemy.

Having nurtured this point of view during the war, Stimson charged those who later criticized the use of the bomb with two errors. First, these critics asked the wrong question: it was not whether surrender could have been obtained without using the bomb, but whether a different diplomatic and military course from that followed by the Truman administration would have achieved an earlier surrender. Second, the basic assumption of these critics was false: the idea that American policy should have been based primarily on a desire not to employ the bomb seemed as "irresponsible" as a policy controlled by a positive desire to use it. The war, not the bomb, Stimson argued, had been the primary focus of his attention; as secretary of war his responsibilities permitted no alternative.

Stimson's own wartime diary nevertheless indicates that from 1941 on, the problems associated with the atomic bomb moved steadily closer to the center of his own and Roosevelt's concerns. As the war progressed, the implications of the weapon's development became diplomatic as well as military, postwar as well as wartime. Recognizing that a monopoly of the atomic bomb gave the United States a powerful new military advantage, Roosevelt and Stimson became increasingly anxious to convert it to diplomatic advantage. In December 1944 they spoke of using the "secret" of the atomic bomb as a means of obtaining a *quid pro quo* from the Soviet Union. But viewing the bomb as a potential instrument of diplomacy, they were not moved to formulate a concrete plan for carrying out this exchange before the bomb was used. The bomb had "this unique peculiarity," Stimson noted several months later in his diary; "Success is 99% assured, yet only by the first actual war trial of the weapon can the actual certainty be fixed." Whether or not the specter of postwar Soviet ambitions created "a positive desire" to ascertain the bomb's power, until that decision was executed "atomic diplomacy" remained an idea that never crystallized into policy.

Although Roosevelt left no definitive statement assigning a postwar role to the atomic bomb, his expectations for its potential diplomatic value can be recalled from the existing record. An analysis of the policies he chose from among the alternatives he faced suggests that the potential diplomatic value of the bomb began to shape his atomic-energy policies as early as 1943. He may have been cautious about counting on the bomb as a reality during the war, but he nevertheless consistently chose policy alternatives that would promote the postwar diplomatic potential of the bomb if the predictions of scientists proved true. These policies were based on the assumption that the bomb could be used effectively to secure postwar diplomatic aims; and this assumption was carried over from the Roosevelt to the Truman administration.

Despite general agreement that the bomb would be an extraordinarily important diplomatic factor after the war, those closely associated with its development did not agree on how to use it most effectively as an instrument of diplomacy. Convinced that wartime atomic-energy policies would have postwar diplomatic consequences, several scientists advised Roosevelt to adopt policies aimed at achieving a postwar international control system. Churchill, on the other hand, urged the president to maintain the Anglo-American atomic monopoly as a diplomatic counter against the postwar ambitions of other nations—particularly against the Soviet Union. Roosevelt fashioned his atomic-energy policies from the choices he made between these conflicting recommendations. In 1943 he rejected the counsel

of his science advisers and began to consider the diplomatic component of atomic-energy policy in consultation with Churchill alone.
This decision-making procedure and Roosevelt's untimely death have
left his motives ambiguous. Nevertheless it is clear that he pursued
policies consistent with Churchill's monopolistic, anti-Soviet views.

The findings of this study thus raise serious questions concerning
generalizations historians have commonly made about Roosevelt's diplomacy: that it was consistent with his public reputation for cooperation and conciliation; that he was naive with respect to postwar Soviet
behavior; that, like Wilson, he believed in collective security as an
effective guarantor of national safety; and that he made every possible
effort to assure that the Soviet Union and its allies would continue to
function as postwar partners. Although this article does not dispute
the view that Roosevelt desired amicable postwar relations with the
Soviet Union, or even that he worked hard to achieve them, it does
suggest that historians have exaggerated his confidence in (and perhaps his commitment to) such an outcome. His most secret and
among his most important long-range decisions—those responsible for
prescribing a diplomatic role for the atomic bomb—reflected his lack
of confidence. Finally, in light of this study's conclusions, the widely
held assumption that Truman's attitude toward the atomic bomb was
substantially different from Roosevelt's must also be revised.

Like the grand alliance itself, the Anglo-American atomic-energy partnership was forged by the war and its exigencies. The threat of a German atomic bomb precipitated a hasty marriage of convenience between British research and American resources. When scientists in
Britain proposed a theory that explained how an atomic bomb might
quickly be built, policy makers had to assume that German scientists
were building one. "If such an explosive were made," Vannevar Bush,
the director of the Office of Scientific Research and Development,
told Roosevelt in July 1941, "it would be thousands of times more
powerful than existing explosives, and its use might be determining."
Roosevelt assumed nothing less. Even before the atomic-energy project was fully organized he assigned it the highest priority. He wanted
the program "pushed not only in regard to development, but also
with due regard to time. This is very much of the essence," he told
Bush in March 1942. "We both felt painfully the dangers of doing

nothing," Churchill recalled, referring to an early wartime discussion with Roosevelt about the bomb.

The high stakes at issue during the war did not prevent officials in Great Britain or the United States from considering the postwar implications of their atomic-energy decisions. As early as 1941, during the debate over whether to join the United States in an atomic-energy partnership, members of the British government's atomic-energy committee argued that the matter "was so important for the future that work should proceed in Britain." Weighing the obvious difficulties of proceeding alone against the possible advantages of working with the United States, Sir John Anderson, then lord president of the council and the minister responsible for atomic-energy research, advocated the partnership. As he explained to Churchill, by working closely with the Americans British scientists would be able "to take up the work again [after the war], not where we left off, but where the combined effort had by then brought it."

As early as October 1942 Roosevelt's science advisers exhibited a similar concern with the potential postwar value of atomic energy. After conducting a full-scale review of the atomic-energy project, James B. Conant, the president of Harvard University and Bush's deputy, recommended discontinuing the Anglo-American partnership "as far as development and manufacture is concerned." Conant had in mind three considerations when he suggested a more limited arrangement with the British: first, the project had been transferred from scientific to military control; second, the United States was doing almost all the developmental work; and third, security dictated "moving in a direction of holding much more closely the information about the development of this program." Under these conditions it was difficult, Conant observed, "to see how a joint British-American project could be sponsored in this country." What prompted Conant's recommendations, however, was his suspicion—soon to be shared by other senior atomic-energy administrators—that the British were rather more concerned with information for postwar industrial purposes than for wartime use. What right did the British have to the fruits of American labor? "We were doing nine-tenths of the work," Stimson told Roosevelt in October. By December 1942 there was general agreement among the president's atomic-energy advisers that the British no longer had a valid claim to all atomic-energy information.

Conant's arguments and suggestions for a more limited partnership were incorporated into a "Report to the President by the Military Policy Committee." Roosevelt approved the recommendations on December 28. Early in January the British were officially informed that the rules governing the Anglo-American atomic-energy partnership had been altered on "orders from the top."

By approving the policy of "restricted interchange" Roosevelt undermined a major incentive for British cooperation. It is not surprising, therefore, that Churchill took up the matter directly with the president and with Harry Hopkins, "Roosevelt's own, personal Foreign Office." The prime minister's initial response to the new policy reflected his determination to have it reversed: "That we should each work separately," he threatened, "would be a sombre decision."

Conant and Bush understood the implications of Churchill's intervention and sought to counter its effect. "It is our duty," Conant wrote Bush, "to see to it that the President of the United States, in writing, is informed of what is involved in these decisions." Their memorandums no longer concentrated on tortuous discussions differentiating between the scientific research and the manufacturing stages of the bomb's development but focused on what to Conant was "the major consideration . . . that of *national security and postwar strategic significance.*" Information on manufacturing an atomic bomb, Conant noted, was a "military secret which is in a totally different class from anything the world has ever seen if the potentialities of this project are realized." To provide the British with detailed knowledge about the construction of a bomb "might be the equivalent to joint occupation of a fortress or strategic harbor in perpetuity." Though British and American atomic-energy policies might coincide during the war, Conant and Bush expected them to conflict afterward.

The controversy over the policy of "restricted interchange" of atomic-energy information shifted attention to postwar diplomatic considerations. As Bush wrote to Hopkins, "We can hardly give away the fruits of our developments as a part of postwar planning except on the basis of some overall agreement on that subject, which agreement does not now exist." The central issue was clearly drawn. The atomic-energy policy of the United States was related to the very fabric of Anglo-American postwar relations and, as Churchill would insist, to postwar relations between each of them and the Soviet Union. Just as the possibility of British postwar commercial competition had played a major role in shaping the U.S. policy of restricted interchange, the specter of Soviet postwar military power played a major role in shaping the prime minister's attitude toward atomic-energy policies in 1943.

"We cannot," Sir John Anderson wrote Churchill, "afford after the war to face the future without this weapon and rely entirely on America should Russia or some other power develop it." The prime minister agreed. The atomic bomb was an instrument of postwar diplomacy that Britain had to have. He could cite numerous reasons for his determination to acquire an independent atomic arsenal after the war, but Great Britain's postwar military-diplomatic position with respect to the Soviet Union invariably led the list. When Bush and Stimson visited London in July, Churchill told them quite frankly that he was "vitally interested in the possession of all [atomic-energy] information because this will be necessary for Britain's independence in the future as well as for success during the war." Nor was Churchill evasive about his reasoning: "It would never do to have Germany or Russia win the race for something which might be used for international blackmail," he stated bluntly and then pointed out that "Russia might be in a position to accomplish this result unless we worked together." In Washington, two months earlier, Churchill's science adviser Lord Cherwell had told Bush and Hopkins virtually the same thing. The British government, Cherwell stated, was considering "the whole [atomic-energy] affair on an after-the-war military basis." It intended, he said, "to manufacture and produce the weapon." Prior to the convening of the Quebec Conference, Anderson explained his own and Churchill's view of the bomb to the Canadian prime minister, Mackenzie King. The British knew, Anderson said, "that both Germany and Russia were working on the same thing," which, he noted, "would be a terrific factor in the postwar world as giving an absolute control to whatever country possessed the secret." Convinced that the British attitude toward the bomb would undermine any possibility of postwar cooperation with the Soviet Union, Bush and Conant vigorously continued to oppose any revival of the Anglo-American atomic-energy partnership.

On July 20, however, Roosevelt chose to accept a recommendation from Hopkins to restore full partnership, and he ordered Bush to "renew, in an inclusive manner, the full exchange of information with the British." A garbled trans-Atlantic cable to Bush reading "review" rather than "renew" gave him the opportunity to continue his negotiations in London with Churchill and thereby to modify the president's order. But Bush could not alter Roosevelt's intentions. On August 19, at the Quebec Conference, the president and the prime minister agreed that the British would share the atomic bomb. Despite Bush's negotiations with Churchill, the Quebec Agreement revived the principle of an Anglo-American atomic-energy partnership, albeit the British were reinstated as junior rather than equal partners.

The president's decision was not a casual one taken in ignorance. As the official history of the Atomic Energy Commission notes: "Both Roosevelt and Churchill knew that the stake of their diplomacy was a technological breakthrough so revolutionary that it transcended in importance even the bloody work of carrying the war to the heartland of the Nazi foe." The president had been informed of Churchill's position as well as of Bush's and Conant's. But how much closer Roosevelt was to Churchill than to his own advisers at this time is suggested by a report written after the war by General Leslie R. Groves, military director of the atomic-energy project. "It is not known what if any Americans President Roosevelt consulted at Quebec," Groves wrote. "It is doubtful if there were any. All that is known is that the Quebec Agreement was signed by President Roosevelt and that, as finally signed, it agreed practically in toto with the version presented by Sir John Anderson to Dr. Bush in Washington a few weeks earlier."

The debate that preceded the Quebec Agreement is noteworthy for yet another reason: it led to a new relationship between Roosevelt and his atomic-energy advisers. After August 1943 the president did not consult with them about the diplomatic aspects of atomic-energy policy. Though he responded politely when they offered their views, he acted decisively only in consultation with Churchill. Bush and Conant appear to have lost a large measure of their influence because they had used it to oppose Churchill's position. What they did not suspect was the extent to which the president had come to share the prime minister's view.

It can be argued that Roosevelt, the political pragmatist, renewed the wartime atomic-energy partnership to keep relations with the British harmonious rather than disrupt them on the basis of a postwar issue. Indeed it seems logical that the president took this consideration into account. But it must also be recognized that he was perfectly comfortable with the concept Churchill advocated—that military power was a prerequisite to successful postwar diplomacy. As early as August 1941, during the Atlantic Conference, Roosevelt had rejected the idea that an "effective international organization" could be relied upon to keep the peace; an Anglo-American international police force would be far more effective, he told Churchill. By the spring of 1942 the concept had broadened: the two "policemen" became four, and the idea was added that every other nation would be totally disarmed. "The Four Policemen" would have "to build up a reservoir of force so powerful that no aggressor would dare to challenge it," Roosevelt told Arthur Sweetser, an ardent internationalist. Violators first would be quarantined, and, if they persisted in their disruptive activities, bombed at the rate of a city a day until they agreed to behave. The president told Molotov about this idea in May, and in November he repeated it to Clark Eichelberger, who was coordinating the activities of the American internationalists. A year later, at the Teheran Conference, Roosevelt again discussed his idea, this time with Stalin. As Robert A. Divine has noted: "Roosevelt's concept of big power domination remained the central idea in his approach to international organization throughout World War II."

Precisely how Roosevelt expected to integrate the atomic bomb into his plans for keeping the peace in the postwar world is not clear. However, against the background of his atomic-energy policy decisions of 1943 and his peace-keeping concepts, his actions in 1944 suggest that he intended to take full advantage of the bomb's potential as a postwar instrument of Anglo-American diplomacy. If Roosevelt thought the bomb could be used to create a more peaceful world order, he seems to have considered the threat of its power more effective than any opportunities it offered for international cooperation. If Roosevelt was less worried than Churchill about Soviet postwar ambitions, he was no less determined than the prime minister to avoid any commitments to the Soviets for the international control of atomic energy. There could still be four policemen, but only two of them would have the bomb.

The atomic-energy policies Roosevelt pursued during the remainder of his life reinforce this interpretation of his ideas for the postwar period. The following three questions offer a useful framework for analyzing his intentions. Did Roosevelt make any additional agreements with Churchill that would further support the view that he intended to maintain an Anglo-American monopoly after the war? Did Roosevelt demonstrate any interest in the international control of atomic energy? Was Roosevelt aware that an effort to maintain an Anglo-American monopoly of the atomic bomb might lead to a postwar atomic arms race with the Soviet Union?

An examination of the wartime activities of the eminent Danish physicist, Niels Bohr, who arrived in America early in 1944 as a consultant to the atomic-bomb project, will help answer these questions. "Officially and secretly he came to help the technical enterprise," noted J. Robert Oppenheimer, the director of the Los Alamos atomic-bomb laboratory, but "most secretly of all . . . he came to advance his case and his cause." Bohr was convinced that a postwar atomic armaments race with the Soviet Union was inevitable unless Roosevelt and Churchill initiated efforts during the war to establish the international control of atomic energy. Bohr's attempts to promote this idea in the United States were aided by Justice Felix Frankfurter.

Bohr and Frankfurter were old acquaintances. They had first met in 1933 at Oxford and then in 1939 on several occasions in London and the United States. At these meetings Bohr had been impressed by the breadth of Frankfurter's interests and, perhaps, overimpressed with his influence on Roosevelt. In 1944 the Danish minister to the United States brought them together, once again, at his home in Washington. Frankfurter, who appears to have suspected why Bohr had come to America and why this meeting had been arranged, had learned about the atomic-bomb project earlier in the war when, as he told the story, several troubled scientists had sought his advice on a matter of "greatest importance." He therefore invited Bohr to lunch in his chambers and, by dropping hints about his knowledge, encouraged Bohr to discuss the issue.

After listening to Bohr's analysis of the postwar alternatives—an atomic armaments race or some form of international control—Frankfurter saw Roosevelt. Bohr had persuaded him, Frankfurter reported, that disastrous consequences would result if Russia learned on her own about the atomic-bomb project. Frankfurter suggested that it was a matter of great importance that the president explore the possibility of seeking an effective arrangement with the Soviets for controlling the bomb. He also noted that Bohr, whose knowledge of Soviet science was extensive, believed that the Russians had the capability to build their own atomic weapons. If the international control of atomic energy was not discussed among the Allies during the war, an atomic arms race between the Allies would almost certainly develop after the war. It seemed imperative, therefore, that Roosevelt consider approaching Stalin with a proposal as soon as possible.

Frankfurter discussed these points with the president for an hour and a half, and he left feeling that Roosevelt was "plainly impressed by my account of the matter." When Frankfurter had suggested that the solution of this problem might be more important than all the plans for a world organization, Roosevelt had agreed. Moreover he had authorized Frankfurter to tell Bohr, who was scheduled to return to England, that he might inform "our friends in London that the President was most eager to explore the proper safeguards in relation to X [the atomic bomb]." Roosevelt also told Frankfurter that the problem of the atomic bomb "worried him to death" and that he was very eager for all the help he could have in dealing with it.

The alternatives placed before Roosevelt posed a difficult dilemma. On the one hand, he could continue to exclude the Soviet government from any official information about the development of the bomb, a policy that would probably strengthen America's postwar military-diplomatic position. But such a policy would also encourage Soviet mistrust of Anglo-American intentions and was bound to make postwar cooperation more difficult. On the other hand, Roosevelt could use the atomic-bomb project as an instrument of cooperation by informing Stalin of the American government's intention of cooperating in the development of a plan for the international control of atomic weapons, an objective that might never be achieved.

Either choice involved serious risks. Roosevelt had to balance the diplomatic advantages of being well ahead of the Soviet Union in atomic-energy production after the war against the advantages of initiating wartime negotiations for postwar cooperation. The issue here, it must be emphasized, is not whether the initiative Bohr suggested would have led to successful international control, but rather whether

Roosevelt demonstrated any serious interest in laying the groundwork for such a policy.

Several considerations indicate that Roosevelt was already committed to a course of action that precluded Bohr's internationalist approach. First, Frankfurter appears to have been misled. Though Roosevelt's response had been characteristically agreeable, he did not mention Bohr's ideas to his atomic-energy advisers until September 1944, when he told Bush that he was very disturbed that Frankfurter had learned about the project. Roosevelt knew at this time, moreover, that the Soviets were finding out on their own about the development of the atomic bomb. Security personnel had reported an active Communist cell in the Radiation Laboratory at the University of California. Their reports indicated that at least one scientist at Berkeley was selling information to Russian agents. "They [Soviet agents] are already getting information about vital secrets and sending them to Russia," Stimson told the president on September 9, 1943. If Roosevelt was indeed worried to death about the effect the atomic bomb could have on Soviet-American postwar relations, he took no action to remove the potential danger, nor did he make any effort to explore the possibility of encouraging Soviet postwar cooperation on this problem. The available evidence indicates that he never discussed the merits of the international control of atomic energy with his advisers after this first or any subsequent meeting with Frankfurter.

How is the president's policy, of neither discussing international control nor promoting the idea, to be explained if not by an intention to use the bomb as an instrument of Anglo-American postwar diplomacy? Perhaps his concern for maintaining the tightest possible secrecy against German espionage led him to oppose any discussion about the project. Or he may have concluded, after considering Bohr's analysis, that Soviet suspicion and mistrust would be further aroused if Stalin were informed of the existence of the project without receiving detailed information about the bomb's construction. The possibility also exists that Roosevelt believed that neither Congress nor the American public would approve of a policy giving the Soviet Union any measure of control over the new weapon. Finally Roosevelt might have thought that the spring of 1944 was not the proper moment for such an initiative.

Though it would be unreasonable to state categorically that these considerations did not contribute to his decision, they appear to have been secondary. Roosevelt was clearly, and properly, concerned about secrecy, but the most important secret with respect to Soviet-American relations was that the United States was developing an atomic bomb. And that secret, he was aware, already had been passed on to Moscow. Soviet mistrust of Anglo-American postwar intentions could only be exacerbated by continuing the existing policy. Moreover an attempt to initiate planning for international control of atomic energy would not have required the revelation of technical secrets. Nor is it sufficient to cite Roosevelt's well-known sensitivity to domestic politics as an explanation for his atomic-energy policies. He was willing to take enormous political risks, as he did at Yalta, to support his diplomatic objectives.

Had Roosevelt avoided all postwar atomic-energy commitments, his lack of support for international control could have been interpreted as an attempt to reserve his opinion on the best course to follow. But he had made commitments in 1943 supporting Churchill's monopolistic, anti-Soviet position, and he continued to make others in 1944. On June 13, for example, Roosevelt and Churchill signed an Agreement and Declaration of Trust, specifying that the United States and Great Britain would cooperate in seeking to control available supplies of uranium and thorium ore both during and after the war. This commitment, taken against the background of Roosevelt's peace-keeping ideas and his other commitments, suggests that the president's attitude toward the international control of atomic energy was similar to the prime minister's.

Churchill had dismissed out of hand the concept of international control when Bohr talked with him about it in May 1944. Their meeting was not long under way before Churchill lost interest and became involved in an argument with Lord Cherwell, who was also present. Bohr, left out of the discussion, was frustrated and depressed; he was unable to return the conversation to what he considered the most important diplomatic problem of the war. When the allotted half hour elapsed, Bohr asked if he might send the prime minister a memorandum on the subject. A letter from Niels Bohr, Churchill bitingly replied, was always welcome, but he hoped it would deal with a subject other than politics. As Bohr described their meeting: "We did not even speak the same language."

Churchill rejected the assumption upon which Bohr's views were founded—that international control of atomic energy could be used as a cornerstone for constructing a peaceful world order. An atomic monopoly would be a significant diplomatic advantage in postwar diplomacy, and Churchill did not believe that anything useful could be gained by surrendering this advantage. The argument that a new weapon created a unique opportunity to refashion international affairs ignored every lesson Churchill read into history. "You can be quite sure," he would write in a memorandum less than a year later, "that any power that gets hold of the secret will try to make the article, and this touches the existence of human society. This matter is out of all relation to anything else that exists in the world, and I could not think of participating in any disclosure to third or fourth parties at the present time."

Several months after Bohr met Churchill, Frankfurter arranged a meeting between Bohr and Roosevelt. Their discussion lasted an hour and a half. Roosevelt told Bohr that contact with the Soviet Union along the lines he suggested had to be tried. The president also said he was optimistic that such an initiative would have a "good result." In his opinion Stalin was enough of a realist to understand the revolutionary importance of this development and its consequences. The president also expressed confidence that the prime minister would eventually share these views. They had disagreed in the past, he told Bohr, but they had always succeeded in resolving their differences.

Roosevelt's enthusiasm for Bohr's ideas was more apparent than real. The president did not mention them to anyone until he met with Churchill at Hyde Park on September 18, following the second wartime conference at Quebec. The decisions reached on atomic energy at Hyde Park were summarized and documented in an *aide-mémoire* signed by Roosevelt and Churchill on September 19, 1944. The agreement bears the markings of Churchill's attitude toward the atomic bomb and his poor opinion of Bohr. "Enquiries should be made," the last paragraph reads, "regarding the activities of Professor Bohr and steps taken to ensure that he is responsible for no leakage of information particularly to the Russians." If Bohr's activities prompted Roosevelt to suspect his loyalty, there can be no doubt that Churchill encouraged the president's suspicions. Atomic energy and Britain's future position as a world power had become part of a single equation for the prime minister. Bohr's ideas, like the earlier idea of restricted interchange, threatened the continuation of the Anglo-American atomic-energy partnership. With such great stakes at issue Churchill did not hesitate to discredit Bohr along with his ideas. "It seems to me," Churchill wrote to Cherwell soon after Hyde Park, "Bohr ought to be confined or at any rate made to see that he is very near the edge of mortal crimes."

The *aide-mémoire* also contained an explicit rejection of any wartime efforts toward international control: "The suggestion that the world should be informed regarding tube alloys [the atomic bomb], with a view to an international agreement regarding its control and use, is not accepted. The matter should continue to be regarded as of the utmost secrecy." But Bohr had never suggested that the world be informed about the atomic bomb. He had argued in memorandums and in person that peace was not possible unless the Soviet government—not the world—was officially notified only about the project's existence before the time when any discussion would appear coercive rather than friendly.

It was the second paragraph, however, that revealed the full extent of Roosevelt's agreement with Churchill's point of view. "Full collaboration between the United States and the British Government in developing tube alloys for military and commercial purposes," it noted, "should continue after the defeat of Japan unless and until terminated by joint agreement." Finally the *aide-mémoire* offers some insight into Roosevelt's intentions for the military use of the weapon in the war: "When a bomb is finally available, it might perhaps, after mature consideration, be used against the Japanese, who should be warned that this bombardment will be repeated until they surrender."

Within the context of the complex problem of the origins of the cold war the Hyde Park meeting is far more important than historians of the war generally have recognized. Overshadowed by the Second Quebec Conference on one side and by the drama of Yalta on the other, its significance often has been overlooked. But the agreements reached in September 1944 reflect a set of attitudes, aims, and assumptions that guided the relationship between the atomic bomb and American diplomacy during the Roosevelt administration and, through the transfer of its atomic legacy, during the Truman administration as well. Two alternatives had been recognized long before Roosevelt and

Churchill met in 1944 at Hyde Park: the bomb could have been used to initiate a diplomatic effort to work out a system for its international control, or it could remain isolated during the war from any cooperative initiatives and held in reserve should cooperation fail. Roosevelt consistently favored the latter alternative. An insight into his reasoning is found in a memorandum Bush wrote following a conversation with Roosevelt several days after the Hyde Park meeting: "The President evidently thought he could join with Churchill in bringing about a US-UK postwar agreement on this subject [the atomic bomb] by which it would be held closely and presumably to control the peace of the world." By 1944 Roosevelt's earlier musings about the four policemen had faded into the background. But the idea behind it, the concept of controlling the peace of the world by amassing overwhelming military power, appears to have remained a prominent feature of his postwar plans.

In the seven months between his meeting with Churchill in September and his death the following April Roosevelt did not alter his atomic-energy policies. Nor did he reverse his earlier decision not to take his advisers into his confidence about diplomatic issues related to the new weapon. They were never told about the Hyde Park agreements, nor were they able to discuss with him their ideas for the postwar handling of atomic-energy affairs. Though officially uninformed, Bush suspected that Roosevelt had made a commitment to continue the atomic-energy partnership exclusively with the British after the war, and he, as well as Conant, opposed the idea. They believed such a policy "might well lead to extraordinary efforts on the part of Russia to establish its own position in the field secretly, and might lead to a clash, say 20 years from now." Unable to reach the president directly, they sought to influence his policies through Stimson, whose access to Roosevelt's office (though not to his thoughts on atomic energy) was better than their own.

Summarizing their views on September 30 for the secretary of war, Bush and Conant predicted that an atomic bomb equivalent to from one to ten thousand tons of high explosive could be "demonstrated" before August 1, 1945. They doubted that the present American and British monopoly could be maintained for more than three or four years, and they pointed out that any nation with good technical and scientific resources could catch up; accidents of research, moreover, might even put some other nation ahead. In addition atomic bombs were only the first step along the road of nuclear weapons technology. In the not-too-distant future loomed the awesome prospect of a weapon perhaps a thousand times more destructive—the hydrogen bomb. Every major center of population in the world would then lie at the mercy of a nation that struck first in war. Security therefore could be found neither in secrecy nor even in the control of raw materials, for the supply of heavy hydrogen was practically unlimited.

These predictions by Bush and Conant were more specific than Bohr's, but not dissimilar. They, too, believed that a nuclear arms race could be prevented only through international control. Their efforts were directed, however, toward abrogating existing agreements with the British rather than toward initiating new agreements with the Soviets. Like Bohr they based their hope for Stalin's eventual cooperation on his desire to avoid the circumstances that could lead to a nuclear war. But while Bohr urged Roosevelt to approach Stalin with the carrot of international control before the bomb became a reality, Bush and Conant were inclined to delay such an approach until the bomb was demonstrated, until it was clear that without international control the new weapon could be used as a terribly effective stick.

In their attempt to persuade Roosevelt to their point of view Bush and Conant failed. But their efforts were not in vain. By March 1945 Stimson shared their concerns, and he agreed that peace without international control was a forlorn hope. Postwar problems relating to the atomic bomb "went right down to the bottom facts of human nature, morals and government, and it is by far the most searching and important thing that I have had to do since I have been here in the office of Secretary of War," Stimson wrote on March 5. Ten days later he presented his views on postwar atomic-energy policy to Roosevelt. This was their last meeting. In less than a month a new president took the oath of office.

Harry S. Truman inherited a set of military and diplomatic atomic-energy policies that included partially formulated intentions, several commitments to Churchill, and the assumption that the bomb would be a legitimate weapon to be used against Japan. But no policy was definitely settled. According to the Quebec Agreement the president had the option of deciding the future of the commercial aspects of the atomic-energy partnership according to his own estimate of what was fair. Although the policy of "utmost secrecy" had been confirmed at Hyde Park the previous September, Roosevelt had not informed his atomic-energy advisers about the *aide-mémoire* he and Churchill signed. Although the assumption that the bomb would be used in the war was shared by those privy to its development, assumptions formulated early in the war were not necessarily valid at its conclusion. Yet Truman was bound to the past by his own uncertain position and by the prestige of his predecessor. Since Roosevelt had refused to open negotiations with the Soviet government for the international control of atomic energy, and since he had never expressed any objection to the wartime use of the bomb, it would have required considerable political courage and confidence for Truman to alter those policies. Moreover it would have required the encouragement of his advisers, for under the circumstances the most serious constraint on the new president's choices was his dependence upon advice. So Truman's atomic legacy, while it included several options, did not necessarily entail complete freedom to choose from among all the possible alternatives.

"I think it is very important that I should have a talk with you as soon as possible on a highly secret matter," Stimson wrote to Truman on April 24. It has "such a bearing on our present foreign relations and has such an important effect upon all my thinking in this field that I think you ought to know about it without further delay." Stimson had been preparing to brief Truman on the atomic bomb for almost ten days, but in the preceding twenty-four hours he had been seized by a sense of urgency. Relations with the Soviet Union had declined precipitously during the past week, the result, he thought, of the failure of the State Department to settle the major problems between the Allies before going ahead with the San Francisco Conference on the United Nations Organization. The secretary of state, Edward R. Stettinius, Jr., along with the department's Soviet specialists, now felt "compelled to bull the thing through." To get out of the "mess" they had created, Stimson wrote in his diary, they were urging Truman to get tough with the Russians. He had. Twenty-four hours earlier the president met with the Soviet foreign minister, V. M. Molotov, and "with rather brutal frankness" accused his government of breaking the Yalta Agreement. Molotov was furious. "I have never been talked to like that in my life," he told the president before leaving.

With a memorandum on the "political aspects of the S-1 [atomic bomb's] performance" in hand and General Groves in reserve, Stimson went to the White House on April 25. The document he carried was the distillation of numerous decisions already taken, each one the product of attitudes that developed along with the new weapon. The secretary himself was not entirely aware of how various forces had shaped these decisions: the recommendations of Bush and Conant, the policies Roosevelt had followed, the uncertainties inherent in the wartime alliance, the oppressive concern for secrecy, and his own inclination to consider long-range implications. It was a curious document. Though its language revealed Stimson's sensitivity to the historic significance of the atomic bomb, he did not question the wisdom of using it against Japan. Nor did he suggest any concrete steps for developing a postwar policy. His objective was to inform Truman of the salient problems: the possibility of an atomic arms race, the danger of atomic war, and the necessity for international control if the United Nations Organization was to work. "If the problem of the proper use of this weapon can be solved," he wrote, "we would have the opportunity to bring the world into a pattern in which the peace of the world and our civilizations can be saved." To cope with this difficult challenge Stimson suggested the "establishment of a select committee" to consider the postwar problems inherent in the development of the bomb. If his presentation was the "forceful statement" of the problem that historians of the Atomic Energy Commission have described it as being, its force inhered in the problem itself, not in any bold formulations or initiatives he offered toward a solution. If, as another historian has claimed, this meeting led to a "strategy of delayed showdown," requiring "the delay of all disputes with Russia until the atomic bomb had been demonstrated," there is no evidence in the extant records of the meeting that Stimson had such a strategy in mind or that Truman misunderstood the secretary's views.

What emerges from a careful reading of Stimson's diary, his memorandum of April 25 to Truman, a summary by Groves of the meeting, and Truman's recollections is an argument for overall caution in American diplomatic relations with the Soviet Union: it was an argument against any showdown. Since the atomic bomb was potentially the most dangerous issue facing the postwar world and since the most desirable resolution of the problem was some form of international control, Soviet cooperation had to be secured. It was imprudent, Stimson suggested, to pursue a policy that would preclude the possibility of international cooperation on atomic-energy matters after the war ended. Truman's overall impression of Stimson's argument was that the secretary of war was "at least as much concerned with the role of the atomic bomb in the shaping of history as in its capacity to shorten the war." These were indeed Stimson's dual concerns on April 25, and he could see no conflict between them.

Despite the profound consequences Stimson attributed to the development of the new weapon, he had not suggested that Truman reconsider its use against Japan. Nor had he thought to mention the possibility that chances of securing Soviet postwar cooperation might be diminished if Stalin did not receive a commitment to international control prior to an attack. The question of why these alternatives were overlooked naturally arises. Perhaps what Frankfurter once referred to as Stimson's habit of setting "his mind at one thing like the needle of an old victrola caught in a single groove" may help to explain his not mentioning these possibilities. Yet Bush and Conant never raised them either. Even Niels Bohr had made a clear distinction between the bomb's wartime use and its postwar impact on diplomacy. "What role it [the atomic bomb] may play in the present war," Bohr had written to Roosevelt in July 1944, was a question "quite apart" from the overriding concern: the need to avoid an atomic arms race.

The preoccupation with winning the war obviously helped to create this seeming dichotomy between the wartime use of the bomb and the potential postwar diplomatic problems with the Soviet Union raised by its development. But a closer look at how Bohr and Stimson each defined the nature of the diplomatic problem created by the bomb suggests that for the secretary of war and his advisers (and ultimately for the president they advised) there was no dichotomy at all. Bohr apprehended the meaning of the new weapon even before it was developed, and he had no doubt that scientists in the Soviet Union would also understand its profound implications for the postwar world. He was also certain that they would interpret the meaning of the development to Stalin just as scientists in the United States and Great Britain had explained it to Roosevelt and Churchill. Thus the diplomatic problem, as Bohr analyzed it, was not the need to convince Stalin that the atomic bomb was an unprecedented weapon that threatened the life of the world but the need to assure the Soviet leader that he had nothing to fear from the circumstances of its development. By informing Stalin during the war that the United States intended to cooperate with him in neutralizing the bomb through international control, Bohr reasoned that its wartime use could be considered apart from postwar problems.

Stimson approached the problem rather differently. Although he believed that the bomb "might even mean the doom of civilization or it might mean the perfection of civilization" he was less confident than Bohr that the weapon in an undeveloped state could be used as an effective instrument of diplomacy. Until its "actual certainty [was] fixed," Stimson considered any prior approach to Stalin as premature. But as the uncertainties of impending peace became more apparent and worrisome, Stimson, Truman, and the secretary of state-designate, James F. Byrnes, began to think of the bomb as something of a diplomatic panacea for their postwar problems. Byrnes had told Truman in April that the bomb "might well put us in a position to dictate our own terms at the end of the war." By June, Truman and Stimson were discussing "further *quid pro quos* which should be established in consideration for our taking them [the Soviet Union] into [atomic-energy] partnership." Assuming that the bomb's impact on diplomacy would be immediate and extraordinary, they agreed on no less than "the settlement of the Polish, Rumanian, Yugoslavian, and Manchurian problems." But they also concluded that no revelation would be made "to Russia or anyone else until the first bomb had been successfully laid on Japan." Truman and Stimson based their expectations on how they saw and valued the bomb; its use against Japan, they reasoned, would transfer this view to the Soviet Union.

Was an implicit warning to Moscow, then, the principal reason for deciding to use the atomic bomb against Japan? In light of the ambiguity of the available evidence the question defies an unequivocal answer. What can be said with certainty is that Truman, Stimson, Byrnes, and several others involved in the decision consciously considered two effects of a combat demonstration of the bomb's power: first, the impact of the atomic attack on Japan's leaders, who might be persuaded thereby to end the war; and second, the impact of that attack on the Soviet Union's leaders, who might then prove to be more cooperative. But if the assumption that the bomb might bring the war to a rapid conclusion was the principal motive for using the atomic bomb, the expectation that its use would also inhibit Soviet diplomatic ambitions clearly discouraged any inclination to question that assumption.

Policymakers were not alone in expecting a military demonstration of the bomb to have a salubrious effect on international affairs. James Conant, for example, believed that such a demonstration would further the prospects for international control. "President Conant has written me," Stimson informed the news commentator Raymond Swing in February 1947, "that one of the principal reasons he had for advising me that the bomb must be used was that that was the only way to awaken the world to the necessity of abolishing war altogether." And the director of the atomic-energy laboratory at the University of Chicago made the same point to Stimson in June 1945: "If the bomb were not used in the present war," Arthur Compton noted, "the world would have no adequate warning as to what was to be expected if war should break out again." Even Edward Teller, who has publicly decried the attack on Hiroshima and declared his early opposition to it, adopted a similar position in July 1945. "Our only hope is in getting the facts of our results before the people," he wrote to his colleague, Leo Szilard, who was circulating a petition among scientists opposing the bomb's use. "This might help to convince everybody that the next war would be fatal," Teller noted. "For this purpose actual combat use might even be the best thing."

Thus by the end of the war the most influential and widely accepted attitude toward the bomb was a logical extension of how the weapon was seen and valued earlier—as a potential instrument of diplomacy. Caught between the remnants of war and the uncertainties of peace, scientists as well as policy makers were trapped by the logic of their own unquestioned assumptions. By the summer of 1945 not only the conclusion of the war but the organization of an acceptable peace seemed to depend upon the success of the atomic attacks against Japan. When news of the successful atomic test of July 16 reached the president at the Potsdam Conference, he was visibly elated. Stimson noted that Truman "was tremendously pepped up by it and spoke to me of it again and again when I saw him. He said it gave him an entirely new feeling of confidence." The day after receiving the complete report of the test Truman altered his negotiating style. According to Churchill the president "got to the meeting after having read this report [and] he was a changed man. He told the Russians just where they got on and off and generally bossed the whole meeting." After the plenary session on July 24 Truman "casually mentioned to Stalin" that the United States had "a new weapon of unusual destructive force." Truman took this step in response to a recommendation by the Interim Committee, a group of political and scientific advisers organized by Stimson in May 1945 to advise the president on atomic-energy policy. But it is an unavoidable conclusion that what the president told the premier followed the letter of the recommendation rather than its spirit, which embodied the hope that an overture to Stalin would initiate the process toward international control. In less than three weeks the new weapon's destructive potential would be demonstrated to the world. Stalin would then be forced to reconsider his diplomatic goals. It is no wonder that upon learning of the raid against Hiroshima Truman exclaimed: "This is the greatest thing in history."

As Stimson had expected, as a colossal reality the bomb was very different. But had American diplomacy been altered by it? Those who conducted diplomacy became more confident, more certain that through the accomplishments of American science, technology, and industry the "new world" could be made into one better than the old. But just how the atomic bomb would be used to help accomplish this ideal remained unclear. Three months and one day after Hiroshima was bombed Bush wrote that the whole matter of international relations on atomic energy "is in a thoroughly chaotic condition." The wartime relationship between atomic-energy policy and diplomacy had been based upon the simple assumption that the Soviet government would surrender important geographical, political, and ideological objectives in exchange for the neutralization of the new weapon. As a result of policies based on this assumption American diplomacy and prestige suffered grievously: an opportunity to gauge the Soviet Union's response during the war to the international control of atomic energy was missed, and an atomic-energy policy for dealing with the Soviet government after the war was ignored. Instead of promoting American postwar aims, wartime atomic-energy policies made them more difficult to achieve. As a group of scientists at the University of Chicago's atomic-energy laboratory presciently warned the government in June 1945: "It may be difficult to persuade the world that a nation which was capable of secretly preparing and suddenly releasing a weapon as indiscriminate as the [German] rocket bomb and a million times more destructive, is to be trusted in its proclaimed desire of having such weapons abolished by international agreement." This reasoning, however, flowed from alternative assumptions formulated during the closing months of the war by scientists far removed from the wartime policy-making process. Hiroshima and Nagasaki, the culmination of that process, became the symbols of a new American barbarism, reinforcing charges, with dramatic circumstantial evidence, that the policies of the United States contributed to the origins of the cold war.

15

From Harlem to Montgomery

DOMINIC J. CAPECI, JR.

• No history of the United States since World War II could possibly be complete without an account of the black struggle for equality. In 1954, the United States Supreme Court ruled unconstitutional the "separate but equal" school that had typified the nation officially since 1898 and in fact throughout its history. In 1956, the Montgomery bus boycott in Alabama brought national attention to segregated facilities in public conveyances, and soon thereafter sit-ins and "freedom rides" kept up a constant pressure for integration in the South. And in 1963, at the giant March on Washington, Dr. Martin Luther King spoke from the steps of the Lincoln Memorial to proclaim the goal: "Free at last."

The March on Washington was followed by the Civil Rights Act of 1964, the Voting Registration Act of 1965, the explosive riots in Los Angeles, Detroit, and Newark in the mid-1960s, and the rise of a militant black nationalist movement that signaled political and social changes between blacks and whites in the United States. Southern blacks, protected by federal marshals, registered to vote and in succeeding years put into office hundreds of black officials and whites responsive to their black constituencies.

In the following essay, Dominic J. Capeci, Jr., reminds us that men of God were in the forefront of the civil rights struggle. For centuries, black ministers had been the spokesmen of their people, and perhaps the only occupational group not dependent upon whites for support. Capeci notes the many similarities between the two most famous black leaders

Reprinted by permission from *The Historian* 41 (August 1979), 721–737.

AUTHOR'S NOTE: The author wishes to thank Clifford I. Whipple, Professor of Psychology at Southern Missouri State University for advice and information on the sociopsychological developments of Powell and King.

of the past half-century—Adam Clayton Powell, Jr., and
Martin Luther King, Jr.—and shows how their differences in
methods and rhetoric reflected varying influences in their up-
bringing.

While much has been written about Martin Luther King, Jr., and the
Montgomery Bus Boycott of 1956, historians have ignored Adam
Clayton Powell, Jr., and the Harlem Bus Boycott of 1941. The two
boycotts were marked by similar leadership and occurred in decades
of despair but in periods of major socioeconomic change. Although
it was much smaller in size and more local in impact, a study of the
Harlem boycott yields important information on Powell's leadership
before his political career and, more significantly, on earlier protest
philosophies and tactics. A comparison of the boycotts reveals both
the continuity and unity in black protest and leadership and the
diversity that marks different eras and locales.

Though Powell and King came of age in different generations and
regions, they experienced similar formative influences that ultimately
led them to nonviolent protest. Both were named after their fathers,
each of whom had risen from sharecropping to become renowned
Baptist ministers in Harlem and Atlanta, respectively. Reverend Adam
Clayton Powell, Sr., and Reverend Martin Luther King, Sr., were
assertive, protective parents. Thus young Powell was spoiled "utterly
and completely," while King, Jr., enjoyed life's comfort in "an extraordinarily peaceful and protected way." Both were precocious,
entering college in their mid-teens and earning advanced degrees in
religion. More significant, both underwent serious racial and religious
growing pains. As a youngster, Powell had been roughed up by blacks
for being "white" and by whites for being "colored." Later at Colgate
University he passed for white until his father came to lecture on race
relations. The negative reaction of Powell's white roommate to his true
identity was a "tremendous" shock. Perhaps the trauma was almost as
great as the earlier, unexpected death of his sister Blanche, which
triggered in Powell a religious reaction: "The church was a fraud, my
father the leading perpetrator, my mother a stupid rubber stamp."
King, too, was scarred during his early years. When the mother of his
white playmates informed King (then six years old) that as they grew

older they could no longer play together, he ran home crying. Although never estranged from his father, as a teenager King considered the church irrelevant and wondered whether religion "could serve as a vehicle for modern thinking."

As young adults, Powell and King overcame these problems. At Colgate, Powell experienced a revelation, which led to his ordination in 1931. He served as assistant pastor of his father's Abyssinian Baptist Church and earned a master's degree in religious education at Columbia University. In 1937, he succeeded his father as pastor. Adopting the elder Powell's commitment to the social gospel, he forged his congregation into "a mighty weapon" and led numerous nonviolent direct action protests for black employment opportunities during the Great Depression. As part of the larger "Jobs-for-Negroes" movement, Powell joined with Reverend William Lloyd Imes of the St. James Presbyterian Church and A. Philip Randolph of the Brotherhood of Sleeping Car Porters to organize the Greater New York Coordinating Committee for Employment. By 1941 Powell overestimated that four years of picketing by the committee had brought Harlem "ten thousand jobs." This commitment and leadership earned him enormous popularity and, among church women, the title "Mr. Jesus."

King matured along similar lines, for Dr. Benjamin E. Mays and others at Morehouse College successfully molded his concept of religion. King was ordained and became the assistant pastor at his father's Ebenezer Baptist Church. He then attended Crozer Theological Seminary and received a doctorate in theology from Boston College. Although the elder King was only infrequently involved in organized protest, he and Alberta King had instilled dignity and pride in their son. King remembered his father admonishing a policeman for calling him "boy"; pointing to his son, the elder King ejaculated, "That's a boy there. I'm Reverend King." Eventually, King drew on nonviolent direct action for the Montgomery boycott and became immensely popular. "L. L. J.," or "Little Lord Jesus" as church women called him, had moved to the center stage of black leadership.

While Powell and King, then, experienced similar upbringings, a comparison of the bus boycotts in Harlem and Montgomery provides an opportunity to analyze their leadership, protest philosophies, and tactics.

The Harlem bus boycott of 1941 was prompted by black degradation, rising expectations, and a heritage of black protest. Throughout the 1930s, black New Yorkers subsisted on marginal economic levels. As late as 1940, 40 percent of the city's black population received relief or federal monies for temporary jobs. Moreover, most blacks were relegated to menial positions. In Harlem, the largest black community of over two hundred thousand persons, hope was generated, nevertheless, as black leaders and white officials—like Mayor Fiorello H. La Guardia—pressed for change and as World War II held out promise for greater black employment opportunities.

Blacks had a longstanding grievance against the Fifth Avenue Coach Company and the New York Omnibus Corporation. In 1935, the Mayor's Commission on Conditions in Harlem reported that the Coach Company was "fixed in its policy of the exclusion of Negroes from employment." At the time of the bus boycott six years later, the Coach Company and the Omnibus Corporation together employed only sixteen blacks, mostly as janitors, none as drivers or mechanics, out of a labor force of thirty-five hundred persons. Hence, on March 10, 1941, when the Transportation Workers Union (TWU), under the leadership of Michael J. Quill, went on strike against the bus companies, black leaders moved quickly to the union's support. The National Negro Congress, for example, "wholeheartedly" supported the strike, which lasted for twelve days and halted the service of thirteen hundred buses.

Under Roger Straugh's leadership, the Harlem Labor Union (HLU) began picketing local bus stops before the TWU strike had ended, demanding the employment of black bus drivers and mechanics. The Greater New York Coordinating Committee for Employment led by Powell and the Manhattan Council of the National Negro Congress directed by Hope R. Stevens joined with HLU to form the United Bus Strike Committee (UBSC). The formal boycott, however, did not begin until March 24, four days after TWU had agreed to arbitration and two days after bus service had resumed. Moreover, Powell emerged as the spokesman for the boycotters, providing, in Urban Leaguer Elmer A. Carter's estimation, "dynamic leadership."

Before the boycott began, Powell received a quid pro quo from Quill. In return for black support of the TWU strike, the boycott would receive union backing. Later, on March 24, Quill assured

Powell that blacks employed by the bus companies would be considered for union membership so long as they had clean records and had never been scabs. That evening, over fifteen hundred persons gathered at the Abyssinian Baptist Church and agreed to boycott the buses until blacks were hired as drivers and mechanics.

Powell's tactics drew from the Jobs-for-Negroes movement, in which many members of the United Bus Strike Committee had participated. Picket lines surrounded Harlem's bus stops, soup kitchens fed volunteers, and black chauffeurs and mechanics were registered. An "emergency jitney service" of privately owned automobiles transported some boycotters, but the key to the boycott's success was New York City's subway system and taxi companies which provided efficient, relatively inexpensive alternative transportation. Before the boycott terminated, volunteers painted placards, donated approximately $500, and gave the use of their automobiles. The month-long campaign kept sixty thousand persons off the buses each day at a loss of $3,000 in daily fares. It also drew together five hundred persons from various backgrounds and both races, as bandleaders, ministers, postal clerks, housewives, beauticians, and nurses walked the picket line. Celebrities, like musician Duke Ellington, actively supported the boycott.

Well aware of the significance of the church in black society, Powell made the Abyssinian Baptist Church one of two boycott headquarters. It was the location of the first and second boycott rallies. It provided volunteers experienced in protest, communications, and physical resources and, of course, became the base of Powell's operations and the center of his power.

Powell stressed the philosophy of nonviolent direct action. Blacks were to use only peaceful, legal avenues of redress. By appealing to "the Grace of God" and "the power of the masses," Powell combined religious and political themes; this combination of righteousness and self-help would enable "a black boy . . . to roll a bus up Seventh Avenue." Picket lines, as well as Powell's rhetoric, however, implied militancy. Those flouting the boycott, he declared, should be converted, "one way or another." Three years after the boycott, Powell summarized his nonviolent, though strident, philosophy in *Marching Blacks*: "No blows, no violence, but the steady unrelenting pressure of an increasing horde of people who knew they were right" would bring change.

The boycott was threatened first by violence and then by a misleading newspaper story. Following a UBSC rally at the Abyssinian Baptist Church on March 31, individuals hurled objects at several buses along Lenox Avenue. Fifty patrolmen dispersed those responsible, some of whom had attended the rally. "FEAR ANOTHER HARLEM RIOT," screamed the *Age*'s headlines. Of more concern to Powell and others was the *Amsterdam News* story of April 5. It announced that the bus companies had agreed to employ over two hundred black drivers and mechanics, providing that TWU waive the seniority rights of more than three hundred former bus employees waiting to be rehired. Such an agreement had been discussed, but no final decision had been reached. USBC leaders moved quickly to maintain the boycott. They labeled the story "a lie," reorganized pickets, distributed leaflets, asked ministers to inform their congregations of "the true facts," and planned a mass meeting.

Despite crisis, the boycott and negotiations continued. Once Ritchie agreed to hire blacks, the major obstacle was TWU seniority policies. On April 17, Powell informed five thousand persons at the Golden Gate Ballroom that an agreement was imminent. Signed twelve days later, the agreement waived the seniority rights of all except ninety-one TWU drivers furloughed by the bus companies; after these men were reinstated, one hundred black drivers were to be hired. The next seventy mechanics employed would also be black, and thereafter, blacks and whites would be taken on alternately until 17 percent of the companies' labor force—exclusive of clerical staff—was black. This quota represented the percentage of black residents in Manhattan. Black workers would be enrolled as TWU members, although the bus companies exercised "sole discretion as to the type of Negro employees to be hired." The agreement would not take precedence over prior management-labor commitments provided they were nondiscriminatory. Of course, all boycott activities would cease. Powell declared that the agreement was made possible by new TWU contracts providing shorter hours and by additional municipal franchises enabling the bus companies to employ three hundred more persons.

Several factors made the Harlem boycott successful. Powell's agreement with Quill prevented bus company officials from playing blacks against whites in the TWU strike and the bus boycott. Throughout the strike, Quill raised the possibility of the bus companies employing strikebreakers. Blacks traditionally had been exploited as scabs, and some of the bus terminals were strategically located in Harlem. Indeed, at least one Harlem correspondent informed Mayor La Guardia that two thousand black men could "start the bus lines in 5, 10, or 20 hours." Powell's agreement significantly reduced the possibility of TWU's strike being broken by force, and reciprocally, it assured that the bus boycott would not fail because of traditional union opposition toward blacks.

Powell's agreement with Quill also held out the hope that blacks would support labor in the upcoming subway negotiations between La Guardia and TWU leaders. During the previous June, the municipal government had bought and unified the Brooklyn-Manhattan Transit Corporation and the Interborough Rapid Transit Company, which had been operated by TWU and the Brotherhood of Locomotive Engineers. When La Guardia contended that neither the right to strike nor a closed shop could be permitted among civil service employees, labor officials retorted that the mayor had reneged on his obligations and anticipated a precedent-breaking conflict with the municipal government when the original contract expired on June 20, 1941. TWU leaders believed that mayoral reference to the bus strike as "bull-headed, obstinate and stupid" was designed to weaken their position in the coming subway negotiations. Obviously, public opinion would be crucial in that dispute. Hence, some blacks, like the *Age* editor, saw TWU support for the bus boycott as a trade-off for black support in the forthcoming union battle with the mayor.

Changing opinions and the impact of World War II helped make the Powell-Quill agreement possible. The racial attitudes of TWU leaders had been improving since 1938 when the union unsuccessfully sent blacks to be employed as drivers at the World's Fair. By World War II, Powell understood how uncomfortable society was in opposing a totalitarian, racist Nazi regime while practicing racial discrimination. "America," he stated later, "could not defeat Hitler abroad without defeating Hitlerism at home." Of equal importance, TWU leadership could pare seniority lists by three hundred unemployed members and make room for black employees because defense orders stimulated the economy and selective service calls reduced union ranks. According to the *Afro-American* editor, the difficulty in finding bus drivers and mechanics provided blacks with unforeseen opportunities.

The boycott assured those opportunities. By early May, seven black mechanics had been hired by the bus companies and ten blacks were expected to begin chauffeur training within a week. Six months later, forty-three blacks had been employed in various classifications, including mechanic's helpers. Finally, on February 1, 1942, after all the ninety-odd furloughed white operators had been given opportunity for reemployment, the first ten black drivers employed by the Coach Company and the Omnibus Corporation began their routes.

That victory was historical. It drew blacks, labor, and management together in a successful effort to break down discriminatory employment practices in privately owned bus companies, and indirectly, it accelerated a similar trend that had already begun in the municipally owned transportation systems under La Guardia's leadership. The boycott also held out promise for "Negro-labor solidarity." Moreover, it effectively utilized the tactics and philosophies of the Jobs-for-Negroes movement, focused on the concept of equal opportunity, established the idea of a quota system, and provided safeguards for protecting blacks in their newly won jobs. All these elements were also attempted in the 1930s and 1960s, indicating the continuum in black protest that links militant means with traditional ends and nonviolent direct action tactics with greater participation in larger society. By exploiting both TWU ambitions and war manpower exigencies, Powell, Straugh, and Stevens created numerous jobs for black workers. But it was Powell who played the leading role, as he had done for the past decade, speaking out and organizing protests that brought approximately seventeen hundred jobs to Harlem. Exactly because of that record, blacks enthusiastically supported his successful candidacy for City Council in November 1941. His delivery of tangible gains merits mention, for as councilman and, later, congressman he had the reputation for imparting only catharsis to his constituents. Finally, Powell's boycott sparked other protests; numerous blacks agreed with the editor of the *Pittsburgh Courier*, who said, "If this can be done in New York, it can be done in other cities." Indeed, in May the National Association for the Advancement of Colored People launched a nationwide picket campaign against defense industries that held government contracts but refused to hire blacks; Powell journeyed to Chicago to help the Negro Labor Relations League launch a jobs campaign; and the Colored Clerks Circle of St. Louis prepared to boycott a local cleaning company. Official entry of the United States into World War II prevented the emergence of what might have been widespread black protest akin to that of the 1950s and 1960s.

Nearly fifteen years later, when Rosa Parks refused to give up her seat to a white passenger on the Montgomery Bus Line, another phase of black protest began. It was led by Martin Luther King, Jr., who was unknown and inexperienced when leadership of the Montgomery Improvement Association was thrust on him in December of 1955. When he arrived in Montgomery during the previous year to accept the pastorate of the Dexter Avenue Baptist Church, it was "the cradle of the Confederacy." Of one hundred and thirty thousand residents, blacks comprised 40 percent. Segregated and scattered throughout the city, they were exploited economically and lacked even the semblance of geographic, political, or social unity. Jim Crow practices prevailed, particularly on the bus lines where operators possessed police powers for enforcing segregation. A long history of passenger abuse by bus drivers was well known to blacks who had been beaten, ridiculed, and stranded. Coretta Scott King accurately contended that black passengers were treated worse than cattle, "for nobody insults a cow." Earlier efforts to protest this treatment had failed because of black disunity and white power.

Juxtaposed to years of degradation, however, were rising expectations. If the United States Supreme Court's decision against segregated public school systems in *Brown* v. *Topeka* (1954) did not affect Montgomery immediately, it signaled a major change in race relations. More immediate, however, was the emergence of what King termed "a brand new Negro" whose struggle for dignity was obstructed by self-deceiving whites who continued to live in the past. Hence some blacks and many whites were surprised when the arrest of Rosa Parks triggered protest. During the eighteen years that he had lived in the South, columnist Carl Rowan "had never seen such spirit among a group of Negroes."

That spirit was mobilized by the Montgomery Improvement Association (MIA) which grew out of the efforts of E. D. Nixon, a pullman porter who presided over the local NAACP, and Jo Ann Robinson, an English professor at Alabama State College and president of the Women's Political Council. They arranged a meeting of black ministers, who adopted Reverend Ralph Abernathy's idea of the MIA, elected King as its president, and organized a mass meeting of black residents. On Sunday, December 5, over four thousand people crammed into the Holt Street Baptist Church to endorse a boycott until the bus lines guaranteed (1) courteous treatment, (2) a first-come-first-served seating arrangement (blacks in the rear, whites in the front), and (3) employment of black operators on predominantly black routes. Moderate, mostly symbolic, alterations in the Jim Crow system were sought.

The MIA tactics resembled those of earlier black protest movements, including Powell's. As Lawrence D. Reddick has pointed out, Montgomery was "ideally fitted" for a bus boycott: its sizable black population comprised 70 percent of all bus passengers, while its layout of 27.9 square miles enabled residents to reach most places by foot. An effective boycott, however, needed alternative means of transportation. In its initial stages, black cab companies agreed to carry black passengers for the price of the ten cents bus fare. A car pool supplemented the taxi service, becoming the major mode of transportation after municipal officials outlawed the lower taxi fares. Over three hundred automobiles moved in and out of forty-eight dispatch and forty-two collection stations. Financial support originated among the protestors, but as their efforts drew national and international attention, donations came from various sources. In one year, the MIA had spent $225,000. From December 5, 1955, to December 21, 1956, the boycott cost the Montgomery Bus Lines over a quarter of a million dollars in fares, the City of Montgomery several thousand dollars in taxes, and the downtown white merchants several million dollars in business. It also boosted black businesses and reduced the social distance between classes within the black society.

It was no coincidence that the protest spirit emanated from the Church, southern black society's most independent institution and primary means of communication. It became routine for blacks to share a ride or walk daily and attend mass meetings at a different church each Monday and Thursday. The boycott became inseparable from the secular and religious life of black society, maximizing the participation of everyone from domestic to clergymen. Not surprisingly, church-owned vehicles in the car pool were dubbed "rolling churches."

Emphasizing the concepts of love and justice, King forged a philosophy of nonviolent direct action, stressing self-help, condemning violence, focusing on evil—rather than evil-doers—and espousing "love for America and the democratic way of life." He realized the limits of black power, the history of white repression, and the need for legitimacy in the eyes of white America. Perhaps for these reasons, MIA leaders originally sought a first-come-first-served seating arrangement "under segregation" and watched those blacks who might have resorted to violence. Both the demands for desegregation in seating arrangements and the Gandhian dimension of King's philosophy evolved after the boycott had begun. Nonviolence, already implicit in the Christian teaching that underlay the boycott, was formally articulated by King as a result of the influences of Bayard Rustin and the Reverend Glenn E. Smiley of the Fellowship of Reconciliation.

Despite solid organization and philosophical appeal, the boycott confronted several problems. King later admitted having been "scared to death by threats against myself and my family." Indeed, on January 30, 1956, as Coretta King and baby Yolanda inhabited the premises, the King home was bombed. In addition, King had to deal with a legal system that sanctioned Jim Crow. As a result of Title 14, Section 54, of the Alabama Code prohibiting boycotts, King and eighty-eight others were convicted of unlawful activities. Later the car pool was halted by court injunction. What saved the boycott was the slow wit of the municipal officials and the federal injunction banning segregated buses which was upheld by the United States Supreme Court. Nor did the boycott receive meaningful support from the white community. A handful of whites, like Reverend Robert Graetz, pastor of the black Lutheran Trinity Church, "paid dearly" for participating in the boycott. Other whites assisted the protest unwittingly by chauffeuring their domestics to and from work. For the most part, however, whites either opposed the boycott or, if sympathetic to it, were afraid to say so publicly.

Internal pressures also proved troublesome. Early in the boycott, as abusive phone calls, long hours of work, and relentless efforts to maintain unity began to mount, King despaired and confided in God, "I've come to the point where I can't face it alone." At this time King experienced a revelation, which enabled him "to face anything." Jealousy on the part of some black ministers threatened the boycott periodically. The gravest incident occurred on January 21 when King was informed that Mayor W. A. Gayle and three black ministers had agreed on a settlement to end the boycott. That evening and the following Sunday morning, MIA leaders successfully alerted the black community to this hoax.

These pressures notwithstanding, the boycott was successful, with support coming from numerous quarters. Congressman Adam Clayton Powell, Jr., for example, pressed President Dwight D. Eisenhower to protect the eighty-odd blacks indicted for boycott activities. When Eisenhower refused to comply, Powell publicly chided him for "trying to wash his hands like Pilate of the blood of innocent men and women in the Southland." He then organized a "National Deliverance Day of Prayer" for March 28, which was commemorated in several cities, including Atlanta, Chicago, and New York. Powell collected and sent $2,500 to MIA. Early the next month, he asked all members of the House of Representatives for contributions to help rebuild seven black churches in Montgomery that had been bombed by terrorists, and later recorded that only two Congressmen honored his request. Before the year ended, he and several other nationally known blacks spoke in Montgomery. In sum, the Montgomery bus boycott brought to the surface black awareness that had been stirring since World War II.

As significant was the recent shift in the United States Supreme Court under Chief Justice Earl Warren. Just as Mayor Gayle had deduced that the boycott could be crushed by enjoining the car pool for being unlicensed, the higher court upheld a United States District Court decision that laws in Alabama requiring segregation on buses were unconstitutional. This decision of November 13, 1956, meant victory for MIA, but King continued the boycott until a federal order arrived in Montgomery six weeks later; on December 21, MIA leaders rode the bus in victory.

That victory sparked the Civil Rights Movement. The Montgomery bus boycott provided a leader in King, a philosophy in nonviolence, a tactic in direct action, and, as important, a tangible triumph. Blacks were poised for change, needing, in Lerone Bennett's words, "an act to give them power over their fears." The boycott, of course, did much more, for under King's leadership it achieved legitimacy and prepared both races for a prolonged assault on inequality. That King succeeded in the South, and succeeded with the United States Supreme Court's assistance, underscored a major theme for the coming decade. That the Montgomery City Bus Line so adamantly and successfully refused any agreement regarding the hiring of black bus drivers indicated both the obstacles and limits for changes that lay ahead. Nevertheless, the boycott spawned the Southern Christian Leadership Conference, "a sustaining mechanism," and elevated the struggle for racial equality to the national level.

The Harlem boycott of 1941 came nowhere near achieving this, for it was much smaller and failed to sustain a national protest movement. Nor was it supported throughout the black community. Yet similarities between it and the Montgomery experience abound, particularly those dealing with leadership. Powell and King came from deeply Christian, middle-class families that provided physical security while imposing high parental expectations. As precocious youngsters, both Powell and King experienced anxiety and guilt. Each questioned his father's vocation, perhaps feeling incapable of living up to the parental reputation or, as most likely in Powell's case, repressing hostility toward a domineering father. Each tried to escape: Powell by passing for white and King by engaging in masochistic tendencies. (King jumped out of an upstairs window once, blaming himself for an accident involving his grandmother; at another time, he blamed himself for being at a parade when she died of illness.) As young adults, however, both men sublimated this inner turmoil and embraced the church and their fathers, becoming independent from the latter, yet reflecting them. Perhaps, as psychoanalyst Erich Fromm has theorized about other historical figures, their long-sought-after personal independence emerged in their struggle for collective black liberation.

Powell and King believed that collective liberation could only come through the black church with its "enormous reservoirs of psychic and social strength." Such liberation would free both races, for blacks possessed the divinely inspired mission of achieving equality through the redemption of white society. As the largest black Protestant church in the United States, the Abyssinian Baptist Church boasted a membership of thousands, which provided Powell with impressive human and financial resources. King's Dexter and Avenue Baptist Church, however, was more representative of black congregations, comprising one thousand persons and limited finances. In order to be effective, Powell and King successfully established coalitions with other religious and secular groups.

If the church became the vehicle for change, it was black folk religion that provided the sinew for protest. Powell and, more directly, King, converted traditional black religiosity into "a passion for justice." Speaking to northern, urban congregations, Powell avoided "Valley-and-Dry-Bones sermons," stressing instead "nicely chosen Negro idioms about everyday issues." Powell could be moved by his own words and weep publicly. King spoke a more "religious language" that struck at the heart of southern black culture. Reverend Andrew Young, a member of the Southern Christian Leadership Conference, observed that no one could have mobilized black southerners by arguing about segregation and integration, but when King preached about "leaving the slavery of Egypt" or "dry bones rising again" everybody understood his language. Both Powell and King possessed what historian Joseph R. Washington, Jr., has called "that Baptist hum which makes what is said only as important as how it is said." The inflections of their voices, the cadence of their deliveries, the nuances of their messages, the animation of their gestures were eagerly anticipated and instinctively understood by multitudes who shared a special cultural and historical relationship with their preachers. Powell and King, then, mobilized black people and became their surrogates, "interpreting their innermost feelings, their passions, their yearnings" as well as channeling their emotions into viable protest.

Protestant theology and Gandhian tactics provided the means by which Powell and King could channel the passion for justice. Both men advocated the social gospel, contending that any religion ignoring the socioeconomic conditions that shackle humanity was, in King's rhetoric, "a dry-as-dust religion." Nonviolent direct action was not a new tactic in black protest, but it was one that permitted Powell, King, and their supporters to become social gospel activists. Following King's successful boycott, blacks increasingly favored an active role by the church in social and political issues during the years 1957 to 1968.

If the boycotts shared a similar religious heritage, they also reflect the respective personality characterizations of Powell and King. Political scientist Hanes Walton, Jr., notes that Powell used nonviolence for practical reasons as "a potent, energetic tool," while King embraced it as "an end in itself, endowed with superior moral qualities." Powell did not advocate violence, but on occasion his rhetoric was intimidating and implied the use of intimidation. King, of course, would tolerate no such deviation from passive resistance. King's commitment notwithstanding, Powell more accurately reflected the reasons for which blacks utilized nonviolent direct action. In the aftermath of the Montgomery boycott, for example, over 70 percent of the black respondents surveyed in that city recognized the usefulness of nonviolence since black people lacked the "power to use violence successfully." According to sociologist E. Franklin Frazier, "Gandhism as a philosophy and a way of life is completely alien to the Negro"; black religious heritage accounts for the presence of nonviolent direct action in the civil rights movement.

That King much more than Powell envisaged—as did Mahatma Gandhi—"a life service to humanity on a level which called for a self-discipline of rare order" was partly due to socioecological factors. Even in 1941, Harlem, the "Negro Mecca" of the world, was a more secure environment for black people than was Montgomery fifteen years later. Powell had been raised in that security and had successfully used the avenues of redress that were available in the North. King had been brought up in southern segregation, where survival depended upon staying in one's place and where protest efforts had little result. Powell never experienced the pressures and fears that haunted King daily; Powell had enemies, but none who threatened his family or bombed his home. Exactly because of his own background and fears, King understood the need to allay southern white fears if blacks were to avoid pogroms and race relations were to progress: "If you truly love and respect an opponent, you respect his fears too."

King's upbringing emphasized inner control, the kind that enabled him to bear parental whippings with "stoic impassivity." Reverend King, Sr., stressed discipline, and the precarious social environs demanded self-regulation. Hence King originally questioned the emotionalism in the black church and later, in the boycott, took great pains to direct it into safe arenas. Finally, the religious and secular elements in the southern black church appear to have been much more interdependent than elsewhere, which partly accounts for King's commitment to nonviolence as a way of life. This commitment may have been—as in Gandhi's experience—marked by ambivalence, for King stressed love partly for the purpose of controlling hate (perhaps his own). In Powell's case, the opposite was true. As a child, he was spoiled, and lived in an environment that did not demand inner control for survival. He never led a humble life but, rather, publicly flouted the racial mores of white society. Nor was his religion as all-encompassing as King's; it was more secular and compartmentalized, reflecting the tremendous impact that migration and urbanization had had upon the northern black church. Powell released anger more directly by stressing direct action, while King tended to displace it by putting emphasis on nonviolence or, more precisely, on what Gandhi called Satyagraha—love-force. It is, then, no coincidence that Powell later singled out Marcus Garvey as the greatest mass leader, demonstrated his independence by clearly identifying an enemy, and spoke militantly of change. King, however, referred only to Booker T. Washington in his first major address in the boycott—"Let no man pull you so low as to make you hate him," stressed racial reconciliation by describing forces of evil, and prayed for opponents. Hence it is not surprising that the name of Powell's organization, the United Bus Strike Committee, projected an assertive, challenging image and that the Harlem boycott focused on the tangible bread-and-butter issue of jobs. By contrast, King's efforts emphasized uplift, as implied in the title, Montgomery Improvement Association, and sought more symbolic, civil rights objectives.

Powell had undertaken the Harlem boycott as his last major protest as a social gospel activist at the end of the Jobs-for-Negroes campaign. He would soon begin a political career as councilman in New York City, and World War II would soon reduce protest to rhetoric as black leaders feared that their efforts would be labeled traitorous. King was thrust into the Montgomery boycott, his first meaningful protest, which began the civil rights movement. Larger and more significant historically than anything that Powell had done, King embraced that movement and its principles until they died together on April 4, 1968. While the contributions of King are obvious, those of Powell have been forgotten by many. Nevertheless, King knew of

Powell's efforts. "Before some of us were born, before some of us could walk or talk," King recalled in the 1960s, "Adam Powell wrote *Marching Blacks*, the charter of the black revolution that is taking place today." One can imagine Powell, in his accustomed modesty, ejaculating an "Amen."

16

The TV Quiz Show Scandals of the 1950s

RICHARD S. TEDLOW

• In 1884, Paul Nipkow of Germany received an American patent for the electromagnetic transmission of visual images. But until the development of the electron tubes known as phototubes there was no way of amplifying the current sufficiently. The decade 1930–1940 saw the laboratory perfection of television equipment, but World War II obviously interrupted commercial applications of the device. Only after 1950 did television become a major industry, an important method of communication, and the most popular form of entertainment in the United States. Indeed, a persuasive argument can be made for the proposition that only the automobile has had a greater influence on twentieth-century American life.

When television was in its infancy, quiz shows caught the public fancy. Unlike the familiar programs of the 1980s, however, those like The $64,000 Question promised truly substantial rewards for the victors. Week after week millions of citizens were glued to their sets, wondering whether the remarkable persons on their screens would go for broke or settle for sums already won.

Chicanery and scandal intervened to bring the quiz shows into disrepute and to threaten the development of a major industry. The central figure in the controversy was a brilliant young instructor at Columbia University who happened to be a member of a renowned intellectual family. Why did

From "Intellect on Television: The Quiz Show Scandals of the 1950s." Reprinted by permission of *American Quarterly*, Richard S. Tedlow, and the University of Pennsylvania. Copyright 1976, Trustees of the University of Pennsylvania.

AUTHOR'S NOTE: The author would like to thank Professor Stephen J. Whitfield of the Brandeis University American Studies Department for his help in preparing this article.

Charles Van Doren cheat in 1956? More importantly, why did television executives insist that contestants participate in a scheme to deceive the public? Richard Tedlow's brief essay points out the continuing dilemma of television—how to balance integrity and quality with the demand for high audience ratings.

On the 7th of June, 1955, *The $64,000 Question* made its debut on the CBS television network. No programming idea could have been more thoroughly foreshadowed by previous shows. Since the mid-1930s radio had been exploiting the American passion for facts with contests and games. For years, small amounts of cash or manufacturer-donated merchandise had been given away through various formats. What was new about *Question* was the size of the purse. The giveaway had taken a "quantum jump"; losers received a Cadillac as a consolation prize.

Question's format was simple. The producers selected a contestant who chose a subject about which he or she answered increasingly difficult questions which were assigned monetary values ranging from $64 to $64,000. The contestant could quit without attempting the succeeding plateau, but if he chose to continue and missed, he forfeited his winnings and was left with only his Cadillac.

By a few deft touches, the producers heightened the aura of authenticity and tension. The questions used were deposited in a vault of the Manufacturers Trust Company and brought to the studio by a bank officer flanked by two armed guards. As the stakes increased, the contestant entered a glass-enclosed "isolation booth" on stage to the accompaniment of "ominous music which hinted at imminent disaster" in order to prevent coaching from the audience. Since the contestant returned week after week rather than answering all the questions on one broadcast, the audience was given time to contemplate whether he would keep his winnings or go on to the next plateau and also a chance to worry about how difficult the next question might be.

The program became an immediate hit. In September, an estimated 55 million people, over twice as many as had seen the Checkers speech, viewing 84.8% of the television sets in operation at the time, saw

Richard S. McCutchen, a 28-year-old marine captain whose category was gourmet foods, become the first grand prize winner.

Most early contestants were seemingly average folks who harbored a hidden expertise in a subject far removed from their workaday lives. Thus McCutchen was asked about *haute cuisine* rather than amphibious assault. This separation was no accident. Its purpose was not only to increase the novelty of the show by providing something odd to the point of being freakish but also to integrate the viewer more intimately into the video melodrama. Everyone who had ever accumulated a store of disconnected, useless information could fantasize about transforming it into a pot of gold.

In a few months, *Question* had created a large new "consumption community," Daniel Boorstin's label for the nonideological, democratic, vague, and rapidly shifting groupings which have characterized twentieth-century American society. Suddenly a third of the country had a common bond about which total strangers could converse. Paradoxically, in order to belong to this community, the individual had to isolate himself physically from others. Families stayed at home to watch the show, rather than celebrating it in the company of a large crowd. Movie theaters reported a precipitous decline in business, and stores and streets were empty when it came on the air.

Everyone whose life was touched by the show seemed to prosper. In addition to their prize money, some contestants received alluring offers to do public relations work for large companies or to star in movies. *Question*'s creator, an independent program packager named Louis Cowan, became president of CBS-TV, an indication of how pleased the network executives were to present so successful a show. Even the banker who brought the sealed questions from the vault found himself promoted to a vice presidency. But the greatest beneficiary was the sponsor.

In March of 1955, the show was purchased by Revlon, which soon began reaping the rewards of well-constructed advertising on a popular television program. Several products quintupled their sales, and advertising for one had to be discontinued because it sold out nationally. George F. Abrams, the company's vice president in charge of advertising, gloated that *Question* "is doing a most fantastic sales job. It certainly is the most amazing sales success in the history of the cosmetics industry. There isn't a single Revlon item that hasn't benefitted." Net sales for 1955 increased 54% over the previous year, and in 1956 they soared another 66%. When Revlon shares were first offered on the New York Stock Exchange at the end of 1955, the issue's success was "so great it was almost embarrassing."

Question's greatest liability was its own success; it spawned imitators around the world. In the United States, a spate of programs featuring endless variations of gift-giving for answering questions further retarded "TV's already enfeebled yearning to leaven commercialism with culture." Most of these have mercifully been consigned to oblivion, but one rivaled *The $64,000 Question* in the impact it made upon the nation.

The *21* program was developed by another firm of independent program packagers, Barry and Enright, Inc. The format was different, especially in having two contestants compete against each other and no limit on their winnings, but the basic idea was the same. Questions were given point values, and the points were worth money. Once again, the "wiles of a riverboat gambler" were combined with the memory of sundry bits of information which was passed off as intellectual acumen, with the result a spectacularly profitable property.

Barry and Enright leased the show to Pharmaceuticals, Inc., now known as the J. B. Williams Company, and it first appeared on NBC on October 12, 1956. Pharmaceuticals, whose most well-known product was Geritol, soon had good reason to be pleased with its quiz show. *21* did not attain quite the ratings of *Question*, but it competed successfully against *I Love Lucy*, one of the most popular programs in television history, and attracted much notice. Although its advertising director was reluctant to give complete credit to the program for the increased sales of Geritol, it could hardly have hurt. Sales in 1957 bettered the previous year's mark by one-third.

Unlike *Question*, *21* did not shun the highly educated, and one of its contestants became a symbol to the nation of the profitability of intellectual achievement. Charles Van Doren provided evidence that an intellectual could be handsome, that he could get rich, and that he could be a superstar. Like a football player, the intellectual athlete could win fame and wealth. Van Doren's family could lay genuine claim to membership in an American aristocracy of letters. Descended from seventeenth-century Dutch immigrants, Van Doren's uncle Carl was a literary critic whose 1939 biography of Benjamin Franklin won a Pulitzer Prize. His father Mark won the Prize for poetry the following year, and he was equally famous for his accomplishments in the classroom as a professor of English at Columbia. The wives of the Van Doren brothers were also literary, rounding out a remarkably cultivated quartet. Van Doren's family divided its time between a country estate in Connecticut and a Greenwich Village townhouse where guests over the years included Sinclair Lewis, Mortimer Adler, Joseph Wood Krutch, and Morris Ernst. The family was the symbol of intellectual vitality.

Van Doren established himself on the program by defeating the swarthy, seemingly impoverished previous champion Herbert Stempel on December 5, 1956, after having played three tie matches with Stempel on November 28. It was smooth sailing for the weeks that followed.

> On the TV screen [Eric Goldman has written] he appeared lanky, pleasant, smooth in dress and manner but never slick, confident but with an engaging way of understating himself. The long, hard questions would come at him and his eyes would roll up, squeeze shut, his forehead furrow and perspire, his teeth gnaw at his lower lip. Breathing heavily, he seemed to coax information out of some corner of his mind by talking to himself in a kind of stream-of-consciousness. Like a good American, he fought hard, taking advantage of every rule. . . . Like a good American, he won without crowing. And, like a good American, he kept on winning, drowning corporation lawyers or ex-college presidents with equal ease on questions ranging from naming the four islands of the Balearic Islands to explaining the process of photosynthesis to naming the three baseball players who each amassed more than 3,500 hits. Charles Van Doren was "the new All-American boy," the magazines declared, and to millions he was that indeed.

Van Doren's victories on the quiz show brought him greater rewards than had accrued to any of his predecessors. He received thousands of letters from parents and teachers around the world, thanking him for popularizing the life of the mind. Little services such as dry cleaning, which he had had to pay for when supporting himself on his $4,400 yearly salary as an English instructor at Columbia, were now donated *gratis* by star-struck shopkeepers. Several colleges expressed an interest in hiring him away from Columbia, and he found himself referred to in print as "Doctor" despite not yet having earned his Ph.D. And then, of course, there was the money. Van Doren won $129,000 during his 14 weeks on 21. Soon after he left, he was awarded a $50,000 contract to appear on the *Today* show, where for five minutes each morning he would speak of science, literature, history. "I think I may be the only person," he once remarked, "who ever read 17th century poetry on a network television program—a far cry from the usual diet of mayhem, murder and rape."

Rumors of improper practices surfaced soon after the quiz shows made their debut. By the end of 1956, articles were appearing in the trade and general circulation press discussing the "controls" exercised by the producers to keep popular contestants alive and eliminate the unpopular. "Are the quiz shows rigged?" asked *Time* magazine in the spring of 1957, a year in which the networks were investing a small fortune in them. The answer: producers could not "afford to risk collusion with contestants," and yet, because of pretesting, they were able to ask questions which they knew the contestants would or would not know. They could thus manipulate the outcome "far more effectively than most viewers suspect." The report noted, however, that Van Doren "feels certain that no questions were being formfitted to his phenomenal mind."

A number of contestants had been disappointed at their treatment on the shows. The most important of these, and the John Dean of this piece, was the man Van Doren first defeated, Herbert Stempel.

Stempel's motives were very mixed. One was money. He had quickly squandered his winnings and had failed in an attempt to blackmail more out of producer Dan Enright. A more important reason was his bruised ego. Stempel had been forced to portray himself as a poor boy from Brooklyn, when in fact he had married into a well-to-do family and was from Queens. Enright insisted that he wear ratty suits and a cheap wristwatch to project this image and that he address the emcee, Jack Barry, deferentially as Mr. Barry while other contestants called him Jack. He had an I.Q. of 170 and was infuriated by having to "miss" answers he knew "damn well." And he was beside himself at the unearned praise accorded Van Doren. Here was "a guy that had a fancy name, Ivy League education, parents all his life, and I had the opposite." He would hear passing strangers remark that he was the man who had lost to this child of light, and he could not stand it. But it was more than greed or envy that prompted Stempel to turn state's evidence. Even before he was ordered to "take a dive" and before he had ever heard of Charles Van Doren, he was telling friends that the show was fixed. Stempel knew all the real answers about the quiz shows, and he was bursting to show the nation how smart he was.

In 1957, Stempel tried to interest two New York newspapers in the truth, but both papers refused to print what would have been one of the biggest scoops of the decade because they feared libel action. It is a commentary on the state of investigative journalism at the time that not until August, 1958, after the discovery that a giveaway show called *Dotto* was fixed, was Stempel able to make his charges in public. At this time also, New York County District Attorney Frank Hogan began an investigation, and the inexorable process of revelation had been set in motion. For almost a year, the grand jury interviewed about 150 witnesses. The producers tried to arrange a cover-up by persuading the show's alumni to perjure themselves. Many of the most well known did just that. It was one thing to fix a quiz show, however, and quite another to fix a grand jury probe. Realizing that the day of reckoning was at last approaching, the producers hurried back to change their testimony. This they did without informing the contestants, leaving them, to put it mildly, out on a limb.

For reasons which remain unclear, the judge sealed the grand jury's presentment, but the Subcommittee on Legislative Oversight (over the FCC) of the House Interstate and Foreign Commerce Committee determined to get to the bottom of the matter. Its public hearings, held in Washington in October and November of 1959, attracted worldwide attention.

On October 6, a bitter Herbert Stempel exposed the whole sordid story of *21*. He had originally applied to take part in what he thought was an honest game but was approached by Enright who talked him into becoming an actor rather than a riverboat gambler. Every detail of his performances was prearranged: his wardrobe, his diffidence, his hesitations, and his answers. He was instructed on the proper way to mop his brow for maximum effect, and he was guaranteed to sweat because the air conditioning in the isolation booth was purposely kept off. From his testimony, it became clear that Van Doren was implicated as well. On the following two days, other contestants, producer Enright, and his assistant Albert Freedman testified to the fix. No one contradicted Stempel.

In the months preceding the hearings Van Doren had consistently and ever more vehemently proclaimed that no matter what others had done, his appearances on 21 had been strictly legitimate. When Stempel's charges were first published in the papers, Van Doren was "horror struck. . . . I couldn't understand why Stempel should want to proclaim his own involvement." A representative of D.A. Hogan interviewed him toward the end of the year, and he denied everything. He retained a lawyer, to whom he lied about his involvement, and then proceeded to perjure himself before the New York County Grand Jury in January 1959. He was assured by Enright and Freedman that they too would cover up.

Van Doren's day of reckoning came on November 2, 1959, before the subcommittee. Herb Stempel hurried down from New York City to get a seat from which he could clearly see his former adversary. Pale and jittery, Van Doren walked into the crowded hearing room and delivered himself of one of the most bathetic confessions in the history of American public speech.

He wished that he could erase the past three years but realizing the past to be immutable resolved to learn from it. When he had first contacted Barry and Enright, he had assumed that their programs were honest. Before his appearance on 21, Albert Freedman summoned him to his apartment and, taking him into the bedroom, explained that Stempel had to be defeated in order to make the show more popular. Van Doren asked to go on the air honestly, but Freedman said he had no chance to defeat the brilliant Stempel. "He also told me that the show was merely entertainment and that giving help to quiz contests was a common practice and merely a part of show business." Besides, said Freedman, Van Doren had an opportunity to help increase respect for intellectual life and education. "I will not," said Van Doren, "bore this committee by describing the intense moral struggle that went on inside me." The result of that struggle was history. Freedman coached him on how to answer questions to increase the suspense and several times gave him a script to memorize. When Van Doren missed the questions which were slated for the evening, Freedman "would allow me to look them up myself. A foolish sort of pride made me want to look up the answers when I could, and to learn as much about the subject as possible."

> As time went on the show ballooned beyond my wildest expectations. . . . [F]rom an unknown college instructor I became a celebrity. I received thousands of letters and dozens of requests to make speeches, appear in movies, and so forth—in short, all the trappings of modern publicity. To a certain extent this went to my head.

He realized, however, that he was misrepresenting education and was becoming more nervous about the show. He urged the producers to let him quit, but it was only after they could arrange a sufficiently dramatic situation that he was defeated.

Van Doren's brief testimony was the climax of the subcommittee's investigation as it was of this scandal as a whole. Nevertheless, the hearings continued, including an investigation of The $64,000 Question. Question was also fixed, and although the details differed from the 21 case, the deception was no less pervasive.

It is no exaggeration to say that the American public was transfixed by the revelation of quiz show fraud. A Gallup Poll found the highest level of public awareness of the event in the history of such surveys. Questioned about the shows at successive news conferences, President Eisenhower said he shared "the American general reaction of almost bewilderment" and compared the manipulations to the Black Sox scandal of 1919. The quiz show episode affords an opportunity to discuss feelings toward Van Doren, the hero unmasked, and also the general arguments which swirled around television at decade's turn.

For Van Doren, humiliation came in the wake of confession. Just as institutions had been happy to associate themselves with quiz show geniuses, they hurried to dissociate themselves when the geniuses turned out to be hustlers. NBC fired Van Doren, while Columbia "accepted his resignation." The actions of these two institutions were scrutinized along with those of Van Doren in the period following his confession.

From the first, both NBC and CBS had maintained the highly implausible stand that they were fooled about the shows along with the public. They unquestionably could have uncovered the rigging had they really wanted to, and in the end they were left holding the bag. They had lost millions of dollars and, what was worse, had suffered what at the time loomed as a potentially mortal blow to a very pleasant way of making a lot of money. The popular uproar threatened to force government to restrict the broadcasting prerogatives of management. In this state of affairs, Van Doren had to go. CBS took the next step by eliminating quiz shows altogether, from which NBC refrained.

Few were surprised by NBC's stand. The network was, after all, a business, and Van Doren had become a liability. Columbia's treatment of him aroused different issues. Some students had no patience with him, but hundreds rallied to his defense with petitions and demonstrations. They pointed out that his teaching was excellent and that having made public relations capital out of his victories, Columbia would be craven to desert him now. The Columbia College dean, however, maintained, "The issue is the moral one of the honesty and integrity of teaching." The dean found Van Doren's deceptions contrary to the principles a teacher should have and should try to instill in his students.

The academic community holds in especial contempt, as *Love Story* author Eric Segal was to discover, those "willing to play the fool" for limitless publicity. In defense of Columbia's action, political scientist Hans J. Morgenthau published two essays purporting to show that Van Doren had actually violated "the moral law" as handed down from Moses, Plato, Buddha, and other worthies. Apparently no such law would have been violated had Van Doren's participation in what thinking people very well knew was a cheap stunt been unrigged. If any crime had been committed in the quiz show episode, it was surely the broad conspiracy to portray as genuine intellectual activity the spouting of trivia. But while the shows were on and winning high ratings, there was neither from Morgenthau nor Columbia a peep of protest.

The most devastating but also perhaps the fairest indictment of Van Doren's role was penned by a Columbia colleague, Lawrence S. Hall, who demonstrated that Van Doren's confession had been as thoroughly fraudulent as his conduct on 21. He had not confessed because of a letter from a fan of his on the *Today* show as he had claimed but only because of a congressional subpoena. "To the very

end he never did perform the ethical free act of making up his mind.
. . . Van Doren did not *decide* to tell the truth; what he did was
adapt himself to the finally inescapable necessity of telling it." Worst
of all, asserted Hall, was his "concealing under [the] piously reflexive
formulas" of his silken prose "the most maudlin and promiscuous
ethical whoredom the soap opera public has yet witnessed."

Unlike Hall the average American seemed rather sympathetic. A
Sindunger poll asked respondents to rate those most blameworthy for
the fixes. Asked to assess the responsibility of network, sponsor, producer, and Van Doren, only 18.6% blamed Van Doren the most
while 38.9% blamed him the least. A substantial number even favored
a continuation of shows, rigged or not. Many man-in-the-street inter-
viewees said they would have done no differently, and most newspaper
editorials treated him extraordinarily gently.

Investigators discovered not a single contestant on *21*, and only
one on *The $64,000 Question*, who refused to accept money once
they learned the shows were fixed. Most were quite "blithe" about it.
Pollsters at the end of the 1950s were finding the belief widespread
that the individual did not feel it was his place to condemn. Moral
relativism, it seemed, rather than adherence to Professor Morgenthau's moral absolutism, was the rule. So many people lived polite
lies that though it may have been titillating to discover them, they
were hardly worth preaching about.

Other factors, in addition to this general willingness to partake in
a fraud such as the quiz shows, help explain why the outrage was
muted and transient. First, as Boorstin has pointed out, television
unites many people in a community, but their union is tenuous and
easily forgotten. Secondly, although many were taken in by the seeming reality of the shows, they had believed and been disabused so
many times in the past that the shock soon wore off. For underneath
the belief in the shows there probably lingered skepticism. Robert
Merton observed in 1946 that cynicism about public statements from
any source, political or commercial, was pervasive. Television was a
new medium which some may have thought was simply too big to play
the rules of the oldtime newspaper patent medicine advertiser. The
quiz shows taught them that it was not, and some critics asserted that
it was the naked selfishness of commercial radio and television, more
than the machinations of particular producers or contestants, that

was truly to blame. The quiz shows excited to a new pitch of intensity long-running arguments about commercial broadcasting and the public interest.

The growth of commercial broadcasting cannot be explored here at length, but suffice it to say that it was opposed every step of the way by intellectuals, educators, and journalists who deplored what they saw as the perversion of a medium of great potential for the sake of the desire of private business to push products. As early at the 1920s, when radio was first coming into its own, articulate voices spoke up against its use for advertising. Bruce Bliven thought such "outrageous rubbish" should be banned from the air, and at least one congressman considered introducing legislation to that end. Herbert Hoover, whose Commerce Department supervised the granting of broadcast licenses, felt that radio would die if it allowed itself to be "drowned in advertising chatter," but he favored self-regulation rather then government action. The Radio Act of 1927 demanded that licensees operate their stations not solely for profit but with due regard for the "public interest, convenience, and necessity."

As charted by broadcasting's foremost historian, Erik Barnouw, the ascendancy of commercial programming was established in a fit of absence of mind. "If such a system [as exists today] had been outlined in 1927 or 1934, when our basic broadcasting laws were written," he concluded, "it certainly would have been rejected." Critics believed that the quiz shows and the radio "payola" scandals that followed proved that broadcasting was too important to be left in the hands of those whose primary, if not sole, motive was to turn a profit for the stockholders.

Television executives insisted that the scandals were the exception in a generally well run industry, but critics thought they were the tip of the iceberg. In themselves, the scandals were relatively unimportant, held the *New Republic.* "A real investigation would center on the simple question: why is television so bad, so monstrous?" It was the thirst for profit which forced the industry to a state of thralldom to the ratings. It was profit which mandated such dreadful children's programming. Advertising agencies and their clients, with profit always uppermost in mind, forced absurd restrictions on what could be broadcast. When commentators complained about the astounding amount of violence on the tube, defenders warned of the danger of censorship. Critics replied that the most stultifying censorship was already being exercised in behalf of the manufacturers of the pointless nostrums of an overindulgent society. In its quest for ratings, television seemed consistently to avoid satisfying the intelligent minority.

The industry had now been caught red-handed, Walter Lippmann wrote, in "an enormous conspiracy to deceive the public in order to sell profitable advertising to the sponsors." The situation which had made this shameful occurrence possible could not be allowed to survive intact. Television had "to live up to a higher, but less profitable, standard." What America needed was prime time TV produced "not because it yields private profits but because it moves toward truth and excellence." What was needed, said Lippmann, was public service television.

Industry spokesmen had traditionally defended themselves as true democrats. The president of CBS, Frank Stanton, soon after *The $64,000 Question* was first aired, declared, "A program in which a large part of the audience is interested is by that very fact . . . in the public interest." By such a standard, the quiz show can be seen not as "cynical malpractices . . . in one corner of television," as Robert Sarnoff tried to represent them, but rather as the perfect expression of the industry.

Sarnoff recognized the charges being hurled at TV in 1959 and 1960 as the "long-familiar [ones] of mediocrity, imbalance, violence, and overcommercialism." These charges had been unjustified in the past and were unjustified in 1960, but because "those who press them are now armed with the cudgels represented by the quiz-show deceptions" they could not be sloughed off. Sarnoff's response was to promise careful scrutiny of such programs in the future and vigorous self-regulation. As a special bonus to the viewing public in a gesture to wipe the slate clean, he offered to donate time for a series of debates between the major Presidential candidates of 1960, which eventually resulted in the televised confrontations between Kennedy and Nixon.

Sarnoff's offer was enthusiastically welcomed by such politicians as Stewart Udall, who had been working for a suspension of equal time regulations in order to permit broadcast debates between Democratic and Republican Presidential nominees in the upcoming election.

Paradoxically, the four "Great Debates" which ensued showed unmistakably the influence of the supposedly discredited quiz programs. The similarity in formats was obvious. As in 21, two adversaries faced each other and tried to give point-scoring answers to questions fired at them under the glare of klieg lights. The debates bore as little relationship to the real work of the presidency as the quiz shows did to intellectuality. Boorstin has remarked on how successful they were "in reducing great national issues to trivial dimensions. With appropriate vulgarity, they might have been called the $400,000 Question (Prize: a $100,000-a-year job for four years)." No President would act on any question put to him by the reporters without sustained and sober consultation with trusted advisors. But the American people, conditioned by five years of isolation booth virtuosity, expected the "right" answer to be delivered pithily and with little hesitation. They did not want to be told that some questions did not have simple answers—or any answers at all.

The technological advances which led to radio and television grew out of the tinkerings of amateur experimenters. These two new forms of mass communication, with unprecedented drama and immediacy, developed independently of the desire to say anything. In 1854, Henry David Thoreau wrote, "We are in great haste to construct a magnetic telegraph from Maine to Texas; but Maine and Texas, it may be, have nothing important to communicate." This observation has been yet more relevant during the last half century. Except for the military, which was always seeking more direct means for locating ships at sea and soldiers on the battlefield, no one knew what to broadcast and telecast. The federal government, dominated by the ideology of free enterprise, declined to fill this void. To be sure, regulations did prohibit certain messages over the air, but there has never been a national statement on the positive purposes of the new media which the industry was obliged to take seriously.

Business soon discovered that broadcasting was a powerful instrument for increasing sales. Those advertisers who had financed the print media, including manufacturers of patent medicines, cosmetics, and cigarettes, quickly adopted the same role with radio and television. Left to their own devices, they sought programs which would constitute a congenial frame for their selling message. They soon hit upon the idea, among others, of parlor games, of which the quiz shows were direct descendants.

Such programs had been popular since the thirties, but in the 1950s, clever producers learned how to make them even more so. They combined large sums of money with the American fondness for facts, dressed up as intellectuality, and the result was *The $64,000 Question* and *21*. When these programs were exposed as frauds, a jaded public, inured to mendacity, was quick to forgive.

Critics have often complained, as they did with vigor after the scandals, that television—"a medium of such great potential"—was being so ill-used. But no one seems to have a clear vision of what that potential is. The lack of direction which characterized the early years of American broadcasting has never been overcome. Commentators such as Lippmann have won their public broadcasting system, but commercial television has not upgraded its fare in order to compete. If anything, public TV may act as a lightning rod deflecting complaints about the commercial industry by providing an outlet for those demanding alternative viewing.

For its part, the industry has usually ignored what enlightened guidance has been available in favor of traditional forms of entertainment guaranteed not to distract the viewer from the advertisements. Thus, recently, quiz and game shows have made a comeback. There has even been talk of resurrecting *The $64,000 Question*, despite the risk of reviving along with it memories of past chicanery. Such programming represents a distressing devotion to Philistinism and a failure of imagination, the solution for which is not in sight.

17

"Our Needs Know No Laws": The Issue of Illegal Mexican Immigration Since 1941

JUAN RAMON GARCIA

• The United States has always had a peculiar relationship with Mexico. Since it first emerged as an independent nation in the first quarter of the nineteenth century, Mexico has had to contend with the policies and ambitions of a northern neighbor that was richer, stronger, more populous, and more advanced. Consequently, every Mexican government has had to adjust its plans and goals to the colossus of the North.

American policies have often been ambivalent, however. In the 1920s and 1930s presidents Calvin Coolidge, Herbert Hoover, and Franklin D. Roosevelt withstood right-wing pressure and allowed Mexico to proceed with social and economic reforms. This "Good Neighbor Policy" was designed to prove that the United States would not intervene in the domestic affairs of a nearby nation even when Washington disapproved of the direction of government policy. Thus it was hoped that the traditional mistrust of a rich and powerful Uncle Sam would be alleviated.

Unfortunately, the rhetoric of American tolerance sometimes exceeded the reality of actual policy. Recently, when Mexican peasants in the northern parts of that country seized the lands on which they worked, President Luis Escheverría legalized their occupation by supporting genuine land reform. But the resulting shock waves in the American business community that was and is dependent on lucrative winter crops from Mexico were felt in Washington. Partly because of pressure from the United States, Escheverría's successor, Lopez Portillo, backed away from the previously strong governmental support for land seizures by peasants.

The inability of most Mexican peasants to achieve a decent

living standard has had an important impact on immigration into the United States. As Professor Juan Ramon Garcia of the University of Arizona argues in the following essay, successive American attempts to control illegal entrants from south of the border have failed because they deal only with symptoms rather than with causes. Mass deportations and contract labor programs, he writes, will not work because the border is so long as to be virtually unpatrollable. The real solution lies in improving the economic position of Mexican nationals, who will otherwise try to improve their lives by crossing over, legally or illegally, into the easily accessible United States.

In 1951 an undocumented worker stood before a judge during his deportation hearing. As the weary judge examined the file, he noted that the man had been charged several times with entering this country illegally. Looking up at him, the judge asked testily, "Don't you respect the laws of this country?" The worker replied, "Our necessities know no laws." Ten years later another undocumented worker, awaiting transportation back to Mexico in a detention center, told an interviewer, "Many people condemn us for trying to make a living. They are so busy in attacking us that they too often forget that we are human beings." In 1978, police in the Chicago area stopped a U-Haul truck carrying eighteen undocumented workers. The men had been locked in the back of the truck for forty-eight hours with no food, little water, and only two slop buckets for their personal needs. They had boarded the truck in Phoenix, where the temperature had been one hundred twelve degrees. It was at least twenty degrees hotter inside the truck. Even the case-hardened cops were moved to compassion by the suffering which these men, most of them less than twenty years of age, had endured. As one of the policemen put it, "I thought I had seen just about everything in twenty-five years on the job. But this is about the worst I've seen done to human beings by other human beings."

The question of illegal immigration from Mexico to this country has been, and continues to be, both vexing and controversial. It is vexing because it has led to abuse, exploitation, and suffering for the people who enter illegally. It is controversial because the problem is rooted in a quagmire of emotional, moral, social, political, economic, and international issues which at times defy description or solution. Throughout this protracted controversy, which dates back in terms of intensity to the early 1940s, a number of remedies have been proposed. To date the majority have either failed to be enacted or have been too limited to resolve a complex and worrisome problem.

The issue of illegal immigration from Mexico has once again generated national concern and interest. In part this is due to increased coverage of the subject by the mass media and to the fact that Americans are in the midst of an economic crisis which affects their jobs, earnings, and livelihoods. As has been the case historically, Americans in economically hard-pressed times are usually more sensitive to those factors which they perceive as responsible for their problems. In their eyes the presence of large numbers of undocumented workers in this country is part of the problem. To critics and opponents of this "uncontrolled influx," undocumented workers deprive American citizens of jobs, overtax social service agencies, increase the tax burden, and contribute to a myriad of social problems which affect the overall quality of life in the United States.

There is of course another side to the argument. Those sympathetic to the plight of undocumented workers argue that they contribute a great deal to the American economy, while deriving few benefits from it. According to them, a large percentage of undocumented workers who are employed in the United States pay a variety of taxes. Yet these people seldom take advantage of the services available to them because of fear of detection and deportation. Moreover, the majority of "illegals" are honest, hard-working, law-abiding people who, under different circumstances, would be considered model citizens. To date neither side in the controversy has been able to fully substantiate its viewpoint.

Groups on both sides of the controversy have made their views clear, and they have increasingly exerted pressure on policymakers. Yet the steps taken by national leaders have been both halting and of necessity limited, for they recognize the issue is explosive and emotional. They realize that no solution will please everyone. Further complicating matters is the fact that the great majority of illegal immigrants are Mexican citizens. In the past this was not a matter of great concern, but the recent discovery of vast oil reserves in Mexico, when coupled with the energy needs of this country, now requires American officials to take greater cognizance of this fact. They cannot afford to alienate an oil-rich Mexico by mishandling a tremendously delicate issue.

The problems confronting the United States in terms of illegal immigration and most of the proposals set forth to resolve them date back to the World War II period. United States entry into the war in 1941 created a tremendous labor shortage, particularly in the agricultural sector. Growers found that they could not compete with the wages paid by industrial employers. Those who had traditionally performed farm work either joined the military or flocked to the urban centers in search of better pay. As a result of intense lobbying pressure and the importance of agriculture to the war effort, the federal government negotiated a contract labor program with Mexico in 1941. Under this treaty Mexico agreed to provide its own nationals to perform work in agriculture and a few other designated areas for specified periods. In return the United States assumed responsibility for placing these individuals on jobs and providing food, shelter, and transportation back to Mexico once the contract period had ended. Braceros, as the temporary workers were called, would be given contracts guaranteeing them fair treatment and clearly spelling out the terms of their employment. Although the bracero program was enacted as a temporary wartime measure, it was continually renewed from 1942 to 1964. During this twenty-two-year period, some 4.5 million migrant workers came to the United States.

From the outset the program was plagued by exploitation, misunderstandings, confusion, and conflicting interests. Furthermore, it did not end the growing influx of illegal entrants from Mexico, as its proponents had predicted. Instead, the bracero program acted as one more catalyst to northern migration. The promise of a contract drew thousands of hopeful applicants to border recruiting stations. As a result there were usually more applicants than there were jobs. Those who failed to obtain a contract were loath to return home empty-handed, for many of them had either borrowed money or invested what little they had to reach the border contracting stations. They therefore opted to cross the border illegally. Thus the guest worker program only served to increase the entry of undocumented workers.

The inconsistent immigration policy followed by the United States also contributed to increased illegal entry after World War II. Then, as now, the United States implemented "special" policies with regard to Mexican immigration whenever the government deemed them necessary and beneficial to groups who held vested interests in the acquisition of cheap labor. For this reason the United States has on several occasions undertaken policies which are contrary to its own immigration laws. More often than not, this special policy has been in the form of ad hoc exemptions and administrative adjustment to those laws. A case in point was the bracero program. Another example can be found in the unilateral recruitment of Mexican workers in 1948 and in 1954.

Because of the failure of the United States to institute penalties against those who hired illegals, the Mexican government decided to terminate the bracero agreement in 1948. But it did not produce the anticipated response. Instead, the United States viewed the ploy as both arbitrary and unjustified, and it threatened to open the border if Mexico did not reinstate the program immediately. When Mexico refused, United States officials ordered the border opened to any bracero seeking employment. Word spread quickly among Mexicans who had anxiously been awaiting contracts. At first only a few bold individuals risked crossing the border in full view of American immigration authorities. When the rest realized that American officials were not going to prevent their entry, a wholesale rush occurred.

As hundreds of Mexicans crossed the river into El Paso, immigration officials placed them under technical arrest and then immediately paroled them to members of the Texas Employment Commission. As a result of the El Paso Incident of October 1948, some five thousand braceros were allowed to enter the United States illegally at the behest of immigration officials, whose job it was to enforce the laws against illegal entry. Although Mexico and the United States worked out their differences shortly thereafter, the lesson of the El Paso Incident was not lost on many. It was obvious that the United States would undertake legal and extralegal measures to acquire laborers whenever the need arose.

This was again clearly demonstrated in 1954 when negotiations over the renewal of the bracero program reached an impasse. As in

1948, American officials threatened that if Mexico terminated the agreement, they would resort to the unilateral recruitment of Mexican workers. To prove its point, the United States announced that contracting would resume on January 2, 1954, in El Centro, California, with or without an international agreement. Mexican officials responded that they were not prepared to negotiate under duress. At the same time Mexico attempted through threats and pleas to deter its people from going to the California border, but to no avail. When negotiations broke off, the United States opened the border at El Centro and seven hundred Mexicans were allowed to enter illegally. Mexico responded by posting armed guards on its side of the border. The presence of troops caused a tense situation, which was exacerbated by United States officials who resorted to a process of instant legalization of anyone who managed to cross the border. The legalization process was accomplished by having Mexicans who entered illegally run back to the official border crossing-point, put one foot on Mexican soil, and then dart back so that they could be legally processed. At times this practice approached the absurd, as depicted in a photograph showing a hapless Mexican being pulled south by a Mexican border official and north by an official of the United States. The look, a combination of fear, confusion, and chagrin, on this man's face, told the whole story.

Between January 23 and February 5, 1954, a series of bloody clashes erupted between Mexican troops and desperate, hungry braceros. According to the *New York Times*, Mexican officials were dismayed and angered at the sight of thousands of their countrymen jammed like "sardines" and gasping for air in the crunch to cross the border for a handful of harvest jobs. Tulio Lopez-Lira, who was in charge of emigration at the Mexican border port, blamed the Americans for the riots. "My countrymen," he said, "have been trapped here by American lies and propaganda that the border would be open to them." Another outspoken critic of the unilateral recruitment policy which instantly accorded legal status to illegal entrants was Congressman John F. Shelley of California. In condemning the recent events in his home state, Shelley leveled a broadside at the myopic view of the federal government on the issue of illegal immigration. "Apparently the government's reasoning is that if we simply remove all restrictions on border crossing, as we have done since expiration of the bracero agreement, all crossings will be legal and we will, therefore, wipe out the wetback problem."

Shelley's observation was essentially correct. Not only had the United States violated its own immigration laws by resorting to uni-lateral recruitment, but it had also implemented other questionable procedures which further encouraged illegal immigration from Mexico. One such procedure involved the legalization of wetbacks, a practice which was implemented by the Immigration and Naturalization Service (INS) in 1947 in an attempt to reduce the number of illegals in this country by "regularizing" their presence. This program was undertaken with the full consent and approval of Mexican officials, who were ostensibly opposed to any measures which would further encourage illegal emigration. The legalization process was formalized through clauses in the bracero agreements of 1947, 1949, and 1950. By 1951, the program had so proved its merits in the eyes of Mexico and the United States that it was incorporated into Public Law 78 (the official title of the bracero agreement) under Section 501. Under this clause the secretary of labor was authorized "to recruit Mexican workers, including illegal entrants who had resided in the United States for the preceding five years, or who had entered originally under legal contract and remained after it expired." Those who supported the legalization program claimed that it helped reduce the number of illegals in the country by making them legalized braceros. Thus the majority of braceros contracted after 1951 were in reality legalized undocumented workers.

This practice seriously undermined the enforcement of immigration laws. One of the strongest condemnations of the policy came from the President's Commission on Migratory Labor, which was ap-pointed in June 1950. In its final report, the commission accused the federal government of having condoned the wetback traffic during the harvest season:

> Wetbacks who were apprehended were given identification slips in the United States by the Immigration and Naturalization Service, which entitled them, within a few minutes, to step back across the border and become contract workers. There was no other way to obtain the indispensable slip of paper except to be found illegally in the United States. Thus violators of the law were rewarded by receiving legal contracts while the same oppor-

tunities were denied law-abiding citizens of Mexico. The United States, having engaged in a program giving preference in contracting to those who had broken the law, had encouraged violation of immigration laws. Our government thus had become a contributor to the growth of an illegal traffic which it has the responsibility to prevent.

While it is evident that the United States exacerbated the problem of illegal entry, Mexico must also share in the blame, for it condoned these practices because of the benefits derived from illegal emigration. For example, the money sent back by illegals to friends, family, and creditors helped Mexico's ailing economy. More importantly, the legal and illegal emigration of Mexicans served as a safety valve, drawing out potentially explosive elements who were unemployed and disgruntled. Finally, the Mexican government netted political gains on the home front by attacking the United States for its failure to end illegal entry and to protect the rights of Mexican nationals within its boundaries. Thus the United States became a convenient and easily assailable scapegoat for Mexico. It should be noted that the above views and circumstances still apply today.

In spite of the intensity and the importance of immigration from Mexico after 1941, the American people considered the wetback influx as largely a local problem confined to the border regions. This lack of concern and interest was mirrored by newspapers, weekly news magazines, and the popular pictorial magazines. But beginning in 1951, media attitudes began to change. Seemingly overnight, the public was inundated with articles and feature stories about undocumented workers. Most of the stories emphasized the ill effects which the "silent invasion" of "aliens" had on American society. These stories charged that illegals were responsible for increased disease rates, crime, narcotics traffic, and welfare costs, and that they served as a cover for subversive elements who were infiltrating the country. Thus what became embedded in the public mind was a negative view about illegal immigration, a view which was reinforced by the widespread use of terms such as "horde," "tide," "invasion," "wetback," "illegal," and "alien" to describe undocumented persons. To most Americans these terms conjured up images of faceless, shadowy, and sinister beings who skulked across the border in the dead of night in order to deprive American citizens of their jobs and livelihood.

Of course not all Americans opposed the entry of undocumented workers. The illegal was the very backbone of economic survival for a number of southwestern communities, and the widespread use and exploitation of illegal labor from Mexico had become a long-accepted norm. Many people in these communities had developed entrenched moral, ethical, and social justifications which supported the hiring and the abuse of undocumented workers. For the most part, those who employed wetbacks were scornful of interlopers who threatened to undercut their labor supply either through legislation penalizing employers or through stepped-up enforcement measures. They believed that the "handling of wetbacks" should be left to them, for they "knew and understood" these people best. Unfortunately for undocumented workers, such understanding was grounded in deeply embedded and negative stereotypes about Mexicans. This was especially true in the Rio Grande Valley of Texas, an area where most of the Mexicans hired were illegals. To employers the Mexicans were childlike, undisciplined, and lazy. Mexicans were also perceived as subhumans who were of little value except in performing hard work. As one valley resident put it, Mexicans did not really mind the hard work, the long hours, and the low pay. They were used to this. After all, he concluded, they "have behind them five hundred years of burden-bearing and animal-like living and just can't adjust to civilization in the way a white man does." Other long-time employers of illegals agreed. In their view Mexicans had enough bad attributes, and efforts to improve their way of life only added to the problem of dealing with them. To their way of thinking, they were doing illegals a favor by hiring them. After all, if things were really that bad in the United States, why did they make such determined efforts to come here?

In 1954 rising unemployment, the continued interest of the mass media, a growing public outcry against the "illegal influx," and the expression by immigration officials that they had begun to lose control of the border all forced the Eisenhower administration to deal with the problem. Attorney General Herbert Brownell adopted a two-pronged approach. The first was the implementation of a massive program to regain control of the border and reduce illegal entry. The program, code-named "Operation Wetback," began in June 1954. It was a large-scale, paramilitary program undertaken by the INS involving concentrated strike forces and raids in areas which had heavy concentrations of illegals. Focusing on the states of California, Texas, Arizona, and New Mexico, the raids lasted throughout the summer and resulted in the deportation and repatriation of more than one million undocumented workers. Although recent research has found that the success of Operation Wetback was greatly exaggerated, it nonetheless represented a major effort by the federal government and the INS to enforce the immigration laws and to restore a semblance of control along the United States–Mexican border. Since 1954 the INS has sporadically conducted similar drives. These drives have usually followed hard on the heels of intense and protracted media attention upon the influx of illegals, rising unemployment, a noticeable downswing in the economy, and public outcry fostered by these conditions. Like Operation Wetback, the ensuing roundups merely represented a stopgap measure designed to placate an aroused public. While such drives do serve limited purposes, they do not address the major causes of illegal entry from Mexico.

While Operation Wetback was being planned and implemented, Herbert Brownell undertook the second part of his program. This was the introduction of legislation to impose penalties against those who "knowingly" employed illegals or were captured in the act of smuggling or harboring them. The legislation was introduced in Congress in 1954 by Republican Senator Arthur Watkins of Utah and Democratic Representative Louis E. Graham of Pennsylvania.

Attempts to introduce penalty legislation against employers during President Harry Truman's tenure had met with resounding defeat, and from the outset it was apparent that Brownell's proposals would also face an uphill battle. Opposing the penalty legislation was a powerful and well-organized group in Congress which was determined to protect the interests of those whose economic survival depended upon a cheap source of labor. As a result of this strong opposition, Brownell's proposals were never enacted. After Operation Wetback, interest in reintroducing penalty legislation quickly faded. The muchpublicized "success" of the deportation drives of 1954 lulled many proponents of such legislation into believing that the influx of illegals was at last under control, and that perhaps penalty legislation, which would always encounter tremendous opposition, was not the solution after all.

They were of course mistaken. Operation Wetback did not signal the end of illegal immigration from Mexico although it presented that impression to many. After 1954, agricultural employers contracted with individual Mexicans. Thus between 1954 and 1960, there occurred a dramatic increase in the number of braceros hired (see Table 1). During this same period INS figures reflected a dramatic decrease in the numbers of undocumented workers apprehended. This tended to support the claims of the INS that the problem of illegal entry was now under control. At the same time these figures bolstered the arguments of those who favored the continuation of a bracero program. Proponents argued that it served as a deterrent to illegal entry, and they warned federal officials that termination of the program

TABLE 1

Number of Braceros Contracted 1951–1964		Number of Undocumented Persons 1951–1964	
Year	Contracted	Year	Contracted
1951	190,745[a]	1951	500,628
1952	197,100	1952	543,538
1953	201,380	1953	875,318
1954	309,033	1954	1,075,168
1955	398,650	1955	242,608
1956	445,197	1956	72,442
1957	436,049	1957	44,451
1958	432,857	1958	37,242
1959	437,643	1959	30,196
1960	315,846	1960	29,651
1961	291,420	1961	29,877
1962	194,978	1962	30,272
1963	186,865	1963	39,124
1964	177,736	1964	43,844
Total	4,215,499		

a Includes 46,076 contracted under 1948 agreement prior to July 15.
SOURCE: U.S. Department of Labor, "Summary of Migratory Station Activities."

SOURCE: U.S. Immigration and Naturalization Service.

would only reopen the floodgates to illegal entry. These arguments and the power of probracero groups proved effective and resulted in the continuation of the program until 1964.

As if to underscore the warnings of probracero groups, apprehension of illegals began to increase in 1963 and 1964. On the surface it seemed that the program had in fact been a deterrent to illegal entry. Yet appearances were deceiving, as other critical factors had been responsible for the apparent decline of illegal immigration from Mexico. One factor was that after 1954 the Border Patrol returned to routine operations, largely abandoning the concentrated approach as implemented in 1954. The Border Patrol also continued the legalization of apprehended wetbacks, which meant that a good proportion of the braceros contracted were in reality illegals whose presence in this country had been regularized. Another reason for the "decline" of illegal immigration was the introduction of increased labor-saving technology, which reduced needs in the unskilled agricultural labor market.

After 1959 there was a rapid decline in the number of braceros contracted, in part because of labor-saving technology and the more rigid enforcement of wage guarantees. The government also began to tighten certification requirements for establishing the need to import and hire braceros. Thus prior to the end of the bracero program in 1964, many employers had again begun to resort to an increased use of undocumented workers. Among those employed were large numbers of commuters who had entered the United States by using a border-crossing permit. The permits, which were fairly easy to acquire, permitted the holder to enter the United States for the purposes of entertainment, shopping, visiting, or business. Holders of this permit were prohibited from working while in this country or from traveling more than twenty-five miles from the border. Those holding the permit were allowed to enter the United States for periods not to exceed seventy-two hours.

Obviously, the temptation proved too great for many. Once here they mailed the cards back to Mexico to avoid having them confiscated in case of apprehension by INS authorities. As no records were kept of the number of people entering or leaving the United States on a daily basis, it proved almost impossible to determine how many had entered legally and remained illegally. The unavailability of records in this area added to the numerical illusion that illegal entry, as shown by apprehensions, had declined.

Further adding to the incentive to enter illegally was the enactment of more stringent immigration restrictions by the United States in 1965 and 1968. Under the new regulations, applicants were given preference if they were blood relatives of citizens or legal residents already in the United States. Members of preferred professions such as engineering and medicine were also given higher priority. Preference was also shown to applicants who had employers who would sponsor them. People who did not fall into any of these categories were free to apply as well, although their chances for legal admission, given the long waiting lists, were almost nil. Many were unwilling to make application upon such slim chances, especially given the high cost and the complicated procedures.

Factors in Mexico also served to spur illegal emigration. The growth in Mexico's economy between 1950 and 1960 was not sufficient to keep up with its population growth, which had more than doubled between 1940 and 1963, rising from twenty-two to forty-five million. Therefore, the lack of employment opportunities, a rapidly expanding population, and Mexico's economic overdependence on the United States, when coupled with the availability of work in the United States and a largely unpatrolled border, all served once again to attract Mexican nationals in increasing numbers.

By the late 1960s, illegal immigration had increased significantly. Labor organizations and social reform groups once again called for measures to deal with what they saw as a problem of major proportions. Yet their concern was not shared by important government officials or the general public. The boom economy of the 1960s appeared capable of absorbing and utilizing an enlarged labor force, regardless of its source. Furthermore, the hostile environment toward undocumented persons had for the moment dissipated. Americans were more concerned with the domestic and foreign issues raised by the Vietnam War.

As the war ground to an end, as some semblance of domestic tranquility returned, and as the nation began to experience the economic problems inherent in adjusting to a peacetime economy, illegal immigration once again became an issue of major public and governmental concern. Newspaper stories and government reports reflected a steady increase in the number of undocumented persons apprehended each year. According to INS estimates, the number of illegal aliens apprehended increased from about two hundred thousand in 1968 to five hundred thousand in 1972. Accompanying these reports were renewed attacks from various groups. As in the past, undocumented workers were accused of overburdening social and welfare agencies, of depriving Americans of jobs, and of driving up rates of crime and disease. Some claimed that if this large-scale influx continued unchecked, it would lead to the formation of "welfare reservations" and "wetback subcultures" which would be breeding grounds for discontent, alienation, and potential revolution. Adding to the "alien scare" were the statements of high-ranking immigration officials who sought additional funding for their programs. One of the more vociferous was Leonard Chapman, the head of the INS. In 1972 he warned that the United States was undergoing a "growing, silent invasion of illegals" and called upon Americans to demand swift action to halt it, for there "was no time to lose."

The scare tactics and warnings had their desired effects. Stepped-up INS campaigns against undocumented workers followed, studies were commissioned, various state and federal subcommittees held hearings, and some states enacted legislation against those who "knowingly" employed illegals. For the most part, the reports and the hearings stirred a great deal of interest, debate, and controversy but did little to resolve the problem. The penalty legislation enacted at the state level also did little to discourage employment of illegals because it contained vague language and numerous loopholes which made prosecution and conviction very difficult. Instead, a number of these state laws were used by unscrupulous employers to intensify their discrimination against Hispanic people. According to one observer, some employers used the laws as a pretext for refusing to hire minorities, claiming that applicants had failed to prove beyond a shadow of a doubt that they were indeed legal residents or citizens of the United States.

At the federal level, Congressman Peter Rodino and Senator Edward F. Kennedy introduced bills in 1972 and 1974 respectively designed to regularize the status of aliens already in the United States and to impose sanctions against employers who hired illegals. Neither of the proposals won wide support in Congress. Although they continued to stir interest and controversy, repeated efforts to have the bills enacted failed. By mid-1975 the question of illegal immigration from Mexico had once again become a major issue both here and in Mexico. Deadlocked over what path to follow, Congress deferred any action. It instead adopted a wait-and-see posture.

In 1977 President Jimmy Carter introduced a series of measures which he hoped would prove acceptable to a majority of people. Similar to those proposed under Truman and Eisenhower, they called for increased personnel to patrol the border, legislation to penalize those who employed illegals, and closer cooperation with those countries from which undocumented persons came. A fourth measure entailed granting "amnesty" to illegal aliens. Under this provision, undocumented persons who entered before 1970 and who had resided in the United States continually since their arrival would be permitted to remain. They could also begin the process of becoming naturalized citizens. The plan also proposed that aliens who entered between 1970 and 1977 would be permitted to remain in the United States, but only on a temporary basis. A more definite ruling on their future status would come after the federal government "had studied the matter further." Finally, under Carter's plan, those who entered illegally after 1977 would be subject to immediate deportation.

President Carter's plan was vigorously discussed and received widespread criticism from a variety of groups and organizations. Critics of the plan assailed it as either too amorphous, too lenient, or too stringent. As debate raged around the proposals, the Carter administration came under attack from other sectors. When economic conditions in the country deteriorated further, the energy problem deepened, and affairs in the Middle East worsened, Carter's proposal on illegal immigration fell by the wayside. There was little that the beleaguered president could do to gain support for any of his proposals, and thus no legislative action was taken on them.

Yet even if Carter's proposals had been enacted, it is doubtful that they would have had any significant impact on the problem of illegal immigration. For example, it is unlikely that Congress would have enacted a stringent and effective law against employers of illegals. It is also doubtful that a large number of undocumented persons would have taken advantage of the amnesty provisions. First of all, applying for amnesty would have meant exposure to INS officials. To a group of people long conditioned to remaining invisible, such a step would have been threatening and dangerous. Furthermore, the burden of proof in terms of continuous residency before 1970 would have fallen totally on those seeking citizenship status. There was always the chance that such proof would not be accepted by immigration officials, in which case applicants would be subject to deportation. To many the process involved appeared complicated, the risks great, and the benefits minimal and uncertain. For those who had entered after 1970 the assignment of a temporary resident status was not worth the risk of identifying themselves, especially since there was little or no indication of what might happen to them after the government "had studied the matter." For obvious reasons, Carter's plan was even less appealing to those who entered after 1977.

The proposal for increasing border patrol personnel also had its weaknesses. For example, increasing personnel and equipping them with sophisticated hardware would have no impact whatsoever in controlling those who entered the United States legally by using their temporary tourist or student cards, and then overstayed, thus becoming illegals. Critics also pointed out that although this proposal would make it more difficult for those without cards to enter illegally, it would not deter them. If anything, the program would only increase the profits of "coyotes" (commercial smugglers), who already operated lucrative businesses assisting undocumented persons in crossing the border. Finally, Carter's plan contained little that would have attacked the problem at its roots. His plan did not sufficiently address itself to reducing the major push factors extant in Mexico which contribute to illegal emigration.

President Ronald Reagan's proposal also fails to address the basic causes of the problem. There is little or no discussion of helping Mexico battle its economic underdevelopment, or of alleviating the large trade imbalance which exists between it and the United States. There is also little indication that Mexico will receive increased capital from the World Bank to invest in projects such as its integrated rural development program, which thus far appears to be helping its economically depressed rural sectors. Reagan's proposals place emphasis on the unilateral approach to reducing the problem—an approach which has met with little success in the past.

In addition, Reagan's plans contain serious flaws which will exacerbate the problem. Because of the "serious dimensions" of the situation, he has requested that the government be given wide-ranging emergency powers. Among them is the authority to establish detention centers for illegals without requiring environmental studies in advance. This proposal, if enacted, might not bode well for those illegals unfortunate enough to be captured and detained. Without proper safeguards, these places might lapse into pestilential and poorly maintained camps. Reagan's program also calls for stiff fines against those who employ illegals. Yet he has provided a palatable alternative in an effort to gain the support of powerful interest groups who would vehemently resist sanctions against employers. Reagan has proposed a two-year experimental guest worker program that would bring in fifty thousand braceros to the United States each year. If successful, the program would then be expanded to bring in between five hundred thousand and one million guest workers annually. Thus the program would substitute one source of cheap labor for another.

The Reagan administration claims the guest worker program would help reduce illegal entry. Yet it might serve to encourage illegal entry, much as the bracero program of 1942 to 1964 did. In essence, there are likely to be more applicants than jobs. For those who fail to obtain a contract, the tendency will be to enter illegally. Moreover, guest workers may opt to remain illegally after their contract term has expired. Finally, the program would create a class of highly exploited laborers since extensive contract guarantees might not be included in the agreement or, if included, might not be strictly enforced given Reagan's emphasis on deregulation of the private sector. It is interesting to note that the president's proposal of a guest worker program comes at a time when the United States is experiencing high employment.

In conclusion, past experience has adequately demonstrated the ineffectiveness of mass deportations, restrictive measures, contract labor programs, and a unilateral approach in providing long-term solutions to the problem of illegal immigration. Undocumented persons will continue to seek better opportunities in the United States so long as those opportunities are lacking or denied them at home. That is one of the consequences of a contiguous and negotiable border separating a rich nation from a poor one.

18

The Last War, the Next War, and the New Revisionists

WALTER LA FEBER

• During the 1960 presidential campaign, John F. Kennedy repeatedly criticized the Eisenhower administration for too great a reliance on nuclear weapons. After his election, the new president implemented a policy of flexible response to so-called wars of national liberation. When guerrilla conflict began in Vietnam, President Kennedy sent airplanes, artillery, and 16,000 "advisers" to bolster Premier Diem's regime.

The war continued to widen, and in 1963 Lyndon B. Johnson inherited a shaky Saigon regime dependent upon American support. Rather than face charges of appeasement in world affairs, President Johnson increased the Southeast Asian involvement. In August 1964, in response to an alleged attack on an American destroyer, President Johnson ordered the bombing of North Vietnam. This prompted the Senate to pass—with only two dissenting votes—the Gulf of Tonkin Resolution, which granted the chief executive extraordinary powers to protect the national interest. By 1967, more than a half-million United States servicemen were trying to prevent a Communist takeover, "contain" China, and convince other governments of America's resolve to defend its friends.

As everyone now realizes, this huge effort was unsuccessful, and the cost in the lives of young men and in more than a decade of runaway inflation was enormous. But there has been less agreement as to why the rich and powerful United States, with its technologically sophisticated weaponry and its absolute command of the air and the sea, could not bring

Reprinted by permission of *democracy*, 43 West 61st Street, NY, NY 10023. Copyright 1980. Walter LaFeber is Professor of History at Cornell and author of *America, Russia and the Cold War, 1945–1980* (John Wiley Publishers, 1981), among other works.

to heel a small, poor, and backward nation that was divided against itself. *The following essay by Cornell University historian Walter LaFeber is perhaps the finest piece yet written about this unfortunate episode.*

As if to prove Lord Acton's dictum that "the strong man with the dagger is followed by the weak man with the sponge," a remarkable rewriting of the Vietnam war's history is under way. It is especially remarkable because the new revisionists are either ignorant of American policy in the conflict or have chosen to forget past policies in order to mold present opinion. More generally, they are rewriting the record of failed military interventionism in the 1950 to 1975 era in order to build support for interventionism in the 1980s. More specifically, the new revisionists are attempting to shift historical guilt from those who instigated and ran the war to those who opposed it.

Immediately after South Vietnam fell in 1975, Secretary of State Henry Kissinger urged Americans to forget the quarter-century-long war. That advice was no doubt related to his other concern at the time: committing U.S. military power to Angola and the Horn of Africa. Congress had fortunately learned from experience and stopped Kissinger from involving the country in an African Vietnam. The next year, however, influential authors began to discover that Vietnam's history was more usable than Kissinger had imagined. General William Westmoreland, who commanded U.S. forces during the worst months of fighting in the 1960s, set the line when he argued in his memoirs and public speeches that the conflict was not lost on the battlefield, but at home where overly sensitive politicians followed a "no-win policy" to accommodate "a misguided minority opposition . . . masterfully manipulated by Hanoi and Moscow." The enemy, Westmoreland claimed, finally won "the war politically in Washington."

Part of Westmoreland's thesis was developed with more scholarship and cooler prose by Leslie H. Gelb and Richard K. Betts in *The Irony of Vietnam: The System Worked*. It was not the "system"—that is, the Cold War national security establishment—that failed, the authors argued. Failure was to be blamed on the American people, who never understood the war and finally tired of it, and on the Presidents who supinely followed the people. Thus the "system" worked doubly well: the professional bureaucrats gave the correct advice, as they were paid to do, and the Presidents followed the public's wishes, as democratic theory provides that they should.

Westmoreland's argument that the antiwar groups wrongly labeled Vietnam an illegal and immoral conflict was developed by Guenter Lewy's *America in Vietnam*. Lewy, however, was so honest that his own evidence destroyed the thesis. Although he wrote that U.S. soldiers followed civilized modes of war even though this sometimes meant virtual suicide, Lewy also gave striking examples of how the troops ruthlessly destroyed villages and civilians. "It is well to remember," he wrote, "that revulsion at the fate of thousands of hapless civilians killed and maimed" because of American reliance upon high-technology weapons "may undercut the willingness of a democratic nation to fight communist insurgents." That becomes a fair judgment when "thousands" is changed to "hundreds of thousands." Lewy nevertheless held grimly to his thesis about the war's morality and legality, even as he reached his closing pages: "the simplistic slogan 'No more Vietnams' not only may encourage international disorder, but could mean abandoning basic American values." It apparently made little difference to Lewy that those basic American values had been ravaged at My Lai, or at Cam Ne, where a Marine commander burned down a village and then observed in his after-action report that "it is extremely difficult for a ground commander to reconcile his tactical mission and a people-to-people program." Lewy's conclusions, not his evidence, set a tone that was widely echoed, particularly after the foreign policy crises of late 1979.

The Soviet invasion of Afghanistan was seized upon with almost audible sighs of relief in some quarters. *Commentary*, which had publicly introduced Lewy's argument in 1978, published a series of essays in early 1980 that developed some of his conclusions, especially the view that if the Vietnam experience inhibited future U.S. interventions, it "could mean abandoning basic American values." In an essay that thoughtfully explored the meaning of his own antiwar protests in the 1960s, Peter Berger nevertheless drew the conclusion that the American defeat in Vietnam "greatly altered" the world balance of power, and that "American power has dramatically declined, politically as well as militarily." Charles Horner condemned President Jimmy Carter's early belief that Vietnam taught us the limits of U.S. power. "That view," Horner claimed, "is the single greatest restraint on our capacity to deal with the world, and that capacity will not much increase unless the view behind it is changed, thoroughly and profoundly." Horner did his best to reinterpret the meaning of Vietnam, but it was *Commentary*'s editor, Norman Podhoretz, who best demonstrated how history could be rewritten to obtain desired conclusions.

"Now that Vietnam is coming to be seen by more and more people as an imprudent effort to save Indochina from the horrors of Communist rule rather than an immoral intervention or a crime," Podhoretz wrote in the March 1980 issue, "the policy out of which it grew is also coming to be seen in a new light." He believed that the "policy— of defending democracy [*sic*] wherever it existed, or of holding the line against the advance of Communist totalitarianism by political means where possible and by military means when necessary," was based on the Wilsonian idea that "in the long run," U.S. interests depended on " 'the survival and the success of liberty' in the world as a whole." This revisionist view of Vietnam, Podhoretz argued, is helping to create a "new nationalism"—the kind of outlook that "Woodrow Wilson appealed to in seeking to 'make the world safe for democracy' and that John F. Kennedy echoed.

Podhoretz's grasp of historical facts is not reassuring; the essay has three major errors in its first three pages. George A. Carver, Jr.'s essay subtitled "The Teachings of Vietnam," in the July 1980 issue of *Harper's*, only adds to that problem. An old C.I.A. hand who was deeply involved in Vietnam policy planning, Carver is identified in *Harper's* only as "a senior fellow" at Georgetown University's Center for Strategic and International Studies. That identification is nevertheless of note, for the Center serves as an important source of personnel and ideas for what passes as Ronald Reagan's foreign policy program. In the article, Carver set out to "dispel Vietnam's shadows" so the United States could again exercise great power and influence. When he mentioned earlier policy, Carver simply postulated that South Vietnam fell to North Vietnamese conventional forces, not to "any popular southern rebellion," and that "the press and media, and their internal competitive imperatives" misrepresented the real progress the U.S. forces were making in the war. Beyond that, the analysis consists of empty generalizations (Americans are encumbered in their foreign policy by "theological intensity" and "childlike innocence"), and it climaxes with the insight that "the world is cruel."

Read closely, Carver's warning about the dangers of "theological intensity" contradicts Podhoretz's call for a new Wilsonianism. But in the wake of the Iranian and Afghanistan crises, few read these calls to the ramparts of freedom very closely. The essays were more valuable for their feelings than for their historical accuracy. The new revisionists wanted to create a mood, not recall an actual past, and their success became dramatically apparent when that highly sensitive barometer of popular feelings, commercial television, quickly put together a new sitcom on the war, "The Six O'Clock Follies." One reviewer labeled it a "gutlessly cynical comedy," signaling that "suddenly we are supposed to be able to laugh at Vietnam." As the *Washington Post*'s critic observed, however, since the conflict has "been deemed a safe zone . . . all three networks have Vietnam sitcoms in the works" for 1980–1981. Television was placing its seal of approval on a revisionism that promised to be commercially as well as ideologically satisfying.

Given this new mood, it was natural that those who wielded, or planned to wield, power were also prepared to help wring the sponge. In 1978 Zbigniew Brzezinski had lamented privately to Senate staff members that the floundering administration needed a *Mayagüez* incident so Carter, as Ford had in 1975, could get tough with Communists (preferably, apparently, from a small country), and rally Americans behind a battle flag. By the end of 1979, Carter had not one but two such opportunities with the Iranian hostage issue and the Soviet invasion of Afghanistan, and as usual Americans indeed closed ranks behind the President. In mid-December, Brzezinski observed that the country was finally getting over its post-Vietnam opposition to military spending and overseas intervention.

Three months later, Ronald Reagan, in his only major foreign policy speech prior to the Republican Convention, urged a return to Wilsonianism—what one reporter characterized as a belief that Americans have "an inescapable duty to act as the tutor and protector of the free world in confronting . . . alien ideologies." To carry out this mission, Reagan proclaimed, "we must rid ourselves of the 'Vietnam syndrome.'" He of course meant the old "syndrome," not the new syndrome of the revisionists that the war was to be admired for its intent if not its outcome. A frustrated job seeker at the Republican Convention best captured the effects of the new revisionism. A reporter teased Henry Kissinger about his prediction in the early 1970s that if the war did not end well for Americans there would be a fierce right-wing reaction. "It turned out just about the way I predicted it would," Kissinger replied. The former Secretary of State, however, contributed to the mood that threatened to confine him to academia. In recent writings and speeches, Kissinger has argued that if the Watergate scandal had not driven Nixon from office, South Vietnam would not have been allowed to fall. His claim cannot, of course, be completely disproved, but it is totally unsupported by either the post-1973 military and political situation in Vietnam, or the antiwar course of American policies, including Nixon's, that appeared long before the Watergate scandal paralyzed the administration.

The arguments of the new revisionists—or the new nationalists, as some prefer to be called (in perhaps unconscious reference to the New Nationalism of Theodore Roosevelt and Herbert Croly that pledged an imperial "Big Stick" foerign policy)—dominated the foreign policy debates and, indeed, the Carter-Brzezinski foreign policies in early 1980. Because those arguments rest heavily on interpretations of the Vietnam conflict, their use of the war's history deserves analysis. This can be done on two levels: the new revisionists' explicit claims, and the events they choose to ignore.

The most notable explicit theme is captured by Westmoreland's assertion that the war was lost because of pressure from a "misguided minority opposition" at home, or by Peter Berger's more careful statement that "the anti-war movement was a primary causal factor in the American withdrawal from Indochina." Since at least the mid-1960s, detailed public opinion polls have existed that show that Americans supported a tough policy in Vietnam. In this, as in nearly all foreign policies, the public followed the President. As Herbert Y. Schandler concluded after his careful study of public opinion between 1964 and 1969, "If the administration is using increasing force, the public will respond like hawks; if it is seeking peace, the public responds like doves." When Lyndon Johnson tried to convince doubters by whip-

ping out the latest opinion polls showing support for the war, he did
not have to make up the figures. George Ball has testified that the
antiwar protests only "dug us in more deeply" and intensified the
administration's determination to win. Ball, who served as Under
Secretary of State under Johnson, rightly calculated that "only late
in the day did widespread discontent . . . appreciably slow the escalation of the war." Even those who dissented in the 1960s were more
hawk than dove. Richard Scammon and Ben Wattenberg's analysis of
the 1968 election concluded that a plurality of the Democrats who
voted for Eugene McCarthy in the primaries supported George Wallace in November, and that finding is corroborated by polls revealing
that a majority of those who opposed the conduct of the war also
opposed protests against the war. Westmoreland's "misguided minority opposition" was of significantly less importance than a much larger
group that wanted him to have whatever he needed to end the war.
It simply is not true, as Barry Goldwater claimed at the 1980 Republican Convention, that the "will" to win the war was missing in the
1960s.

By 1970–1971, antiwar opposition had increased, but it did not stop
Nixon from expanding the conflict into Cambodia and Laos. One
statistic stands out: before Nixon sent in the troops, 56 percent of
college-educated Americans wanted to "stay out" of Cambodia, and
after he committed the forces, 50 percent of the same group supported
the Cambodian invasion. When Nixon carpet-bombed North Vietnam two years later and for the first time mined the North's ports,
59 percent of those polled supported the President, and only 24 percent opposed him, even though it was clear that the mining could
lead to a confrontation with the Russians and Chinese, whose ships
used the harbors.

The effectiveness of the antiwar movement has been greatly over-
rated by the new revisionists, and the movement has consequently
served as the scapegoat for them as well as for the national security
managers whose policies failed in Vietnam. Given the new revisionist
arguments, it needs to be emphasized that the United States lost in
Vietnam because it was defeated militarily, and that that defeat occurred because Americans could not win the war without destroying
what they were fighting to save—or, alternatively, without fighting for
decades while surrendering those values at home and in the Western

alliance for which the cold war was supposedly being waged. The anti-war protesters only pointed up these contradictions; they did not create them.

The new revisionists argue that the nation has largely recovered from the disaster. Carl Gershman writes that "as the polls reveal, the American people have now overwhelmingly rejected the ideas of the new [Carter-Vance-Young] establishment." The strategy of the post-Vietnam "establishment" is to contain communism only in selected areas, and by using nonmilitary means if possible. The polls actually reveal considerable support for this strategy. In January 1980, after the invasion of Afghanistan, a CBS/*New York Times* survey showed that about two-fifths of those polled wanted to respond with non-military tactics, two-fifths wanted to "hold off for now," and less than one-fifth favored a military response. Lou Harris discovered that within six weeks after the seizure of the hostages in Iran, support for military retaliation dropped off sharply. Quite clearly, if the new nationalists hope to whip up public sentiment for using military force wherever they perceive "democracy" to be threatened, they have much work yet to do. Most Americans have not overwhelmingly rejected nonmilitary responses, even after being shaken by the diplomatic earthquakes of 1979–1980. And they appear too sophisticated to agree with Podhoretz's Wilsonian assumption that "American interests in the long run [depend] on the survival and the success of liberty in the world as a whole." A majority of Americans seem to agree with that part of the post-Vietnam "establishment" represented by Vance and Young that it is wiser to trust nationalisms in the Third World than to undertake a Wilsonian crusade to rescue those nationalisms for an American-defined "liberty."

There is a reason for this confusion among new revisionist writers. They focus almost entirely on the Soviet Union instead of on the instability in Third World areas that the Soviets have at times turned to their own advantage. Such an approach allows the new revisionists to stress military power rather than the political or economic strategies that are most appropriate for dealing with Third World problems. The new nationalists, like the old, pride themselves on being realists in regard to power, but their concept of power is one-dimensional. Once this military dimension becomes unusable, nothing is left. A direct military strategy is appropriate for dealing with the Soviets in certain cases—for example, if the Red Army invaded Western Europe or Middle East oil fields. That strategy, however, has existed since the days of Harry Truman; the Vietnam war, regardless of how it is reinterpreted, has nothing new to teach us about that kind of massive response. A quarter-century ago, when the United States took its first military steps into Vietnam, Reinhold Niebuhr warned that the policy placed "undue reliance on purely military power" and therefore missed the fundamental political point: a U.S. military response was incapable of ending "the injustices of [Asia's] decaying feudalism and the inequalities of its recent colonialism." Niebuhr's advice was of course ignored. The supposed realists of the day proceeded to commit military power in Vietnam—to *contain China*. For, in the mid-1960s, China was the villain for the national security managers, as the Soviets are now for the new revisionists.

The reason for the failure of U.S. military power was not that it was severely limited. Lyndon Johnson bragged that he put 100,000 men into Vietnam in just one hundred and twenty days. Those troops were supported by the most powerful naval and air force ever used in Asia. Laos became the most heavily bombed country in history, North Vietnam's ports and cities were bombed and mined almost yard by yard, and Nixon dropped a ton of bombs on Indochina for every minute of his first term in the White House. Neither the will nor the power was missing. As Michael Herr wrote in *Dispatches*, "There was such a dense concentration of American energy there, American and essentially adolescent, if that energy could have been channeled into anything more than noise, waste and pain, it would have lighted up Indochina for a thousand years." Vietnam provides a classic lesson in the misuse of military power, but that lesson is being overlooked by the new revisionists.

And if they have misunderstood the conflict's central political and military features, so have the new revisionists lost sight of the historical context. They stress that Vietnam caused the decline of American power. It is quite probable, however, that when historians look back with proper perspective on the last half of the twentieth century, they will conclude that U.S. foreign policy problems in the 1970s and 1980s resulted not from the Vietnam experience, but more generally from political misperception and from an overestimation of American power. The *hubris* produced by the American triumph in the Cuban missile crisis contributed to such misestimation, but the problems also resulted from the failure to understand that U.S. power began a relative decline in the late 1950s and early 1960s. It was during those earlier years that the American economy and international trade began a decline that only accelerated—not started—in the 1970s; that such important allies as Japan and West Germany directly attacked American markets and helped to undermine the dollar; that the Western alliance displayed its first signs of slipping out of Washington's control; and that the Third World rapidly multiplied its numbers and decided—as the creation of OPEC in 1969 demonstrated—that it no longer had to join either one of the superpower camps. Future historians will consequently see the Vietnam war as one result, not a cause, of the relative decline of American power that began in the late 1950s. They will also probably conclude that space ventures, and the achievement of independence by nearly one hundred nations in the Third World, were of greater historical significance than the Vietnam conflict or the U.S.-USSR rivalry that obsesses the new revisionists.

Even with their narrow focus on the lessons of Vietnam, it is striking how much the new revisionists omit from their accounts of the war. They say relatively little about the South Vietnamese. The war is viewed as an eyeball-to-eyeball confrontation between Americans and Communists, and the turn comes when the Americans, undone by what Carver calls their "childlike innocence," blink. This approach resembles watching two football teams but not noticing the ball that is being kicked and passed around. The new revisionists have downplayed the inability of the South Vietnamese to establish a stable and effective government amid a massive U.S. buildup, the Vietnamese hatred for the growing American domination, and the massive desertions from the South's army in 1966–1967, even when the U.S. forces arrived to help. As early as 1966, non-Communist student leaders accurately called the country's presidential elections "a farce directed by foreigners." By 1971, a Saigon newspaper ran a daily contest in which readers submitted stories of rape or homicide committed by

Americans. As Woodrow Wilson learned in 1919, some people just do not want to be saved—at least by outsiders with whom they have little in common.

The new revisionists also overlook the role the allies played in Vietnam. There is a good reason for this ommission: of the forty nations tied to the United States by treaties, only four—Australia, New Zealand, South Korea, and Thailand—committed any combat troops. The major European and Latin American allies refused to send such forces. We later discovered that the South Koreans, whom Americans had saved at tremendous cost in 1950, agreed to help only after Washington bribed them with one billion dollars of aid. The key Asian ally, Japan, carefully distanced itself from the U.S. effort. This was especially bitter for American officials, for Truman and Eisenhower had made the original commitment to Vietnam in part to keep the area's raw materials and markets open for the Japanese. Relations between Tokyo and Washington deteriorated rapidly. When Lyndon Johnson asked whether he could visit Japan in 1966, the answer came back, "inconceivable." An article in the authoritative *Japan Quarterly* stated that if the United States became involved in another war with China, divisions in Japanese public opinion "would split the nation in two" and lead to "disturbances approaching a civil war in scale."

As Jimmy Carter admitted in early 1980, the United States needs strong support from allies if it hopes to contain the Soviets in the Middle East. It would be well, therefore, to note carefully the allied view of U.S. policy in Vietnam and elsewhere before embarking on a Wilsonian crusade to make "democracy" safe everywhere. Having chosen to ignore the lesson that Vietnam teaches about the allies, the new revisionists resemble traditional isolationists, who, as scholars have agreed, were characterized by a desire for maximum freedom of action, minimum commitment to other nations ("no entangling alliances"), and a primary reliance on military force rather than on the compromises of political negotiations.

Finally, these recent accounts neglect the war's domestic costs. The new revisionists stress the decline of the American "will" to win, but they say little about how the economic disasters and a corrupted presidency produced by the war influenced that "will." As early as January 1966, Lyndon Johnson admitted that "because of Vietnam we cannot do all that we should, or all that we would like to do" in building a more just society at home. As the phrase went at the time, Americans—those "people of plenty"—suddenly discovered they could not have both guns and butter. The butter, or, more generally, the Great Society program, was sacrificed. A Pentagon analysis drawn up under the direction of Secretary of Defense Clark Clifford after the 1968 Tet offensive faced the problem squarely. It concluded that militarily the war could not be won, "even with the 200,000 additional troops" requested by Westmoreland. A drastic escalation, moreover, would result not only in "increased defiance of the draft," but in "growing unrest in the cities because of the belief that we are ignoring domestic problems." A "domestic crisis of unprecedented proportions" threatened. If the new revisionists and Reagan Republicans plan to manipulate the war's history to obtain higher defense budgets and unilateral commitments overseas, they should discuss this crucial characteristic of the war's course: it was determined less by campus protesters than by the growing realization that the costs worsened the conditions of the poorest and most discriminated against in American society until an "unprecedented" crisis loomed. Clifford turned against the war after businessmen he respected suddenly became scared and dovish. Clifford learned, but there is little evidence that the new revisionists understand the choices that were embedded in what they dismiss as the "Vietnam syndrome."

As persons who attack centralized power in the federal government, the new revisionists and the Reagan Republicans should at least discuss the effect of Vietnam on the imperial presidency. They could note, for example, that nothing centralizes power more rapidly than waging the cold war militarily, unless it is waging hot war in Korea and Vietnam. In 1967, Under Secretary of State Nicholas Katzenbach told the Senate that the power given by the Constitution to Congress to declare war was "an outmoded phraseology." In 1969–1972, Nixon used "national security" as the rationale for ordering a series of acts that resulted in nearly forty criminal indictments. Vietnam raised the central question in American foreign policy: How can the nation's interests be defended without destroying the economic and political principles that make it worth defending? In their extensive study of Vietnam, the new revisionists have chosen to ignore that question.

They have instead concentrated on an objective that is as simple as it is potentially catastrophic; the removal of the restraints of history, so that the next war can be waged from the start with fewer limitations. They are offering a particular interpretation of the last war, so the next war can be fought differently. This purpose helps explain why these writers stress the narrow military aspects of the war and ignore the larger problems of historical context, the Western allies, economic costs, and political corruption. Westmoreland again set the tone with his remark that "if we go to war . . . we need heed the old Oriental saying, 'It takes the full strength of a tiger to kill a rabbit' and use appropriate force to bring the war to a timely end." In his reassessment of the tragedy, Ambassador Robert Komer condemned the "institutional factors—bureaucratic restraints" that made success impossible. Lewy argued that the struggle was considered a mistake at the time because of "the conviction that the war was not being won and apparently showed little prospect of coming to a successful conclusion." If only the restraints had been lifted, the new revisionists imply, the war—which they consider morally and politically justified—could have been fought to a successful conclusion. This inference is drawn with little attention to either the inherent contradictions in Vietnam military strategy (for example, that villages had to be destroyed to be saved) or the nonmilitary aspects of the conflict. It comes perilously close to an end-justifies-the-means argument.

By trying to make the last war more acceptable, the new revisionists are asking us to make the next war legitimate, even before we know where it will be or what it will be fought for. A Chinese official once told Henry Kissinger that "one should not lose the whole world just to gain South Vietnam." Nor, it might be added, should men with sponges try to legitimize their global cold-war policies by whitewashing the history of the war in South Vietnam.